# Prentice Hall Reference Guide to Grammar and Usage

## with exercises

### Third Edition

## MURIEL HARRIS
Purdue University

Prentice Hall
Upper Saddle River, New Jersey 07458

*Library of Congress Cataloging-in-Publication Data*

HARRIS, MURIEL
    Prentice Hall reference guide to grammar and usage / Muriel
Harris.—3rd ed.
      p.     cm.
    Includes index.
    ISBN 0-13-234642-7 (pbk.)
    1. English language—Grammar.   2. English language—Usage.
I. Title.
PE1112.H293   1997
428.2—dc20
                            96-8319
                               CIP

Production editor: Joan E. Foley
Editorial director: Charlyce Jones Owen
Acquisitions editor: Mary Jo Southern
Director of marketing: Gina Sluss
Director of production and manufacturing: Barbara Kittle
Development editor: Kara Hado
Senior managing editor: Bonnie Biller
Manufacturing manager: Nick Sklitsis
Prepress and manufacturing buyer: Lynn Pearlman
Copyeditor: Kathryn Graehl
Creative design director: Leslie Osher
Interior and cover designer: Carole Anson
Cover art: Ximena de la Piedra Tamvakopoulos

## TO SAM, DAVID, BECKY AND DAN
### —AND NOW HANNAH TOO—
### AS ALWAYS—AND EVER

This book was set in 10/11 New Baskerville by Carlisle Communications, Ltd.,
and was printed and bound by Courier Companies, Inc. The cover
was printed by Phoenix Color Corp.

Printed in the United States of America
10  9  8  7  6  5  4  3  2  1


ISBN 0-13-234642-7 (with exercises)
ISBN 0-13-258989-3 (without exercises)


Prentice-Hall International (UK) Limited, *London*
Prentice-Hall of Australia Pty. Limited, *Sydney*
Prentice-Hall Canada Inc., *Toronto*
Prentice-Hall Hispanoamericana, S.A., *Mexico*
Prentice-Hall of India Private Limited, *New Delhi*
Prentice-Hall of Japan, Inc., *Tokyo*
Simon & Schuster Asia Pte. Ltd., *Singapore*
Editora Prentice-Hall do Brasil, Ltda., *Rio de Janeiro*

# CONTENTS

# TO THE INSTRUCTOR

The new material in the third edition of this reference guide was added partly in response to requests from users of previous editions and partly to assist writers with a wider range of strategies to use as they move through various writing processes. In Part One, "The Writing Process," writers are encouraged to view the various suggestions and strategies as possibilities to try when planning, writing, and revising and to select those that are most appropriate for them. My approach here has been to help students recognize that everyone composes differently and to find out what works best for them. The suggestions and strategies also encourage writers to work collaboratively, to move away from the limited—and limiting—notion that writers work alone.

This attention to the complex interaction of writers and readers is further emphasized in the greatly expanded sections on research writing and argumentation. The greater attention in this edition to topics writers need to consider when preparing research papers and when writing argumentation reflects the increased emphasis on such writing. In response to the growing diversity of student populations, this edition also expands the sections relevant to students learning English as a second language. For easier reference, those aspects of English grammar and usage ESL students turn to most often are collected in a separate section, though these students will also find relevant hints directed to them throughout the book.

Finally, because writing tools have changed dramatically with the advent of word processing on computers, this edition provides extended assistance with using computers through all stages of the writing process, from planning strategies to gathering information online to document design. Included in Chapter 43, in the discussion on searching the Internet for information, is a box that lists useful addresses on the World Wide Web, where students can start their on-line searching. Here I'm drawing on my experience in developing an online writer's resource, Purdue University's OWL (On-line Writing Lab). Our OWL offers dozens of handouts on writing skills, links to useful resources for information (and for job searches), and links to the most widely used sites for searching the Internet. You are welcome to direct your students to this site, which can be reached by e-mail, FTP, Gopher, and the World Wide Web:

| | |
|---|---|
| World Wide Web: | http://owl.english.purdue.edu |
| Gopher: | owl.english.purdue.edu |
| FTP: | owl.english.purdue.edu |
| E-mail: | owl@cc.purdue.edu |

Through all the editions, when writing this reference guide to grammar and usage, I've kept in mind the countless numbers of students whom I've worked with elbow to elbow as a writing lab tutor and also the stacks of papers I've read as a teacher. Included here are those points of grammar and rules I have seen students struggling with and all the suggestions, proofreading techniques, and cautionary advice about pitfalls to avoid that I've passed along to them. Drawing on the experience derived from more years than I care to count, I've empha-sized topics that I know are major sources of confusion and included strategies I also know students find useful. This book is thus the result of many years of field testing and is also a collection of hints and strate-gies that students have shared with me.

The book reflects my efforts to produce a reference guide that all writers can use, even when they don't know much grammatical termi-nology. In the Purdue Writing Lab we answer hundreds of grammar hotline calls, and we sit with hundreds more students who know the word or phrase or punctuation usage they want to check but don't know how to find the page or section they need in a handbook. Where possi-ble, students should be able to actively consult a guide to grammar while they are editing their writing rather than wait passively for some-one else to locate and name their errors.

To help students leap this hurdle, I've created two guides, "Question and Correct" and "Compare and Correct." In the "Question and Correct" list, students can find many of their questions with accompa-nying references to the sections in the book they need. But it is some-times difficult to phrase a question, so I have also included "Compare and Correct," another means to locate the appropriate pages in the book. Here students will find examples of typical troublesome constructions that may be similar to theirs. Again, references will guide them to appropriate places in the book.

Students who have had an instructor or writing lab tutor help them identify the point of grammar or usage they want to check can use the index, the table of contents, and the list of correction symbols to find the appropriate page or section.

The organization of the book is also intended to help writers easily locate the information they need. **The Writing Process** reviews the concerns of all writers as they move through various stages of writing. **Sentence Accuracy, Clarity, and Variety** provides rules and suggestions for constructions beyond the word level. **Parts of Sentences** explains parts of speech; grammatical terms having to do with single words; and concepts about phrases, clauses, and sentence types. **Punctuation** covers guidelines for the most frequently used forms in these areas. **Mechanics and Spelling** covers mechanics, such as capitals and abbreviations, as well as proofreading, the use of spell checkers, and useful spelling rules. **Style and Word Choice** offers suggestions for avoiding sexist language, wordiness, and clichés, along with guidelines on tone and word choice. **Research and Documentation** moves through the processes of finding a topic, searching for information, taking notes, and documenting sources. **ESL Concerns** includes those aspects of English grammar most needed by students learning English as a second language. The appendices cover other important material. Appendix A, **Argument,** presents a discussion of writers' concerns when writing argumentation papers. Appendix B, **Document Design,** covers various aspects of paper formatting. Appendix C, **Résumés,** discusses the various parts of a résumé and includes examples relevant to students with different work experiences. The **Glossary of Usage** and **Glossary of Grammatical Terms** round out the handbook.

Students will find this book to be user-friendly, clear, and concise. In the HINTS boxes they'll find useful strategies and errors to avoid, and in the exercises they will learn interesting bits of information about lighter topics—such as the origin of the phrase "It's a doozy" and reasons for the increasing popularity of pigs—and about relevant, current topics—such as the problems of waste disposal. The exercises are set up so that students can practice several different types of skills: proofreading, sentence combining, and in the "pattern practice," writing their own sentences using various rules.

This version of the book is what publishers call the "third edition," but those of us involved with writing call these later drafts "revisions."

As with other revising I do, this was an opportunity to clean up minor infelicities, to clarify some explanations, and—most important—to add new material where needed. The most major additions reflect directions writing programs have taken—to emphasize discussions of writing processes in handbooks, to focus on collecting information and citing sources in research papers, to stress concerns for writing argumentation, to include information relevant to writing with computers and collecting information online, and to remain aware of the needs of the many students learning English as a second language. With these additions as well as those in the second edition, I now feel confident that the book is more inclusive both in terms of the audience it is aimed at and the types of writing assignments for which it can offer help. I'm delighted that I had this opportunity to revise.

This book, then, is a guide to writing as well as to the editing and proofreading stages of writing. As I explain in the "To the Student" introduction, editing is only one of the writing processes and is most commonly performed after writers have composed their thoughts into words on paper. My advice to students is to attend to editing at the last stages, when they are close to a final draft of a paper. But research has made us aware of how nonlinear writing processes are, and some degree of editing and polishing may occur throughout various drafts. Our job, as teachers, is to keep our students from thinking that editing for grammatical correctness is the heart of writing. Part One of this book, on writing processes, is intended to help with that. We also need to remind our students that reference guides are useful and necessary tools, but ultimately no book can answer all questions or include every sticky or unusual case. Having an instructor or a writing center tutor to talk to is also necessary.

Among the useful supplements specific to this handbook available from Prentice Hall are the following:

❖ *Practicing Grammar and Usage* (by Muriel Harris). This booklet of supplementary exercises accompanies the Third Edition of the *Prentice Hall Reference Guide to Grammar and Usage*, matching both topics and approach. You'll find all exercises in paragraph form with answer keys at the back. These booklets can be purchased by students, or you can copy individual exercises from your free booklet as needed when you adopt the *Reference Guide*. (The pages are formatted for ease of copying.)

❖ *Online Handbook.* This computerized reference system is compatible with most word processing packages and permits students to access information in the *Reference Guide* as they compose on a word processor. Available in Windows, Macintosh, and IBM versions.

❖ *Blue Pencil* and *Blue Pencil Authoring System* (by Robert Bator and Mitsura Yamada). *Blue Pencil* is an interactive editing program that allows students to practice their writing skills by making revisions in paragraph-length passages on the computer screen. If students have trouble with a particular concept, they can request additional instruction from the program. *The Blue Pencil Authoring System,* a for-sale item for instructors, allows you to create your own exercises for the *Blue Pencil* program. Available in Macintosh and IBM versions.

In addition to the text-specific supplements, the following **Prentice Hall Resources for Composition** are available to qualifying adopters. Contact your local Prentice Hall representative for details.

❖ *The Research Organizer* (by Sue D. Hopke of Broward Community College). This handy booklet offers guidance on the research paper and provides space for students to record their research strategy, notes, citations, outlines, and drafts all in one place. Instructors using the *Reference Guide* may copy this supplement free of charge for their class, or students may purchase the entire booklet at a minimal cost.

❖ *Model Research Papers,* Second Edition (by Jeanette Lewis). This collection of nine student research papers in various fields offers models of documentation, stylistic conventions, and formal requirements for different disciplines. Instructors using the *Reference Guide* may copy this supplement free of charge for their class, or students may purchase the entire booklet at a minimal cost.

❖ *Prentice Hall/Simon & Schuster Transparencies for Writers* (by Duncan Carter of Portland State University). This set of 100 two- and four-color transparencies features exercises, examples, and suggestions for student writing that focus on all aspects of the writing process—from generating ideas and shaping an outline to preparing a draft and revising, editing, and documenting the final paper. These transparencies also cover grammar, punctuation, and mechanics via overlays that show how sentence and paragraph errors can be corrected most effectively.

❖ *Bibliotech2.* Using this computerized bibliography generator, students follow prompts to format their bibliography in either

MLA, APA, or CBE documentation style. Students can print the bibliography directly from the program or save it to an ASCII file that can then be converted to the word processing file of their choice. Available in Macintosh and IBM versions.

❖ *Prentice Hall Workbook for ESL Writers* (by Stacy Hagen and Bernice Ege-Zavala of Edmond Community College). This workbook, available for purchase by students, offers exercises on grammar and writing problems particularly troublesome to non-native speakers of English.

❖ *Student Economy Packages.* When you adopt the *Reference Guide* and another Prentice Hall composition text, the publisher makes them available in a shrink-wrapped package at a 10 percent discount off the total price.

❖ *Webster's Compact School and Office Dictionary.* This brief paperback dictionary is available at only $2.70 over the price of the *Reference Guide* when the two are shrink-wrapped together.

❖ *Webster's New World Dictionary Third College Edition.* This full-size hardcover dictionary is available for student purchase at a discounted price of $9.05 when ordered with the *Reference Guide.*

## Acknowledgments

This book first took shape in the mind of Phil Miller, President of Humanities and Social Science, as he patiently listened to all my griping about grammar handbooks. His quiet wisdom and calm persistence brought this book into existence. Lynn Greenberg Rosenfeld, Senior Editor, English, saw the first edition of the manuscript through many formative stages, and her levelheaded good sense still pervades the book. Kate Morgan, the Development Editor, took on the heroic task of page-by-page editing of that first edition as well as huge-scale matters of organization and content. Her refinements continue to grace the pages, though I still lay claim to any faults she did not weed out. Later editions benefited from the perspectives of Alison Reeves as she took on the work of Senior Editor, English, and the careful eye, close editing, and useful suggestions of Kara Hado, Development Editor, are evident throughout this version. I've benefited also from the helpful comments, corrections, and suggestions of reviewers and users—including writing center tutors—who have added their voices and insights throughout this book: Robert Dial, University of Akron; James Helvey, Davidson County Community

College; Michael Williamson, Indiana University of Pennsylvania; Connie Eggers, Western Washington University; Christopher Thaiss, George Mason University; Lyle W. Morgan II, Pittsburg State University; Joe Lostracco, Austin Community College; Joyce Powell, North Lake University; Marion Perry, Erie Community College; Carol Franks, Portland State University; Donald Fucci, Ramapo College; Vivian Brown, Laredo Junior College; Walter Beale, University of North Carolina at Greensboro; Tracy Baker, University of Alabama at Birmingham. Others who were particularly helpful as I prepared the second edition are Rebecca Innocent, Southern Mississippi University; Jami Josifek, University of California at Irvine; and Barbara Moreland, University of Texas at Arlington. I am also glad to have this opportunity to acknowledge the help of Virginia Underwood Allen (Iowa State University) with methods of explaining grammar, and the input of tutors from the Babson College writing center, under the direction of Joel Nydahl, who offered useful additions to the questions in the "Question and Correct" guide. I'd like to thank reviewers for the third edition, including Sheila Carter-Tod, Hollins College; Mary Dunn, College of Lake County; Matthew Hearn, Valdosta State University; Will Hochman, University of Southern Colorado; Eileen Moeller, Syracuse University; Sharon Shapiro, Naugatuk Valley Community-Technical College; Neal Snidow, Butte Community College; and Nancy Wood, University of Texas at Arlington. For the third edition, faculty, graduate students, and writing lab tutors at Purdue University who generously shared with me their wisdom and experience about writing and writing on computers include Lori Baker, Stuart Blythe, Johndan Johnson-Eilola, Barbara L'Eplattenier, Richard Morris, Edwin Nagelhout, Michelle Sidler, and Murray Shugars. Others who have kindly contributed useful suggestions and comments include Karl Beckson, Nan Hackett, Susan Pratt, Sara Sandstrom, and Kim Way (Concordia College), and Tamzon Wilensky (Purdue University). I also owe a large debt of gratitude to the production department staff who transformed my sheets of computer printout into visually attractive, visually informative pages. Finally, I must acknowledge the extensive amount of assistance I've gotten from student writers who over the years have patiently listened to my attempts to help them and who revised into coherent papers the endless questions, doodles, diagrams, handouts, and bits of advice I kept giving them. As for my husband,

Samuel, and our children—David and Rebecca, her husband Daniel, and their daughter Hannah—I prefer to think that my appreciation for them and for what they mean to me is always evident in our lives, not on pages of books.

*Muriel Harris*

THE NEW YORK TIMES and PRENTICE HALL are sponsoring A CONTEMPORARY VIEW, a program designed to enhance student access to current information of relevance in the classroom. Through this program, the core subject matter provided in the text is supplemented by a collection of time-sensitive articles from one of the world's most distinguished newspapers, **THE NEW YORK TIMES.** These articles  demonstrate the vital, ongoing connection between what is learned in the classroom and what is happening in the world around us.

So that students can enjoy the wealth of information of **THE NEW YORK TIMES** daily, a reduced subscription rate is available. For information, call toll-free: 1-800-631-1222.

**PRENTICE HALL** and **THE NEW YORK TIMES** are proud to co-sponsor **A CONTEMPORARY VIEW.** We hope it will make the reading of both textbooks and newspapers a more dynamic, involving process.

# TO THE STUDENT

This handbook may look like others you've used or seen, but there are some differences in this book that will make it easier—and more helpful—for you to use:

**This book assumes that you are like all other writers and that you are unlike all other writers.**

❖ All writers need to be aware of the various writing processes they use, but every writer is different from every other writer. So, in Part One, you'll find some suggestions for writing and for using computers to write that will be helpful for you in particular but other strategies that won't work as well for you.

❖ All writers struggle with writing. Perhaps there are a few people somewhere who can sit down and dash off well-written drafts. Most of us, however, need to write and rewrite and to edit our writing before handing it on to others.

❖ All writers make the final choices and decisions about their writing, but writers also benefit from interacting with others who read their writing and offer feedback. Some writers benefit from collaborating with others during the early stages of planning and drafting; other writers prefer to save such collaboration until their papers are farther along.

**This handbook is designed for easy use.**

❖ This book is arranged so that you can look up answers to your questions without knowing the necessary grammatical terms. If you have a specific question, turn to the "Question and Correct" list inside the fold-out back cover. If you don't know what to ask but you know your sentence or paragraph just doesn't seem right, turn to the red-edged pages called "Compare and Correct." (There is, of course, an index if you know the point of grammar you want to check.)

❖ Most of the grammatical terms you need are explained in Part Three. Others are explained as you need them.

❖ The explanations in this book are stated as concisely as possible. You won't be spending extra time reading a lot of unnecessary prose.

❖ The information is presented with visual aids such as charts, tables, lists, and different ink shades to help you locate what you need quickly.

**This handbook concentrates only on the most essential points of grammar and the most frequently made errors.**

❖ This book focuses on the questions and problems writers most frequently have.

❖ You won't find an exhaustive list of grammatical terms of seldom-used rules in this book. However, if you want definitions of grammatical terms such as *participle, gerund,* and so on, see the Glossary of Grammatical Terms at the back of this book.

**This book offers explanations and strategies and includes HINTS to follow.**

❖ Rules are explained, not just stated.

❖ This book offers strategies to use. Sometimes it's easier to remember a rule and apply it; sometimes it's easier just to have a strategy to follow. For example, you can either follow the rule for spelling *desert* and *dessert,* or you can try one writing center tutor's strategy: she remembers that just as she likes seconds for dessert, she uses a second *s* for *dessert.* Look for other strategies in the HINT boxes.

❖ Other HINTS are reminders to help you avoid errors that writers frequently make.

❖ This book is intended to answer most questions, though you may need to consult your teacher or writing center tutor for further explanation or specific information. No book can include answers to all writing questions or to all the messy exceptions to rules of English grammar.

**This book offers suggestions for how computers and online sources can help you write.**

✤  You may be fairly comfortable with writing on computers or at the beginning stages of word processing, but the suggestions for using computers to plan, write, revise, and edit your writing will offer new approaches that can increase the usefulness of the computer.

✤  Online search tools in libraries and on the Internet are extremely helpful but can be intimidating when you first jump in. The advice in this book, in the section on writing research papers, should help you, but your library and your access to the Internet may make conditions somewhat different at your site. Some addresses for useful World Wide Web sites you can go to when searching the Internet are listed in Chapter 43, and in Appendix C on résumés, you will find a few World Wide Web sites that list job openings. There are also numerous OWLs (online writing labs) with a variety of resources. You can start with the OWL I helped to develop at Purdue University. Here you will find links to most of these OWLs, as well as links to dozens of handouts on writing skills, links to sources of information, and links to sites that will search the Internet for you. To reach Purdue University's OWL, use the following Internet addresses:

| | |
|---|---|
| World Wide Web: | http://owl.english.purdue.edu |
| Gopher: | owl.english.purdue.edu |
| FTP: | owl.english.purdue.edu |
| E-mail: | owl@cc.purdue.edu |

**This book offers exercises in a useful format.**

✤  To practice your understanding of various topics, try the exercises at the end of each chapter and check your answers with the Answer Key.

✤  You'll notice that the exercises are not lists of separate sentences. Instead, you'll be checking your understanding by practicing proofreading and pattern practice skills with paragraphs. The subjects of these paragraphs are of general interest and may even add to your storehouse of minor facts with which to amaze your friends. (For example, you'll read about the magnificent old Duesenberg automobile, the Turkish origins of Santa Claus, the art of whistling, the popularity of pigs as pets, and nonimpact aerobics.)

As you can tell from this description, the goal of this book is to be a useful companion for you when you write. As you edit your papers before turning them over to your readers, you may have questions such as "Do I need a comma here?" or "Something doesn't seem right in that sentence—what's wrong?" If you don't know the grammatical terms to look up in the index, try the suggestions for using this book in the next section. If needed, browse through the "Question and Correct" or "Compare and Correct" sections.

## Some Cautionary Advice

All textbook writers would like to think that what they have written supplies all the answers and solves all the reader's problems. Their book is all that students need. That must be a great feeling, but you and I know that in the case of any reference guide to grammar and usage, such as this book, knowledge of grammar is only one aspect of writing—and not the most important one, either. The writer's real task is to use writing to give shape to thoughts, to focus on topics and present them clearly and coherently. For most writers, this means moving through a variety of processes to compose, develop, and organize ideas and writing several drafts—at least—with feedback, when possible, from readers as the drafts are revised and evolve into more finished products.

In this book you'll find some useful help with these writing processes, and the most effective time to use the rules for grammar and mechanics is when you are working on final or near-final drafts, polishing them for grammatical correctness, proofing for correct punctuation and spelling, and sharpening your word choices and sentence constructions. At the earlier stages of composing, you don't want to interrupt your thought processes or the flow of the ideas evolving on the page to worry about choosing the right pronoun. There is also no point in checking the punctuation of a sentence in an early draft if it may disappear in the next draft. When you have a well-developed, well-organized topic and have done all the necessary revision, you are finally ready to concentrate on matters such as sentence correctness, word choices, punctuation, spelling, and the appearance of the page. Then, you can benefit from the portions of this book that are designed to help you edit your writing to conform to standard English. When your sentences are clearly phrased and correctly punctuated and when your words are appropriately chosen and correctly spelled, your readers can more easily understand—and appreciate—your ideas.

*Muriel Harris*

# PART ONE

## THE WRITING PROCESS

This part on the writing process offers suggestions about writing that may be new to you and may turn out to be more helpful than methods you now use when writing. Some suggestions may help other writers, but not you. A major part of learning to write effectively is learning what works for you. That may mean putting aside some well-meaning advice you've read or heard or tried in the past. For example, some writers prefer to start with outlines while others need to write for a while to find their direction and can then turn to making an outline. Some writers find that discussing their thoughts about a subject with someone else helps them develop those ideas. Others need to work alone and then seek feedback later. There is no one "correct" way to write, and the same writer may use different approaches for different situations. But no matter how differently writers work through the various writing processes, there are considerations all writers must think about. These processes are discussed here, along with a variety of strategies for writing.

Because many writers now use computers as they write, Chapter 4 covers writing process strategies to use when planning, drafting, revising, and editing with a computer.

1

# 1 Purposes and Audiences (purp)

## 1a Purpose

Writing is a powerful multipurpose tool that helps us discover and explore more fully what we are thinking so that we learn as well as express our feelings and thoughts. We write to convey information, to persuade others to believe or act in certain ways, to help ourselves and others remember, and to create works of literary merit. Through writing, we can achieve a variety of purposes:

- *Summarizing:* Stating concisely the main points of a piece of writing
- *Defining:* Explaining the meaning of a word or concept
- *Analyzing:* Breaking the topic into parts and examining how these parts work or interact
- *Persuading:* Offering convincing support for a point of view
- *Reporting:* Examining all the evidence and data on a subject and presenting an objective overview
- *Evaluating:* Setting up and explaining criteria for evaluation and then judging the quality or importance of the object being evaluated
- *Discussing/Examining:* Considering the main points, implications, and relationships to other topics
- *Interpreting:* Explaining the meaning or implications of a topic

# 1b Topic

The subject of a piece of writing may be a topic the writer chooses, or it may be assigned. If you are asked to choose your own topic and don't readily have something in mind, assume that an interviewer or reporter is asking you one of the following questions. Your answer might begin as suggested here.

- What is a problem you'd like to solve?
  *". . . is a problem, and I think we should . . ."*
- What is something that pleases, puzzles, irritates, or bothers you?
  *"What annoys (or pleases) me is . . ."*
- What is something you'd like to convince others of?
  *"What I want others to agree on is. . ."*
- What is something that seems to contradict what you read or see around you?
  *"Why does . . ." (or) "I've noticed that . . . but . . ."*
- What is something you'd like to learn more about?
  *"I wonder how . . ."*
- What is something you know about that others around you may not know?
  *"I'd like to tell you about . . ."*

# 1c Thesis

After you've selected a topic to write about, you also have to decide on a comment that you'll make about it. Then, you will have a thesis. Sometimes the comment part of a thesis is developed in a writer's mind early in the writing process, and sometimes it becomes clear as the writer works through various writing processes.

| *Topic* | *Comment* |
|---|---|
| Television commercials | should not insult competing brands or companies. |
| Effective document design | helps technical writing present complex material more clearly. |

---

**HINT 1: When you start to write, ask yourself:**
- Who am I in this piece of writing? (A friend? An impartial observer? Someone with knowledge to share? A writer with a viewpoint to recommend? An angry customer?)

*continued on next page*

---

- Who is my intended audience? (Peers? A potential boss? A teacher? Readers of my local newspaper? Colleagues in an office? People who are likely to agree with me? Or disagree? Or are neutral?)
- What is the purpose of this writing? (To convince? Amuse? Persuade? Inform?)
- What are some other conditions that will shape this writing? (The assignment, length, due date, format, evaluation criteria)

Narrowing the topic is an important stage of writing because no one can write an effective paper that is vague or promises to cover too much. Some of your answers to the questions in the previous HINT box will help you narrow your subject. If the assigned length is three pages, you have to limit your topic more than if you are asked to write a fifteen-page paper. If your audience is not all college students but specifically college students who depend on financial aid from the government, your topic is also narrowed. Being specific is a way to limit the scope of a topic. Instead of writing a short paper about how the Internet can promote learning in high school classes, you could write about a more specific topic, such as how the World Wide Web is used in high school biology classes.

# 2 Writing Processes and Strategies (w pr)

As we write, we engage in a variety of actions. We plan, draft, organize, revise, edit, perhaps go back to plan some more, revise, maybe reread what we've written, reorganize, put the draft aside for a while, write, and so on. All of these writing processes are part of the larger act of producing a piece of writing, and there is great variety in how writers move back and forth through these processes. Because moving through all these processes takes time, most writers (especially better ones) realize that they have to start early and that they'll be engaged in some hard work. Additional suggestions for writing process strategies to use when you are working on a computer are included in Chapter 4.

# 2a Planning

During the planning process, you find the material you want to include in your writing. The following useful strategies can help you find material.

- **Brainstorming**  Once you have a general topic in mind, one way to start planning is to turn off the editor in your brain (that voice that rejects ideas before you've had a chance to consider or develop them) and let thoughts tumble out either in conversation or on paper. Ideas tend to generate other ideas, and a variety of thoughts will surface. Some writers need to write down whatever occurs to them so that they won't forget all the material they will later sort through. The writing may be in sentences or set down as notes and phrases, depending on which format the writer finds most useful. During a brainstorming session with a writing center tutor, one writer took the following notes as she considered whether she would support term limits for the members of the United States Congress:

  *For term limits*
  - *Prevents one person from gaining too much power and representing only one faction of the public.*
  - *Keeps bringing newcomers into office so they represent different parts of the public in their district.*
    - *New political views*
    - *That means that the groups who give political donations will change.*
  - *In the last term that person can put his or her energies into working on laws and not just on getting elected.*
  - *Stay in office too long, maybe not doing important work?*

  *Against term limits*
  - *People really get to know their job and have seniority.*
  - *Leaders (Speaker of the House . . . who else? majority leader? powerful committee heads?) have to have a lot of experience to do a good job.*

  *Some facts to find out*
  - *How many Congressional representatives stay in office a long time?*
  - *What happens to them after long terms in office?*
  - *Do leaders really have to have a lot of experience? (Check on role of advisors and staff.)*

- **Freewriting**  Some writers find that they produce useful material when they start writing and keep writing without stopping. The writing is "free" in that it can go in any direction that occurs to the writer as she writes. The important part of freewriting is to keep going. You can also use freewriting as a "mind dump," recording everything you know about the subject you're going to write about. One student writer began his freewriting for an assignment about analyzing a stereotype he had encountered as follows:

*My dream even from when I was a child was always to be a farm manager. Back in seventh grade I remember my social studies class was having a class discussion of vocations in life. Never once did anyone talk about a profession in the line of agriculture, so when I asked, "What about farm management?" I was blasted with laughter and crude comments. The comments they made were false stereotypes that people have. People think all ag students are "countrified" or are just "farm boys." Just "hicks." Another stereotypical view is that farmers are lazy, just plant and sit around at the local coffee shop and gossip. My father's farm is very diversified. We grow mint, onions, and corn. The mint and onions keep us busy all year. Many farmers get a job in town to supplement their farm income. Farmers need to keep complicated records and take hard ag courses in college. Computers are an important part of farming today.*

- **Listing**  Some writers begin by searching their minds for what they know about the subject and listing those points on paper. That also helps to clarify what they will need to find out before they begin to write. The following list was developed by a writer working on an application to a school of veterinary medicine:

*What experiences have I had with animals?*
*- Summer assistant in local vet's office*
*- Cleaned equipment.*
*- Helped with animals during treatment.*
*- Got to know how much work is involved.*
*- My own pets*
*- Learned to care for a variety of animals.*
*- Should I list my coursework? High school clubs?*
*- Helped a cousin show her sheep.*
*- Had to groom two sheep.*

- **Clustering and branching**  Clustering establishes the relationships between words and phrases. Begin by writing a topic in the middle of a sheet of paper and circling it. Then as related ideas come to mind, draw lines to connect these ideas to other ideas in a nonlinear way. Other ideas will become the center of their own clusters of ideas as the topic branches out. When you keep an open mind, ideas spill out on the page. You can rework them in a more orderly way by putting the main idea at the top of the page and reordering the branches. The writer who created the following cluster was exploring the topic of divorce and its effects on children.

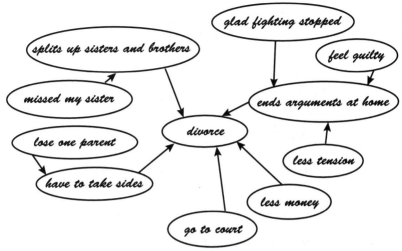

- **Conversation/collaboration**  While some writers prefer to plan by themselves, others benefit from talking with a peer response group, a writing center tutor, or a friend. Talk produces more talk, and if the listener asks questions, even more ideas can develop in the writer's mind. If you find talk useful and you are in a situation where you can't engage in conversation, try picturing yourself addressing an imaginary audience.

- **Writer's notebook/journal**  Ideas tend to float to the surface of our minds when we're engaged in other activities, such as walking to class, cooking, or taking a shower. You can capture those thoughts by recording them in a writer's notebook as soon as you can. Some good writers carry a small notebook to jot down these reminders. Others regularly keep journals, writing brief entries at least once a day. You can refer to your journal or notebook for ideas when you write.

- **Reading**  An important source of material for your writing is the reading you do. You can search out relevant information in libraries or on the Internet. You may also find connections to your topic when you read the daily newspaper, a magazine, or readings for other classes. Your writer's notebook then becomes a particularly useful place to record these connections.

- **Outlining**  Some writers benefit from producing an outline as the first stage in planning. They may or may not follow that outline, and it may change as the paper develops, but the outline is a useful

2a
pr

planning tool. You can also use an outline after an early draft to see how your paper will be structured. The following outline was prepared for a report on how to increase donations to a local food bank for the poor:

*Show problem*
- *Need for food for local homeless*
  - *Present level of food needed*
    - *2,000 per month request food*
    - *No. of homeless children increasing*
  - *Donations not keeping up with demand*
  - *Largest local donor, a restaurant, has closed*
- *Projections for future unemployment when auto plant closes*

*Solutions*
- *Ask local media (newspaper, TV station) to show problem*
- *Send requests to local churches and synagogues*
- *Explore new commercial sources*
  - *Local supermarkets*
  - *College residence hall cafeterias*
  - *Restaurants*
- *Ask for volunteer collectors of food*

- **Who? what? when? where? how? why?**   These question words, often used by journalists in gathering information for news articles, can be useful in provoking us to think more fully about a topic. *Who* or *what* might be involved or affected? *Why?* Is the location (*where?*) important? *How? What* connects the people or things involved? Try using these question words in a variety of combinations, and jot down your answers. For a paper about the effects on human skin of too much exposure to sun, the writer asked herself these questions as she gathered information:

  *What damage can sun cause to human skin? Why?*
  *What illnesses result?*
  *How serious are these?*
  *Who is most likely to be affected?*
  *How can these illnesses be treated?*
  *How widespread is the problem?*
  *What are the warning signs?*

- **Types of evidence**   As you plan, you may find it helpful to clarify the kinds of information, if any, to be included in your paper. Will you draw primarily on personal experience gained from the direct observation of your world (what you see, hear, and read), or will you depend on reading, researching the work of others in the library, or gathering your own data from interviews or research?

- **Divide and conquer**  For writing projects that seem overwhelming, you may find that making a list of the steps involved in completing the project is a useful planning strategy. Breaking the writing into groups of manageable tasks makes it easier to plunge into each one. Your list also provides a road map for how to proceed. When and how will you collect evidence? Will you go to the library tomorrow afternoon? What will you need to read before you start writing? What questions do you want to discuss with a writing center tutor?

# 2b Drafting

Some writers prefer to do most of their planning in their heads, and as a result, they have the general shape of a paper in mind when they start writing. Others have to write and rewrite early drafts before a working draft begins to take shape. In general, early drafts are very rough as you add, change, and rework. Some writers are ready to share their early drafts with others, to get advice, to hear how the draft sounds when read aloud by a writing center tutor, a peer response group, or themselves, and to get more ideas for revision. Other writers aren't ready to share their early drafts, and they prefer to delay reader input until a later draft. Because many good writers work collaboratively, they seek readers of their drafts before they are finished.

Writers who have time to put a draft aside for a while also find that new suggestions pop up or that something they hear or read triggers suggestions for new material to add to the draft. This is yet another reason for starting early—to allow for that "percolating" time. In addition, when you have a short period away from a draft, you gain distance so that you can be more objective about what revisions are needed. When you reread a freshly written draft, it is hard to separate what is still in your head from what is on the page, and it is even harder to see what is missing or in need of reworking.

# 2c Organizing

As your draft takes shape, it may follow the outline you wrote, or the outline may need to be reworked. Or you may be a writer who outlines after some drafting. At whatever stage an outline is most useful, it helps you see if the organizational structure is sound and if any sections need more material. An outline can be an informal list of major points with the minor ones listed and indented under major points. If you are using a computer, put the outline on the screen and experiment with cutting and pasting parts of the outline in different places until you see a logical flow that makes sense to you. (See Chapter 4 for more strategies for writing on computers.) If you have a large collection of evidence and notecards to organize, try color-coding the cards or sorting them according to the sections of the paper in which they will be used.

# 2d Revising

A particularly important part of writing is revising, which means re-seeing the whole and then reworking it. Because this can be difficult to do, some writers make the mistake of handing in an early draft that hasn't been adequately revised. The low grades they get are not indications of being inadequate writers but a result of handing in a paper too early in the writing process. (If you are a purchaser of computer software, think of similar problems caused when software is released too early, before the bugs are worked out. The program would have been much more successful if the developers had worked on it more before release.)

During the revision process, many writers are helped considerably by collaborative feedback from others. Writers who publish their works often get feedback and helpful advice from their editors, and scholars who submit articles and books to scholarly publications ask colleagues to read their manuscripts. Reader response can be very useful when you are revising your paper. You may have classroom opportunities for working with a response group, and you can visit your writing center to talk with a tutor who can also provide you with reader feedback. Or you might have conferences with your teacher. There are a variety of ways to get reader feedback, but it's important to remember that finally, you are the writer, and you must decide which advice to listen to and which to put aside.

To revise effectively, first go through all the major qualities of good writing, those aspects referred to as the higher-order concerns (HOCs) by Thomas J. Reigstad and Donald McAndrew. (The lower-order concerns, or LOCs, are discussed in the section on editing.) Use the revision checklist in the HINT box that follows to review the HOCs.

---

**HINT: Revision Checklist (HOCs = Higher-Order Concerns)**

**Purpose**: What is the purpose of this paper? Do the thesis and audience fit the purpose? Have you achieved the purpose? If not, what's needed?

**Thesis**: Is the thesis clearly stated? Has it been narrowed sufficiently? Is it appropriate for the assignment? Can you summarize your thesis if asked? If you think of the thesis as a promise that you will discuss this statement, have you really kept all parts of that promise?

**Audience**: Who is the audience for this paper? Is the audience appropriate for this topic? Is it clear who the intended audience is? What assumptions have you made about the members of your audience? Did you tell them what they already know? Is that appropriate? If you are writing for your teacher or some expert in the field, does he or she expect you to include background material? (An essay exam or other writing in which the purpose is to evaluate the writer's knowledge should include such information even when the reader knows the material too.) Did you leave out anything your audience needs to know?

**Organization**: What is the central idea of each paragraph? Does that idea contribute to the thesis? Do the paragraphs progress in an organized, logical way? Are there any gaps or jumps from one part to another? Is the reader likely to get lost in any part? Do your transitions indicate when the writing moves to a new aspect of the topic?

**Development**: Are there places where more details or examples or specifics would help? Have you left out anything your audience needs to know? Are there details that are not relevant and should be omitted?

## 2e Editing and Proofreading

Editing is the fine-tuning process of writing. When you edit, you attend to what has been called the lower-order concerns (LOCs), that is, details of grammar, usage, punctuation, spelling, and other mechanics. The most effective time to edit is when you're done revising so that you have shaped the paper and won't be making any more large-scale changes. It is far more efficient to fine-tune sentences you know will be in the final version than to edit work that might be deleted in a later draft. Yet another reason for not editing until the paper is close to completion is that you may be reluctant to delete sentences or words you have already corrected. Even if a sentence needs to be rewritten or doesn't belong in the paper, there's a natural tendency to want to leave it in because it is grammatically correct. Don't let yourself fall into that trap. Errors in grammar and usage send the wrong message to your readers about your general level of competence in using language, and such errors will cause you to get lower grades.

Proofreading is the final editing process of writing, the last check for missing words, misspellings, format requirements, and so on. If you have a list of references you consulted while writing your paper, this is the time to do a final check on the information and the format of the entries. To check your spelling, try the proofreading suggestions listed

**2e**
**pr**

in 38a. If you use a spell checker in your word processing program, re-member that spell checkers cannot flag problems with wrong forms of words such as *it's/its* or *advice/advise.* If you use a grammar checker, re-member that such programs catch some but not all grammar problems and can only offer suggestions. For example, the program may high-light constructions such as *there is/there are,* but it cannot tell you whether your choice is appropriate.

---

**HINT: Editing and Proofreading Checklist (LOCs = Lower-Order Concerns)**

Don't try to check for everything as you edit and proofread your final draft. It's more efficient to know your typical problem areas and to use strategies for finding and correcting any errors. The HINT boxes in this book give you numerous strategies to try. In addition, try these general suggestions:

- Put the paper aside for a bit. It's easier to see problems when the paper is not as fresh.
- To help your eye slow down and see each word, read the paper aloud. Try sliding a card down each line as you reread. Then, as you read aloud, your eyes and ears will both be working to help you.
- If you tend to leave out words, point to each word as you read. Be sure that you see a written version of every word you say.
- As you read, have a list in mind of the particular problems you tend to have when writing. Which grammatical problems have frequently been marked by teachers? Which aspects of gram-mar do you frequently have to check in a handbook? Here are some of the most common problems to look for in your papers:

| | |
|---|---|
| fragments | omitted commas |
| subject-verb agreement | verb tenses |
| comma splices | spelling errors |
| misplaced apostrophes | run-on sentences |
| pronoun reference | unnecessary commas |
| omitted words | missing transition words |

- Keep this book close by as you edit and proofread. If you have a question and don't know which section to check, see the **"Question and Correct"** section inside the back cover of this book. If you have a written example, check the **"Compare and Correct"** section in the red-edged pages at the back of this book to find a similar example.

# 3 Paragraphs (para)

Each paragraph in a paper is a group of sentences that work together to develop one idea or topic within the larger piece of writing. Effective paragraphs are unified, coherent, and developed.

## 3a Unity

A unified paragraph focuses on one topic and does not include unnecessary or irrelevant material. To check the unity of each of your paragraphs, ask yourself what the paragraph is about. You should be able to answer in a sentence that either is implied or appears in the paragraph as the topic sentence. Any sentence not related to this topic sentence is probably a digression that doesn't belong in the paragraph.

## 3b Coherence

Every paragraph should be written so that each sentence flows smoothly into the next. If your ideas, sentences, and details fit together clearly, your readers can follow along easily without getting lost. To help your reader, use the suggestions in Chapter 14 for repeating key words and phrases and using synonyms, pronouns, and transitional devices between sentences and paragraphs.

## 3c Development

A paragraph is well developed when it covers the paragraph topic fully, using details, examples, evidence, and other specifics the reader needs as well as generalizations to bind these specifics together. You can check the development of each of your paragraphs by asking yourself what else your reader might need or want to know about that topic. Some specifics help to explain or support the more general statements, and other specifics help to make bland generalizations come alive.

## 3d Introductions and Conclusions

Some writers need to write their introduction before the body of the paper, and others find it easier to write their introduction after revising the body. Some writers even write the introduction last. As you draft your introduction and conclusion, consider the following points:

- **Introduction:** The purpose of the introduction is to bring the reader into the writer's world, to build interest in the subject (why should the reader read this?), and to announce the topic. Interesting details, a startling statistic, a question, an anecdote, or a surprising statement are some of the "hooks" writers can use to catch the reader's interest.

- **Conclusion:** Your paper needs a conclusion to let the reader know the end is near, much the same way as a piece of music needs a conclusion or a conversation needs a clear signal that you're about to leave or hang up. Conclusions can either look backward or forward.

> **Looking Backward:** If the paper has been a complex discussion, you can look back by summarizing the main points to remind the reader of what was discussed. Or you can look back to emphasize important points you don't want the reader to forget. Or, to heighten the sense of conclusion, you can come full circle by referring back to something in the introduction.

> **Looking Forward:** If the paper is short or doesn't need a summary, you can pose a question for the reader to consider, or you can offer advice or suggest actions the reader can take based on your discussion, argument, or proposal.

# 3e Patterns of Organization

Paragraphs can be organized in a great variety of ways: following chronological order; moving from general to specific information or from specific to general; or following some spatial order such as top to bottom, side to side, or front to back. The patterns illustrated in the following paragraphs are ways of thinking about and organizing ideas. You can also use these patterns during planning as you think about your topic. The information about the current job market and future employment trends contained in these sample paragraphs was found during a brief search of resources on the Internet. See Chapter 43 for a discussion about searching methods.

- **Narration** Narratives tell stories (or parts of stories) with events usually arranged in chronological order to make a point that relates to the whole paper.

> *With the rapid growth in opportunities for physical therapists, a recent graduate in this field found that her job search was a particularly pleasant experience. Offered dozens of jobs around the*

*country, she began by deciding where she wanted to travel as well as where she might want to live. On her interview trips, she explained, "I was treated royally. Recruiters in three different cities—Atlanta, Seattle, and Tucson—paid all my expenses for on-site interviews." When she opted to stay in Seattle for some sightseeing, her hotel and food expenses were paid for two additional days. After her Seattle trip, she went to Atlanta, where recruiters offered her a particularly generous relocation package and sign-on bonus. Her experience is one more example of the fact that while job searching in many fields today is disheartening, the need for physical therapists is causing employers to compete for applicants.*

- **Description**  Description includes details about people, places, things, or scenes drawn from the senses: sight, sound, smell, touch, and taste.

  *In the offices and laboratories of many companies, people now work in groups, sitting around a table, talking and trading ideas. Working with colleagues can be enjoyable when the group keeps its sense of humor and maintains an informal atmosphere. Bottles of flavored spring water are passed out, doughnut crumbs are scattered over reports and charts, and aging pizza boxes are stacked up along the conference room wall. But that does not mean real work isn't getting done. There is an art to group work because everyone has to learn how to work smoothly with a diversity of personalities. One worker may want to dominate the conversation or try to assert his ideas, his loud voice like a refrain above all the other noise as he insists that everyone listen to him. Another person may find that as a woman, in order to be heard she has to be more aggressive than a male colleague might have to be. So she leans forward, elbows on the table, to insert her voice in the conversation. Early in the morning, some members of the group are trying to wake up by slurping coffee, and late in the afternoon, others want to give up and take the work home. But even with the continuous need to work on blending different people into the group, employers are finding that the results are usually better than if each employee were left alone to do his or her part of the work.*

- **Cause and effect**  Cause-and-effect paragraphs trace causes or discuss effects. The paragraph may start with effects and move backward to analyze causes or start with causes and then look at the effects. The following paragraph starts with a cause, the age of the American population, and then looks at the effects of demographics on the job market.

  *The growth and direction of the job market in the future is greatly affected by population trends, so government agencies such as the Bureau of Labor Statistics study population changes in or-*

der to determine where the growth in jobs will be in the next century. A major factor that influences jobs is the age of the population. Because the number of Americans over 85 will increase about four times as fast as the total population, there will be a major increase in the demand for health services. With the shift to relatively fewer children and teenagers, there will also be greater demand for products and services for older people. For example, older people with stable incomes will travel more and have more money for consumer goods, so some jobs will focus more on tending to their needs. The job market, present and future, is shaped by the age of America's population, present and future.

- **Analogy** Use analogies to compare things that may initially seem to have little in common but that can offer fresh insights when compared.

It's a mistake to think that the best way to look for a job is to apply for available openings. Over 75 percent of the jobs being filled every year are not on those lists. A better way of looking for a job is very much like inventing a successful item to sell in the marketplace. The "hot" best-sellers are not merely better versions of existing ones; they are totally new, previously unthought-of consumer goods or services. In the same way, the majority of the jobs being filled are not ones that existed before, and like a successful new children's toy or some new piece of electronic equipment, they did not exist because no one realized the work needed to be done. Good executives, managers, and business owners often have ideas for additional positions, but they haven't yet developed those ideas into full-blown job descriptions. Like the inventor who comes up with the concept for a new consumer product, a job seeker can land a position by asking potential employers about changing needs in their corporation and suggesting that he or she can take on those responsibilities. Finding a new need is definitely a strategy that works as well for job seekers as it does for inventors.

- **Example and illustration** Frequently, writers discuss an idea by offering examples to support the topic sentence. Or the writer may use an illustration—which is an extended example.

**Examples**

According to the Bureau of Labor Statistics, America's workers will become an increasingly diverse group. While white non-Hispanic men have historically been the largest segment of the labor force—about 78 percent—that will not be true in the next century. By 2005, Hispanics will add about 6.5 million workers, an increase of 64 percent over current levels. Within the next ten years or so, African-Americans, Hispanic-Americans, and Asian-Americans will account for roughly 35 percent of all labor force entrants. Another factor that will increase the diversity of the workplace will be the growing number of women. Although the number of women under the age of 40 entering the working world began to grow more slowly than in the past, women are expected to fill about 48 percent of all jobs by 2005. These and other groups will continue to diversify America's labor pool.

### Illustration

The Bureau of Labor Statistics study of employment trends for the future reports that the fastest-growing areas for jobs will be in occupations that require higher levels of education. Office and factory automation as well as offshore production have greatly reduced the number of people needed in jobs that can be filled by high school graduates. Now, the need is for more executives, administrators, managers, and people with professional specialties—occupations that all require people with higher education. Moreover, in a complex world dominated by high-tech electronics and international markets, a high school education is no longer adequate. High school graduates will increasingly find themselves limited to the service sector, working in areas such as fast-food service, where the pay is low and there is little potential for advancement. The trend toward the need for people with higher education is expected to continue for the foreseeable future.

- **Classification and Division**   Classification involves grouping or sorting items into a group or category based on unifying principles. Division starts with one item and divides it into parts.

### Classification

As America moves from being a nation that produces goods to a nation that produces services, the major growth in employment will be in the service-producing industries. Included in this group, according to the Bureau of Labor Statistics, are five major categories of service employment. First, there are the service industries, which include the health services needed by a growing and aging population; all the business service industries that supply personnel for offices and for computer and data processing; the education field, which will need more teachers for more students as the population continues to grow; and also the social services areas such as child care and family services. The second major category of service-producing jobs includes those in wholesale and retail trade, spurred in part by rising incomes and the rapid increase in sales of clothing, appliances, and automobiles. Finance, insurance, and real estate make up the third major category, and government is a fourth area of service in which the number of jobs will increase. Finally, the category of transportation, communications, and public utilities will be a major area for expansion of jobs, with truck transportation accounting for 50 percent of the new jobs in this area while jobs in communications decline about 12 percent.

## Division

As we look more closely at the area of marketing and sales occupations, which the Bureau of Labor Statistics defines as a growing service area, we can see that it includes a wide variety of jobs. People who work in this area sell goods and services in stores, on the phone, and by catalogs and mail order. They also purchase commodities and properties for resale, act as wholesalers for others, and scout out new stores and franchises to open. Travel agents as well as financial services counselors aim to increase consumer interest in their goods and services. Others study the market for growth trends and consumer needs or analyze sales both in the United States and abroad. Marketing and sales occupations indeed span a broad spectrum of interests, though they all have the consumer in mind.

- **Process Analysis** A process paragraph analyzes or describes a process or the way something works. Such paragraphs can also explain how to complete some process and are ordered chronologically.

When you scout the job market, here are some steps to follow to improve your opportunities for finding the job you want. First, do not limit yourself to the jobs listed by various companies. Those lists represent only a small percentage of the jobs available, and they will draw dozens—maybe even hundreds—of applicants. Instead, draw up a list of companies you'd like to work for by browsing through their yearly reports and other materials available in a job counselor's office. Don't forget the Yellow Pages, particularly if you know the city where you want to work. Then, call the company and ask for the name of someone likely to be the hiring authority. If possible, get some name other than that of the personnel manager—that person's job is often to screen out unqualified candidates. Next, send a clear, well-focused resume directly to that person, and don't be bashful about listing your accomplishments in terms of that company's needs. In the cover letter, state why you are the ideal person for that organization. Make your reader see why the company will be better off with you, not anyone else. Be sure to conclude the cover letter with a request for an interview and explain that you will be following up with a phone call within the next few days. At the interview, explore all the options you can, helping the other person see how you might fit in, even if there is no vacancy at the present time. You might help the person create a new position for which you'd be the best applicant. Finally, be sure to write a short letter thanking the interviewer for meeting with you.

- **Compare and contrast** One way to discuss two subjects is to compare them by looking at their similarities. You can also contrast them by looking at their differences. There are two options for organizing such a paragraph: (1) present first one subject and then the other, or (2) discuss both subjects at the same time, item by item.

**Two Subjects, One at a Time**

A government study of occupations in forestry and logging indicate that they represent two rather different areas of work. Forestry technicians compile data on the characteristics of forests, such as size, content, and condition. Generally, they are the decision makers, traveling through sections of forest to gather basic information about species of trees in the forest, disease and insect damage, seedling mortality, and conditions that may cause forest fires. One of their main responsibilities is to determine when a tract of forest is ready to be harvested. Less skilled than forest technicians are forest workers whose work includes more physical labor. They plant new tree seedlings to reforest timberland; remove diseased or undesirable trees; spray herbicides where needed; and clear away brush and debris from camp trails, roadsides, and camping areas. Like forest technicians, though, their work requires long hours out of doors in all kinds of weather.

**Two Subjects, Point by Point**

Many students who graduate with economics majors take one of two very different types of jobs, either as government economists or as market research analysts for large companies. Those who go to work for the government assess economic conditions in the United States and abroad and estimate the economic effects of specific changes in legislation or public policy. Marketing research analysts, on the other hand, are concerned with the design, promotion, price, and distribution of a product or service. Another area of difference is that government economists analyze data provided by government studies while marketing research analysts often design their own surveys and questionnaires or conduct interviews. But, whether they work as economists for the government or as analysts for private companies, most people in this field find that they often work under pressure of deadlines and tight schedules. In spite of the pressure, some economists and analysts combine full-time jobs with part-time or consulting work in academia or other settings.

- **Definition** A definition of a term places it in a general class and then differentiates it from others in that class, often with the use of examples and comparisons.

Skill in problem solving is a crucial mental ability that job interviewers look for when they meet applicants, but it is not clear *what this mental process is. Problem solving is an ability that assists a person in defining what the problem is and how to formulate steps to solve it. Included in this complex cognitive act are a number of characteristic mental abilities. Being flexible— remaining open to new possibilities— is a great asset in solving a problem, though a good problem solver also draws on strategies that may have worked in other settings. In addition, problem solving involves keeping the goal clearly in mind so that a person doesn't get sidetracked into exploring related problems that don't achieve the desired goal. Employers want problem solvers because having such a skill is far more valuable than having specific knowledge. Problem-solving abilities cannot be taught on the job, whereas specific knowledge often can be, and specific knowledge can become outdated, unlike the ability to solve problems.*

# 4 Writing with Computers (comp)

Using word processing software on a computer is an efficient way to write. You can add, delete, revise, and move blocks of words around with great ease and speed. You will probably find your drafts easier to read as you revise. Even if you cannot type well (and many successful computer users can't), a computer can be both a convenience and an aid throughout the writing process. But remember to save your files—often—and make backup copies of your files, even when you've carefully saved them. Disks can go bad, and files can get lost.

Listed here are a number of strategies to try in all aspects of the writing process.

## 4a Planning with Computers

- **Freewriting and brainstorming**  If freewriting or brainstorming are useful strategies for you (see 2a), do this on the computer. You can use a cut-and-paste feature to place parts of those planning notes into a draft as needed. Some writers find that they can freewrite more easily if they turn down the brightness on their computer screen so that it's dark and they cannot see what they type. You may also want to create separate files for different topics within the freewriting.

- **Writing an e-mail message**  As you think about your assignment or topic, write an e-mail message to someone in your class or to a friend. Use that e-mail message to try out ideas as you would in a conversation with peer group members or a writing center tutor. Encourage the person who receives your e-mail to ask questions that help you clarify your ideas. If you want a copy of one of your messages, send it to your own e-mail address as well.

- **Planning visually**  Use a draw or paint program to do some visual planning such as clustering and branching (see 2a).

- **Making an outline**  Set up headings for an outline in large bold letters. Later, when you go back to fill in the subheadings and subpoints, you will be able to see the larger structure of the paper. Some word processing programs let you go back and forth between a screen showing only the headings and screens showing the detailed material within sections.

- **Keeping a journal**  If keeping a journal helps you, start a journal file for each assignment and include thoughts and questions that occur to you as you work. Include a plan for how you will proceed through the assignment, and if there are stages or steps to complete, write a "to do" list. Include phrases and ideas that occur to you and that may fit into the paper with some cutting and pasting from one file to another.

- **Storing notes**  As you gather material from your reading and other research sources, develop a separate file or make use of a feature in your word processing program to store those notes.

## 4b Drafting with Computers

- **Creating a scrap file**  As you start drafting, make two separate files, one for the paper you are writing and the other for scraps—words, sentences, and paragraphs—that you discard as you draft. Use the scrap file by cutting and pasting into it anything that doesn't seem to fit in as you write. This scrap file can be a very useful storage space for materials that should be deleted from the paper you are writing now but that may be useful for other assignments. You may also want a scrap file for key words, words that come to mind and that can be useful when needed, or for phrases that may come in handy as section headings in your paper.

- **Adding notes**  As you work, you may come up with a suggestion you want to consider or a question that needs to be checked, but you don't want to stop writing. You can include a reminder to yourself by writing a note on the screen in bold letters or in parentheses. Be sure to delete these notes before you submit a final draft.

- **Splitting screens**  Consider this strategy if it helps you to look at information or additional writing in one file while you draft in another file. If you can view multiple files on your screen at the same time, you can look at the material in your scrap, outline, or note files. This is especially useful because you can cut, paste, and copy between files.

## 4c Organizing with Computers

- **Mixing up the order of paragraphs or sentences**  Make a new copy of your file and then, in the new file, use the cut-and-paste feature to move paragraphs around. You may see a better organizing principle than the one you had been using. Do the same with sentences within paragraphs.

- **Checking your outline**  Look again at the bold-lettered headings of the outline you made during planning (or create one now), and reassess whether your outline is adequate and well organized.

## 4d Revising with Computers

- **Starting at the beginning of a file**  Each time you open your file, you are at the beginning of the draft. Start there and read until you come to the section where you will be working. Rereading has several advantages. It helps you get back into the flow of thought, and it permits you to re-see what you've written so that you can do some revising as you read forward.

- **Renaming a file**  Each time you open your file, save it with a new file name so that you always know which is the most recent version you've worked on. If your first draft is Draft1, the next time you open that file, save it as Draft2. Then, the next time you can save it as Draft3, and so on.

- **Printing out hard copies to read**  It may help you to look at a printed copy of your paper as you revise so that you can see the development and organization, as well as get a sense of the whole paper. If you do print out a draft of your paper, however, resist the temptation to hand in that draft because it looks neat and seems to have a finished appearance.

- **Using page or print view to check paragraphs**  Switch to the page or print view so that you can see a whole page on the screen. Do the paragraphs look about the same length? Is one noticeably shorter than the others? Does it need more development? Is there a paragraph that seems to be disproportionately long?

- **Highlighting sentence length** Working with a copy of your main file, hit the return key after every sentence so that every sentence looks like a separate paragraph. Are all of your sentences the same length? If so, do you need variety? Do they all start the same way? Do you need to use different sentence patterns? (See Chapter 15 on sentence variety.)

# 4e Editing and Proofreading with Computers

- **Using online tools** There are a number of online tools you can use while editing, such as spell checkers and grammar checkers. However, grammar checkers are often not very effective because it is hard to distinguish between appropriate and inappropriate advice they offer. Some word processing programs come with a thesaurus that is useful for looking up synonyms for words you've been using too much or for finding more specific words than the ones you have used.

- **Changing the appearance of key features of your writing** Put active verbs in bold letters, put passive constructions in italics, use larger fonts for descriptive words, underline your thesis statement, and so on. By changing the appearance of these features, you may find that some of your writing habits need to be changed too. Perhaps you use too many passives or you don't use enough descriptive words.

- **Editing on hard copy** It may be easier for you to print out a draft and mark that for editing changes, in addition to printing out previous drafts when revising. If you do, put marks in the margins to indicate lines where changes are to be made so that you can easily find them again.

# PART TWO

## SENTENCE ACCURACY, CLARITY, AND VARIETY

This part will help you write and revise your sentences so that they are accurate, complete, clear, and effective. The topics cover common sentence errors, parts of sentences, words acting within sentences, whole sentences, and relationships between sentences.

# 5 Comma Splices and Fused Sentences (cs/fs)

A **comma splice** and a **fused sentence** (also called a **run-on**) are punctuation problems in compound sentences. (See 25b on compound sentences.)

There are three patterns for commas and semicolons in compound sentences:

**1.** Independent clause⊙ and   independent clause.
                      but
                      for
                      or
                      nor
                      so
                      yet

**2.** Independent clause⊙   independent clause.

**3.** Independent clause⊙ however,   independent clause.
                      therefore,
                      moreover,
                      thus,
                      consequently,
                      (etc.)

### Commas in Compound Sentences

Use a comma when you join two independent clauses (clauses that would be sentences by themselves) with any of the following seven joining words:

| and | but | for | or | nor | so | yet |
|-----|-----|-----|-----|-----|-----|-----|

> The game was over, **but** the crowd refused to leave.

Some variations:

- If both independent clauses are very short, you may omit the comma.

  > Lucinda may come or she may stay home.

- Some people prefer to use a semicolon when one of the independent clauses already has a comma.

  > Every Friday, depending on the weather, Sam likes to play tennis; but sometimes he has trouble finding a partner.

> **HINT:** Don't put commas before every *and* in your sentences. *And* is frequently used in ways that do not require commas.

### Semicolons in Compound Sentences

If you use any connecting words other than *and, but, for, or, nor, so,* or *yet,* or if you don't use any connecting words, you'll need a semicolon.

> The game was over; **however,** the crowd refused to leave.

> The game was over; the crowd refused to leave.

## 5a Comma Splices

The **comma splice** is a punctuation error that occurs either when independent clauses are joined only by a comma and no coordinating conjunction or when a comma is used instead of a semicolon between two independent clauses.

> **Comma Splice:** In Econ 150, students meet in small groups for an extra
> *and*
> hour each week, ∧ this helps them learn from each other.

**Comma Splice:** The doctor prescribed a different medication ; however, it's not helping.

# 5b Fused or Run-on Sentences

> The **fused** or **run-on sentence** is a punctuation error that occurs when there is no punctuation between independent clauses.

**Fused or Run-on Sentence:** I didn't know which job I wanted , and (or) ; I couldn't decide.

There are several ways to fix comma splices, fused sentences, and run-ons:

- Add one of the seven joining words (*and, but, for, or, nor, so, yet*) (and be sure to use a comma).
- Separate the independent clauses into two sentences.
- Change the comma to a semicolon. (See 28a.)
- Make one clause dependent upon another clause. (See 23b and 26b.)

## Exercise 5.1: Proofreading Practice

*In the following paragraph there are some compound sentences that require commas. Add commas where they are needed.*

(1) Cocoa beans have been grown in the Americas for several thousand years. (2) They were considered a treasure and were cultivated by the Aztecs for centuries before the Spanish discovered them in Mexico. (3) Cocoa reached Europe even before coffee or tea and its use gradually spread from Spain and Portugal to Italy and France and north to England. (4) In 1753 the botanist Linnaeus gave the cocoa plant its scientific name, *Theobroma cacao,* the food of the gods. (5) The tree is cacao, the bean is cocoa, and the food is chocolate but it bears no relation to coca, the source of cocaine. (6) Most cacao is grown within ten degrees of the equator. (7) In the late nineteenth century the Portuguese took the plant to some islands off Africa and it soon became an established crop in the Gold Coast, Cameroon, and Nigeria, where the temperature and humidity are ideal for it.

## Exercise 5.2: Pattern Practice

*Combine some of the short sentences listed here (and change a few words, if you need to) so that you have five compound sentences that follow the pattern shown here. Be sure to punctuate correctly with a comma.*

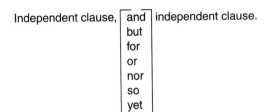

Independent clause, | and | independent clause.
                    | but |
                    | for |
                    | or  |
                    | nor |
                    | so  |
                    | yet |

There are many varieties of chocolate.
All varieties come from the same bean.
All varieties are the product of fermentation.
Once fermented, beans must be dried before being packed for shipping.
Chocolate pods cannot be gathered when they are underripe or overripe.
Chocolate pods are usually harvested very carefully by hand.
In the processing different varieties of chocolate are produced.
Dutch chocolate has the cocoa butter pressed out and alkali added.
Swiss chocolate has milk added.
Conching is the process of rolling chocolate over and over against itself.
Conching influences the flavor of chocolate.
Chocolate is loved by millions of people all over the world.
Some people are allergic to chocolate.

# 6 Subject-Verb Agreement (agr)

**Subject-verb agreement** occurs when the subject and verb endings agree in number and person.

## 6a Singular and Plural Subjects

The subject of every sentence is either singular or plural, and that determines the ending of the verb.

### (1) Singular

Singular nouns, pronouns, and nouns that cannot be counted, such as *news, time,* and *happiness* (see Chapter 50), take verbs with singular endings.

I chew.    Water drips.    Time flies.    You laugh.    The news is dull.

## (2) Plural

Plural nouns and pronouns take verbs with plural endings.

We know.      The cups are clean.      They stretch.      The stamps stick.

# 6b Buried Subjects

It is sometimes difficult to find the subject word when it is buried among many other words. In that case, disregard prepositional phrases; modifiers; *who, which,* and *that* clauses; and other surrounding words.

❖ Almost **all** of Art's many friends who showed up at the party last night at
    *(subject)*

Andy's **brought** gifts.
        *(verb)*

[In this sentence, *Almost* is a modifier, *of Art's many friends* is a prepositional phrase, and *who showed up at the party at Andy's* is a *who* clause that describes *friends.*]

---

**HINT:** For a present tense sentence, you can't have two -*s* endings at the same time, one on the subject and the other on the verb. Plural subject nouns have an -*s* at the end and so do many third person, present tense, singular verbs. So, a plural subject can't have a singular verb, and a singular subject can't have a plural verb.

Chimes ring.      The boy jumps.

---

**HINT 1:** It's easier to find the verb first, so locate the verb by asking *who* or *what* is the doer of the verb. The verb is also the word that changes when you change the time of the sentence, from present to past or past to present.

**HINT 2:** Eliminate phrases starting with the following words because they are normally not part of the subject.

| | | |
|---|---|---|
| including | along with | together with |
| accompanied by | in addition to | as well as |
| except | with | no less than |

**Everyone** in our family, including my sister, **has taken** piano lessons.
*(subject)*                                        *(verb)*

# 6c Compound Subjects

Subjects joined by *and* take a plural verb (X *and* Y = more than one, plural).

The (dog) and the (squirrel) are running around the tree.

The (company) and its (subsidiary) manufacture auto parts.

Sometimes, though, the words joined by *and* act together as a unit and are thought of as one thing. If so, use a singular verb.

(Peanut butter and jelly) is a popular filling for sandwiches.

# 6d *Either/Or* Subjects

When the subject words are joined by *either . . . or, neither . . . nor,* or *not only . . . but,* the verb agrees with the closest subject word.

Either **Alice** or her (children) are going to bed early.

Neither the **choir** nor the (director) is ready for the performance.

Not only the **clouds** but also the (snow) was gray that day.

# 6e Clauses and Phrases as Subjects

When a whole clause or phrase is the subject, use a singular verb.

(What I want to know) is why I can't try the test again.

(Saving money) is difficult to do.

(To live happily) seems like a worthwhile goal.

However, if the verb is a form of *be* and the noun afterward (the complement) is plural, the verb has to be plural.

What we saw <u>were</u> pictures of the experiment.    [What we saw = pictures]

# 6f Indefinites as Subjects

Indefinite words with singular meanings such as *each, every,* and *any* take a singular subject when (1) they are the subject word or (2) they precede the subject word.

**Each** has her own preference.

Each **book** is checked in by the librarian.

However, when indefinite words such as *none, some, most,* or *all* are the subject, the number of the verb depends on the meaning of the subject.

**Some** of the book is difficult to follow.  [The subject of the sentence here is a portion of the book and is therefore thought of as a single unit and has a singular verb.]

**Some** of us are leaving now.  [The subject of this sentence is several people and is therefore thought of as a plural subject with a plural verb.]

**All** she wants is to be left alone.

**All** my sweaters are in that drawer.

# 6g Collective Nouns and Amounts as Subjects

**Collective nouns** are nouns that refer to a group or a collection (such as *team, family, committee,* and *group*). When a collective noun is the subject and refers to the group acting as a whole group or single unit, the verb is singular.

Our **family** has just bought a new car.

In most cases, a collective noun refers to the group acting together as a unit, but occasionally the collective noun refers to members acting individually. In that case, the verb is plural.

The **committee** are unhappy with each other's decisions.

[The subject here is thought of as different people, not a single unit.]

When the subject names an amount, the verb is singular.

Twenty-five **cents** is cheap.          Four **bushels** is enough.
More than 125 **miles** is too far.      Six **dollars** is the price.

# 6h Plural Words as Subjects

Some words that have an *-s* plural ending, such as *civics, mathematics, measles, news,* and *economics,* are thought of as a single unit and take a singular verb.

**Physics** <u>is</u> fascinating.      The **news** <u>is</u> disheartening.
**Measles** <u>is</u> unpleasant.      Modern **economics** <u>shows</u> contradictions.

Some words, such as those in the following list, are treated as plural and take a plural verb, even though they refer to one thing. (In many cases, there are two parts to these things.)

**Jeans** <u>are</u> fashionable.      **Eyeglasses** <u>are</u> inexpensive.
**Pants** <u>cover</u> his tan.      **Shears** <u>cut</u> cloth.
**Scissors** <u>cut</u> paper.      **Thanks** <u>are</u> not necessary.
**Clippers** <u>trim</u> hedges.      **Riches** <u>are</u> his dream.

# 6i Titles, Company Names, and Words as Subjects

For titles of written works, names of companies, and words used as terms, use singular verbs.

***All the King's Men*** <u>is</u> the book assigned for this week.

**General Foods** <u>is</u> hiring people for its new plant.

**"Cheers"** <u>is</u> a word he often says when leaving.

# 6j Linking Verbs

Linking verbs agree with the subject rather than the word that follows (the complement).

Her **problem** <u>is</u> frequent injuries.

Short **stories** <u>are</u> my favorite reading matter.

# 6k There Is/There Are/It

The verb depends on the complement that follows the verb.

**There** <u>is</u> an excellent old movie on TV tonight.

**There** <u>are</u> too many old movies on TV.

However, *it* as the subject always takes the singular verb, regardless of what follows.

**It** <u>was</u> the bears in the park that knocked over the garbage cans.

# 61 *Who, Which, That* and *One of . . . Who/Which/That* as Subjects

When *who, which,* and *that* are used as subjects, the verb agrees with the previous word they refer to (the antecedent).

They are the students **who** <u>study</u> hard.

He is the student **who** <u>studies</u> the hardest.

In the phrase *one of those who* (or *which* or *that*), it is necessary to decide whether the *who, which,* or *that* refers only to the one or to the whole group. Only then can you decide whether the verb is singular or plural.

Rena is one of those shoppers who buy only things that are on sale.

one of those shoppers who buy

[In this case, Rena is part of a large group, shoppers who buy only things that are on sale, and acts like them. Therefore, *who* takes a plural verb because it refers to shoppers.]

The *American Dictionary* is one of the dictionaries on the shelf that includes Latin words.

one . . . that includes

[In this case the *American Dictionary*, while part of the group of dictionaries on the shelf, is specifically one that includes Latin words. The other dictionaries may or may not. Therefore, *that* refers back to that *one* dictionary and takes a singular verb.]

## Exercise 6.1: Proofreading Practice

*In the following paragraph choose the correct verb that agrees with the subject.*

How children's drawings develop (1. is, are) a fascinating subject. For example, a two-year-old and sometimes even a three-year-old (2. does not, do not) create any recognizable forms when scribbling, and most of the children recently studied by a child psychologist (3. seem, seems) not to be aware of the notion that a line stands for the edge of an object. Typically, by the age of three, children's spontaneous scribbles along with their attempts at drawing a picture (4. become, becomes) more obviously pictorial. When a child has drawn a recognizable shape, either the child or some nearby adult (5. attempt, attempts) to label the shape with a name. By the age of three or four, there (6. is, are) attempts to draw images of a human, images that look like a tadpole and consist of a circle and two lines for legs. Psychologists, especially those who (7. study, studies) the development of people's concepts of reality, (8. conclude, concludes) that young children's tad-pole-like drawings (9. is, are) a result of inadequate recall of what people look like. However, Clayton Peale is one of a number of psychologists who (10. insist, insists) that young children do have adequate recall but (11. isn't, aren't) interested in realism because they prefer simplicity. Once the desire for realism (12. set, sets) in, it leads to the more complex drawings done by older children.

## Exercise 6.2: Pattern Practice

*Using the following patterns for correct subject-verb agreement, write two sentences of your own.*

Pattern A: Compound subject joined by *and* with a plural verb

> The whole flower exhibit and each display in it were carefully planned for months.

Pattern B: An amount as a subject with a singular verb

> Ten dollars is a small price to pay for that.

Pattern C: A title, company name, or word with a singular verb

> *The Mysteries of the Universe* is a new educational TV series.

Pattern D: An item that is a single unit but is thought of as plural (such as pants, scissors, and jeans) with a plural verb

> The scissors need sharpening.

Pattern E: Plural words (such as *physics, economics,* and *measles*) with a singular verb

> The news of the election results is being broadcast live from the election board office.

Pattern F: *Either . . . or, neither . . . nor,* or *not only . . . but*—with a verb that agrees with the nearest subject

> Either Todd or his friends are capable of handling that job.

Pattern G: A whole clause as the subject with a singular verb

> Whatever the finance committee decides to do about the subject is acceptable to the rest of us.

Pattern H: A *who, what,* or *that* clause with a verb that agrees with the correct antecedent

> *Psycho* is one of those movies that shock viewers no matter how many times they watch reruns.

# 7 Sentence Fragments (frag)

A **sentence fragment** is an incomplete sentence.

To recognize a fragment, consider the basic requirements of a sentence:

- A sentence is a group of words with at least one independent clause (see 23a).

> After buying some useful software for her computer, <u>Elena splurged on</u>
> (independent clause)
> <u>several computer games to play</u>.

- A clause has at least one subject and a complete verb, plus an object or complement if needed. (See Chapter 21.)

> During the evening, the <u>mosquitoes</u> <u>avoided</u> the <u>campfire</u>.
>         *(subject)*   *(verb)*      *(object)*

## 7a Unintentional Fragments

- **The fragment without a subject or verb**
  This type of fragment lacks a subject or verb.

> **Fragment:** The five days spent on the beach just relaxing and soaking up the sun.

[*Days* is probably the intended subject here, but it has no verb.]

> **Revised:** The five <u>days</u> spent on the beach just relaxing and soaking up
>           *(subject)*
> the sun <u>was</u> the best vacation I had in years.
>      *(verb)*

> **Fragment:** She selected a current news item as the topic of her essay. Then wondered if her choice was wise.

[The second of these two word groups is a fragment because it has no subject for the verb *wondered*.]

> **Revised:** She selected a current news item as the topic of her essay. Then <u>she</u> <u>wondered</u> if her choice was wise.
>              *(subject)* *(verb)*

---

**HINT 1:** When you proofread for fragments, be sure that the word group has both a subject and a complete verb. Remember that *-ing* words are not complete verbs because they need a helping verb. (See 16b.)

**HINT 2:** To find subjects and predicates in sentences with one-word verbs, make up a *who* or *what* question about the sentence. The predicate is all the words from the sentence used in the *who* or *what* question, and the subject is the rest:

My grandmother lived in a house built by her father.
[Who lived in a house built by her father?]

**Predicate:** lived in a house built by her father

**Subject:** My grandmother

7a
fra

- **The fragment caused by a misplaced period**
  Most fragments are caused by detaching a phrase or dependent clause from the sentence to which it belongs. A period has been put in the wrong place, often because the writer thinks a sentence has gotten too long and needs a period. Such fragments can be corrected by removing the period between the independent clause and the fragment.

  ❖ Ever since fifth grade I have participated in one or more team sports,
     *, beginning*
     ~~Beginning~~ with the typical grammar school sports of basketball and

     volleyball.

     [The second word group is a detached phrase that belongs to the sentence preceding it.]

  ❖ Travelers to Europe should consider visiting in the spring or fall,
     *because*
     ~~Because~~ airfares and hotels are often cheaper then.

     [The second word group is a dependent clause that was detached from the sentence before it.]

**HINT 1:** To proofread for fragments caused by misplaced periods, read your paper backward, from the last sentence to the first. You will be able to notice the fragment more easily when you hear it without the sentence to which it belongs. Most, but not all, fragments occur **after** the main clause.

**HINT 2:** To find dependent clauses separated from the main clause, look for the marker word typically found at the beginning of the dependent clause. (See 23b(2).) If it is standing alone with no independent clause, attach it to the independent clause that

*continued on next page*

completes the meaning. Typical marker words that begin dependent clauses are the following:

| | | | |
|---|---|---|---|
| after | because | since | what |
| although | before | though | when |
| as | even though | unless | whether |
| as if | if | until | while |

**Fragment:** Denise had breakfast at the doughnut shop near Hafter
Hall. ~~After~~ *after* she went to her 8 A.M. biology class.

**HINT 3:** Another way to identify a dependent clause is to be sure that it is not an independent clause that answers a yes/no question.

They often spend Sunday afternoons watching football games on TV.

Do they often spend Sunday afternoons watching football games on TV?

[This question yields a yes/no answer and is therefore an independent clause.]

Because they often spend Sunday afternoons watching football games on TV.

Do because they often spend Sunday afternoons watching football games on TV?

[This is not a reasonable question and is not, therefore, an independent clause.]

# 7b Intentional Fragments

Writers occasionally write an intentional fragment for its effect on the reader. Intended fragments should be used only when the rest of the writing clearly indicates that the writer could have written a whole sentence but preferred a fragment. In the following three sentences the second word group is an intended fragment. Do you like the effect it produces?

**Fragment:** Jessica walked quietly into the room, unnoticed by the rest of the group. *Not that she wanted it that way.* She simply didn't know how to make an effective entrance.

## Exercise 7.1: Proofreading Practice

*In these clusters of sentences, there are both complete sentences and fragments. After you read each sentence, circle either F (fragment) or C (complete sentence).*

A. (1) Pollution is a problem we have not really worked on (F or C). (2) Surely there is something that can be installed in factory smokestacks so that all the chemicals can be filtered out first (F or C). (3) Instead of just pouring right out in the open (F or C). (4) But factories are only part of the problem (F or C). (5) Every time you watch one of those big 747s take off, a big stream of smoke comes barreling out (F or C). (6) Or a big stream of pollution (F or C). (7) When a bus takes off, a cloud of black smoke comes pouring out (F or C). (8) Right through your car's vent into where you are sitting (F or C).

B. (1) Americans used to believe that the future would bring better jobs, better homes, and a better life for their children (F or C). (2) This confidence no longer exists (F or C). (3) Polls that have been reported in the news recently indicating that fewer Americans feel they are better off today than they were five years ago (F or C). (4) Many see themselves as lower on the ladder (F or C). (5) Maybe even with worse living conditions or further decline in the future (F or C).

## Exercise 7.2: Pattern Practice

*Read the following paragraph and note the pattern of dependent and independent clauses (see Chapter 23) in each sentence. Practice by following those patterns to write your own sentences, and check to see that you have not written any fragments. As a guide to help you, the first sentence has been done. For your own sentences, you may wish to write about some modern convenience you particularly like (or dislike) or some modern convenience you wish someone would invent.*

**Sample answer:**

*Sentence 1:*

**Pattern:** Independent clause + dependent clause

**Sample Sentence:** Those hot-air dryers in public restrooms are a Grade A nuisance because it's impossible to dry your face without messing up your hair.

(1) In France the National Electronic Directory has made the phone book obsolete because computer terminals are replacing the books. (2) Instead of a phone book, customers can choose a small computer hooked to their phones. (3) Using this computer they can call the directory along with a thousand other services such as banks, theater ticket offices, stock reports, and databases. (4) The National Electronic Directory holds all twenty-five million French phone listings, and it handles about four million inquiries a month. (5) The directory finds the name of people anywhere in France, has a simple command structure, and is updated daily. (6) The equipment is given to customers free, although there is a charge for each minute a call is made to the directory or any of the other services.

# 8 Dangling and Misplaced Modifiers (dm)

## 8a Dangling Modifiers

A **dangling modifier** is a word or word group that refers to (or modifies) a word or phrase that has not been clearly stated in the sentence.

When an introductory phrase does not name the doer of the action, the phrase then refers to (or modifies) the subject of the independent clause that follows.

> **Having finished** the assignment, Jill turned on the TV.

[*Jill*, the subject of the independent clause, is the doer of the action in the introductory phrase.]

However, when the intended subject (or doer of the action) of the introductory phrase is not stated, the result is a dangling modifier.

> **Having finished** the assignment, the TV was turned on.

[This sentence says that the TV finished the homework. Since it is unlikely that TV sets can get our work done, the introductory phrase has no logical or appropriate word to refer to. Sentences with dangling modifiers say one thing while the writer means another.]

Characteristics of dangling modifiers:

- They most frequently occur at the beginning of sentences but can also appear at the end.
- They often have an *-ing* verb or a *to* + verb phrase near the start of the phrase.

> **Dangling Modifier:** After getting a degree in education, more experience in the classroom is needed to be a good teacher.
>
> **Revised:** After getting a degree in education, Sylvia needed more experience in the classroom to be a good teacher.

**Dangling Modifier:** To work as a lifeguard, practice in CPR is required.

**Revised:** To work as a lifeguard, you are required to have practice in CPR.

There are two strategies for revising dangling modifiers:

1. Name the doer of the action in the dangling phrase.

**Dangling Modifier:** Without knowing the guest's name, it was difficult for Maria to introduce him to her husband.

**Revised:** Because Maria did not know the guest's name, it was difficult to introduce him to her husband.

2. Name the appropriate or logical doer of the action as the subject of the independent clause.

**Dangling Modifier:** Having arrived late for practice, a written excuse was needed.

**Revised:** Having arrived late for practice, the team member needed a written excuse.

## Exercise 8.1: Proofreading Practice

*In the following paragraph there are several dangling modifiers. Identify them by underlining them.*

According to some anthropologists, the fastball may be millions of years older than the beginning of baseball. To prove this point, prehistoric toolmaking sites, such as Olduvai Gorge in Tanzania, are offered as evidence. These sites are littered with smooth, roundish stones not suitable for flaking into tools. Suspecting that the stones might have been used as weapons, anthropologists have speculated that these stones were thrown at enemies and animals being hunted. Searching for other evidence, historical accounts of primitive peoples have been combed for stories of rock throwing. Here early adventurers are described as being caught by rocks thrown hard and fast. Used in combat, museums have collections of these "handstones." So stone throwing may have been a major form of defense and a tool for hunting. Being an impulse that still has to be curbed, parents still find themselves teaching their children not to throw stones.

## Exercise 8.2: Pattern Practice

*Using the patterns of the sample sentences given here, sentences in which the modifiers do not dangle, write your own sentences. The first sentence is done as an example.*

1. After seeing that there were no good movies on television that night, Brook rented a video for his VCR.

### Sentence in the Same Pattern:

While walking home with her friends, Pam remembered the book she needed from the library.

2. To do well in biology, students have to be able to memorize many unfamiliar terms.
3. Unlike opera, rock videos usually don't have main characters or plots.
4. Undecided about his major, Marcos registered for courses in several fields.
5. The movie was a thriller, having lots of blood and gore.

# 8b Misplaced Modifiers

A **misplaced modifier** is a word or word group placed so far away from what it refers to (or modifies) that the reader may be confused.

Modifiers should be placed as closely as possible to the words they modify in order to keep the meaning clear.

**Misplaced Modifier:** The assembly line workers were told that they had been fired by the personnel director.

[Were the workers told by the personnel director that they had been fired, or were they told by someone else that the personnel director had fired them?]

**Revised:** The assembly line workers were told by the personnel director that they had been fired.

Misplaced modifiers are often the source of comedians' humor, as in the classic often used by Groucho Marx and others:

The other day I shot an elephant in my pajamas. How he got in my pajamas I'll never know.

Single-word modifiers should be placed immediately before the words they modify. Note the difference in meaning in these two sentences:

I earned nearly $30.    [The amount was almost $30, but not quite.]

I nearly earned $30.    [I almost had the opportunity to earn $30, but it didn't work out.]

---

**HINT:** Some one-word modifiers that may get misplaced:

| | | | |
|---|---|---|---|
| almost | hardly | merely | only |
| even | just | nearly | simply |

---

## Exercise 8.3: Proofreading Practice

*In these sentences there are some misplaced or unclear modifiers. Underline them and indicate a more appropriate place in the sentence by drawing an arrow to that place.*

After finishing a huge dinner, he <u>merely</u> ate a few cherries for dessert.

(1) The man who was carrying the sack of groceries with an umbrella walked carefully to his car. (2) He only bought a small amount of food for his lunch because he was going to leave town that afternoon. (3) He whistled to his huge black dog opening the car door and set the groceries in the trunk. (4) The dog jumped into the trunk happily with the groceries.

## Exercise 8.4: Pattern Practice

*Choose one of the one-word modifiers listed in the HINT box, and use the word in several places in a series of sentences to create different meanings. Write out the meaning of each sentence.*

**Example (using the word *almost*):**

**Almost** everyone in the office earned a $500 bonus last year.    [Most of the people earned a $500 bonus, but a few people did not.]

Everyone in the office **almost** earned a $500 bonus last year.    [There was almost a chance to earn a bonus, but it didn't work out. Therefore, no one earned a bonus.]

Everyone in the office earned **almost** a $500 bonus last year.    [Everyone earned a bonus, but it was less than $500.]

# 9 Parallel Constructions (//)

## 9a Parallel Structure

**Parallel structure** is the use of the same grammatical form or structure for equal ideas in a list or comparison.

The balance of equal elements in a sentence helps to show the relationship between ideas. Often the equal elements repeat words or sounds.

**Parallel:** The instructor carefully explained <u>how to start the engine</u> and
                                                                    *(1)*

   <u>how to shift gears</u>.
        *(2)*

[1 and 2 are parallel phrases in that both start with *how to:*

* <u>how to</u> start the engine
* <u>how to</u> shift gears]

**Parallel:** <u>Getting the model airplane off the ground</u> was even harder than
              *(1)*

   <u>building it from a kit.</u>
        *(2)*

[1 and 2 are parallel phrases that begin with *-ing verb* forms:

* <u>Getting</u> the model airplane off the ground
* <u>building</u> it from a kit]

**Parallel:** She often went to the aquarium <u>to watch the fish,</u> <u>to enjoy the</u>
                                              *(1)*              *(2)*

   <u>solitude,</u> and <u>to escape from her roommate</u>.
                            *(3)*

[1, 2, and 3 are parallel phrases that begin with *to* + verb.]

Parallelism is needed in the following:

* Items in a series or list

   **Parallel:** Items often overlooked when camping include the following:

   **1.** All <u>medications</u> normally taken on a daily basis

   **2.** <u>Books</u> to read during leisure time

   **3.** <u>Quinine tablets</u> to purify water

      [parallelism with a series of nouns in a list]

   **Parallel:** The three most important skills for that job are

- being able to adapt to new requirements

- knowing appropriate computer languages

- keeping lines of communication open

  [parallelism with *-ing* verbs]

- *Both . . . as/either . . . or/whether . . . or/neither . . . nor/not . . . but/not only . . . but also* (correlative conjunctions)

  **Parallel: Both** by the way he dressed **and** by his attempts at humor, it was clear that he wanted to make a good impression.

  [parallelism with *by the . . .* phrases]

- *And, but, or, nor, yet* (coordinating conjunctions)

  **Parallel:** Job opportunities are increasing in the health fields **but** decreasing in many areas of engineering.

  [parallelism using *-ing* verbs]

- Comparisons using *than* or *as*

  **Parallel:** The mayor noted that it was easier to agree to the new budget **than** to attempt to veto it.

  [parallelism in a comparison with *to* + verb]

# 9b Faulty Parallelism

**Nonparallel structure** (or **faulty parallelism**) occurs when like items are not in the same grammatical form or structure.

❖ Many companies are reducing their labor force as well as *eliminating* ~~eliminate~~ some
   *(1)*                                                                      *(2)*
   employee benefits.

❖ When the investigator took over, he started his inquiry by calling the
                              *requesting*                                    *(1)*
   witnesses back and ~~requested~~ that they repeat their stories.
                        *(2)*

❖ The article looked at <u>future uses of computers</u> and <s>what</s> their role <s>will be</s> in

                                 *(1)*                                       *(2)*

<u>the next century</u>.

---

**HINT 1:**  As you proofread, **listen** to the sound when you are link-ing or comparing similar elements. Do they balance by sounding alike? Parallelism often adds emphasis by the repetition of similar sounds.

**HINT 2:**  As you proofread, **visualize** similar elements in a list. Check to see that the elements begin in the same way.

Isaiah wondered whether it was better <u>to tell</u> his girlfriend that he for-got or <u>if</u> he should make up some excuse.

[Isaiah wondered whether it was better

- <u>to tell</u> his girlfriend that he forgot
               (or)
- <u>if</u> he should make up some excuse]

**Revised:** Isaiah wondered whether it was better <u>to tell</u> his girlfriend that he forgot or <u>to make up</u> some excuse.

---

## Exercise 9.1: Proofreading Practice

*In this paragraph, underline the parallel elements in each sentence.*

One of the great American cars was the J-series Duesenberg. The cars were created by Fred and August Duesenberg, two brothers from Iowa who began by making bicycles and who then gained fame by building racing cars. Determined to build an American car that would earn re-spect for its excellent quality and its high performance, the Duesenbergs completed the first Model J in 1928. The car was an awesome machine described as having a 265-horsepower engine and a top speed of 120 mph. Special features of the car were its four-wheel hydraulic brakes and extensive quantities of lightweight aluminum castings. The masterpiece was the Duesenberg SJ, reputed to have a 320-horsepower engine and to accelerate from zero to 100 mph in 17 seconds.

## Exercise 9.2: Pattern Practice

*Using these sentences as patterns for parallel structures, write your own sentences using the same patterns. You may want to write about some favorite vehicle of your own, such as a car or bike.*

1. A common practice among early Duesenberg owners was to buy a bare chassis and to ship it to a coach builder, who would turn the chassis into a dazzling roadster, cabriolet, or dual-cowl phaeton.

2. Duesenbergs that were originally purchased for six thousand dollars or so and that are now being auctioned off for more than a million dollars are still considered to be superb examples of engineering brilliance.

3. After the Duesenberg first appeared on the market and people realized its excellence, the phrase "It's a doozy" became part of American slang.

# 10 Consistency (Avoiding Shifts) (shft)

**Consistency** in writing involves using the same (1) pronoun person and number, (2) verb tense, (3) tone, (4) voice, and (5) indirect or direct form of discourse.

## 10a Shifts in Person or Number

Avoid shifts between first, second, and third person pronouns, and between singular and plural.

The following chart shows three "persons" in English pronouns:

| PRONOUN PERSON | | |
| --- | :---: | :---: |
| | **Singular** | **Plural** |
| **First person** (the person or persons speaking) | I, me | we, us |
| **Second person** (the person or persons spoken to) | you | you |
| **Third person** (the person or persons spoken about) | he, she, it | they, them |

Some readers view first or second person writing as too personal or informal and suggest that writers use third person for formal or academic writing. Second person, however, is appropriate for giving instructions or helping readers follow a process:

First, (you) open the hood of the car and check the water level in the battery.

[The pronoun *you* can be used or omitted.]

First person is appropriate for a narrative about your own actions and for essays that explore your personal feelings and emotions. Some teachers encourage writers to use first person to develop a sense of their own voice in writing.

## (1) Unnecessary Shift in Person

Once you have chosen to use first, second, or third person, shift only with a good reason.

❖ In a <u>person's</u> life, the most important thing ~~you do~~ *he or she does* is to decide on a type of
     *(3rd)*                                  *(2nd)*
job.

[This is an unnecessary shift from third to second person.]

## (2) Unnecessary Shift in Number

To avoid pronoun inconsistency, don't shift unnecessarily in number from singular to plural (or from plural to singular).

❖ ~~The working woman faces~~ *Working women face* many challenges to advancement in a career.
               *(sing.)*
When <u>they</u> marry and have children, <u>they</u> may need to take a leave of
  *(pl.)*                            *(pl.)*
absence and stay home for several months.

[The writer uses the singular noun *woman* in the first sentence but then shifts to the plural pronoun *they* in the second sentence.]

# 10b Shifts in Verb Tense

Because verb tenses indicate time, keep writing in the same time (past, present, or future) unless the logic of what you are writing about requires a switch.

Narrative writing can be in the past or present, with time switching if needed. Explanatory writing (exposition) that expresses general truth is usually kept in present time, though history is written in past time.

**Necessary Shift:** Many people today <u>remember</u> very little about the Vietnam War except the filmed scenes of fighting they <u>watched</u> on television news at the time.

[The verb *remember* reports a general truth in the present, and the verb *watched* reports past events.]

**Unnecessary Shift:** While we <u>were watching</u> the last game of the World Series, the picture suddenly <u>gets</u> fuzzy.

[The verb phrase *were watching* reports a past event, and there is no reason to shift to the present tense verb *gets.*]

**Revised:** While we <u>were watching</u> the last game of the World Series, the picture suddenly <u>got</u> fuzzy.

# 10c Shifts in Tone

Once you choose a formal or informal tone for a paper, keep that tone consistent in your word choices. A sudden intrusion of a very formal word or phrase in an informal narrative or the use of slang or informal words in a formal report or essay indicates the writer's loss of control over tone.

❖ The job of the welfare worker is to assist in a family's struggle to obtain *children's* funds for the ~~kids'~~ food and clothing.

[The use of the informal word *kids'* is a shift in tone in this formal sentence.]

# 10d Shifts in Voice

Don't shift unnecessarily between active and passive voice in a sentence. (See 16d for a review of active and passive verbs.)

**Active:** He <u>insisted</u> that he was able to perform the magic trick.

**Passive:** The magic trick <u>was not considered</u> to be difficult by him.

❖ He <u>insisted</u> that he was able to perform the magic trick, which *he did not consider* ~~was not considered~~ to be difficult ~~by him~~.

When choosing between passive and active, remember that many readers prefer active voice verbs because they are clearer, more direct, and more concise. The active voice also forces us to think about who the doer of the action is. For example, in the following sentence the writer uses passive rather than considering who the doer is:

Many arguments are offered against abortion.   [By whom?]

But there are occasions to use passive:

• When the doer of the action is not important or is not known

The pep rally was held before the game.

For the tournament game, more than five thousand tickets were sold.

• When you want to focus on the action, not the doer

The records were destroyed.

• When you want to avoid blaming, giving credit, or taking responsibility

The candidate conceded that the election was lost.

• When you want a tone of objectivity or wish to exclude yourself

The experiment was performed successfully.

It was noted that the results confirmed our hypothesis.

# 10e Shifts in Discourse

When you repeat the exact words that someone says, you are using **direct discourse**, and when you change a few of the words in order to report them indirectly, you are using **indirect discourse**. Mixing direct and indirect discourse results in unnecessary shifting, a problem that causes lack of parallel structure as well.

**Direct Discourse:** The instructor said, "Your reports are due at the beginning of next week. Be sure to include your bibliography."

**Indirect Discourse:** The instructor said that our reports are due at the beginning of next week and that we should be sure to include our bibliographies.

**Unnecessary Shifting:** The instructor said that our reports are due at the beginning of next week and be sure to include your bibliography.

[This sentence also mixes together a statement and a command, two different moods. For more on mood, see 16e.]

## Exercise 10.1: Proofreading Practice

*As you read the following paragraph, proofread for consistency and correct any unnecessary shifts. Underline the inconsistent word and write a more consistent form above it. You may also want to omit some words or phrases.*

Many people think that recycling material is a recent trend. However, during World War II more than 43 percent of America's newsprint was recycled, and the average person saved bacon grease and other meat fat, which they returned to local collection centers. What you would do is to pour leftover fat and other greasy gunk from frying pans and pots into tin cans. Today, despite the fact that many trendy people are into recycling, only about 10 percent of America's waste is actually recycled. The problem is not to get us to save bottles and cans but to convince industry to use recycled materials. There is a concern expressed by manufacturers that they would be using materials of uneven quality and will face undependable delivery. If the manufacturer would wake up and smell the coffee, they would see the advantages for the country and bigger profits could be made by them.

# 11 Faulty Predication (pred)

**Faulty predication** occurs when the subject and the rest of the clause (the *predicate*) don't make sense together.

**Faulty Predicate:** The <u>reason</u> for her sudden success <u>proved</u> that she was talented.

[In this sentence the subject, *reason,* cannot logically prove "that she was talented."]

**Revised:** Her sudden success proved that she was talented.

Faulty predication often occurs with forms of the verb *to be* because this verb sets up an equation in which the terms on either side of the verb should be equivalent:

| *Subject* | | *Predicate* |
|-----------|-----|-------------|
| $2 \times 2$ | = | 4 |
| $2 \times 2$ | is | 4 |

Dr. Streeter   is   our family doctor.

**Faulty Predication:** Success is when you have your own swimming pool.

[The concept of success involves much more than having a swimming pool. Having a pool can be one example or a result of success, but it is not the equivalent of success.]

**Revised:** One sign of success is having your own swimming pool.

> **HINT:** Faulty predication often occurs in sentences with the following constructions:
>
> is when . . .     is why . . .     is where . . .     is because . . .
>
> It is best to avoid these constructions in academic writing.
>
> *that*
> **Faulty Predication:** The reason I didn't show up is ~~because~~ I overslept.

## Exercise 11.1: Proofreading Practice

*Rewrite the following examples of faulty predication so that they are correct sentences.*

1. Relaxation is when you grab a bowl of popcorn, put your feet up, and watch football on television for two hours.
2. Computer science is where you learn how to program computers.
3. One of the most common ways to improve your math is getting a tutor.
4. The next agenda item we want to look at is to find out the cost of purchasing decorations.
5. His job consisted mainly of repetitious assembly line tasks.

## Exercise 11.2: Pattern Practice

*The patterns of the following five sentences avoid faulty predication. Practice these patterns by completing the second sentence in each set. Be sure to use the same pattern even though your subject matter will be different.*

1. A good science fiction movie is one that has an exciting plot and realistic special effects.
   A good _____ is _____ .
2. His job as a receptionist is to direct people to the right office.
   His job as a _____ is _____.
3. One sign of her excellent memory is her ability to remember the punch lines of all the jokes she hears.
   One sign of her _____ is _____ .
4. The reason I didn't buy those boots is that they are overpriced.
   The reason _____is that _____.
5. Stage fright is a kind of apprehension accompanied by a dry mouth, sweaty hands, and a fluttery stomach.
   _____ is _____.

# 12 Coordination and Subordination

## 12a Coordination (coord)

When an independent clause is added to another independent clause to form a sentence, both clauses are described as **coordinate** because they are equally important and have the same emphasis.

### (1) Appropriate Coordination

Independent clauses are joined together by coordinators and appropriate punctuation (see Chapters 5, 23a, and 26a). Two types of words join coordinate clauses:

- *Coordinating conjunctions* (the seven coordinating words used after a comma) are:

  and        but        for        or        nor        so        yet

- *Conjunctive adverbs* (coordinating words used after a semicolon) include:

  consequently   otherwise   however   thus
  furthermore    therefore   moreover  nevertheless

The following sentences illustrate appropriate coordination because they join two clauses of equal importance and emphasis.

> Kathy is doing well as a real estate broker, and she hopes to become wealthy before she is thirty-five.

> Some people take vitamin C tablets for colds; however, other people prefer aspirin.

### (2) Inappropriate Coordination

**Inappropriate coordination** occurs when two clauses that are either unequal in importance or have little or no connection with each other are joined together as independent clauses.

Inappropriate coordination can be corrected by making one clause dependent on the other. However, if there is little connection between the clauses, they may not belong in the same sentence or paragraph.

**Inappropriate Coordination:** Winter in Texas can be very mild, and snow often falls in New England during the autumn.

[The connection between these two clauses is very weak; they don't belong together unless the writer can show more connection.]

**Inappropriate Coordination:** Jim was ill, and he went to the doctor.

**Revised:** Because Jim was ill, he went to the doctor.

[In this case the first clause can be shown to depend on the second clause.]

## (3) Excessive Coordination

**Excessive coordination** occurs when too many equal clauses are strung together with coordinators. As a result, a sentence can ramble on and become tiresome or monotonous.

Excessive coordination can be corrected by breaking the sentence into smaller ones or by making the appropriate clauses into dependent ones.

**Excessive Coordination:** Kirsten is an exchange student from Holland, and she is visiting the United States for the first time, so she decided to drive through the Southwest during vacation.

**Revised:** Kirsten, an exchange student from Holland visiting the United States for the first time, decided to drive through the Southwest during vacation.

# 12b Subordination (sub)

When one clause has less emphasis or is less important in a sentence, it is **subordinate** to or dependent on the other clause.

## (1) Appropriate Subordination

The relationship of a dependent or subordinate clause to a main clause is shown by the marker word that begins the subordinate clause. (See 23b and 25b.) Some common marker words (called *subordinating conjunctions*) are:

| | | |
|---|---|---|
| after | before | unless |
| although | if | until |
| as | once | when |
| as though | since | whether |
| because | though | while |

<u>Although I like snow</u>, I enjoy Florida vacations in winter.

Mr. Stratman, <u>who never missed a football game</u>, was one of the team's greatest supporters.

The house <u>that she grew up in</u> was torn down.

## (2) Inappropriate Subordination

**Inappropriate subordination** occurs when the more important clause is placed in the subordinate or dependent position and has less emphasis.

**Inappropriate Subordination:** A career <u>that combines a lot of interaction with people and opportunities to use my creative talents</u> is my goal.

**Revised:** My career goal is to combine a lot of interaction with people and opportunities to use my creative talents.

## (3) Excessive Subordination

**Excessive subordination** occurs when a sentence has a string of clauses subordinate to each other. As a result, readers have difficulty following the confusing chain of ideas dependent on each other.

To revise excessive subordination, place the string of dependent clauses in separate sentences with independent clauses.

**Excessive Subordination:** These computer software companies should inform their employees about advancements and promotions with the company because they will lose them if they don't compete for their services since the employees can easily find jobs elsewhere.

**Revised:** These computer software companies should inform their employees about advancements and promotions with the company. If these companies don't compete for the services of their employees, the companies will lose them because the employees can easily find jobs elsewhere.

## Exercise 12.1: Proofreading Practice

*In the following paragraph there are some sentences with inappropriate coordination and subordination. Rewrite these sentences so that the paragraph has appropriate coordination and subordination.*

(1) Most people think of pigs as providers of ham, bacon, and pork chops, and they think of pigs as dirty, smelly, lazy, stupid, mean, and stubborn, but there's more to pigs than this bad press they've had, so we should stop and reevaluate what we think of pigs. (2) President Harry Truman once said that no man should be allowed to be president who does not understand hogs because this lack of understanding indicates inadequate appreciation of a useful farm animal. (3) Some people are discovering that pigs make excellent pets. (4) In fact, pigs have been favorite characters in children's fiction, and many people fondly remember Porky Pig and Miss Piggy, the Muppet creation, as well as the heroic pig named Wilbur in E. B. White's *Charlotte's Web*. (5) Now there are clubs for those who keep pigs as pets, and they are not just on farms where they have long been favorites as pets for farm children, who are likely to be fond of animals. (6) People with pigs as pets report that their pigs are curious, friendly little animals that are quite clean despite the "dirty as a pig" saying, though they are also not very athletic and have a sweet tooth. (7) Pigs can be interesting pets and are useful farm animals to raise.

## Exercise 12.2: Pattern Practice

*To practice using subordination and coordination appropriately, use these suggested patterns in your own sentences. You can build your sentences from the short sentences offered here.*

**1.** Coordination: Join independent clauses with any of the following words (or others listed on previous pages).

| , and | , but | , or |
|---|---|---|
| ; moreover, | ; however, | ; therefore, |

**2.** Subordination: Subordinate dependent clauses to independent clauses by using any of the following words (or others listed on previous pages) at the beginning of the dependent clause.

| after | once | when |
|---|---|---|
| although | since | whether |
| as | that | which |
| because | though | while |
| before | unless | who |
| if | until | whose |

You can use these clauses to build your paragraph:

Plastic used to be considered a cheap, shoddy material.
Now plastic is taking the place of traditional materials.
Cars are made of plastic.
Boats, airplanes, cameras, fishing rods, watches, suitcases, toothpaste tubes, and plates are made of plastic.

Plastic has replaced the glass in eyeglasses.
Plastic has replaced the wood in tennis rackets.
Plastic has replaced cotton and wool in our clothing.
Plastic seems new.
Plastic has been with us for a long time.
Amber is a natural form of plastic.
Celluloid is a nearly natural plastic.
Celluloid was developed in 1868 as a substitute for ivory in billiard balls.
Celluloid proved to be too flammable.
New types of plastic have mushroomed.
The use of plastics has steadily increased.
By the mid-1970s plastic had become the nation's most widely used material.

# 13 Sentence Clarity (clar)

The suggestions offered in this section will improve the clarity of your sentences. These suggestions are based on what is known about how to help readers follow along more easily and understand sentence content more fully.

## 13a Moving from Known (Old) to Unknown (New) Information

To help readers understand your writing, begin your sentences with something that is generally known or familiar before you introduce new or unfamiliar material later in the sentence. Then, when that new material is known, it becomes familiar, or "old," and you can go on to introduce more new material.

Note how these sentences move from familiar (or old) information to new:

**Familiar ——▶ Unfamiliar:**

Every semester, after final exams are over, I'm always faced with the problem of what to do with lecture notes. These old notebooks might be useful some day, but they just keep piling up on my bookcase. Some day, it will collapse under the weight of information I might never need.

On the other hand, this example is not as clear:

**Unfamiliar ◄——— Familiar:**

Second-rate entertainment is my categorization of most movies I've seen lately, but occasionally, there are some with worthwhile themes. In the Southwest, the mysterious and rapid disappearance of an Indian culture is the topic of a recent movie I saw that I would say has a worthwhile theme.

You probably found these sentences hard to read because the familiar information comes after the new information.

# 13b Using Positive Instead of Negative

Use the positive (or affirmative) instead of the negative because negative statements are harder for people to understand.

**Unclear Negative:** Less attention is paid to commercials that lack human interest stories.

**Revised:** People pay more attention to commercials with human interest stories.

# 13c Avoiding Double Negatives

Use only one negative at a time in your sentences.

Using more than one negative word creates a double negative, which is grammatically incorrect and leaves the reader with the impression that the writer isn't very literate. Some double negatives are also hard to understand.

**Double Negative:** He did not have no money.

**Revised:** He had no money. (or) He did not have any money.

**Double Negative:** I don't think he didn't have no money left after he paid for his dinner.

[This sentence is particularly hard to understand because it uses both a double negative and negatives instead of positives.]

**Revised:** I think he had some money left after he paid for his dinner.

**HINT 1:** Watch out for contractions with negatives in them. If you use the following contractions, do not use any other negatives in your sentence.

| | | |
|---|---|---|
| aren't | don't | wasn't |
| couldn't | hadn't | weren't |
| didn't | hasn't | won't |
| doesn't | isn't | wouldn't |

*any*
❖ She doesn't want ~~no~~ more riders in the car.

**HINT 2:** Watch out for other negative words:

| | | |
|---|---|---|
| hardly | no place | nothing |
| neither | nobody | nowhere |
| no one | none | scarcely |

*any*
❖ They hardly had ~~no~~ popcorn left.

# 13d Using Verbs Instead of Nouns

Try to use verbs if possible rather than noun forms. Actions expressed as verbs are more easily understood than actions named as nouns.

**Unnecessary Noun Form:** The decision was made to adjourn.

**Revised:** They decided to adjourn.

| *Some Noun Forms* | *Verbs to Use Instead* |
|---|---|
| The determination of . . . | They determine . . . |
| The approval of . . . | They approve . . . |
| The preparation of . . . | They prepare . . . |
| The discovery of . . . | They discover . . . |
| The analysis of . . . | They analyze . . . |

# 13e Making the Intended Subject the Sentence Subject

Be sure that the real subject or the doer of the action in the verb is the grammatical subject of the sentence.

Sometimes the real subject of a sentence can get buried in prepositional phrases or other less noticeable places.

**Subject Buried in a Prepositional Phrase:**

For real music lovers, <u>it is</u> preferable to hear a live concert instead of a tape.

[The grammatical subject here is *it*, which is not the real subject of this sentence.]

A revision brings the real subject out of the prepositional phrase. The following example shows one possibility.

**Revised:** <u>Music lovers prefer</u> to hear a live concert instead of a tape.

**Real Subject Buried in the Sentence:**

<u>It seems</u> like ordering from catalogs is something that Chris does too much.

If the real subject, Chris, becomes the sentence subject, the entire sentence becomes more clear.

**Revised:** <u>Chris seems</u> to order too much from catalogs.

# 13f Using Active Instead of Passive

The active verb (see 16d) is often easier to understand than the passive because the active voice explains who is "doing" the action.

**Active:** The committee <u>decided</u> to postpone the vote.
         *(active)*

**Not as clear:** The decision that <u>was reached</u> by the committee was to
                *(passive)*
         postpone the vote.

## Exercise 13.1: Proofreading Practice

*The following paragraph has numerous problems with clarity. Each of the sentences in the paragraph could be revised by using one or more of the suggestions in this chapter. List the section numbers of all the suggestions that could be followed to improve each of these sentences.*

(1) Beyond boomerangs and koala bears, knowledge about Australia was not common among Americans until a few years ago. (2) All that was changed by the appearance in the United States of Australian movies such as *My Brilliant Career* and *Mad Max.* (3) In addition, there was the appearance on American television of commercials of Paul Hogan, the Australian entertainer, reminding us that the America's Cup in yachting had been lost by the Americans to the Australians. (4) Now, American tourists are pouring into Australia, and hardly any big travel agency doesn't offer package tours "down under." (5) They are

obviously happy to have discovered this new continent for sightseeing. (6) Not to be missed are sights to dazzle Americans, such as the Great Barrier Reef, a 1,250-mile reef teeming with tropical fish, and the outback. (7) A vast collection of deserts and bush country where the aborigines live is also to be visited, with lovely cities such as Sydney and Melbourne for the traveler.

## Exercise 13.2: Pattern Practice

*Look back through this chapter at the patterns for the changes you suggested in Exercise 13.1. Use those patterns to revise the paragraph above so that it is clearer.*

# 14 Transitions (trans)

**Transitions** are words and phrases that build bridges between sentences, parts of sentences, and paragraphs. These bridges show relationships and help to blend sentences together smoothly.

Several types of transitions are illustrated here.

## 14a Repetition of a Key Term or Phrase

Among the recent food fads sweeping America is the interest in **exotic foods**. While not everyone can agree on what **exotic foods** are, most of us like the idea of trying something new and different.

## 14b Synonyms

Since the repetition of a key word or phrase can become boring, use a synonym (a word or phrase having essentially the same meaning) to add variety while not repeating.

One food Americans are not inclined to try is **brains**. A Gallup Poll found that 41 percent of the people who responded said they would never try **brains**. Three years later, the percentage of those who wouldn't touch **gray matter** had risen to 49 percent.

## 14c Pronouns

Pronouns such as *he, she, it, we,* and *they* are useful devices when you want to refer back to something mentioned previously. Similarly, *this, that, these,* and *those* can be used as links.

In addition to brains, there are many other foods that <u>Americans</u> now find
(1)
more distasteful than <u>they</u> did several years ago. For example, more
(1)
people now say they would never eat <u>liver, rabbit, pig's feet, or beef kidneys</u>
(2)
than said so three years ago. Even restaurant workers who are exposed to

<u>these</u> delicacies aren't always wild about <u>them.</u>
(2)                                                    (2)

# 14d Transitional Words and Phrases

English has a huge storehouse of words and phrases that cue the reader
to relationships between sentences. Without these cues the reader may
be momentarily puzzled or unsure of how sentences relate to each
other. For example, read these two sentences:

> John is very tall. He does not play basketball.

If it took you a moment to see the connection, try reading the same two
sentences with a transitional word added:

> John is very tall. However, he does not play basketball.

The word *however* signals that the second sentence contradicts or con-
trasts with the first sentence. Read the following:

> The state government was determined not to raise taxes. Therefore, . . .

As soon as you reached the word *therefore,* you knew that some conse-
quence or result would follow.

The transitions listed in the following chart are grouped according
to the categories of relationships they show.

| TRANSITIONS | |
|---|---|
| *Adding* | and, besides, in addition, also, too, moreover, further, furthermore, next, first, second, third, finally, last, again, and then, likewise, similarly |
| *Comparing* | similarly, likewise, in like manner, at the same time, in the same way |

| Contrasting | but, yet, however, still, nevertheless, on the other hand, on the contrary, in contrast, conversely, in another sense, instead, rather, notwithstanding, though, whereas, after all, although |
| Emphasizing | indeed, in fact, above all, add to this, and also, even more, in any event, in other words, that is, obviously |
| Ending | after all, finally, in sum, for these reasons |
| Giving examples | for example, for instance, to illustrate, that is, namely, specifically |
| Pointing to cause and effect, proof, conclusions | thus, therefore, consequently, because of this, hence, as a result, then, so, accordingly |
| Showing place or direction | over, above, inside, next to, underneath, to the left, to the right, just behind, beyond, in the distance |
| Showing time | meanwhile, soon, later, afterward, now, in the past, then, next, before, during, while, finally, after this, at last, since then, presently, temporarily, after a short time, at the same time, in the meantime |
| Summarizing | to sum up, in brief, on the whole, as has been noted, in conclusion, that is, finally, as has been said, in general, to recapitulate, to conclude, in other words |

**HINT:** In this list you'll notice words such as *and* and *but*, which some people prefer not to use to begin sentences. Others think these are useful words to achieve variety and smooth transitions between sentences.

Although jet lag is a nuisance for travelers, it can be a disaster for flight crews. **But** flight crews can reduce the effects of jet lag by modifying their sleep patterns. **And** airlines are beginning to recognize the need for in-flight naps.

# 14e Transitions in and between Paragraphs

## (1) Transitions between Sentences in a Paragraph

Your paragraphs are more easily understood when you show how every sentence in the paragraph is connected to the whole. To signal the connections, use **repetition, synonyms, pronouns,** and **transitional words and phrases.** In the following example, these connections are highlighted.

◯ = repetition          ( ) = pronouns

▢ = synonyms          ▢ = transitional words and phrases

While drilling into Greenland's layers of ice, scientists recently pulled up evidence from the last ice age showing that the island's climate underwent extreme shifts within a year or two. (This) unexpected finding is based on evidence from ice cores that the climate often shifted from glacial to warmer weather in just a few years. In addition, other evidence indicates that the annual amount of snow accumulation also changed abruptly at the same time. As the climate went from cold to warm, the amount of snowfall jumped abruptly by as much as 100 percent. This change happened because more snow falls during warmer periods when the atmosphere holds more water. From this evidence, scientists therefore conclude that warming and cooling of the earth may be able to occur much faster than had been previously thought.

## (2) Transitions between Paragraphs

As you start a new paragraph, you should also show the link to previous paragraphs, and an effective place to do this is in the first sentence of the new paragraph. Use the following strategies for including transitions between paragraphs.

- **Use repetition as a hook.** One way to make a connection is to reach back to the previous paragraph, referring to an element from there in the beginning of your next paragraph. Some writers think of this as using a hook. They "hook" an element from above and bring it down—through the use of repetition—to the next paragraph, providing a connecting thread of ideas.

Suppose your paper discusses the changing role of women in combat. In a paragraph on the history of women's roles in warfare, you conclude with the example of Harriet Tubman, an African-American who led scouting raids into enemy territory during the Civil War. In the next paragraph you want to move to new roles for women in modern combat. Your opening sentence can "hook" the older use of women as scouts and tie that to their new role as pilots in the Gulf War:

While a few women served in more limited roles as <u>scouts</u> in previous
*("hook" to previous paragraph)*
wars, in the Gulf War women took on more extensive roles as pilots flying supplies, troops, and ammunition into combat zones.

- **Use transitional words to show direction.** Because every paragraph advances your paper forward, the first sentence can be used to point your readers in the direction of your whole essay. Think of the first sentence of every paragraph as being like a road map, indicating to your readers where they are headed.

    For example, suppose your next paragraph in a paper on campaign reform presents a second reason in your argument against allowing large personal contributions to political candidates. Use a transitional word to show that you are building a list of arguments:

    <u>Another reason</u> political candidates should not receive large personal contributions is . . .

    [The underlined words show that the writer is adding another element.]

    Or suppose that your next paragraph is going to acknowledge that there are also arguments for the opposing side in this topic. You would then be going in the opposite direction or contrasting one side against the other:

    <u>Not everyone, however,</u> is in favor of making personal contributions to candidates illegal. Those who want to continue the practice argue that . . .

    [The underlined words signal a turn in the opposite direction.]

## Exercise 14.1: Proofreading Practice

*To practice recognizing different types of transitions, read the following paragraph and underline the transitions. Categorize them by putting the appropriate numbers under the words you mark, using these numbers:*

1. Repetition of key term or phrase
2. Synonyms
3. Pronouns
4. Transitional words or phrases

International airports may soon have a high-tech machine that is really an unusually reliable nose. This sophisticated machine sniffs for drugs and will provide a more accurate means of trapping narcotics smugglers than has been possible so far. The walk-through narcotics vapor detector pulls in air samples from a passenger's clothes as he or she passes through. Several feet past the first sampling, the passenger is again sampled by having air blown across his or her body. Then, these vapor samples are funneled into a device called a thermionic sensor. If the sensor sets off an alarm, the passenger is searched. However, it is not always certain that drugs will be found because there can be an occasional false alarm. But officials hope that the electronic nose will strike fear in the hearts of would-be smugglers. If so, this high-tech nose will act as a deterrent as well as a detector.

## Exercise 14.2: Pattern Practice

*In the following paragraph, the connections or transitional links are missing in paragraph 1, but they are added in paragraph 2. Paragraph 3, like paragraph 1, needs transitions. Use the types of transitional links described in Chapter 14 and illustrated in paragraph 2 to revise paragraph 3. Your revision will be paragraph 4.*

**Paragraph 1:**

I like autumn. Autumn is a sad time of year. The leaves turn to brilliant yellow and red. The weather is mild. I can't help thinking ahead to the coming of winter. Winter will bring snowstorms, slippery roads, and icy fingers. In winter the wind chill factor can make it dangerous to be outside. I find winter unpleasant. In the autumn I can't help thinking ahead to winter's arrival. I am sad when I think that winter is coming.

**Paragraph 2:**

Although I like autumn, it is also a sad time of year. Of course, the leaves turn to brilliant yellow and red, and the weather is mild. Still, I can't help thinking ahead to the coming of winter with its snowstorms, slippery roads, and icy fingers. Moreover, in winter the wind chill factor can make it dangerous to be outside. Because I find these things unpleasant, in the autumn I can't help thinking ahead to winter's arrival. Truly, I am sad when I think that winter is coming.

**Paragraph 3:**

Caring for houseplants requires some basic knowledge about plants. The plant should be watered. The plant's leaves should be cleaned. The spring and summer bring a special time of growth. The plant can be fertilized then. The plant can be repotted. The diameter of the new pot should be only two inches larger than the pot the plant is presently in. Some plants can be put outside in summer. Some plants cannot be put outside. If you are familiar with basic requirements for houseplants, you will have healthy plants.

# 15 Sentence Variety (var)

Sentences with the same word order and length produce the kind of monotony that is boring to readers. To make your sentences more interesting, add variety by making some longer than others and by finding alternatives to starting every sentence with the subject and verb.

## 15a Combining Sentences

- You can combine two sentences (or independent clauses) into one longer sentence.

   ❖ Doonesbury cartoons laugh at contemporary politicians. The *, but the* victims of the satire probably don't read the cartoon strip.

> **HINT:** To join an independent clause to another with *and, but, for, or, nor, so,* or *yet,* use a comma. Use a semicolon if you do not use connecting words or if you use other connecting words such as *therefore* and *however.*

- You can combine the subjects of two independent clauses in one sentence when the verb applies to both clauses.

   **Original:** During the flood, the Wabash River overflowed its banks. At the same time, Wildcat Creek did the same.

   **Revised:** During the flood, both the Wabash River and Wildcat Creek overflowed their banks.

- You can join two predicates when they have the same subject.

   **Original:** Ken often spends Sunday afternoons watching football on TV. He spends Monday evenings the same way.

   **Revised:** Ken often spends both Sunday afternoons and Monday evenings watching football on TV.

## 15b Adding Words

- You can add a description, a definition, or other information about a noun after the noun.

❖ Dr. Lewis *, our family dentist,* recently moved to Florida.

❖ I plan to visit New York *, a city with a wide variety of ethnic restaurants.*

❖ Professor Nguyen ⟲ is a political science teacher ⟲ . ~~She~~ gives lectures in the community on current events.

- You can add a *who, which,* or *what* clause after a noun or turn another sentence into a *who, which,* or *what* clause.

❖ Ed *, who takes his job very seriously,* always arrives at his desk at 7:55 A.M.

❖ The experiment failed because of Murphy's law *, which* ~~. This law~~ states that buttered bread always falls buttered side down.

- Sometimes, you can delete the *who, which, what* words, as in the following example:

❖ The National Football League, ~~which is~~ popular with TV fans, is older than the American Football League.

- You can add phrases and clauses at the beginning of the sentence. For example, you can begin with a prepositional phrase. Some prepositions you might use include the following:

| In . . . | Because of . . . | On . . . |
| At . . . | In addition to . . . | From . . . |
| For . . . | Under . . . | Between . . . |

<u>In addition to</u> soup and salad, she ordered bread sticks and coffee.

<u>From</u> an advertiser's point of view, commercials are more important than the TV programs.

- You can begin with infinitives (*to* + verb) or with phrases that start with *-ing* and *-ed* verbs.

<u>To attract</u> attention, the hijackers ordered the plane to fly to Africa.

<u>Tired</u> of hearing her dog whining, she finally opened the door and let the cold, wet pooch in the house.

- You can add transitional words (see Chapter 14) at the beginning of sentences.

<u>However,</u> I don't want to make a decision too quickly.

<u>In addition</u>, the new model for that sports car will have a turbo boost.

- You can begin with dependent clauses by starting these clauses with dependent markers such as the following:

| after . . . | because . . . | since . . . | when . . . |
| although . . . | if . . . | until . . . | while . . . |

<u>After</u> the parade was over, the floats were quickly taken apart.

<u>When</u> spring comes, I'll have to start searching for a summer job.

# 15c Changing Words, Phrases, and Clauses

- You can move adjectives after the *is* verb to the front of the sentence so that they describe the subject noun.

**Original:** The homecoming queen was surprised and teary-eyed. She waved enthusiastically to the crowd.

**Revised:** Surprised and teary-eyed, the homecoming queen waved enthusiastically to the crowd.

- You can expand your subject to a phrase or clause.

<u>Hunting</u> is his favorite sport.

<u>Hunting grouse</u> is his favorite sport.

<u>To hunt grouse in the early morning mists</u> is to really enjoy the sport.

<u>Whoever has hunted grouse in the early morning mists</u> knows the real joys of the sport.

<u>That grouse hunting is enjoyable</u> is evident from the number of people addicted to the sport.

- You can change a sentence to a dependent clause (see 23b) or put it before or after the independent clause.

❖ *Because he* ~~He~~ overslept yesterday morning and missed class. ~~He~~ *, he* did not hear the announcement of the exam.

❖ *Although* America is overly dependent on foreign oil. ~~Scientists~~ *, scientists* have not yet found enough alternative sources of energy.

## Exercise 15.1: Pattern Practice

*In the paragraphs included here, paragraph 1 (which you will probably find very choppy and boring) is composed of sentences in a very similar pattern. Paragraph 2, a revision of paragraph 1, follows the strategies for achieving variety that are described in this chapter. As you read through paragraph 2, identify the various strategies used to achieve sentence variety. Use those and other strategies described in this chapter to revise paragraph 3, which (like paragraph 1) is composed of sentences in a very similar pattern.*

**Paragraph 1:**

(1) Whistling is a complex art. (2) It involves your lips, teeth, tongue, jaw, rib cage, abdomen, and lungs. (3) It occasionally also involves your hands and fingers. (4) Whistling sounds are produced by the vibration of air through a resonating chamber. (5) This resonating chamber is created by your mouth or hands. (6) One factor is particularly crucial. (7) This factor is the type of space produced in your mouth by your tongue. (8) Whistling is usually thought of as a means of entertainment. (9) It can also be a means of communication. (10) Some people include whistling as part of their language. (11) Others use whistling to carry messages over long distances.

**Paragraph 2 (Revision of Paragraph 1):**

(1) Whistling is a complex art that involves your lips, teeth, tongue, jaw, rib cage, abdomen, and lungs, and occasionally your hands and fingers. (2) Whistling sounds are produced by the vibration of air through the resonating chamber created by your mouth or hands. (3) One particularly crucial factor is the type of space produced in your mouth by your tongue. (4) Although whistling is usually thought of as a means of entertainment, it can also be a means of communication. (5) Some people include whistling as part of their language, and others use whistling to carry messages over long distances.

**Paragraph 3:**

Scientists neglect whistling. Amateurs and hobbyists do not neglect it. There are whistling contests all over the United States. Accomplished whistlers whistle classical music, opera, jazz, Broadway show tunes, polkas, and even rock and roll at these contests. People whistle very differently. Some people pucker their lips. Other people use their throat, hands, or fingers to produce whistling sounds. These whistling sounds resemble the flute. Whistling has several advantages. One advantage is that it is a happy sound. Whistlers never lose their instrument. Their instrument doesn't need to be cleaned or repaired. Their instrument costs nothing. It is easily transported. Learning how to whistle is hard to explain. Whistling is something you pick up either at a young age or not at all.

# PART THREE

## PARTS OF SENTENCES

If you have a racing bike, you may know about derailleurs and caliper brakes, and if you use computers, you may know about modems, bytes, and RAM. The more we know about a subject, the more specialized terms we learn, and this is true of grammar as well. However, to be users we don't all need to be specialists. But as we learn to effectively use our bikes, our computers, and our language, we do need to understand some basic concepts about each of them. Having a working vocabulary of some terms speeds us through explanations of these concepts.

In this chapter, you will learn both the basic terms you'll need and useful concepts about sentence parts. With this background knowledge, you'll understand the explanations of grammatical rules here and in other chapters.

# 16 Verbs (v)

A **verb** is a word or group of words that expresses action, shows a state of existence, or links the subject (usually the doer of the action) to the rest of the sentence.

The first step in distinguishing complete sentences from incomplete ones is recognizing the verb. Many sentences have more than one verb, but they must have at least one. Verbs provide several kinds of essential information in a sentence:

- Some verbs express action.

  Tonya **jogs** every day.

  I **see** my face in the mirror.

- Some verbs (called linking verbs) indicate that a subject exists or link the subject (the who or what) and the rest of the sentence together.

  She **feels** sad.

  The shark **is** hungry.

- Verbs indicate time.

  They **went** home.    [past time]

  The semester **will end** in May.    [future time]

- Verbs indicate number.

  Matt always **orders** anchovy pizza.    [singular—only one doer of the action, Matt]

Qun and Medhi always **order** sausage pizza.    [plural—two doers of the action, Qun and Medhi]

- Verbs indicate the person for the subject (the who or what, usually the doer of the action).

**First person:** *I* or *we*
I **love** to cook.

**Second person:** *you*
You **love** to cook.

**Third person:** *he, she, it, they*
He **loves** to cook.

---

**HINT:** You can find the verb (or part of it, when the verb has more than one word) by changing the time expressed in the sentence (from the present to the past, from the past to the future, and so on). In the following examples the word that changes is the verb, and the sentence expresses something about the past or present because of the verb form.

| *Present* | *Past* |
|---|---|
| Tamar **jogs** every day. | Tamar **jogged** every day. |
| I **see** my face in the mirror. | I **saw** my face in the mirror. |
| She **feels** sad. | She **felt** sad. |
| The shark **is** hungry. | The shark **was** hungry. |

---

# 16a Verb Phrases

A **verb phrase** is several words working together as a verb.

He **has gone** home.

I **am enjoying** my vacation.

They **should have attended** the movie with me.

# 16b Verb Forms

**Verb forms** are words that are not complete verbs in themselves and may be part of a verb phrase or may appear elsewhere in the sentence.

## (1) -ing Verbs

Forms of the verb that end in -ing, called *gerunds,* are never complete verbs by themselves. To be part of the verb phrase, the -ing form needs a helping verb and is then part of a progressive tense verb (see 16c). The -ing form may also be used alone elsewhere in the sentence.

The computer program **is working** smoothly.

[*Working* is a verb form because it is only a part of the verb phrase. *Is working* is the whole verb phrase because of the helping verb *is.*]

**Feeling** guilty is one of his favorite pastimes.

[*Feeling* is part of the subject. It is a verb form but not a verb.]

Everyone enjoys **laughing.**

[*Laughing* is the direct object of the verb. (The direct object completes the meaning or receives the action of the verb.) *Laughing* is a verb form but not a verb.]

---

**HINT:** Some incomplete sentences, called *fragments,* are caused by using only an -ing verb form with no helper.

*is showing* (or) *shows*
❖ Harlan, with his fast track record yesterday, **showing** all the practice and effort of the last three months.

[This is not a complete sentence because *showing* is not a complete verb.]

For more information on fragments, see Chapter 7.

---

## (2) -ed Verbs

To show past tense, most verbs have an -ed or -d added to the base form. (The base form is the main entry in the dictionary.) With no helping verb, the -ed or -d form is the simple past tense. When the -ed form has a helping verb such as *has* or *had,* it is part of one of the perfect tenses (see 16c). The -ed or -d form can also be used alone elsewhere in the sentence.

She **has jumped** farther than any other contestant so far.

[*Jumped* is part of the verb phrase, and *has jumped* is the complete verb phrase.]

I read that chapter, the one **added** to last week's assignment.

[*Added* is not part of the verb phrase.]

## (3) *to* + Verb

Another verb form, called the *infinitive,* has *to* added to the base form. This infinitive form is used with certain verbs (see 47c).

I was supposed **to give** her the ticket.

[*Was supposed to give* is the whole verb phrase.]

**To forgive** is easier than **to forget.**

[*To forgive* and *to forget* are not part of the verb phrase.]

## Exercise 16.1: Proofreading Practice

*To practice your ability to identify verbs, verb phrases, and verb forms, underline the verbs and verb phrases in the following sentences. Circle the verb forms both in verb phrases and elsewhere in the sentence. As an example, the first sentence is already marked. Remember, many sentences have more than one verb or verb phrase.*

*Remember to ask yourself the following questions:*

- *To find a verb or verb phrase:* Which word or group of words expresses action, shows a state of existence, or links the subject, the doer of the action, to the rest of the sentence?
- *To find a verb form:* Which words end in *-ing* or *-ed* or have *to* + verb? Which of these are not complete verbs in themselves?

(1) For a long time psychologists have wondered what memories are and where they are stored in the human brain. (2) Because it is the basis of human intellect, memory has been studied intensely. (3) According to one psychologist, memory is an umbrella term for a whole range of processes that occur in our brains. (4) In particular, psychologists have identified two types of memory. (5) One type is called declarative memory, and it includes memories of facts such as names, places, dates, and even baseball scores. (6) It is called declarative because we use it to declare things. (7) For example, a person can declare that his or her favorite food is fried bean sprouts. (8) The other type is called procedural memory. (9) It is the type of memory acquired by repetitive practice or conditioning, and it includes skills such as riding a bike or typing. (10) We need both types of memory in our daily living because we need facts and we use a variety of skills.

## Exercise 16.2: Pattern Practice

*The following paragraph is in the present tense. Change it to the past tense by underlining the verbs and writing the past tense verb above the word that is changed. As an example, the first sentence is already marked.*

*studied*

(1) To learn more about memory, a psychologist <u>studies</u> visual memory by watching monkeys. (2) To do this, he uses a game that requires the monkey to pick up a block in order to find the food in a pail underneath. (3) After a brief delay the monkey again sees the old block on top of a pail and also sees a new block with a pail underneath it. (4) The new block now covers a pail with bananas in it. (5) The monkey quickly learns each time to pick up the new block in order to find food. (6) This demonstrates that the monkey remembers what the old block looks like and also what distinguishes the new block. (7) The psychologist concludes that visual memory is at work.

# 16c Verb Tense

**Verb tense** indicates the time of the verb: past, present, or future.

The four tenses for the past, present, and future are as follows:

- Simple
- Progressive:  *be* + *-ing* form of the verb
- Perfect: *have*
           *had* + the *-ed* form of the verb
           *shall*
- Perfect progressive: *have*
                       *had* + *been* + *-ing* form of the verb

The following chart shows verb forms:

| VERB FORMS | | | |
|---|---|---|---|
| | **Present** | **Past** | **Future** |
| **Simple:** | I walk. | I walked. | I will walk. |
| **Progressive:** | I am walking. | I was walking. | I will be walking. |
| **Perfect:** | I have walked. | I had walked. | I will have walked. |
| **Perfect progressive:** | I have been walking. | I had been walking. | I will have been walking. |

## (1) Present Tense

**Simple Present**

- Present action or condition: She **counts** the votes. They **are** happy.
- General truth: States **defend** their rights.

- Habitual action: He **drinks** orange juice for breakfast.
- Future time: The plane **arrives** at 10 P.M. tonight.
- Literary or timeless truth: Shakespeare **uses** humor effectively.

**Form:** This is the form found in the dictionary and is often called the base form. For third person singular subjects (*he, she, it*), add an *-s* or *-es*.

| | |
|---|---|
| I, you, we, they **walk.** | I, you, we, they **push.** |
| He, she, it **walks.** | He, she, it **pushes.** |

> **ESL HINT:** Students learning English as a second language may have difficulty in determining when American culture determines that something is a general, literary, or timeless truth and should be expressed in simple present tense. If so, a teacher or writing center tutor can help.

**Present Progressive**

- Activity in progress, not finished, or continued: The committee **is studying** that proposal.

**Form:** This form has two parts: *is* (or) *are* + *-ing* form of the verb.

We **are going.**    He **is singing.**

**Present Perfect**

- Action that began in the past and leads up to and includes the present: The company **has sold** that product since January.
- Habitual or continued action started in the past and continuing into the present: She **has** not **smoked** a cigarette for three years.

**Form:** Use *have* (or) *has* + *-ed* form of regular verbs (called the *past participle*).

I **have eaten.**    He **has** not **called.**

**Present Perfect Progressive**

- Action that began in the past, continues to the present, and may continue into the future: They **have been considering** that purchase for three months.

**Form:** Use *have* (or) *has* + *been* + *-ing* form of the verb.

He **has been running.**    They **have been meeting.**

## (2) Past Tense

**Simple Past**

- Completed action: We **visited** the museum during the summer.

- Completed condition: It **was** cloudy yesterday.

**Form:** Add *-ed* for regular verbs. For other forms, see the list of irregular verbs in this section.

> I **walked.**    They **awoke.**

### Past Progressive

- Past action that took place over a period of time: They **were driving** through the desert when the sandstorm hit.
- Past action that was interrupted by another action: The engine **was running** when he left the car.

**Form:** Use *was* (or) *were* + *-ing* form of the verb.

> She **was singing.**    We **were running.**

### Past Perfect

- Action or event completed before another event in the past: When the meeting began, she **had** already **left** the building.

**Form:** Use *had* + *-ed* form of the verb (past participle).

> He **had** already **reviewed** the list when Mary came in.

### Past Perfect Progressive

- Ongoing condition in the past that has ended: The diplomat **had been planning** to visit when his government was overthrown.

**Form:** Use *had* + *-ing* form of the verb.

> They **had been looking.**    She **had been speaking.**

## (3) Future Tense

### Simple Future

- Actions or events in the future: The recycling center **will open** next week.

**Form:** Use *shall* (or) *will* + base form of the verb. (In American English, *will* is commonly used for all persons, but in British English, *shall* is often used for the first person.)

> I **will choose.**    They **will enter.**

### Future Progressive

- Future action that will continue for some time: I **will be expecting** your call.

**Form:** Use *will* or *shall* + *be* + *-ing* form of the verb.

He **will be studying.**    They **will be driving.**

### Future Perfect

- Actions that will be completed by or before a specified time in the future: By Thursday, we **will have cleaned up** the whole filing cabinet.

**Form:** Use *will* (or) *shall* + *have* + *-ed* form of the verb (past participle).

They **will have walked.**    We **will have finished.**

### Future Perfect Progressive

- Ongoing actions or conditions until a specific time in the future: In June we **will have been renting** this apartment for a year.

**Form:** Use *will* (or) *shall* + *have* + *been* + *-ing* form of the verb.

They **will have been paying.**    She **will have been traveling.**

## (4) Irregular Verbs

The most often used irregular verbs have the forms shown in the following chart:

| IRREGULAR VERB FORMS | | | | |
|---|---|---|---|---|
| | **Present** | | **Past** | |
| *Verb* | *Singular* | *Plural* | *Singular* | *Plural* |
| to be | I am<br>you are<br>he, she,<br>it is | we are<br>you are<br>they are | I was<br>you were<br>he, she,<br>it was | we were<br>you were<br>they were |
| to have | I have<br>you have<br>he, she,<br>it has | we have<br>you have<br>they have | I had<br>you had<br>he, she,<br>it had | we had<br>you had<br>they had |
| to do | I do<br>you do<br>he, she,<br>it does | we do<br>you do<br>they do | I did<br>you did<br>he, she,<br>it did | we did<br>you did<br>they did |

## IRREGULAR VERBS

| Base (or Present) | Past | Past Participle |
| --- | --- | --- |
| arise | arose | arisen |
| awake | awoke | awoken |
| be | was, were | been |
| beat | beat | beaten |
| become | became | become |
| begin | began | begun |
| bend | bent | bent |
| bet | bet | bet |
| bind | bound | bound |
| bite | bit | bitten (or) bit |
| bleed | bled | bled |
| blow | blew | blown |
| break | broke | broken |
| bring | brought | brought |
| build | built | built |
| burst | burst | burst |
| buy | bought | bought |
| cast | cast | cast |
| catch | caught | caught |
| choose | chose | chosen |
| cling | clung | clung |
| come | came | come |
| cost | cost | cost |
| creep | crept | crept |
| cut | cut | cut |
| deal | dealt | dealt |
| dig | dug | dug |
| dive | dived (or) dove | dived |
| do | did | done |
| draw | drew | drawn |
| drink | drank | drunk |
| drive | drove | driven |
| eat | ate | eaten |
| fall | fell | fallen |
| feed | fed | fed |
| feel | felt | felt |
| fight | fought | fought |
| find | found | found |
| fling | flung | flung |
| fly | flew | flown |
| forbid | forbade | forbidden |

| Base (or Present) | Past | Past Participle |
|---|---|---|
| forget | forgot | forgotten |
| forgive | forgave | forgiven |
| freeze | froze | frozen |
| get | got | gotten |
| give | gave | given |
| go | went | gone |
| grind | ground | ground |
| grow | grew | grown |
| hang | hung | hung |
| have | had | had |
| hear | heard | heard |
| hide | hid | hidden |
| hit | hit | hit |
| hold | held | held |
| hurt | hurt | hurt |
| keep | kept | kept |
| know | knew | known |
| lay | laid | laid |
| lead | led | led |
| leave | left | left |
| lend | lent | lent |
| let | let | let |
| lie | lay | lain |
| lose | lost | lost |
| make | made | made |
| mean | meant | meant |
| meet | met | met |
| mistake | mistook | mistaken |
| pay | paid | paid |
| prove | proved | proved (or) proven |
| put | put | put |
| quit | quit | quit |
| read | read | read |
| ride | rode | ridden |
| ring | rang | rung |
| rise | rose | risen |
| run | ran | run |
| say | said | said |
| see | saw | seen |
| seek | sought | sought |
| sell | sold | sold |
| send | sent | sent |

*continued on next page*

*continued from previous page*

| Base (or Present) | Past | Past Participle |
|---|---|---|
| set | set | set |
| shake | shook | shaken |
| shed | shed | shed |
| shine | shone | shone |
| shoot | shot | shot |
| shrink | shrank | shrunk |
| shut | shut | shut |
| sing | sang | sung |
| sink | sank (or) sunk | sunk |
| sit | sat | sat |
| sleep | slept | slept |
| slide | slid | slid |
| speak | spoke | spoken |
| spend | spent | spent |
| spin | spun | spun |
| split | split | split |
| spread | spread | spread |
| spring | sprang | sprung |
| stand | stood | stood |
| steal | stole | stolen |
| stick | stuck | stuck |
| sting | stung | stung |
| stink | stank | stunk |
| strike | struck | struck |
| swear | swore | sworn |
| sweep | swept | swept |
| swim | swam | swum |
| swing | swung | swung |
| take | took | taken |
| teach | taught | taught |
| tear | tore | torn |
| tell | told | told |
| think | thought | thought |
| throw | threw | thrown |
| understand | understood | understood |
| wake | woke | waken |
| wear | wore | worn |
| weep | wept | wept |
| win | won | won |
| wind | wound | wound |
| wring | wrung | wrung |
| write | wrote | written |

## Exercise 16.3: Proofreading Practice

*In the following paragraph, choose the correct verbs from the options given in parentheses. Remember that the time expressed in the verb has to agree with the meaning of the sentence.*

The way children (1. learn, will learn) to draw seems simple. But studies show that when given some kind of marker, young children (2. have begun, will begin, begin) by scribbling on any available surface. At first, these children's drawings (3. are, should be, had been) simple, clumsy, and unrealistic, but gradually the drawings (4. have become, should become, become) more realistic. One researcher who (5. will study, could study, has studied) the drawings of one- and two-year-olds concludes that their early scrawls (6. are representing, may represent, had represented) gestures and motions. For example, the researcher notes that one two-year-old child who was observed (7. took, has taken, had taken) a marker and (8. is hopping, hopped, had hopped) it around on the paper, leaving a mark with each imprint and explaining as he drew that the rabbit (9. was going, had gone, could have gone) hop-hop. The researcher (10. had concluded, has concluded, concludes) that the child was symbolizing the rabbit's motion, not its size, shape, or color. Someone who (11. had seen, sees, might see) only dots on a page (12. would not see, has not seen, had not seen) a rabbit and (13. should conclude, would conclude, had concluded) that the child's attempts to draw a rabbit (14. have failed, had failed, failed).

## Exercise 16.4: Pattern Practice

*The following paragraph is written in present tense. At the beginning of the paragraph, add the words "Last year," and rewrite the rest of the paragraph so that it is in past tense. To do so, change all the underlined verbs to past tense.*

One of the most popular new attractions in Japanese recreation parks is a maze for people to walk through. For some people this can be twenty minutes of pleasant exercise, but others take an hour or two because they run in circles. Admission costs about three dollars a person, an amount that makes mazes cheaper than movies. Mazes also last longer than roller coaster rides. One Japanese businessman, first dragged there by his wife, says that he enjoys it because it keeps him so busy that he forgets all his other worries. Some people like to amble in a leisurely way through the maze and let time pass, but most maze players try to get out in the shortest time possible. At the entrance, a machine gives people a ticket stamped with the time they enter. Some people quit in the middle and head for an emergency exit or ask a guard for help. But most rise to the challenge and keep going until they emerge at the other end, hoping to claim a prize.

# 16d  Verb Voice

**Verb voice** tells whether the verb is in the active or passive voice. In the active voice, the subject performs the action of the verb. In the passive voice, the subject receives the action. The doer of the action in the passive voice may either appear in a "by the . . ." phrase or be omitted.

**Active:** The dog bit the boy.

**Passive:** The boy was bitten by the dog. [The subject of this sentence is the boy, but he was not doing the action of biting.]

> **HINT:** In the passive voice the verb phrase always includes a form of the *to be* verb, such as *is, are, was, is being,* and so on. Also, if the doer of the action is named, it is in a "by the . . ." phrase.

# 16e  Verb Mood

The **mood** of a verb tells whether it expresses a fact or opinion (**indicative**); expresses a command, a request, or advice (**imperative**); or expresses a doubt, a wish, a recommendation, or something contrary to fact (**subjunctive**).

- **Indicative:** Verbs in the indicative (or declarative) mood express a fact or opinion and have their subjects stated in the sentence.

    He **needs** a computer to print out his résumé.

    The environmentalists and loggers **could** not **reach** any agreement.

- **Imperative:** Verbs in the imperative mood express a command, make a request, or offer advice. The subject word is not included because the subject is understood to be the reader (you).

    **Open** that window, please.

    **Watch** your step!

    Next, **put** the wheel on the frame.

- **Subjunctive:** In the subjunctive mood, verbs express a doubt, a wish, a recommendation, or something contrary to fact. In the subjunctive, present tense verbs stay in the simple base form and do not indicate the number and person of the subject.

It is important that she **be** (not *is*) here by 9 P.M.

The form requires that a passport photo **accompany** (not *accompanies*) the application.

For past subjunctive, the same form as simple past is used; however, for the verb *be, were* is used for all persons and numbers.

I wish she **had arrived** on time.

If I **were** (not *was*) him, I'd sell that car immediately.

If land **were** (not *was*) cheaper there, they could buy a farm.

## Exercise 16.5: Proofreading Practice

*In the following paragraph, underline verb phrases in each sentence and indicate the voice of the verb by writing "active" or "passive." Ask yourself the following questions:*

- Is the subject receiving any action? If so, it's passive. If not, it's active.
- Is there a doer named in the "by the . . ." phrase? If so, it's passive.

*The mood of most of the verbs is factual (declarative). If you find any verb that states something contrary to fact (subjunctive), write "subjunctive." If you spot a command (imperative), write "imperative."*

(1) America <u>is</u> such a youth-oriented nation that roughly $3 billion <u>is</u>
                    *(active)*
<u>spent</u> every year by consumers who <u>want to eliminate</u> wrinkles. (2) Be-
*(passive)*                                    *(passive)*
tween $1 and $2 billion of this is spent on cosmetic surgery. (3) Now a new drug may offer a better answer. (4) The drug, retinoic acid, was originally marketed as an acne cream and is now being advertised as a treatment to improve skin tone and erase wrinkles. (5) "Buy a facelift in a tube" could be the advertising slogan for this drug, which may reverse the process of aging.

## Exercise 16.6: Sentence Practice

*Combine the short sentences in the following paragraph into longer ones. Underline all the verb phrases in your revised sentences, and label them as active or passive. Try to use mostly active verbs, but you will find that some passive verbs are also useful.*

Retinoic acid is a new drug. It is promising. It is being prescribed by doctors as a wrinkle cream. A company owns it. They call it a wonder drug. Retinoic acid was approved by the Food and Drug Administration (FDA). The FDA approved it as an acne cream. This was done in 1971. Some users over thirty-five told doctors side effects were produced. One side effect for some people was smoother, younger-looking skin. The skin was reported by these people to have fewer wrinkles. Other users said their skin was irritated by the drug. The drug was not evaluated by the FDA as a wrinkle fighter. The drug is being tested now for its ability to make skin look younger. But the drug can be prescribed by doctors for its side effects. The appropriate use of the drug can be determined by doctors. They can recommend it for uses not yet approved by the FDA.

# 16f Modal Verbs

**Modals** are helping verbs that express ability, a request, or an attitude, such as interest, expectation, possibility, or obligation.

The following chart shows some common modal verbs:

| COMMON MODAL VERBS | |
|---|---|
| **Verb** | **Use** |
| shall, should | Express intent to do something, advisability:<br><br>You **should** try to exercise more often. |
| will, would | Express strong intent:<br><br>I **will** return those books to the library tomorrow. |
| can, could | Express capability, possibility, request:<br><br>I **can** lend you my tape of that concert. |
| may, might | Express possibility or permission, request:<br><br>She **may** buy a new computer. |
| must, ought to | Express obligation or need:<br><br>I **ought to** fill the gas tank before we drive into town. |

# 17 Nouns and Pronouns

## 17a Nouns (n)

A **noun** is a word that names a person, place, thing, or idea.

The following words are nouns:

| | | |
|---|---|---|
| Marilyn Monroe | Des Moines | peace |
| Henri | light bulb | justice |
| forest | pictures | French |

(For proper and common nouns, see Chapter 34.)

### (1) Singular, Plural, and Collective Nouns

A **singular noun** refers to one person, place, or thing and is the form you would look up in the dictionary.

A **plural noun** is the form that refers to more than one person, place, or thing.

A **collective noun** refers to a group acting as a unit, such as a committee, a herd, or a jury.

**Exceptions:** Some nouns do not fall in these categories because they refer to abstract or general concepts that cannot be counted and do not have plural forms. Examples are *homework, peace, furniture,* and *knowledge.* (See Chapter 50.)

| *Singular Nouns* | *Plural Nouns* | *Collective Nouns* |
|---|---|---|
| box | boxes | family |
| child | children | senate |

### (2) Noun Endings

Nouns have endings that show plural and possession. (See Chapter 27 on apostrophes and 38d on the spelling of plurals.)

| PLURALS | | |
|---|---|---|
| | **Singular** | **Plural** |
| *-s* or *-es* | one cup<br>a box | many cups<br>two boxes |
| **Changed form** | one child<br>one man | three children<br>some men |
| *-f* or *-fe*→ *v*+ *-es* | one half<br>the leaf | two halves<br>the leaves |
| **Other forms** | one ox<br>the medium | a pair of oxen<br>all the media |
| **No change** | a deer<br>one sheep | several deer<br>two sheep |

**HINT 1:** The *-s* noun ending can be either the plural marker or the possessive *-s* marker. Don't make the mistake of putting an apostrophe in plural nouns:

❖ There was a sale on potato ~~chip's~~. *chips*

**HINT 2:** Some writers do not use—or hear—plural forms in their speech, but standard English requires plural endings in writing. If you tend to omit written plurals, proofread your last drafts. To help your eye see the end of the word, point to the noun with your pen or finger to be sure that you see the plural ending. Some writers need repeated practice to notice the missing plural endings.

**HINT 3:** Although the *-s* marks the plural at the end of many nouns, it is also the ending for singular verbs with *he, she, it,* or a singular noun as the subject.

He walk **s.**

The shoe fit **s.**

An *-s* ending may be needed either at the end of the noun for a plural or at the end of the verb for a singular form. Therefore, both the subject and the verb cannot have an *-s* marker at the end.

**Possession**

The possessive form shows ownership or a close relationship. This is clear when we write "Mary's hat" because Mary owns or possesses the hat, but the possessive is less apparent when we write "journey's end" or "yesterday's news." It is more helpful to think about the "of" relationship between two nouns that exists in the possessive form:

Mary's hat    two days' time
the hat of Mary    time of two days

The possessive marker is either an *'s* or *'*. When the plural *-s* or *-es* is added to the noun, only an apostrophe is added after the plural. For singular nouns ending in *-s*, such as *grass,* the *-s* after the apostrophe is optional. It can be added if it doesn't make pronouncing the word more difficult. (See 27a.)

| *Singular* | *Plural* |
|---|---|
| Miriam's hat | the girls' hats |
| the glass's edge | all the glasses' edges |
| James' story (or) James's story | |
| Aldez' zip code    [Adding an *'s* would make the pronunciation difficult.] | |

---

**HINT:** Everything to the left of the apostrophe is the word and its plural. A proofreading strategy is to check the order of what is written. First, write the word; then add any plural markers; and finally, add the possessive markers afterward.

| | *Word* | *Plural* | *Possessive Marker* |
|---|---|---|---|
| girls' gloves = | girl | s | ' |
| baby's toe = | baby | | 's |

---

# 17b Pronouns (pr)

A **pronoun** takes the place of a noun.

If we had only nouns and no pronouns in English, we would have to write the following sentences:

**Without Pronouns:**

Lee lost Lee's car keys.

When Michael went to the library, Michael found some useful references for Michael's paper.

## (1) Personal Pronouns

**Personal pronouns** refer to people or things:

| Subject Case | Object Case | Possessive Case | |
|---|---|---|---|
| I | me | my | mine |
| you | you | your | yours |
| he | him | his | his |
| she | her | her | hers |
| it | it | its | its |
| we | us | our | ours |
| they | them | their | theirs |

## (2) Demonstrative Pronouns

**Demonstrative pronouns** refer to things:

| this | **This** cup of coffee is mine. |
|---|---|
| that | He needs **that** software program. |
| these | Can I exchange **these** tapes? |
| those | No one ordered **those** soft drinks. |

## (3) Relative Pronouns

**Relative pronouns** show the relationship of a dependent clause (see 23b) to a noun in the sentence:

| that | He knew **that** it was too soon to expect results. |
|---|---|
| which | They took the television set, **which** was broken, to the dump. |
| who | Mrs. Bloom is the friend **who** helped me. |
| whom | That manager, **whom** I respected, was promoted. |
| what | Everyone wondered **what** the loud noise was. |

Sometimes relative pronouns can be omitted when they are understood:

This isn't the sandwich **that** I ordered.
This isn't the sandwich I ordered.

## (4) Interrogative Pronouns

**Interrogative pronouns** are used in questions:

| who | **Who** wrote that screenplay? |
|---|---|
| whose | **Whose** jacket is this? |
| whom | **Whom** do you wish to talk to? |
| which | **Which** movie do you want to see? |
| what | **What** will they do now? |

## (5) Indefinite Pronouns

**Indefinite pronouns** make indefinite reference to nouns:

| | |
|---|---|
| anyone/anybody | The notice said that **anyone** could apply. |
| some | May I have **some**? |
| everyone/everybody | She was delighted that **everybody** showed up. |
| everything | That dog ate **everything** on the table. |
| nothing | There is **nothing** he can't fix. |
| one | Please give me **one**. |
| someone/somebody | Would **somebody** show me how this works? |

**HINT:** Indefinite pronouns are usually singular and require a singular verb:

**Everyone** is going to the game.

However, some indefinite pronouns, such as *both, few,* and *many,* require a plural verb. Other indefinite pronouns, such as *all, any, more, most, none,* and *some,* may be either singular or plural, depending on the meaning of the sentence.

**Singular: Some** of my homework is done.

[Here *some* refers to a portion or a part of the homework. Because a "portion" or a "part" is thought of as a single entity, the verb is singular.]

**Plural: Some** of these plates are chipped.

[Here *some* refers to at least several plates. Because *several* is thought of as plural, the verb is plural.]

**Singular: All** the coffee is brewed.

**Plural: All** the customers are pleased.

## (6) Possessive Pronouns

**Possessive pronouns** do not take an apostrophe:

**its** nose    [not *it's* nose]

that dog of **hers**    [not that dog of *her's*]

the house is **theirs**    [not the house is *theirs'*]

Some writers confuse the possessive pronouns with contractions:

| | | |
|---|---|---|
| **It's** a warm day | = | **It is** a warm day. |
| **There's** a shooting star | = | **There is** a shooting star. |

(See Chapter 27 on apostrophes.)

## (7) Reflexive Pronouns

**Reflexive pronouns,** which end in *-self* or *-selves,* intensify the nouns they refer back to:

| | |
|---|---|
| myself | I soaked **myself** in suntan oil. |
| yourself | Please help **yourself.** |
| itself | The pig stuffed **itself** with feed. |
| themselves | They allowed **themselves** enough time to eat. |

## (8) Reciprocal Pronouns

**Reciprocal pronouns** refer back to individual parts of plural terms:

| | |
|---|---|
| each other | They congratulated **each other.** |
| one another | The group helped **one another** to prepare. |

## Exercise 17.1: Proofreading Practice

*Read the following paragraph; underline all the* -s *and* -es *endings that mark plural nouns, and circle all the* 's, s', *and* ' *possessive markers.*

It is a sad fact of life that what some people call the "everyday courtesies of life" are disappearing faster than finger bowls and engineers' slide rules. People in movie theaters carry on loud conversations, older people on buses rarely have anyone get up and offer them a seat, and few shoppers bother to offer thanks to a helpful salesperson. Some people say that courteous ways seem to have lingered longer in small towns than in big cities and that some regions—notably the South—cling more than others to some remaining signs of polite behavior. But more often we hear complaints that courtesy is declining, dying, or dead. Says one New York executive: "There's no such thing as umbrella courtesy. Everybody's umbrella is aimed at my eye level." And a store owner in another city says that short-tempered waiters in restaurants and impatient salesclerks in stores make her feel as if she's bothering them by asking for service. Common courtesy may be a thing of the past.

## Exercise 17.2: Proofreading Practice

*In the following paragraph there are some missing* -s *and* -es *plural noun endings and missing possessive markers. Add any that are missing.*

Among the people who are most aware of the current lack of every-day politeness are airline flight attendant and newspaper advice columnist. Says one flight attendant: "Courtesy is almost zero. People think you're supposed to carry all their bag on and off the flight, even when you have dozen of other passenger to attend to." One syndicated advice columnist notes that courtesy is so rare these day that when someone is kind, helpful, or generous, it is an event worth writing about to an advice columnist. Some teacher blame televisions poor example, especially the many rude detective who shove people around, bang down all those door, and yell in peoples face. Too many of our current movie hero are not particularly gallant, thoughtful, or polite. As a psychologist recently noted, it is hard to explain to children what good manner are when they don't see such behavior on their television or movie screen.

## Exercise 17.3: Pattern Practice

*In the following paragraph there are many singular nouns. Where it is appropriate, change the singular nouns to plural, add the appropriate noun endings, and change any other words or word endings that need to be altered.*

The foreign tourist who travels in the United States often notices that the American is not as polite as a person from another country. The tourist from Europe, who is used to a more formal manner, is particularly offended by the American who immediately calls the tourist by his or her first name. Impoliteness in the United States extends even to an object. An English businessperson noted that in America a public sign issues a command: "No Smoking" or "Do Not Enter." In England such a sign would be less commanding: "No Smoking Please" or "Please Do Not Enter." An American can also be rude without meaning to be. As a Japanese visitor noticed, the nurse who led him into the doctor's office said, "Come in here." In Japan, the visitor noted, a nurse would say, "Please follow me." The foreign tourist, unfortunately, has a variety of such stories to take back to his or her country.

## Exercise 17.4: Pattern Practice

*Write a sentence using each of the nouns and pronouns listed here. Make the noun plural if it can be used in the plural.*

1. laughter
2. machine
3. chair
4. homework
5. book
6. liberty
7. ice
8. engineering
9. key
10. telephone
11. these
12. whose
13. itself
14. anyone
15. its

# 18 Pronoun Case and Reference

## 18a Pronoun Case (ca)

**Pronoun case** refers to the form of the pronoun needed in a sentence.

The following chart shows the pronoun cases:

| | **Subject** | | **Object** | | **Possessive** | |
|---|---|---|---|---|---|---|
| | *Singular* | *Plural* | *Singular* | *Plural* | *Singular* | *Plural* |
| **First person** | I | we | me | us | my, mine | our, ours |
| **Second person** | you | you | you | you | your, yours | your, yours |
| **Third person** | he<br>she<br>it | they<br>they<br>they | him<br>her<br>it | them<br>them<br>them | his<br>her, hers<br>it, its | their, theirs<br>their, theirs<br>their, theirs |

**PRONOUN CASES**

### (1) Subject Case

**Subject case** of pronouns is used when pronouns are subjects or are used after linking verbs such as *is:*

**She** won the lottery.    [*She* is the subject case pronoun.]

Who's there? It is **I**.    [In the second sentence *I* is the subject case pronoun that comes after the linking verb *is.*]

### (2) Object Case

**Object case** of pronouns is used when pronouns are objects of verbs (receive the action of the verb):

I hugged **her.**    [Object of the verb]

Seeing Dan and **me,** she waved.    [Object of the verb]

- **As indirect object:** When pronouns are indirect objects of verbs (explain for whom or to whom something is done), use the object case:

  I gave **her** the glass.   [Indirect object]

  The indirect object can often be changed to a *to + object pronoun* phrase:

  I gave the glass **to her.**

- **As object of prepositions:** Use the object case when pronouns are used as objects of prepositions (complete the meaning of the preposition):

  Al gave the money to **them.**   [Object of the preposition]

---

**HINT 1:** Remember that *between, except,* and *with* are prepositions and take the object case.

❖ between you and +
                   *me*

❖ except Alexi and ~~she~~
                   *her*

❖ with ~~he~~ and +
       *him*   *me*

**HINT 2:** Don't use *them* as a pointing pronoun in place of *these* or *those.* Use *them* only as the object by itself.

❖ He liked ~~them~~ socks.   (or)   He liked them.
            *those*

---

### (3) Possessive Case

**Possessive case** refers to pronouns used as possessives.

Is this **her** hat?        (or)   Is this **hers**?
We gave **him** our pens.   (or)   We gave him **ours.**

---

**HINT 1:** Possessive case pronouns never take apostrophes.

❖ The insect spread ~~it's~~ wings.
                    *its*

**HINT 2:** Use possessive case before *-ing* verb forms.

❖ The crowd cheered ~~him~~ making a three-point basket.
                    *his*

## (4) Pronouns in Compound Constructions

To find the right case when your sentence has two pronouns or a noun and a pronoun, temporarily eliminate the noun or one of the pronouns as you read it to yourself. You'll hear the case that is needed.

❖ John and ~~him~~ *he* went to the store.

[If *John* is eliminated, the sentence would be "*Him* went to the store." It's easier to notice the wrong pronoun case this way.]

When in doubt as to which pronoun case to use, some writers mistakenly choose the subject case because it sounds more formal or "correct."

❖ Mrs. Wagner gave the tickets to **Lutecia** and ~~I~~ *me*.

[Once again, try the strategy of dropping the noun, *Lutecia.* You'll be able to hear that the sentence sounds wrong. ("Mrs. Wagner gave the tickets to *I*.") Because *to* is a preposition, the noun or pronoun that follows is the object of the preposition and should be in the object case.]

When a pronoun and noun are used together, use the same strategy of dropping the noun to hear whether the case of the pronoun sounds wrong.

❖ ~~Us~~ *We* **players** gave the coach a rousing cheer.

[When you drop the noun *players,* the original sentence would be "Us gave the coach a rousing cheer." The pronoun is the subject of the sentence and needs the subject case, the pronoun *we.*]

❖ The lecturer told ~~we~~ *us* students to quiet down.

[When you drop the noun *students,* the original sentence would be "The lecturer told we to quiet down." Instead, the sentence needs the pronoun in the object case, *us,* because it is the object of the verb.]

❖ The newest members of the club, **Mahendi** and ~~me~~ *I*, were asked to pay our dues promptly.

[Since the phrase *Mahendi and me* explains the noun *members,* which is the subject of the sentence, the subject case of the pronoun, *I,* is needed.]

❖ The usher had to find programs for the latecomers, Mahendi and ~~I~~ *me*.

[The phrase *Mahendi and I* explains the noun *latecomers,* the object of the preposition *for.* Thus, the pronoun has to be *me,* the object case.]

## (5) Who/Whom

In informal speech some people may not distinguish between *who* and *whom.* But for formal writing, the cases are as follows:

| Subject | Object | Possessive |
|---|---|---|
| who | whom | whose |
| whoever | whomever | |

**Subject Case: Who** is going to the concert tonight?

[*Who* is the subject of the sentence.]

**Object Case: To whom** should I give this ticket?

[*Whom* is the object of the preposition *to.*]

**Possessive Case:** No one was sure **whose** voice that was.

[When *who* introduces a dependent clause after a preposition, use the subject case:

Give this to **whoever** wants it.

---

**HINT:** If you aren't sure whether to use *who* or *whom,* turn a question into a statement or rearrange the order of the phrase:

**Question: (Who, whom)** are you looking for?

**Statement:** You are looking for **whom.**
*(object of the preposition)*

**Sentence:** She is someone **(who, whom)** I know well.

**Rearranged Order:** I know **whom** well.
*(direct object)*

---

## (6) Omitted Words in Comparisons

In comparisons using *than* and *as,* choose the correct pronoun case by recalling the words that are omitted:

He is taller than (**I, me**).

[The omitted words here are "am tall."]

He is taller than **I** (am tall).

Our cat likes my sister more than (**I, me**).

[The omitted words here are "it likes."]

Our cat likes my sister more than (it likes) **me.**

## Exercise 18.1: Proofreading Practice

*In the following paragraph, there are some errors in pronoun case. Underline the incorrect pronoun forms, and write the correct form above the underlined word.*

Have you ever wondered how people in the entertainment industry choose what you and me will see on television, read in books, and hear on tapes and CDs? Some producers and publishers say that the executives in their companies and them rely on instinct and an ability to forecast trends in taste. But we consumers cannot be relied on to be consistent from one month to the next. So, market researchers constantly keep seeking our opinions. For example, they ask we moviegoers to preview movies and to fill out questionnaires. Reactions from we and our friends are then studied closely. Sometimes, the market researchers merely forecast from previous experience what you and me are likely to prefer. Still, some movies fail for reasons that the market researchers cannot understand. When that happens, who does the movie studio blame? The producer will say that the director and him did all they could but that the leading actor failed to attract an audience. Sometimes, though, us moviegoers simply get tired of some types of movies and want more variety.

## Exercise 18.2: Pattern Practice

*Using the patterns given here, write a similar sentence of your own for each pattern.*

Pattern A: A sentence with an object case pronoun after the preposition *between, except,* or *with*

Everyone was able to hear the bird call **except her.**

Pattern B: A sentence with a compound object that includes a pronoun in the object case.

The newspaper article listed Arthur and **him** as the winners of the contest.

Pattern C: A sentence with a comparison that includes a subject case pronoun

Everyone in the room was dressed more warmly than **I.**

Pattern D: A sentence with a comparison that includes an object case pronoun

The bird was more frightened of the dog than **me.**

Pattern E: A sentence with a compound subject that includes a subject case pronoun

During the festival the announcer and **she** took turns thanking all the people who had helped to organize the events.

# 18b Pronoun Reference (ref)

**Pronoun reference** is the relationship between the pronoun and the noun (antecedent) for which it is substituting.

Pronouns substitute for nouns. To help your reader see this relationship clearly, remember the following rules:

- Pronouns should indicate to which nouns they are referring.
- Pronouns should be reasonably close to their nouns.

> **Unclear Reference:** Gina told Michelle that **she** took **her** bike to the library.
>
> [Did Gina take Michelle's bike or her own bike to the library?]
>
> **Revised:** When Gina took Michelle's bike to the library, she told Michelle she was borrowing it.

Be sure your pronoun refers to a noun that has been mentioned on the page and not merely implied. Also, watch out for the vague *they* that doesn't refer to any specific group or the vague *this* or *it* that doesn't refer back to any specific word or phrase.

❖ In Hollywood ~~they~~ *the screenwriters and producers* don't know what the American public really wants in movies.

[Who are the *they* referred to here?]

❖ When the town board inquired about the cost of the next political campaign, the board was assured that ~~they~~ *the politicians* would pay for **their** own campaigns.

[To whom do *they* and *their* refer? Most likely *they* refers to the politicians who will be campaigning, but "politician" is only inferred.]

❖ *serving as a forest ranger*
Martina worked in a national forest last summer, and ~~this~~ may be her career choice.

[What does *this* refer to? Because no word or phrase in the first part of the sentence refers to the pronoun, the revised version has one of several possible answers.]

## (1) Pronoun Number

For collective nouns, such as *group, committee,* and *family,* use either a singular or plural pronoun, depending on whether the group acts as a unit or acts separately as many individuals within the unit.

> The committee reached **its** decision before the end of the meeting.
>
> [Here the committee acted as a unit.]
>
> The committee relied on **their** own consciences to reach a decision.
>
> [Here everyone relied separately on his or her own conscience.]

Remember to be consistent in pronoun number. Don't shift from singular to plural or plural to singular.

❖ After **someone** studies violin for a few months, **she** may decide to try the
*she*                                      *she*      *s*
piano. Then, ~~they~~ can compare and decide which instrument ~~they~~ like
better.

## (2) Compound Subjects

Compound subjects with *and* take the plural pronoun.

> The **table** and **chair** were delivered promptly, but **they** were not the style I had ordered.

For compound subjects with *or* or *nor,* the pronoun agrees with the subject word closer to it:

> The restaurant offered either regular **patrons** or each new **customer** a free cup of coffee with **his** or **her** dinner.

> Neither this **house** nor the **others** had **their** shutters closed.

## (3) Who/Which/That

When *who, which,* or *that* begins a dependent clause, use the word as follows:

- *Who* is used for people (and sometimes animals).

  He is a person **who** can help you.

- *Which* is used most often for nonessential clauses, though some writers also use it for essential clauses (see Chapter 24).

  The catalogue, **which** I sent for last month, had some unusual merchandise.

  [The *which* clause here is nonessential.]

- *That* is used most often for essential clauses.

  When I finished the book **that** she lent me, I was able to write my paper.

  [The *that* clause here is essential.]

**18 ref**

## (4) Indefinite Words

Indefinite words such as *any* and *each* usually take the singular pronoun.

**Each** of the boys handed in **his** uniform.

## (5) Indefinite Pronouns

*He* was traditionally used to refer to indefinite pronouns ending in *-body* and *-one:*

**Everyone** brought **his** own pen and paper.

Use the following strategies to avoid the exclusive use of the masculine pronoun when the reference is to both males and females (a practice seen by many people as sexist; see Chapter 39 on sexist language):

- Use both the masculine and feminine pronoun.

  Everyone has **his** or **her** coat.    [Some people view this as very wordy.]

- Switch to the plural subject and pronoun.

  **All** the people have **their** coats.

- Use the plural pronoun.

  **Everyone** has **their** coat.    [Some people view this as incorrect. Others, such as the National Council of Teachers of English, accept this as a way to avoid sexist language.]

- Use *a, an,* or *the* if the meaning remains clear.

  **Everyone** has **a** coat.

## Exercise 18.3: Proofreading Practice

*In the following sentences, each pronoun should clearly and correctly refer back to a noun in the sentence. If the reference is clear and correct, write a C before the sentence number. If there is a problem with pronoun reference, write an X before the number.*

1. Whenever Frisha tries to speak Spanish with Maya, she has trouble understanding her pronunciation.
2. Although jogging is still a popular means of exercise, some shoe manufacturers say that it is not as popular as it was five years ago.
3. Every person on the committee had read their copy of the report before the meeting.
4. After the coach and the players reviewed the new plays for the third time, they decided that it was enough for one evening.
5. Either George or Miguel can lend you his book before the exam.

## Exercise 18.4: Proofreading Practice

*In the following paragraph there are some pronoun reference problems. Underline all pronouns that do not clearly refer back to nouns, and write clearer or more appropriate nouns or pronouns above the underlined words. You may find that you will need to change some other words as well.*

Rising insurance premiums are taking their toll on the rock and roll concert business, and it is likely to get higher before conditions improve. People who have been buying tickets for the last ten years are angry at paying five or six dollars more for his or her ticket. But insurance companies say that instances of violence and injury at rock concerts and the rising number of people who file claims are causing it. Property damage has created an additional problem and has caused the number of claims to increase tenfold over the last ten years. Each claim may be for a large sum of money, and it is usually awarded by juries sympathetic to damage caused by rock concert audiences. The situation has gotten so bad recently that some concerts have been canceled when they could not get insurance, and in one case, a particular act was cut from the show because they were considered dangerous. This may cause the number of rock concerts to decrease in the future.

# 19 Adjectives and Adverbs (ad)

## 19a Adjectives and Adverbs

**Adjectives** and **adverbs** describe or add information about other words in a sentence. To distinguish adjectives from adverbs, locate the words they describe or modify. Adjectives modify nouns and pronouns. Adverbs modify verbs, verb forms, adjectives, and other adverbs.

Adjectives modifying nouns and pronouns:

| **red** | house | It | was **beautiful.** |
| *(adjective)* | *(noun)* | *(pronoun)* | *(adjective)* |
| **cheerful** | smile | They | were **loud.** |
| *(adjective)* | *(noun)* | *(pronoun)* | *(adjective)* |

Adverbs modifying verbs, verb forms, adjectives, and other adverbs:

| danced | **gracefully** | ran | **very** | **quickly** |
| *(verb)* | *(adverb)* | *(verb)* | *(adverb)* | *(adverb)* |
| **very** | tall | had | **barely** | moved |
| *(adverb)* | *(adjective)* | | *(adverb)* | *(verb form)* |

Many adverbs end in *-ly:*

| *Adjective* | *Adverb* |
| --- | --- |
| rapid | rapidly |
| nice | nicely |
| happy | happily |

But the *-ly* ending isn't a sure test for adverbs because some nouns have an *-ly* ending for the adjective form (*ghost* and *ghostly*), and some adverbs do not end in *-ly* (*very, fast, far*). To be sure, check your dictionary to see whether the word is listed as an adjective or adverb.

To use adjectives and adverbs correctly:

- Use *-ed* adjectives (the *-ed* form of verbs, past participles) to describe nouns. Be sure to include the *-ed* ending.

    used clothing    painted houses    experienced driver

- Use adjectives following linking verbs such as *appear, seem, taste, feel,* and *look.*

    The sofa seemed comfortable.    [sofa = comfortable]

    The water tastes salty.    [water = salty]

Some verbs can be either linking or action verbs depending on the meaning. Note the two different meanings of the verb *looked:*

    The cat looked sleepy.    [cat = sleepy]

    The cat looked eagerly at the canary.    [In this sentence the cat is performing the action of looking.]

- Use adverbs to modify verbs.

> *quickly.*
> ❖ He ran **quick.**   ❖ The glass broke **sudden.**   ❖ She sang **sweet.**
>
> *suddenly.*   *sweetly.*

- Be sure to distinguish between the following adjectives and adverbs:

| Adjectives | Adverbs |
|------------|---------|
| sure | surely |
| real | really |
| good | well |
| bad | badly |

> *surely*
> ❖ She **sure** likes to dance.   ❖ The car runs **bad.**   ❖ He sings **good.**
>
> *badly*   *well*

**9a**
**ad**

---

**HINT:** *Well* can also be an adjective when it refers to good health.

Despite her surgery, she looks well.   [she = well]

---

- When you use adverbs such as *so, such,* and *too,* be sure to complete the phrase or clause.

> *that she left the office early.*
> ❖ Hailey was so tired ∧.

> *that reservations are recommended.*
> ❖ Malley's is such a popular restaurant ∧.

> *to ask for help.*
> ❖ Tran's problem was that he was too proud ∧.

## Exercise 19.1: Proofreading Practice

*The following paragraph has some errors in adverb and adjective forms. Rewrite the paragraph so that all the adjectives and adverbs are correct. Underline the words you have changed.*

We all know that when football players are very tired, their concern coaches call them back to the sidelines and give them pure oxygen to breathe. But new evidence indicates that these exhaust players could just as well be saving their breath. It seems clear that 100 percent oxygen doesn't particularly help athletes. In a controlled test some athletes breathed in very rapid either normal air or pure oxygen. When tested as to how quick the subjects revived, there was no difference. Both groups said they felt good within about three minutes. One of the players who breathed plain air even commented on the fact that he felt so well. The biggest surprise of all was that none of the players being tested could even tell whether they had breathed real pure oxygen or just normal air.

## Exercise 19.2: Pattern Practice

*Using the patterns given here, write a sentence of your own for each pattern.*

Pattern A: Sentence with an *-ed* adjective modifying a noun

The **fertilized** plant grew quickly on my windowsill.

Pattern B: Sentence with an adverb modifying another adverb

The sound echoed **very** clearly.

Pattern C: Sentence with the adverb *so, such,* or *too* that is complete

It was **such** a long concert that I was tempted to leave during intermission.

Pattern D: An *-ed* adjective after a linking verb

The old man seemed **pleased** when the child said hello.

Pattern E: Sentence with the adverb *well*

With some coaching, the game-show contestant answered the questions very **well.**

Pattern F: Sentence with the adverb *badly*

As the horse cleared the hurdle, it got caught on a bar, fell, and hurt its back leg **badly.**

# 19b *A, An, The*

*A, an,* and *the* precede nouns. The choice between *a* and *an* is determined by the word that follows it.

- Use *a* when the word starts with a consonant sound:

| | | |
|---|---|---|
| a book | a horse | a very big house |
| a one-inch pipe | a youth | a PTA parent |
| a union   [Use *a* when the *u* sounds like the *y* in *you*.] | | |

> **HINT:** *A* is used before consonant **sounds**, not just consonants. In the phrase "a one-syllable word," the word *one* starts with a "wah" sound which is a consonant sound. Similarly, in the phrase "a union," the word *union* starts with a "you" sound.

- Use *an* when the word following it starts with a vowel or an un-sounded *h* (as in *honor, hour,* and *honest*):

| | | |
|---|---|---|
| an egg | an hour | an onion |
| an ancient coin | an eagle | an idea |
| an SOS signal   [the *S* here is sounded as "es"] | | |

---

**HINT:** Formerly, *an* was used before unaccented syllables beginning with *h,* as in the following:

an historian              an hotel                    an habitual offender

However, this is becoming less frequent, and *a* is now considered acceptable, as in the following:

a historian               a hotel                      a habitual offender

---

## Exercise 19.3: Proofreading Practice

*In the following paragraph, choose either* a *or* an *to complete the sentences correctly.*

Maintaining (1. a, an) clear complexion, salvaging (2. a, an) usually bad semester, and decorating (3. a, an) dorm room are among the topics treated in one of the magazine world's fastest-growing segments, magazines for college students. This market is fueled by advertisers eager to reach (4. a, an) untapped market of twelve to thirteen million college students with (5. a, an) large disposable income and (6. a, an) earning potential of many billions of dollars after graduation. Most college magazines are quarterlies, distributed free at (7. a, an) campus newsstand or by direct mail as (8. a, an) insert in the college paper. While profits are high, there is some criticism that these magazines are merely (9. a, an) advertising vehicle and do not focus on substantive issues, such as (10. a, an) close look at student loan programs or (11. a, an) honest appraisal of racism on campus.

## Exercise 19.4: Pattern Practice

*Write a sentence using the suggested nouns and also using* a, an, *or* the *before these nouns.*

**Example:** egg, piece of toast, cup

**Sentence:** For breakfast, I ordered an egg, a piece of toast, and a cup of coffee.

1. used car, salesperson, helpful
2. train, hour, Alaska
3. yeast, bread, oven, cookbook

**4.** *A*'s, *F*'s (as letter grades in a college course), grade book
**5.** old barn, young chickens, wire fence

# 19c Comparisons

Adverbs and adjectives are often used to show comparison, and the degree of comparison is indicated in their forms.

In comparisons, most adjectives and adverbs add *-er* and *-est* as endings or combine with the words *more* and *most* or *less* and *least*.
**Positive form** is used when no comparison is made:

a **large** box        an **acceptable** offer

**Comparative form** is used when two things are being compared (with *-er, more,* or *less*):

the **larger** of the two boxes

the **more** (or **less**) **acceptable** of the two offers

**Superlative form** is used when three or more things are being compared (with *-est, most,* or *least*):

the **largest** of the six boxes

the **most** (or **least**) **acceptable** of all the offers

| **ADJECTIVES AND ADVERBS IN COMPARISONS** | | |
|---|---|---|
| **Positive** | **Comparative** | **Superlative** |
| *(for one; uses the base form)* | *(for two; uses -er, more, or less)* | *(for three or more; uses -est, most, or least)* |
| tall | taller | tallest |
| pretty | prettier | prettiest |
| cheerful | more cheerful | most cheerful |
| selfish | less selfish | least selfish |

Curtis is **tall.**

Curtis is **taller** than Rachel.

Curtis is the **tallest** player on the team.

19
ad

| IRREGULAR FORMS OF COMPARISONS | | |
|---|---|---|
| **Positive** | **Comparative** | **Superlative** |
| *(for one)* | *(for two)* | *(for three or more)* |
| good | better | best |
| well | better | best |
| little | less | least |
| some | more | most |
| much | more | most |
| many | more | most |
| bad, badly | worse | worst |

**9c**
**ad**

Some guidelines for choosing between *-er* and *-est* or *more* and *most* (or *less* and *least*) are as follows:

• With one-syllable words, the *-er* and *-est* endings are commonly used.

quick                          quicker                          quickest

• With two-syllable words, some adjectives take *-er* and *-est,* and some use *more* and *most* (or *less* and *least*). Check the dictionary to be sure.

happy                          happier                          happiest
thoughtful                     more thoughtful                 least thoughtful

• For adverbs, *more* and *most* or *less* and *least* are commonly used.

smoothly                       more smoothly                   least smoothly

• For words with three or more syllables, use *more* and *most* or *less* and *least*.

generous                       more generous                   least generous

---

**HINT 1:** Be sure to avoid double comparisons in which both the *-er* and *more* (or *-est* and *most*) are used.

❖ the ~~most~~ farthest    ❖ ~~more~~ quicker

**HINT 2:** Be sure to complete your comparisons by using all the needed words.

                                    *driving down*
❖ Driving down Hill Street is slower than ⌃ Western Avenue.

[The act of driving down one street is being compared to the act of driving down another street. The streets themselves are not being compared.]

*it is in*
❖ The weather here is as warm as ∧ Phoenix.

*those of*
❖ The results of the second medical test were more puzzling than ∧ the first test.

**HINT 3:** Remember to choose the correct pronoun case in comparisons with omitted words. (See 18a.)

Terry jumps higher than **I** (do).

Terry likes Julie more than (he likes) **me.**

## Exercise 19.5: Proofreading Practice

*In the following paragraph there are a number of errors in the words used to show comparisons. Revise the paragraph to correct these errors.*

(1) A new sport, already popular in Canada and sweeping across the United States, is indoor box lacrosse. (2) It is more faster, furiouser, and often a more brutal version of the field game of lacrosse. (3) Box lacrosse is indeed an exciting game, as it is more speedy and more rougher than ice hockey but requires the kind of teamwork needed in basketball. (4) Scores for box lacrosse are more high than those for field lacrosse because the indoor game has a more smaller playing area with the most opportunities for scoring. (5) The team in box lacrosse is also more smaller than field lacrosse; there are only six people on a side in the indoor game and ten people on conventional field lacrosse teams. (6) In addition, box lacrosse is played on artificial turf in ice-hockey rinks, and the sticks are more short and more thinner than conventional field lacrosse sticks. (7) Almost anything goes in this rough-and-tumble indoor sport.

## Exercise 19.6: Pattern Practice

*Listed here is some information to use in sentences of your own. Try to include as many comparisons as you can in your sentence.*

**Example:** Write a sentence comparing the cost of the items listed here. Use the word *expensive* in your sentence.

| | |
|---|---|
| bananas: | $0.25/pound |
| apples: | $0.49/pound |
| pears: | $0.60/pound |

**Sample Sentence:** At the First Street Fruit Market, apples are more expensive than bananas, but bananas are less expensive than pears, which are the most expensive of these three fruits.

**1.** Write a sentence of your own about the magazines described here, and use the word *interesting*.

> *Today's Trends* is very dull.
>
> *Home Magazine* is somewhat interesting.
>
> *Now!* is very interesting.

**2.** Write a sentence of your own about the ages of the three teenagers described here, and use the words *old* and *young*.

> Chip is thirteen years old.
>
> Michelle is fifteen years old.
>
> Ethan is eighteen years old.

**3.** Write a sentence of your own about the movies described here, and use the word *scary*.

> *Terror at Night* is not a very scary movie.
>
> *Teen Horror* is a somewhat scary movie.
>
> *Night of the Avengers* is a very scary movie.

**4.** Write a sentence of your own about the car engines described here, and use the word *powerful*.

> The Hyundai engine is not very powerful.
>
> The Ford engine is fairly powerful.
>
> The Ferrari engine is very powerful.

**5.** Write a sentence of your own about the professors described here, and use the word *clear*.

> Professor Tischler's lectures are not very clear.

Professor Liu's lectures are somewhat clear.

Professor Gottner's lectures are very clear.

# 20 Prepositions (prep)

**Prepositions** connect nouns and pronouns to another word or words in a sentence.

They left **in** the morning.

[The preposition *in* connects *morning* with the verb *left*.]

## 20a Common Prepositions

The following is a list of common prepositions:

| | | |
|---|---|---|
| about | despite | out |
| above | down | out of |
| according to | during | outside |
| across | except | over |
| after | except for | past |
| against | excepting | regarding |
| along | for | round |
| along with | from | since |
| among | in | through |
| apart from | in addition to | throughout |
| around | in case of | till |
| as | inside | to |
| at | in spite of | toward |
| because of | instead of | under |
| before | into | underneath |
| behind | like | unlike |
| below | near | until |
| beneath | next | up |
| beside | of | upon |
| between | off | up to |
| beyond | on | with |
| by | onto | within |
| concerning | on top of | without |

# 20b Idiomatic Prepositions

If choosing the right preposition is difficult, look up the word it is used with (not the preposition) in the dictionary. The following combinations can be troublesome:

| *Wrong* | *Revised* |
|---------|-----------|
| apologize about | apologize for |
| bored of | bored with |
| capable to | capable of |
| concerned to, on | concerned about, over, with |
| in search for | in search of |
| independent from | independent of |
| interested about | interested in, by |
| outlook of life | outlook on life |
| puzzled on | puzzled at, by |
| similar with | similar to |

# 20c Other Prepositions

Selecting other prepositions can also be difficult. See the Glossary of Usage at the back of this book for help with the following combinations:

among, between
compared to, compared with
could have (*not* could of)

different from, different than
off (*not* off of)
should have (*not* should of)

---

**HINT:** In formal writing, avoid putting a preposition at the end of a sentence, if possible.

    **Informal:** This is the argument he disagreed **with.**

    **Formal:** This is the argument **with** which he disagreed.

Some prepositions, however, cannot be rearranged.

    He wants to go **in.**

    The mayor was well thought **of.**

    The results may not be worth worrying **about.**

---

## Exercise 20.1: Proofreading Practice

*In the following paragraph, underline the prepositions that are incorrectly used, and then write in the correct words.*

The mail carrier knew she should of stayed away from the dog barking on the porch, but it was her first day on a new job. She was concerned on delivering all the mail she had in her bag and hoped she would not have to report any problems. Her co-workers had warned her on the animals along her route, especially that dog at Mayfield Street. Between all the problems she seemed to be having, she did not want to let her co-workers know that she was afraid about animals. But when she tried to put the mail at the mailbox, the dog jumped up and grabbed all of it in his mouth. No one had told her the dog was trained to collect the mail and bring it inside the house.

# 21 Subjects (sub)

A **subject** is the word or words that indicate who or what is doing the action of active verbs. The subject of a passive verb is acted upon by the verb.

---

**HINT:** To find the subject, first look for the verb (see Chapter 16), and then ask *who* or *what* is doing the action for active verbs. Ask *who* or *what* is acted on for passive verbs.

Annie worked as an underpaid lifeguard last summer.

1. Locate the verb: *worked* (active).
2. Ask: Who or what *worked?*
3. The answer is "Annie worked," so *Annie* is the subject.

Annie was paid less than minimum wage by the swimming pool manager.

1. Locate the verb: *was paid* (passive).
2. Ask: Who or what *was paid?*
3. The answer is "Annie was paid," so *Annie* is the subject.

---

There are several complications to remember when finding subjects:

- Some subjects have more than one word.

    Juan and Quo realized that despite being roommates, they really liked each other.

    1. Who *realized?* Juan and Quo.
    2. The subject is *Juan and Quo.*

That roommates occasionally disagree is well known.

**1.** What *is* well known? That roommates occasionally disagree.
**2.** The subject is *That roommates occasionally disagree.*

- Some subjects may be buried among describing words before and after the subject word.

  The major (**problem**) with today's parents is their tendency to avoid being like their parents.

  Almost (**all**) of his recordings are now available on compact disks.

  Too many (**farmers**) in that area of the state planted soybeans last year.

- Subjects in commands are not expressed in words because the person being addressed is the reader (*you*). "Turn the page" really means that you, the reader, should turn the page.

  Close the door.   [Who is being told to close the door? You are.]

  Mix the eggs thoroughly before adding milk.   [Who is being told to mix the eggs? You are.]

- Most subjects come before the verb, but some come in the middle of or after the verb. For questions, the subject comes in the middle of or after the verb.

  When is the **band** going to start?

  Are **they** here yet?

- For sentences that begin with *there is, there are,* or *it is,* the subject comes after the verb.

  There is a buzzing **sound** in my left ear.

  Now there are buzzing **sounds** in both ears.

  It is **one** of those medical mysteries, I guess.

- For verbs in the passive voice, the doer of the action is expressed in a phrase beginning with *by,* and the subject receives the action. When we are not interested in who is doing the action or when it is obvious who did it, the *by* phrase is omitted.

  The ball was hit by the boy.   (or)   The ball was hit.

  The experiment was performed by several assistants. (or) The experiment was performed.

## Exercise 21.1: Proofreading Practice

*Underline the subjects of all the verbs in the following sentences. Remember, it's easier to start by finding the verb and then asking* who? *or* what? *As an example, the first sentence is already marked.*

(1) <u>Humans</u> are unique in preferring to use the right hand. (2) Among other animals, each individual favors one hand or another, but in every species other than humans, the split between the right and the left hand is even. (3) Only humans seem to favor the right hand. (4) Even in studies of prehistoric people, anthropologists have found this preference. (5) For example, in ancient drawings over five thousand years old, most people are shown using their right hands. (6) This evidence suggests that handedness is not a matter of cultural pressures but perhaps of some genetic difference. (7) Although left-handedness seems to run in families, it is not clear how hand preference is passed from one generation to the next.

## Exercise 21.2: Pattern Practice

*In each blank, write a subject word or words that could fit the sentence. Try to add a word or phrase describing the subject.*

(1) Almost every week of the year, <u>drunken teenagers</u> cause highway accidents that could have been avoided. (2) These _____ usually say that they thought they were in control, but the _____ they drive still get away from them and cause damage. (3) Worst of all, _____ are the real victims of these accidents because they are just as likely to get hurt. (4) Maybe _____ are right when they say that _____ should not have driver's licenses. (5) There is _____ of wisdom in that statement.

# 22 Phrases (phr)

A **phrase** is a group of related words without a subject and complete verb. The words in phrases act as the subject or verb in a sentence, or they can add information to other parts of the sentence.

Note how the related words in these phrases work together to offer information:

<u>A major earthquake</u> hit the area last night.

[This phrase is the subject of the sentence.]

Listening to music is one form of relaxation.

[This phrase is the subject of the sentence.]

Dr. Prada, a famous brain surgeon, will be on television this evening.

[This phrase tells us more about the subject, Dr. Prada.]

The bike leaning on its side fell over during the rainstorm.

[This phrase also tells us more about the subject.]

They may have been eating when I called.

[This phrase is the verb phrase.]

He always walks with his toes pointed out.

[This phrase gives added information about the verb.]

Her favorite pastime is visiting museums.

[This phrase comes after a linking verb and completes the subject.]

Jenny looks like Crazy Edna, a second cousin of mine.

[This phrase gives added information about another element in the sentence.]

## Exercise 22.1: Proofreading Practice

*In the following paragraph, some of the phrases have been underlined. Each one of those underlined phrases performs one of the six functions listed. Identify the function of the phrase by writing the appropriate number below the phrase. The first sentence has been done as an example.*

   **1.** The phrase acts as the subject.
   **2.** It tells something more about the subject.
   **3.** It acts as the verb.
   **4.** It tells something more about the verb.
   **5.** It completes the subject of a linking verb.
   **6.** It tells something more about another element in the sentence.

(1) Finding a place for our garbage is a problem as old as human
        *1*
beings. (2) On the Pacific coast there are large, round shell mounds
where for centuries Indians had been discarding the bones and
clamshells that constituted their garbage. (3) When people gathered
together in cities, they hauled their waste to the outskirts of town or
dumped it into nearby rivers. (4) In the United States the first mu-

nicipal refuse system was instituted in Philadelphia, <u>a well-organized city</u>. (5) Here slaves were forced to wade <u>into the Delaware River</u> and toss bales of trash into the current. (6) Eventually <u>this dumping into rivers</u> was outlawed, and people looked for new solutions to the garbage problem. (7) Municipal dump sites, <u>unused plots of land far away from houses</u>, were <u>a frequent answer</u>. (8) But the number of landfill sites <u>is decreasing</u> as many dumps are closed because of health hazards or because of cost. (9) America, <u>a land of throwaway containers and fancy packaging</u>, clearly faces a garbage problem, <u>a problem without any obvious answers</u>.

## Exercise 22.2: Pattern Practice

*In each of the following sentences, one of the phrases has been underlined. Describe the function of that phrase, and then make up your own sentence that has a phrase performing the same function. The first sentence has been done as an example.*

1. America <u>is facing</u> a garbage crisis that gets worse each year.
   *(verb phrase)*

   They <u>have lived</u> in Chicago for almost two years.
   *(verb phrase)*

2. In 1960 <u>the average American</u> sent 2.2 pounds of trash to the dump each day, but now it's 5.1 pounds a day.
3. We need new dump sites, but they are <u>hard to find</u> because no one wants a landfill next door.
4. Some cities, <u>the ones without potential new landfill space</u>, have given up looking for nearby sites.
5. These cities <u>have started</u> a new practice, exporting their garbage to other states.
6. For example, in Ohio, trash arrives <u>from New Jersey</u>.
7. Exporting garbage is an answer, <u>a temporary one</u>, until other states start refusing to accept someone else's trash.

# 23 Clauses (cl)

A **clause** is a group of related words that (unlike a phrase) has both a subject and a complete verb.

A sentence may have one or more clauses.

- A sentence with one clause:

    Some <u>students</u> <u>see</u> themselves working in office environments and
    *(subject) (verb)*
    wearing formal business clothes.

- A sentence with two clauses:

    Although <u>it</u> <u>becomes</u> expensive to buy a wardrobe of business clothes,
    *(subject 1) (verb 1)*
    such <u>people</u> <u>enjoy</u> the daily opportunities to dress well.
    *(subject 2) (verb 2)*

- A sentence with one clause embedded in the middle of another clause:

    <u>Students</u>    <u>who</u>    <u>seek</u> well-paying jobs often <u>think</u> of careers in
    *(subject 1) (subject 2) (verb 2)*                    *(verb 1)*
    business and finance.

# 23a Independent Clauses (in cl)

An **independent clause** can stand alone as a complete sentence because
it doesn't depend on anything else to complete the thought.

An independent clause has the following characteristics:

- It has a complete verb and subject.

    <u>No one</u> <u>could understand</u> the message written on the blackboard.
    *(subject) (complete verb)*

- It expresses a complete thought and can stand alone as a sentence.

    He never wanted to lend me any of his cassette tapes.

- Two different groups of connecting words can be used at the beginning of an independent clause:

    **1.** *And, but, for, or, nor, so, yet* (coordinating conjunctions)

    Detasseling corn is exhausting work, **but** she needed the money.

    (For use of the comma with these connectors, see 26a.)

    **2.** *Therefore, moreover, thus, consequently,* etc. (conjunctive adverbs)

    Detasseling corn is exhausting work; **however,** she needed the
    money.

(For the use of the semicolon with these connectors, see Chapter 5 and 28a.)

- An independent clause can be combined with a dependent clause or with another independent clause to form a sentence (see Chapter 25):

  1. An independent clause can be its own sentence.

     The popularity of some cartoon characters lasts for years.

  2. Two independent clauses can form one sentence.

     Mickey Mouse, Donald Duck, and Bugs Bunny are perennial favorites, but other once-popular characters such as Jiggs and Maggie have disappeared.

  3. An independent clause can be joined with a dependent clause.

     Since Garfield the cat and Peanuts have become great favorites, perhaps they will last for several generations like Mickey Mouse.

## Exercise 23.1: Proofreading Practice

*In the following paragraph, there are groups of underlined words that are numbered. Identify each group as a phrase or a clause. The first sentence has been done as an example.*

(1) For years strange noises, <u>which would start in June and last until</u>
                                    *(clause)*
<u>September</u>, filled the air around the waters of Richardson Bay, <u>an inlet of water near Sausalito, California</u>. (2) The noise was heard in the house-
         *(phrase)*
boats, <u>especially those with fiberglass hulls</u>, moored along the southwestern shore of the bay. (3) <u>The noise was usually described as a deep hum like an electric foghorn or an airplane motor</u>. (4) The noise, <u>which would start in late evening</u>, would stop by morning, <u>ruining people's sleep</u>. (5) <u>During the summer of 1984</u> the hum was unusually loud and stirred investigations. (6) Originally, suspicion centered on a nearby sewage plant, <u>which was suspected of dumping sewage at night</u> <u>when no one would notice</u>. (7) Some others thought there were <u>secret Navy experiments going on</u>. (8) An acoustical engineer, <u>studying the mystery sound for months</u>, kept thinking he would find the answer, <u>but he didn't</u>. (9) Finally, a marine ecologist identified the source of the hum as the sound of the plainfin midshipman, <u>a fish also known as the singing toad</u>. (10) <u>The male's singing</u> was the sound everyone heard, he said, <u>though some people still suspect the sewage plant</u>.

## Exercise 23.2: Pattern Practice

*In this paragraph on visual pollution, notice the patterns of clauses that are present:*

**1.** Some sentences have one clause.
**2.** Some have two clauses separated by punctuation.
**3.** Some have one clause in the middle of another.

*Each sentence in the paragraph follows one of these patterns. Identify that pattern by its number, and then write your own paragraph of five or more sentences. Identify the pattern of clauses in each of your sentences by using these same numbers. As a subject for your paragraph, you may want to describe other types of pollution, such as noise pollution caused by dual-exhaust cars, air pollution caused by cigarette smoke or overpowering perfumes, or visual pollution caused by litter.*

(1) One type of pollution that the government has tried to eliminate is the visual pollution of billboards along our highways. (2) In 1965 Congress passed the Highway Beautification Act to outlaw those ugly signs, but the act didn't work. (3) While the federal government paid for the removal of 2,235 old billboards in 1983, the billboard industry was busy putting up 18,000 new signs in the same year. (4) Since then the situation has gotten worse. (5) The 1965 act had all kinds of loopholes; however, the real problem is a requirement in the act to pay billboard companies for removing the signs. (6) Since some communities don't have the funds for this, too many old signs are still standing, along with all the new ones going up.

# 23b Dependent Clauses (dep cl)

A **dependent clause** cannot stand alone as a complete sentence because it depends on another clause in the sentence to complete the thought.

---

**HINT 1:** Dependent clauses have adverbs at the beginning of the clause. (See the explanation of adverb clauses in 23b(2).)

**HINT 2:** Say the dependent clause aloud, and you'll hear that you need to add more information.

"When I got up this morning . . ."   [Are you waiting for more information?]

**HINT 3:** To locate dependent clauses punctuated as sentences, try proofreading your papers backward from the last sentence to the first.

There are two kinds of dependent clauses: adjective and adverb clauses.

## (1) Adjective Clauses (*who/which/that* clauses)

An **adjective clause** gives additional information about a noun or pronoun in the sentence and starts with one of the following words: *who, which, that, whose, whom.*

The singer, **who used to play lead guitar**, now lets the other band members play while she sings.

The group tried a concert tour, **which was a financial disaster**.

The rumor **that the poor ticket sales were due to mismanagement** never appeared in print.

## (2) Adverb Clauses (*because/if/when* clauses)

An **adverb clause** gives more information about other verbs, adjectives, or adverbs in a sentence or another clause.

Adverb clauses start with adverbs such as the following common ones:

| | | | |
|---|---|---|---|
| after | before | though | when |
| although | even if | unless | whenever |
| as | even though | until | whether |
| as if | if | what | while |
| because | since | whatever | |

> **HINT:** You can recognize adverb clauses by these marker words at the beginning. Because of the meaning of these words, they create the need for another clause to complete the thought. Think of the relationship as follows:
>
> **After** X, Y.    [*After* X happens, Y happens.]
>
> **Because** X, Y.    [*Because* X happens, Y happens.]
>
> *continued on next page*

*continued from previous page*

**If** X, Y.    [*If* X happens, Y will happen.]

**After** I eat lunch tomorrow . . .    [What will happen?]

After I eat lunch tomorrow, I will call you.

**Because** it was so dark out . . .    [What happened?]

Because it was so dark out, she tripped on the steps.

**If** I win the lottery . . .    [What will happen?]

If I win the lottery, I'll quit my job and retire.

**When** it began to rain . . .    [What happened?]

When it began to rain, the game was canceled.

Dependent clauses may appear at the beginning of a sentence, before the independent clause, or at the end of the sentence, where they are harder to recognize:

I will call you **after I eat lunch tomorrow.**

She tripped on the steps **because it was so dark out.**

The game was canceled **when it began to rain.**

**HINT:** To punctuate dependent clauses:

- When the adverb clause appears at the beginning of a sentence, it is followed by a comma.
- When the adverb clause follows an independent clause, no punctuation is needed before the adverb clause. (See 26b.)

> **Until gas prices are cheaper,** I will buy only compact cars.
>
> [adverb clause first]
>
> I will buy only compact cars **until gas prices are cheaper.**
>
> [adverb clause last]

## Exercise 23.3: Proofreading Practice

*Identify the dependent clauses in the following paragraph by underlining them and labeling them as either adjective or adverb clauses.*

(1) The tiny lichen is an amazing plant. (2) It can survive in an incredibly difficult environment because it can do things no other plant can do. (3) The lichen, which can anchor itself on a bare rock by etching the rock's surface with powerful acids, grows into the pits that it burns out. (4) Because lichens grow in cold climates above the tree line, they are frozen or covered by snow most of the year. (5) Unlike the cactus in the desert, the lichen has no way of retaining moisture. (6) Because of this, the sun dries lichens into waterless crusts during the day. (7) When there is a drought, lichens may dry out completely for several months. (8) Even under ideal conditions their total daily growing period may last only for an hour or two while they are still wet with morning dew. (9) The lichen, which may take twenty-five years to grow to a diameter of one inch, can live for several thousand years. (10) These amazing plants are able to live in all sorts of difficult places, but not in cities because the pollution may kill them.

## Exercise 23.4: Pattern Practice

*Write your own paragraph with sentences that include dependent clauses. As in Exercise 23.3, identify the dependent clauses by underlining them and labeling them as either adjective or adverb clauses. If possible, use the sentences in Exercise 23.3 as patterns. As a subject for your paragraph, you may wish to describe an animal, a person, or another plant like the lichen that manages to survive under difficult conditions.*

## Exercise 23.5: Proofreading Practice

*Identify the independent clauses in this paragraph by underlining them. If an independent clause is interrupted by a dependent clause, put parentheses around the dependent clause. The first sentence has been done as an example.*

(1) <u>In 1976 Sony</u>, (which is one of Japan's leading electronic companies,) <u>introduced the first consumer videocassette recorder, or VCR</u>. (2) Within a decade, more than one-third of all homes in the United States had VCRs because people have found them such a convenient source of entertainment. (3) When people want to go out in the evening, they can record their favorite programs and watch them at a different time. (4) In addition, families can produce video histories of weddings, anniversaries, and bar mitzvahs, or they can watch sporting events and see replays whenever they want. (5) The price of a VCR, which fell about 80 percent in the first decade, is another factor in making this new electronic gadget so popular, and videotapes can be rented everywhere, from service stations and supermarkets to public libraries. (6) Because it is reasonably cheap, convenient, and a good source of entertainment, the VCR will continue to be a visible part of the American scene.

## Exercise 23.6: Pattern Practice

*Read the following paragraph, and identify the sentence patterns by the kinds of clauses in each sentence. Choose the most appropriate of the following numbers, and write that number above the sentence.*

1. Independent clause as its own sentence
2. Two independent clauses joined into one sentence
3. One independent clause with a dependent clause
4. Two independent clauses and a dependent clause

*The first sentence has been done as an example. Write your own paragraph using these sentence patterns. You may want to write about some other electronic equipment that you like, such as stereos or portable CD players, or you may want to write about another recent addition to the American scene, such as music videos or unusual clothing fashions.*

3

(1) In addition to its popularity as home entertainment, the VCR has many commercial and educational uses because it can display both pictures and sound so easily. (2) Videotapes are useful as sales promoters, and they have successfully been introduced into supermarkets to show shoppers how to prepare kiwi fruits and how to cook bok choy. (3) In sporting goods stores, videotape pitches showing the success of bodybuilding equipment have resulted in greatly increased sales. (4) Moreover, banks have found videotaping useful for security, and supermarkets now routinely videotape customers as they cash checks. (5) Although these commercial uses of VCRs have just recently begun to appear, educational videotapes have been widely used for a long time in classrooms at all levels from primary school to university classes. (6) Self-improvement videos that help people learn aerobic dancing, tennis, golf, cooking, and Spanish are consistently among the best-selling videotapes. (7) The VCR has become a useful commercial and educational tool.

# 24 Essential and Nonessential Clauses and Phrases

## 24a Essential Clauses and Phrases (es)

An **essential clause** or **phrase** (also called a *restrictive*, or *necessary*, clause or phrase) appears after a noun and is essential in the sentence to complete the meaning. An essential clause or phrase cannot be moved to another sentence or omitted because the meaning of the sentence would change.

Compare the meaning of the following two sentences with and without the clause after the noun *people:*

People <u>who can speak more than one language</u> are multilingual.

People are multilingual.

[The second sentence seems odd because not all people are multilingual. The *who* clause in the sentence above is essential because we need it to understand the meaning.]

Please repair all the windows <u>that are broken</u>.

[If the *that* clause is taken out, the sentence is a request to repair all the windows, not just those that are broken. Since the meaning of the sentence is changed when the *that* clause is removed, the *that* clause is essential to the sentence.]

Sylvester Stallone's movie *Rambo II* will be on TV tonight.

[The movie title *Rambo II* is necessary because Sylvester Stallone has appeared in many movies. If the phrase *Rambo II* is taken out of the sentence, it then says that Stallone's only movie will be on TV.]

**24**
**nor**

---

> **HINT 1:** Essential clauses and phrases are not set off by commas.
> **HINT 2:** Clauses starting with *that* are almost always essential.

---

## 24b Nonessential Clauses and Phrases (non es)

A **nonessential clause** or **phrase** (also called a *nonrestrictive* or *unnecessary* clause or phrase) adds extra information but can be removed from a sentence without disturbing the meaning. The information can be put in another sentence.

Compare the following two sentences to see if the primary meaning of the sentence remains the same after the clause is removed:

My cousin Jim, <u>who lives in Denver</u>, is coming for a visit over Thanksgiving vacation.

My cousin Jim is coming for a visit over Thanksgiving vacation.

[The *who* clause is nonessential because it adds information about where Jim lives but is not necessary. The assumption here is that the writer has only one cousin named Jim. If the writer had two cousins named Jim, one who lives in Denver and another in St. Louis, then *who lives in Denver* would be necessary.]

Sandwich Supreme, <u>one of the first of a new chain of gourmet sandwich shops</u>, serves six different types of cheese sandwiches with a choice of three different types of bread.

[If the phrase describing Sandwich Supreme as a part of a chain of gourmet shops is removed from the sentence, the meaning of the main clause remains intact. The phrase is therefore not essential.]

**4b**
**es**

*Rambo II*, <u>starring Sylvester Stallone</u>, will be on TV tonight.

[In this sentence, the phrase noting who stars in the movie can be removed because it merely adds information about the name of one of the actors. Compare this sentence with the example of *Rambo II* as an essential clause in 24a.]

---

**HINT:** Nonessential clauses and phrases are set off by a pair of commas when they appear within a sentence. Only one comma is needed when they appear at the end of a sentence. (See 26c.)

The compact disk, <u>a revolutionary advance in high-fidelity recording</u>, has made records obsolete.

[Here the nonessential phrase appears in the middle of the sentence and needs two commas.]

Consumers are spending millions of dollars now on compact disks, <u>a revolutionary advance in high-fidelity recording</u>.

[Here the nonessential phrase appears at the end of the sentence and needs only one comma.]

---

Some sentences will be punctuated differently depending on the meaning:

Phil's son <u>Steve</u> is playing in the soccer match.

[This sentence states that Phil has more than one son, and the son named Steve is playing in the soccer match.]

Phil's son, <u>Steve</u>, is playing in the soccer match.

[This sentence states that Phil has only one son, and an extra bit of information is that his name is Steve.]

The bank offered loans to the farmers, <u>who were going to plant soybeans</u>.

[This sentence states that all farmers received loans.]

The bank offered loans to the farmers <u>who were going to plant soybeans</u>.

[This sentence states that the bank offered loans only to the farmers planting soybeans, not to those planting other crops.]

## Exercise 24.1: Proofreading Practice

*In the following paragraph there are underlined phrases. Identify these as either essential or nonessential phrases by writing an E (for essential) or N (for nonessential) above each underlined phrase.*

(1) Art fraud, <u>a widespread problem</u>, is probably as old as art itself. (2) Fourteenth-century Italian stonecarvers <u>who wanted to deceive their buyers</u> copied Greek and Roman statues and then purposely chipped their works so they could peddle them as antiquities. (3) Today forgers, <u>who have become specialists in different kinds of fraud</u>, produce piles of moderately priced prints, paintings, statues, and pottery. (4) The people <u>whom they defraud</u> are usually beginning or less knowledgeable collectors. (5) These people, <u>who usually can afford to spend only a few thousand dollars at most for a work of art</u>, have not developed a skilled eye for detecting fraud.

## Exercise 24.2: Pattern Practice

*In the following paragraph there are some underlined clauses and phrases, both essential and nonessential. Practice using clauses and phrases like these in your writing by composing your own sentences in the same patterns as the following sentences. As your topic, you may want to describe another common kind of fraud or deception that exists today.*

(1) Thomas Hoving, <u>the former director of the Metropolitan Museum of Art</u>, estimates that 40 percent of the art <u>that is on the market today</u> is fake. (2) However, much of this fraudulent art is not detected because even buyers <u>who suspect fraud</u> find it difficult to prove that the seller knowingly unloaded a fake on them. (3) Thus collectors <u>who get stuck with dubious pieces of art</u> usually don't go to court. (4) Instead, they attempt to return the piece to the person <u>from whom they bought it</u>. (5) If that isn't possible, some collectors, <u>particularly the less honest ones</u>, pass the piece of art on to another unsuspecting buyer.

# 25 Sentences (sent)

A **sentence** is a group of words that has at least one independent clause and expresses a relatively complete thought.

The following characteristics of sentences help to distinguish them from fragments:

- Although sentences are said to express "a complete thought," sentences normally occur in the context of other sentences that explain more fully. A sentence may therefore seem to need more information because it will refer to other sentences.

    **He was able to do it.**

    [This is a complete sentence because it is an independent clause. We don't know who "he" is or what "he" was able to do, but when this sentence appears with others, more explanation will make the meaning clear.]

- Sentences can start with any word.

    **1.** *And* and *but* are connecting words that can start an independent clause.

    **But** the dog did not bark.

    [This sentence may not seem "complete" because it needs a context of other sentences to explain the whole situation.]

    **2.** *Because, since,* and other markers that begin adverbial clauses can open a sentence as long as an independent clause follows.

    **Because she did not lock her bike,** it was stolen.

    [dependent clause first, then an independent clause]

    **3.** Dependent clauses and phrases can start a sentence as subjects.

    **That it was hot** did not bother the athletes.

    [dependent clause as subject]

    **4.** Transitional words and phrases, such as *first, to sum up,* and *meanwhile,* can begin a sentence.

    **Next,** she lifted the window.

    [We don't know what "she" did first, but again, the context of other sentences will help.]

- Sentences can have pronouns as subjects.

    **He** was proud of his accomplishments.

- Sentences don't have to have any specified length. They can have only a few or many words.

    Go away!    [short complete sentence]

    Whenever it is time to put away my winter clothing after a long, cold winter season, I always have a deep feeling of relief as if I am forcing the cold air to stay away until next year.    [long complete sentence]

- The complete verb in a sentence may be in a contraction.

    He**'s** here.    That**'s** enough.

    [The verb, *is*, is less obvious because it is contracted.]

- Punctuation errors and other problems in a sentence may occur, but these errors do not make a sentence a fragment.

    The current interest in healthful foods has not diminished the sale of fast food, high-fat hamburgers and hot dogs continue to sell well.

    [This sentence is incorrectly punctuated with a comma, but it is still a sentence. See 5a.]

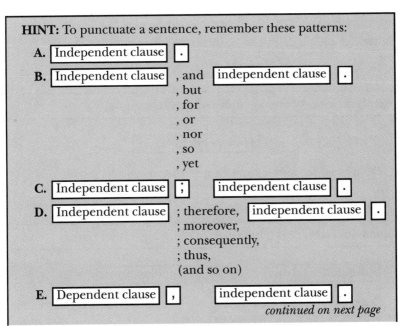

**HINT:** To punctuate a sentence, remember these patterns:

A. Independent clause .

B. Independent clause , and   independent clause .
, but
, for
, or
, nor
, so
, yet

C. Independent clause ;   independent clause .

D. Independent clause ; therefore,   independent clause .
; moreover,
; consequently,
; thus,
(and so on)

E. Dependent clause ,   independent clause .

*continued on next page*

*continued from previous page*

**F.** | Independent clause | | dependent clause | | . |

**G.** | First part of an independent clause | | , | | nonessential | | , |

| rest of the clause | | . |

**H.** | First part of an independent clause | | essential |

| rest of the clause | | . |

For a more complete explanation of sentence punctuation, see Chapters 26 and 28.

# 25a Sentence Purposes

Sentences can be described by their purpose:

- Making a statement (Declarative): The divorce rate is increasing.
- Asking a question (Interrogative): Is anyone home?
- Giving a command (Imperative): Put that book on the table.
- Expressing strong feeling (Exclamatory): That's an amazing feat!

# 25b Sentence Structures

Sentences can be described by their structure.

## (1) Simple Sentences

**Simple sentences** have one independent clause.

| Independent clause |

Doctors are concerned about the rising death rate from asthma.

## (2) Compound Sentences

**Compound sentences** have two or more independent clauses.

| Independent clause | + | independent clause |

Doctors and researchers are concerned about the rising death rate from asthma, but they don't know the reason for it.

## (3) Complex Sentences

**Complex sentences** have at least one independent clause and at least one dependent clause (in any order).

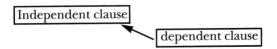

Doctors and researchers are concerned about the rising death rate from asthma because it is a common, treatable illness.

## (4) Compound-Complex Sentences

**Compound-complex sentences** have at least two independent clauses and at least one dependent clause (in any order).

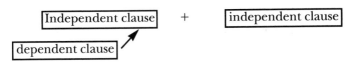

Doctors and researchers are concerned about the rising death rate from asthma because it is a common, treatable illness, but they don't know the reason for the 23 percent increase in the last five years.

## Exercise 25.1: Proofreading Practice

*Identify each of the numbered groups of words with the appropriate letter(s) from this group:*

    I = incomplete sentence
    S = simple sentence
    CP = compound sentence
    CX = complex sentence
    CP-CX = compound-complex sentence

(1) When we have a romantic relationship with another person, we want to know how the other person feels about us. (2) But, as psychologists have found out from their studies, we rarely resort to asking about the other person's feelings. (3) Some people do this, but most people tend to use indirect means. (4) Such as asking a third person's opinion or using some more indirect means of inquiry. (5) A recent study of college students confirmed the tendency among students to use indirect means; moreover, in the study two psychologists learned students' most-often-used indirect tactic, which was to make the other person choose between alternatives, for example, asking the other person to choose

their relationship over something else such as an opportunity to go off for a weekend of skiing. (6) Another way described by the students was testing the other person's limits of endurance in terms of behavior. (7) For example, the student would do something just to see if the other person would put up with it. (8) Yet another kind of testing of relationships was trying to make the other person jealous, and about one-third of the students being studied cited this as a kind of test of the other person's love. (9) The psychologists, who were also looking for instances of people who directly ask the other person about their feelings, found very few examples. (10) Asking the other person directly was reported to be a very difficult thing to do.

## Exercise 25.2: Pattern Practice

*Practice the sentence patterns in the following paragraph by writing your own simple, compound, complex, and compound-complex sentences. Follow the patterns used by these sentences. For your subject matter, you may write about a form of exercise you prefer.*

(1) Many people who have suffered the sprains and aches of aerobic exercising now prefer an alternative form called low-impact aerobics. (2) This involves ways to exercise without causing stress to the body, and it requires strength, endurance, flexibility, and balance. (3) Low-impact exercises involve larger arm motions and leg motions that keep one foot on the floor to reduce bouncing and jumping. (4) Because some people want more upper-body exercise, some low-impact aerobics also include the use of wrist weights. (5) It's not entirely clear that low-impact aerobics deliver the same aerobic benefit as traditional programs, but for those who want to avoid injury or cannot follow the more strenuous routines, it does provide benefit. (6) However, for both traditional aerobics and the low-impact variety, the main cause of injury is still bad shoes, bad floors, bad stretches, and bad instruction.

# PART FOUR

## PUNCTUATION

This part reviews rules for punctuation, those marks we add to the page to guide readers through our sentences.

# 26 Commas (,)

Commas are signals to help readers understand the meaning of written sentences. In the same way that our voices convey meaning by pausing or changing in pitch, commas indicate pauses to help readers understand writing. Thus, the sound of your sentences may help to indicate where commas are needed. But sound isn't always a dependable guide because not every voice pause occurs where a comma is needed and not every comma needs a voice pause. The rules in this section, along with some clues you get from pauses in your voice, will indicate where you'll need commas.

---

### COMMAS AND SEMICOLONS IN SENTENCES

For simple sentences, use pattern 1.
For compound sentences, use patterns 2, 3, and 4.
For complex sentences, use patterns 5, 6, and 7.

1. | Independent clause | .

2. | Independent clause | , **coordinating** | independent clause | .
   **conjunction**:

   and    nor
   but    so
   for    yet
   or

**3.** | Independent clause | ; | | | | independent clause | | . |

**4.** | Independent clause | ; | **independent** | independent clause | | . |
**clause**
**marker:**
however,
nevertheless,
therefore,
consequently,
(etc.)

**5. Dependent marker:** | dependent clause | | , |

| independent clause | | . |
Because
Since
If
When
While
After
(etc.)

**6.** | Independent clause | **dependent** | dependent clause | | . |
**marker:**
because
since
if
when
while
after
(etc.)

**7.** Subject | dependent clause | verb/predicate.

(Use commas before and after the dependent clause if it is
nonessential.)

# 26a Commas in Compound Sentences

There are three ways to join independent clauses together into a compound sentence.

**1.** Use the comma with one of the seven coordinating conjunctions:

| and | for | nor | yet |
| but | or | so | |

_____ (clause) _____ , **and** _____ (clause) _____ .

The television program was dull, but the commercials were entertaining.

After the storm, they collected seashells along the beach, and everyone found some interesting specimens, but the conservationists asked them no to take the shells home.

**Exception:** A comma may be omitted if the two independent clauses are short and there is no danger of misreading.

We were tired so we stopped the game.

She smiled and we all smiled back.

---

**HINT:** To remember the seven coordinating conjunctions, think of the phrase "**fan boys**":

| for | and | nor |
|-----|-----|-----|
| but | or  | yet |
|     |     | so  |

---

**2.** Join independent clauses with a semicolon and a connecting word such as the following:

| however, | therefore, | consequently, |
|----------|------------|---------------|
| thus,    | moreover,  | then,         |

_____ (clause) _____; **thus,** _____ (clause) _____ .

The camping sites were all filled; however, the park ranger allowed latecomers to use empty spaces in the parking lot.

David's new sports car was designed for high speed driving; moreover, it was also designed to be fuel efficient.

---

**HINT:** Use a comma after the connecting word.

---

**3.** Join the independent clauses with a semicolon and no joining words.

_____ (clause) _____ ; _____ (clause) _____ .

Everyone in the room heard the glass shattering; no one moved until it was clear that there was no danger.

For the errors caused by not following one of these three patterns, see Chapter 5.

## Exercise 26.1: Proofreading Practice

*In the following paragraph there are compound sentences that need commas or semicolons. Add the appropriate punctuation.*

An inventor working on a "flying car" says that traveling several hundred miles by commercial airplane is a fairly inefficient way to get around. First you have to drive through traffic to the airport and then you have to park your car somewhere in order to board a plane. You fly to another crowded airport outside a city but then you have to take another automobile to your final destination in town. A more practical solution would be a personal commuter flying vehicle. The inventor, working in a company supported by several government agencies, has developed a vertical takeoff and landing vehicle that has the potential to allow everyone to take to the air. The vehicle can take off and land vertically and it travels five times faster than an automobile. The most recently developed model looks more like a car than a plane however, it operates more like a cross between a plane and a helicopter. Above 125 mph in flight, it flies like a conventional plane and below 125 mph, it maneuvers like a helicopter. It has a number of safety features, such as six engines therefore it can recover if it loses an engine while hovering close to the ground.

## Exercise 26.2: Sentence Combining

*Using the punctuation pattern for commas in compound sentences, combine the following short sentences into longer, compound sentences.*

*Remember, commas in compound sentences follow this pattern:*

_____ (clause) _____ [ , and | but | nor | for | so | or | yet ] _____ (clause) _____.

1. The personal commuter flying vehicle now being designed has room for four passengers.
2. It can fly roughly 850 miles per tank of fuel at a cruising speed of 225 mph.
3. The vehicle can rise above 30,000 feet.
4. It can also hover near the ground.
5. According to the inventor, it has taken two decades of theoretical studies to design the vehicle's shape.
6. It has also taken ten years of wind-tunnel tests to achieve the aerodynamic shape.
7. Government officials foresee an entire transportation network in the future based on the personal flying vehicle.
8. There will have to be automated air traffic control systems for these vehicles.

**9.** The technology for controlling these vehicles already exists.
**10.** The technology will create electronic highways in the sky.

# 26b Commas after Introductory Words, Phrases, and Clauses

A comma is needed after introductory words, phrases, and clauses that come before the main clause.

### Introductory Words

| | | |
|---|---|---|
| Yes, | No, | However, |
| Well, | In fact, | First, |

<u>Well,</u> perhaps he meant no harm. <u>In fact,</u> he wanted to help.

### Introductory Phrases

- Long prepositional phrases (usually four words or more):

    <u>In the middle of a long, dull movie,</u> I decided to get some popcorn.

    <u>Due to his determination not to get a C,</u> he did all the homework.

- Phrases with *-ing* verbals, *-ed* verbals, and *to* + verb.

    <u>Having</u> finished the test before the bell rang, he left the room.

    <u>Tired</u> of never having enough money, she took a second job.

    <u>To get</u> a seat close to the stage, you'd better come early.

### Introductory Clauses

- Introductory dependent clauses that begin with adverbs such as the following:

| | | |
|---|---|---|
| After . . . | Because . . . | Until . . . |
| Although . . . | If . . . | When . . . |
| As . . . | Since . . . | While . . . |

<u>While I was eating,</u> the cat scratched at the door.

Exception: The comma may be omitted when the introductory phrase or clause is short and there is no danger of misreading.

<u>While eating</u> I read the newspaper.

<u>After they retired</u> they moved to Mexico.

> **HINTS:** When dependent clauses come after the main clause, there is no comma.
>
> When the telephone rang, the dog started to bark.
>
> The dog started to bark when the telephone rang.
>
> Use commas after introductory clauses, phrases, and words in the following cases:
>
> - If the introduction is five or more words
> - If there is a distinct voice pause after the introductory part
> - If it is necessary to avoid confusion
>
> **Possibly Confusing:** As I stated the rules can be broken occasionally.
>
> **Revised:** As I stated, the rules can be broken occasionally.
>
> When your sentence starts with an *-ing* verbal, *-ed* verbal, or *to* + verb, be sure you don't have a dangling modifier (see Chapter 8).

## Exercise 26.3: Proofreading Practice

*In the following paragraph there are introductory words, phrases, and clauses that require commas. Add commas where needed.*

(1) A recent study showed that small cars are tailgated more than big ones. (2) Moreover the drivers of subcompact and compact cars also do more tailgating themselves. (3) In the study traffic flow at five different locations was observed, and various driving conditions were included, such as two-lane state roads, four-lane divided highways, and so on. (4) In all more than 10,000 vehicles were videotaped. (5) Although subcompact and compact cars accounted for only 38 percent of the vehicles on the tape their drivers were tailgating in 48 percent of the incidents observed. (6) In addition to having done all this tailgating these drivers were the victims of tailgating 47 percent of the time. (7) Midsize cars made up 31 percent of the cars on the tapes but accounted for only 20 percent of the tailgaters and 24 percent of the drivers being tailgated. (8) Having considered various reasons for this difference the researchers suggest that drivers of other cars may avoid getting close to midsize cars because of the cars' contours. (9) Because midsize cars have more curves in their sloping backs and trunks people may have more trouble seeing around them.

## Exercise 26.4: Pattern Practice

*The following sentences illustrate some of the rules for using introductory commas. Identify the rule by selecting the appropriate letter from the list given here, and then write your own sentence in this pattern.*

Pattern A:    Comma after an introductory word
Pattern B:    Comma after an introductory phrase
Pattern C:    Comma after an introductory clause

1. Because tailgating is a road hazard that is known to cause many accidents, other studies have searched for causes of tailgating.
2. For example, one study examined how people judge distances on the road.
3. Puzzled by the question of why small cars are tailgated so often, researchers studied other drivers' perceptions of how far away small cars appear to be.
4. Despite the fact that many of the people studied were generally able to guess distances accurately, they sometimes perceived small cars to be more than forty feet farther away than they actually were.
5. If drivers tend to think that small cars are really farther away than they actually are, this may explain why small cars are tailgated so often.
6. However, researchers continue to study this problem.

## 26c Commas with Essential and Nonessential Words, Phrases, and Clauses

Nonessential word groups (see 24b) require a pair of commas, one before the nonessential element and the other afterward (unless there is a period). Essential word groups do not have commas to set them off from the rest of the sentence.

---

**HINTS:**

- When an essential clause is removed, the meaning is too general.

  Students **who cheat** harm only themselves.

  [With the word group "who cheat" removed, the sentence would say that students harm themselves. That's too general and does not convey the meaning of the sentence.]

- When a nonessential clause is removed, the meaning is the same.

  The restaurant, which serves only breakfast and lunch, was closed.

  [With the word group "which serves only breakfast and lunch" removed, the sentence still says that the restaurant was closed. The meaning of the main clause is the same.]

- When the word group interrupts the flow of words in the original sentence, it's a nonessential element and needs commas. Some people can hear a slight pause in their voice or a change in pitch as they begin and end a nonessential element.
- When you can move the word group around in the sentence or put it in a different sentence, it is a nonessential element.

   No one, however, wanted to tell her she was wrong.

   No one wanted, however, to tell her she was wrong.

   However, no one wanted to tell her she was wrong.

- When the clause begins with *that*, it is always essential.

   I'll return the sweater **that I borrowed** after I wear it again tonight.

   *That* clauses following verbs that express mental action are always essential:

   I think that . . .       She believes that . . .       He dreams that . . .
   They wish that . . .    We concluded that . . .

- Word groups (called appositives) following nouns that identify or explain the nouns are nonessential and need commas:

   Uncle Ike, a doctor, smoked too much even though he continued to warn his patients not to smoke.   [Uncle Ike = a doctor]

   The movie critic's review of *Heartland*, a story about growing up in Indiana, focused on the beauty of the scenery.   [*Heartland* = a story about growing up in Indiana]

When this word group is the last element in the sentence, keep it attached to the sentence and set it off with a comma. Some fragments are appositives that became detached from the sentence.

❖ She is a good friend. A person whom I trust and admire.
          ,a

## Exercise 26.5: Proofreading Practice

*Some of the sentences in the following paragraph have essential and nonessential words, phrases, and clauses. Underline these elements, write N (for nonessential) or E (for essential), and add commas where they are needed.*

   The use of technical advisers for TV programs is not new. For medical, legal, and police dramas that attempt to be realistic, producers have long called on experts to check the scripts. These experts who read the scripts before production make sure that TV surgeons, lawyers, and police officers use the right terminology and follow standard procedures. Now network shows are also calling on social scientists as consultants to add realism in sitcoms and to help networks conform to criteria that are required by Federal Communications Commission (FCC) standards. The FCC, a federal regulatory agency, says that shows with a potential audience of children even if they are not aired until after the early evening family viewing time must offer some content with educational value. But of course TV still wants to entertain, and sometimes there is some conflict with the writers. On the whole though television scriptwriters have come to recognize and value advice from social scientists and psychologists particularly on important topics such as how children react to divorce, how parents might handle children's drug abuse, or how families deal with emotional crises.

## Exercise 26.6: Pattern Practice

*In Exercise 26.5 there are sentences illustrating the following patterns for punctuating essential and nonessential elements in sentences. Using these patterns and the examples from the paragraph in Exercise 26.5, write your own sentences in the same pattern with correct punctuation.*

Pattern A:   Subject + comma + nonessential clause + comma + verb + object

Pattern B:   Subject + essential clause + verb + object

Pattern C:   Introductory phrase + comma + nonessential word + comma + subject + verb + object

Pattern D:   Subject + verb + object + comma + nonessential phrase

# 26d Commas in Series and Lists

---

Use commas when three or more items are listed in a series.

---

### A Series of Words

Would you prefer the poster printed in yellow, blue, green, or purple?

### A Series of Phrases

He first spoke to Julio, then called his roommate, and finally phoned me.

### A Series of Clauses

She never dreamed she'd be in the movies, she hadn't even tried out for a part, and she was sure she didn't have enough talent to act.

There are some variations in using commas in lists. The comma after the last item before *and* or *or* is preferred, but it may be omitted if there is no possibility of misreading.

Americans' favorite spectator sports are football, baseball, and basketball.

[optional comma]

However, the comma before *and* cannot be omitted in sentences where terms belong together, such as *bread and butter,* or where some misreading is possible.

He talked about his college studies, art, and history.

[This sentence means that he talked about three things: his college studies, art, and history.]

He talked about his college studies, art and history.

[This sentence means that his college studies were in art and history.]

If one or more of the items in a series have commas, semicolons should be used between items.

The group included Bill Packo, the guitarist; Jim Hinders, drums; and Art Clutz, electronic keyboard.

## Exercise 26.7: Proofreading Practice

*In the following paragraph, there are some series of three or more items that need punctuation. Add commas where they are needed.*

Imagine not being able to recognize the face of your sister your boss or your best friend from high school. Imagine looking into a mirror seeing a face and realizing that the face you see is totally unfamiliar. Though this may sound impossible, a small number of people do suffer from a neurological condition that leaves them unable to recognize familiar faces. The condition is called prosopagnosia and results from brain damage caused by infection or stroke. Many people with this problem who have been studied have normal vision reading ability and language skills. They know that a face is a face they can name its parts and they can distinguish differences between faces. But only through other clues—hearing a familiar voice remembering a specific feature like a mustache hearing a name or recalling a particular identifying mark such as an unusual scar—can the people who were studied call up memories of people they should know. Researchers studying this phenomenon have found evidence suggesting that the step leading to conscious recognition of the face by the brain is somehow being blocked.

## Exercise 26.8: Pattern Practice

*The following sentences all have examples of items in a series. Using these sentences as patterns, write your own sentences with correctly punctuated items in series.*

1. His favorite pastimes are sleeping late on weekends, drinking too much beer, and watching game shows on television.
2. She's convinced that it's better to work hard when you're young, to save your money, and then to spend it all when you retire.
3. Do you prefer jogging shoes with leather, canvas, or mesh tops?
4. Some people try to forget their birthdays, some like to have big celebrations, and others don't have any strong preference.

# 26e Commas with Adjectives

Use commas to separate two or more adjectives that describe the same noun equally.

cold, dark water          happy, healthy baby

However, not all adjectives in front of a noun describe the noun equally. When they are not equal (or coordinate) adjectives, do not use commas to separate them.

six big dogs

bright green sweater   [the color of the sweater is bright green]

---

**HINT:** Can you add *and* between the adjectives? Can the adjectives be written in reverse order? If so, separate the adjectives with commas.

- a greedy, stubborn child

  [Either of the following is acceptable:]

  a greedy, stubborn child      (or)      a stubborn, greedy child

- an easy, happy smile

  an easy, happy smile      (or)      a happy, easy smile

But notice the following examples, which do not describe the noun equally.

- a white frame house    [The following is not acceptable: a frame white house]

- two young men    [The following is not acceptable: young two men]

---

## Exercise 26.9: Proofreading Practice

*In the following paragraph, there are sentences with adjectives in front of nouns that need punctuation. Add commas with the adjectives where they are needed, and circle the commas.*

New computer technology has revolutionized the work of secretaries. Previously, dictaphones, electric typewriters, and copy machines made the office an easier more efficient place to work, but secretaries say that e-mail is the breakthrough that has changed the modern large office. Years ago, when a secretary had to mail an inter-office memo, it would be a very tedious job. Printing, collating, addressing, and stuffing envelopes with copies of the memo was a big time-consuming job. Now, with e-mail, a secretary can distribute a memo with a simple quick computer command. But e-mail has some disadvantages too. Some secretaries say that they used to be the center of all important inside information because all memos and correspondence passed through them. Now, bosses can send their own messages, and secretaries can be left out of the loop with important matters. Moreover, a secretary's personal private messages can mistakenly get sent to the whole company.

## Exercise 26.10: Pattern Practice

*Using the patterns given here as guides, write your own phrases correctly punctuated with commas. Write two different phrases for each pattern given.*

**1.** Four little kittens (use a number and another describing word).
**2.** A shiny red door (use a color and another describing word).
**3.** Balding, skinny man (use at least two body features).
**4.** Happy, carefree smile (use at least two emotions).
**5.** Heavy wooden door (use a material and another describing word).

# 26f Commas with Dates, Addresses, Geographical Names, and Numbers

### (1) Commas with Dates

June 12, 1960,   (or)   12 June 1960

[No commas are needed if the day comes before the month.]

May, 1972,   (or)   May 1972

[Commas may be omitted if only the month and year are given.]

The order was shipped out on September 2, 1995, and not received until May 12, 1996.

The application deadline was 15 August 1996 with no exceptions.

## (2) Commas with Addresses

In a letter heading or on an envelope:

Jim Johnson, Jr.
1436 Westwood Drive
Birlingham, ID 98900

In a sentence:

You can write to Jim Johnson, Jr., 1436 Westwood Drive, Birlingham, Idaho 98900 for more information.

## (3) Commas with Geographical Names

Put commas after each item in a place name.

The planning committee has decided that Chicago, Illinois, will be the site for this year's conference and Washington, D.C., for next year's meeting.

## (4) Commas with Numbers

**6f
,**

Separate long numbers into groups of three going from right to left. Commas with four-digit numbers are optional.

4,300,150

27,000

4,401    (or)    4401

## Exercise 26.11: Proofreading Practice

*Add commas in the following paragraph where they are needed.*

The United States Government Printing Office has a catalog of thousands of popular books that it prints. If you'd like a copy of this catalog, write to the Superintendent of Documents United States Government Printing Office Washington DC 20402. There are books on agriculture, business and industry, careers, computers, diet and nutrition, health, history, hobbies, space exploration, and other topics. To pay for the books, you can send a check or money order, but more than 30000 customers every year set up deposit accounts with an initial deposit of at least fifty dollars. Future purchases can then be charged against this account. There are also Government Printing Office bookstores all around the country where you can browse before buying. They do not stock all 16000 titles in their inventory, but they do carry the more popular ones. For example, if you live in Birmingham, you can find the Government Printing Office bookstore in Roebuck Shopping City 9220-B Parkway East Birmingham Alabama 35206. There are other bookstores in Cleveland Ohio and Jacksonville Florida.

### Exercise 26.12: Pattern Practice

*Using the patterns and examples given here, write your own sentences correctly punctuated with commas. Write two different sentences for each pattern given.*

Pattern A: Sentence with a date

Everyone knows that July 4, 1776, was a memorable day in American history.

Pattern B: Sentence with an address

His business address is Fontran Investments, 3902 Carroll Boulevard, Indianapolis, IN 46229.

Pattern C: Sentence with a geographical name

She enjoyed her car trip to Santa Fe, New Mexico, and plans to go again next spring.

Pattern D: Sentence with two numbers of four digits or more

The police estimated that more than 50,000 people took part in the demonstration, but the organizers of the event said they were sure that at least 100,000 had shown up.

# 26g Other Uses for Commas

Commas have other uses in sentences, including the following:

- To prevent misreading:

    **Confusing:** To John Harrison had been a sort of idol.

    **Revised:** To John, Harrison had been a sort of idol.

    **Confusing:** On Thursday morning orders will be handled by Jim.

    **Revised:** On Thursday, morning orders will be handled by Jim. (or)

    **Revised:** On Thursday morning, orders will be handled by Jim.

- To set off sharply contrasted elements at the end of a sentence:

    He was merely ignorant, not stupid.

- To set off a question:

    You're one of the senator's right-hand people, aren't you?

- To set off phrases at the end of the sentence that refer to the beginning or middle of the sentence:

    Shaundra waved enthusiastically at the departing boat, laughing happily.

- To set off direct quotations and after the first part of a quotation in a sentence:

  Becky said, "I'll see you tomorrow."

  "I was able," she explained, "to complete the job on time."

- To set off the opening greeting and closing of a letter:

  Dear David,

  Sincerely yours,

## Exercise 26.13: Proofreading Practice

*The following paragraph needs some punctuation. Add commas where they are needed.*

Have you ever thought about where all those oranges in your orange juice come from? You'd probably say that they come from Florida wouldn't you? Some oranges may, but the world's largest producer of orange juice is now Brazil. Says one of Florida's biggest orange growers "We're going to regain the market sooner than those rookie Brazilians think." Florida growers predict that overplanting and plunging prices have set the stage for a damaging glut in Brazil not in Florida. "We have never had excess juice" claims a major Brazilian grower "and I don't think we ever will." Know-how from American juice companies, along with subsidies from the Brazilian government, is helping Brazilian growers stay on top of the market. Brazilian growers are confident knowing that Florida is more prone to drought and hard freezes. So it looks as if our orange juice will remain partly Brazilian for the foreseeable future.

## Exercise 26.14: Pattern Practice

*Using the patterns and examples given here, write your own sentences correctly punctuated with commas. Write two different sentences for each pattern given.*

Pattern A: To prevent misreading

  After eating, the cat stretched out near the fire and fell asleep.

  [If the comma is left out, is there a possible misreading?]

Pattern B: To set off sharply contrasted elements at the end of the sentence

  Everyone thought the car had stopped, not broken down.

Pattern C: To set off a question

  They were at the game, weren't they?

Pattern D: To set off a phrase at the end of the sentence that refers to the beginning or middle of the sentence

> Jennie decided not to go out in the evening, preferring to enjoy the quiet in her apartment.

Pattern E: To set off direct quotations

> Professor Bendini said, "Don't call me tonight to ask about your grade."

# 26h Unnecessary Commas

Putting in commas where they are not needed can mislead readers because unnecessary commas suggest pauses or interruptions not intended as part of the meaning. (Remember, though, that not every pause needs a comma.)

- Don't separate a subject from its verb:

  **Unnecessary Comma:** The eighteen-year-old in most states ⊙ is now considered an adult.

- Don't put a comma between two verbs:

  **Unnecessary Comma:** We laid out our music and snacks ⊙ and began to study.

- Don't put a comma in front of every *and* or *but*.

  **Unnecessary Comma:** We decided that we should not lend her the money ⊙ and that we should explain our decision.

  [The *and* in this sentence joins two *that* clauses.]

- Don't put a comma in front of a direct object. (Remember, clauses beginning with *that* can be direct objects.)

  **Unnecessary Comma:** He explained to me ⊙ that he is afraid to fly on airplanes because of terrorists.

- Don't put commas before a dependent clause when it comes after the main clause, except for extreme or strong contrast.

  **Unnecessary Comma:** She was late ⊙ because her alarm clock was broken.

  **Extreme Contrast:** She was still quite upset, although she did win an Oscar Award.

- Don't put a comma after *such as* or *especially*.

> **Unnecessary Comma:** There are several kinds of dark bread from which to choose, such as ⊙ whole wheat, rye, oatmeal, and bran bread.

## Exercise 26.15: Proofreading Practice

*In the following paragraph, there are some unnecessary commas. Put an X under the commas that should be removed.*

Although the dangers of alcohol are well known, and have been widely publicized, there may be another danger that we haven't yet realized. Several controlled studies of drunken animals have indicated to researchers, that in an accident there is more swelling and hemorrhaging in the spinal cord, and in the brain, if alcohol is present in the body. To find out if this is true in humans, researchers studied the data on more than one million drivers in automobile crashes. One thing already known is, that drunks are more likely to be driving fast, and to have seat belts unfastened. Of course, their coordination is also poorer than that of sober people, so drunks are more likely to get into serious accidents. To compensate for this, researchers grouped accidents according to type, speed, and degree of vehicle deformation, and found that alcohol still appears to make people more vulnerable to injury. The conclusion of the study was, that the higher the level of alcohol in the person's body, the greater the chance of being injured or killed. In minor crashes, drunk drivers were more than four times as likely to be killed as sober ones. In average crashes, drunk drivers were more than three times as likely to be killed, and in the worst ones, drunks were almost twice as likely to die. Overall, drunks were more than twice as likely to die in an accident, because of the alcohol they drank.

## Exercise 26.16: Pattern Practice

*Using the sentence patterns and examples given here, write your own sentences correctly punctuated with commas. Write two different sentences for each pattern given.*

Pattern A: Subject + verb + object + *and* + verb + object

Before the test <u>Midori</u> <u>studied</u> the botany <u>notes</u> from the lectures and
     *(subject) (verb)*        *(object)*
<u>reread</u> the <u>textbook</u> several times.
*(verb)*    *(object)*

Pattern B: Independent clause + dependent clause

<u>He decided not to live in the dorm</u> <u>because it was so expensive.</u>
  *(independent clause)*          *(dependent clause)*

Pattern C: A sentence with a *that* clause or phrase as a direct object

My high school physical education teacher often told me <u>that eating a good</u>
(<u>*that*</u> clause)
<u>breakfast</u> was an important part of keeping in good shape.

Pattern D: A sentence with a subject that has many words modifying it

Almost <u>everyone</u> attending the recent meeting of the union <u>decided</u> not to
    (*subject*)                                                              (*verb*)
vote for the strike.

# 27 Apostrophes (')

## 27a Apostrophes with Possessives

Use the apostrophe to show possession (see 17a and 17b).

- For singular nouns, use *'s.*

    the book's author     a flower's smell

- For a singular noun ending in *-s*, the *s* after the apostrophe is optional if the *s* doesn't make the pronunciation difficult.

    James's car          (or)     James' car
    the grass's color    (or)     the grass' color

But if adding the *s* after the apostrophe makes the pronunciation difficult, omit the *s*. This happens especially when the next word starts with *s* or *z*.

    Euripides' story    [Trying to say *Euripides's story* is a bit difficult.]

- For plural nouns ending in *-s*, add only an apostrophe.

    both teams' colors     six days' vacation

- For plural nouns not ending in *-s* (such as *children, men, or mice*), use *'s.*

    the children's game     six men's coats

- For the indefinite pronoun (pronouns ending in *-body* and *-one*, such as *no one, someone, and everybody*), use *'s.*

    no one's fault          someone's hat

- For compound words, add *'s* to the last word.

  brother-in-law's job        everyone else's preference

- For joint ownership by two or more nouns, add *'s* after the last noun in the group.

  Mary and Tom's house          bar and restaurant's parking lot

- For individual ownership when several nouns are used, add *'s* after each noun.

  Mary's and Tom's houses.    [This indicates that there are two houses, one belonging to Mary and the other to Tom.]

---

**HINTS:**

1. When you aren't sure if you need the apostrophe, turn the phrase into an "of the" phrase.

   the day's effort  =  the effort of the day

2. Occasionally, you'll have both the "of the" phrase and the apostrophe.

   the painting of Cesar's  [Without the *'s* this phrase would mean that Cesar was pictured in the painting as the subject.]

3. When you aren't sure if the word is plural or not, remember this sequence:

   - First, write the word.
   - Then, write the plural.
   - Then, add the possessive apostrophe marker.

Thus, everything to the left of the apostrophe is the word and its plural, if needed.

| *Word (and plural)* | *Possessive Marker* | *Result* |
| --- | --- | --- |
| cup | 's | cup's handle |
| cups | ' | cups' handles |

---

# 27b Apostrophes with Contractions

Use the apostrophe to mark the omitted letter or letters in contractions.

it's = it is    don't = do not [informal usage]    o'clock = of the clock
'79 = 1979    that's = that is

Jimmy's going = Jimmy is going    [very informal usage]

# 27c Apostrophes with Plurals

Use apostrophes to form the plurals of lowercase letters and abbreviations with periods.

For capital letters, abbreviations without periods, numbers, symbols, and words used as words, the apostrophe before the -s is optional if the plural is clear. In all cases, the 's is neither italicized nor underlined.

Necessary apostrophes:

a's    B.A.'s    A's

Optional apostrophes:

| 9s | (or) | 9's |
| 1950s | (or) | 1950's |
| UFOs | (or) | UFO's |
| ands | (or) | and's |
| &s | (or) | &'s |

> **HINT:** Be consistent in choosing one or the other of these options.

# 27d Unnecessary Apostrophes

Do not use the apostrophe with possessive pronouns or with the regular plural forms of nouns.

Possessive pronouns do not need apostrophes:

| his | hers | its | |
| ours | yours | theirs | whose |

❖ Is that umbrella ~~yours'~~ *yours* or mine?    ❖ I think ~~it's~~ *its* leg is broken.

Remember, *it's* and *who's* are contractions, not possessives:

it's = it is    **It's** a good time to clean out the closet.
who's = who is    **Who's** going to run for vice-president?

Do not use the apostrophe with regular plural forms of nouns that do not show possession.

*Smiths*
❖ The ~~Smiths~~' went to Disney World for vacation.

## Exercise 27.1: Proofreading Practice

*The following paragraph has some words that should show possession. Add apostrophes where they are needed.*

    Although teachers commonly use tests to grade their students learning, taking a test can also help students learn. Peoples memories seem to be more accurate after reading some material and taking a test than after merely reading the material with no testing. In fact, studies have shown that students who take several tests learn even more than those who take only one test after reading material. Although everyones ability to memorize material generally depends on how well the material was studied, scientists research does indicate that test taking aids memory. The type of test is also important because multiple-choice exams help us to put facts together better while fill-in-the-blank questions promote recall of specific facts. These questions ability to test different types of learning suggests that teachers ought to include different types of tests throughout the semester.

## Exercise 27.2: Pattern Practice

*Using the patterns and examples given here, write your own sentences correctly punctuated with apostrophes. Write two different sentences for each pattern given.*

Pattern A: Two singular nouns with *'s*

    If **Daniel's** car doesn't start, we can borrow **Alicia's** van.

Pattern B: A singular noun ending in *-s* with *'*

    Does anyone know Mr. **Myconos's** zip code?

Pattern C: Two plural nouns ending in *-s* with *'*

    Although the **girls'** coats were on sale, all the **boys'** coats were regular price.

Pattern D: A plural noun not ending in *-s* with *'s*

    We helped collect money for the **Children's** Fund.

Pattern E: An indefinite pronoun with *'s*

    I would really appreciate **someone's** help right now.

Pattern F: One compound word with *'s*

    It was the **president-elect's** decision not to campaign on TV.

Pattern G: One example of joint ownership with *'s*

The next morning he felt the **pizza and beer's** effects.

## Exercise 27.3: Proofreading Practice

*In the following informal paragraph, there are contractions that should be marked. Add apostrophes where they are needed.*

Magazine racks used to be for magazines, but that was before mailorder catalogs began invading the market. In 1985, when some catalogs began taking paid ads for such products as liquor and cologne, the line between magazines and catalogs began to blur. In some cases its hard to distinguish the difference. And customers have good reasons to prefer buying catalogs when theres the advantage of having discount coupons tucked in. The catalogs that began appearing on magazine racks in 85 sold for $1 to $3 apiece, but customers would get a $5 discount on their first order. National distributors now estimate that more than five thousand stores and newsstands stock catalogs for such well-known companies as The Sharper Image and Bloomingdale's. Waldenbooks was among the first to display these catalogs on its magazine racks. Its big business now, and magazines have a tough rival to beat.

## Exercise 27.4: Pattern Practice

*Using the patterns and examples given here, write your own sentences correctly punctuated with apostrophes. Write one sentence for each pattern given.*

Pattern A: A sentence with *its* and *it's*

Whenever **it's** raining out, our cat races inside the house to keep **its** fur dry.

Pattern B: A sentence with two contractions

**They're** quite sure they **didn't** owe us any money.

Pattern C: A sentence with *who's* and *whose*

I wonder **whose** skates those are and whether you know **who's** going with us.

## Exercise 27.5: Proofreading Practice

*The following paragraph needs apostrophes to mark plurals. Add the apostrophe even if it is optional.*

In the late 1970s the M.B.A. became one of the most desirable degrees awarded by American universities. In large part this was due to the high salaries offered to new graduates. Students graduating with B.A.s or B.S.s in most fields could expect starting salaries thousands of dollars below the pay of new M.B.A.s, especially those graduating at the top of the class from the more prestigious universities. It was a case of having those hard-earned As translate into better salaries. When huge numbers of M.B.A.s began flooding the market in the mid-1980s, the value of the degree declined somewhat.

## Exercise 27.6: Pattern Practice

*Using the patterns and examples given here, write your own sentences correctly punctuated with apostrophes. Write a sentence for each pattern given.*

Pattern A: The plural of two lowercase letters

On his new typewriter the **e's** and **c's** looked alike.

Pattern B: The plural of two abbreviations without periods

The electronics stores sold their **TVs** at a better discount than their **CDs**.

Pattern C: The plural of a number and a capital letter

There were several **3's** in her new license plate number and some **M's** too.

Pattern D: The plural of a date and a word

He dressed like a **1960s** hippie and sprinkled lots of "**far out's**" and other outdated slang in his speech.

## Exercise 27.7: Proofreading Practice

*Add apostrophes if needed in the following paragraph.*

Erica Johns, a recent contestant on one of the game shows, was embarrassed to see herself in the reruns. There she was on the screen, yelling out the answer and claiming the big prize was hers, even when someone else sounded the buzzer before she did. "Its difficult," she said, "not to act foolish when so much money is involved." But she did win some dance lessons and a cute puppy with its own diamond-studded leash. Still, she wished she had pushed the buzzer and answered the question worth $2,000.

## Exercise 27.8: Pattern Practice

*Using the patterns and examples given here, write your own correctly punctuated sentences. Write your own sentence for each pattern given.*

Pattern A: A sentence with two possessive pronouns

I can never remember whether the car is **hers** or **his**.

Pattern B: A sentence with *it's* and *its*

**It's** never clear whether that dumb dog wants **its** ears scratched or **its** water dish filled.

Pattern C: A sentence with a plural noun that does not show possession and a plural noun that does show possession

There are six pages of **ads** in that magazine with different **dealers'** prices.

# 28 Semicolons (;)

The semicolon is a stronger mark of punctuation than a comma. It is almost like a period but does not come at the end of a sentence. Semicolons are used only between closely related equal elements, that is, between independent clauses and between items in a series. See the chart of "Commas and Semicolons in Sentences" in Chapter 26.

## 28a Semicolons in Compound Sentences

Use the semicolon when joining independent clauses not joined by the seven connectors that require commas: *and, but, for, or, nor, so,* or *yet.*

Two patterns for using semicolons are the following:

- Independent clause + semicolon + independent clause

  He often watched TV reruns; she preferred to read instead.

- Independent clause + semicolon + joining word or transition + comma + independent clause

  He often watched TV reruns; however, she preferred to read instead.

Some joining words or transitional phrases must be preceded by a semicolon:

| | | |
|---|---|---|
| after all, | finally, | in the second place, |
| also, | for example, | instead, |
| as a result, | furthermore, | meanwhile, |
| at any rate, | hence, | nevertheless, |
| besides, | however, | on the contrary, |
| by the way, | in addition, | on the other hand, |
| consequently, | in fact, | still, |
| even so, | in other words, | therefore, |

## Variations in Compound Sentences

A semicolon can be used instead of a comma with two independent clauses joined by *and, but, for, or, nor, so,* or *yet* when one or more of the clauses has its own comma. The semicolon thus makes a clearer break between the two independent clauses.

- Independent clause with commas + semicolon + independent clause:

  <u>Congressman Dow, who headed the investigation, leaked the story to the</u>
  *(independent clause with commas)*
  <u>press</u>; but he would not answer questions during an interview.

A colon can be used between two independent clauses when the second clause restates the first (see Chapter 29).

  Her diet was strictly vegetarian: she ate no meat, fish, poultry, or eggs.

## Exercise 28.1: Proofreading Practice

*In the following paragraph, there are compound sentences that need punctuation. Add semicolons and commas where they are needed.*

Even before children begin school, many parents think they should take part in their children's education and help the children to develop mentally. Such parents usually consider reading to young toddlers important moreover they help the children memorize facts such as the days of the week and the numbers from one to ten. Now it is becoming clear that parents can begin helping when the children are babies. One particular type of parent communication, encouraging the baby to pay attention to new things, seems especially promising in helping babies' brains develop for example handing the baby a toy encourages the baby to notice something new. Some studies seem to indicate that this kind of activity helped children score higher on intelligence tests several years later. Parents interested in helping their babies' brain development have been encouraged by this study to point to new things in the baby's environment as part of their communication with their babies thus their children's education can begin in the crib.

## Exercise 28.2: Pattern Practice

*Using the patterns and examples given here, write your own sentences correctly punctuated with semicolons. Write two sentences for each pattern given.*

Pattern A: Independent clause + semicolon + independent clause

  <u>I didn't know which job I wanted</u>;  <u>I was too confused to decide</u>.
  *(independent clause)*          *(independent clause)*

Pattern B: Independent clause + semicolon + joining word or transitional phrase + comma + independent clause

Three friends recommended that movie; however, I was bored by it.
*(independent clause)*            *(joining word) (indep. clause)*

Pattern C: Independent clause + comma + *and* (or) *but* + independent clause

The shirt is a little small, but he has nothing else to wear.
*(independent clause) (comma)*     *(joining word)*

# 28b Semicolons in a Series

For clarity, use semicolons to separate a series of items in which one or more of the items contain commas. Use semicolons also if items in the series are especially long.

- Items with their own commas:

  Among her favorite videotapes to rent were old Cary Grant movies, such as *Arsenic and Old Lace*; any of Woody Allen's movies; and children's classics, including *The Sound of Music*, *Willy Wonka and the Chocolate Factory*, and *The Wizard of Oz*.

- Long items in a series:

  When planning the bus schedule, they took into consideration the length of travel time between cities where stops would be made; the number of people likely to get on at each stop; and the times when the bus would arrive at major cities where connections would be made with other buses.

# 28c Semicolons with Quotation Marks

If a semicolon is needed, put it after the quotation marks.

Her answer to every question I asked was, "I'll have to think about that"; she clearly had no answers to offer.

# 28d Unnecessary Semicolons

Don't use a semicolon between unequal parts of a sentence, such as between a clause and a phrase or between an independent clause and a dependent clause. Don't use a semicolon in place of a dash, comma, or colon.

They wanted to see the government buildings in the city⊙especially the
*(should be a comma)*
courthouse and the post office.

He kept trying to improve his tennis serve⊙because that was the weakest
*(should be no punctuation)*
part of his game.

When Mike kept spinning his car wheels to get out of the sand, I realized
he was really just persistent⊙not stupid.
*(should be a dash)*

The office clearly needed several more pieces of equipment⊙a computer,
*(should be a colon)*
an answering machine, and a paper shredder.

## Exercise 28.3: Proofreading Practice

*In the following paragraph, there are some unnecessary semicolons to delete and
some necessary semicolons to add. Put an X under semicolons that are incorrect,
and write in the appropriate punctuation above the line. Add semicolons and
other punctuation where needed, and replace any wrong punctuation with semicolons. Underline the added semicolons and other punctuation. Also underline
the semicolons you put in to replace wrong punctuation.*

In the not-too-distant future, when airline passengers board their
flights, they will be able to enjoy a number of new conveniences; such
as choosing their snacks and drinks from on-board vending machines, selecting movies, TV programs, or video games for screens
mounted on the seat in front of them, and making hotel and car-
rental reservations from an on-board computer. Such features are
what aircraft designers envision within the next five years for passenger jets. Their plans, though, may not be realized until much further
in the future; if ever. But the ideas reflect the airline industry's hopes.
If fare wars stop and ticket prices stabilize, passengers may begin
choosing different airlines on the basis of comfort, not cost; if that
happens, airlines will have to be ready with new and better in-flight
features. A Boeing Company executive says that "cabin environment
will be a major factor;" that is, designers must make the cabin so attractive that it will offset lower fares on other airlines. The problem,
however, is added weight caused by some of the suggested features;
such as; computers, video screens, and more elaborate kitchens.
Added weight will mean that the plane consumes more fuel; thus driving up the price of the ticket. Still, some carriers, determined to find
answers, are studying ways to use the new services to generate income; particularly in the area of commercial-supported or pay-
as-you-use video entertainment.

## Exercise 28.4: Pattern Practice

*Using the patterns and examples given here, write your own sentences correctly punctuated with semicolons. Write one sentence for each pattern given.*

Pattern A: Semicolons with a series of items that have their own commas

> The McDonnell Douglas Corporation's new wide-body jet, scheduled to be-gin service soon, is designed for greater passenger comfort and will have refrigerators to hold fresh food; aisles wide enough so that passengers, even heavyset people, can walk past a serving cart; and high-resolution video monitors for every ten rows.

Pattern B: A comma before the phrase *such as*

> Other planes are being built with changes sought by passengers, such as larger overhead storage bins, handrails above the seats, and fresher air in the cabins.

Pattern C: A semicolon after the quotation marks

> One airline executive says that, for now, it's "hard to justify the costs of some suggested innovations"; however, airlines must be ready to meet the challenge if more passengers start choosing their carrier on the basis of comfort.

# 29 Colons (:)

The colon is used in more formal writing to call attention to words that follow it.

## 29a Colons to Announce Elements at the End of a Sentence

Use the colon at the end of a sentence to introduce a list, an explanation (or intensification) of the sentence, or an example.

> The university offers five majors in engineering: mechanical, electrical, civil, industrial, and chemical engineering.

> After weeks of intensive study, there was only one thing she really wanted: a vacation.    [A dash can also be used here, though it is more informal.]

> **HINT:** Think of the colon as the equivalent of the phrase *that is*. For most elements at the end of the sentence, you could have said *that is* where the colon is needed.
>
> When the company president decided to boost morale among the employees, the executive board announced an improvement that would please everyone: pay raises.   [: = that is]

# 29b Colons to Separate Independent Clauses

Use the colon instead of a semicolon to separate two independent clauses when the second amplifies or restates the first clause.

Again, think of the colon as the equivalent of *that is*. An independent clause following a colon may begin with a capital or lowercase letter, although the lowercase letter is preferred.

> Some say that lobbying groups exert too much influence on Congress: they can buy votes as a result of their large contributions to the right senators and representatives.

# 29c Colons to Announce Long Quotations

Use the colon to announce long quotations (more than one sentence) or a quotation not introduced by such words as *said, remarked,* or *stated.*

> The head of the company's research department, Ms. Mann, said: "We recommended budgeting $1 million for the development of that type of software, but we were turned down. We regrouped and tried to think of a new approach to change their minds. We got nowhere."

> He offered an apology to calm her down: "I'm truly sorry that we were not able to help you."

# 29d Colons in Salutations and Between Elements

Use the colon in the salutation of a formal or business letter, in scriptural and time references, between a title and subtitle, with proportions, between city and publisher in bibliographical format, and after an introductory label.

Dear Mayor O'Daly:          6:15 A.M.
Genesis 1:8                 a scale of 4:1
"Jerusalem: A City United"  New York: Midland Books

# 29e Colons with Quotation Marks

If a colon is needed, put it after the closing quotation mark.

"To err is human; to repeat an error is stupid": that was my chemistry teacher's favorite saying in the lab.

# 29f Unnecessary Colons

Do not use the colon after a verb or a phrase like *such as* or *consisted of.*

The people who applied were ⊙ Mr. Orland, Mr. Johnson, and Ms. Lassiter.
*(no punctuation needed)*

She preferred a non-contact sport, such as ⊙ tennis, swimming, or golf.
*(no punctuation needed)*

> **HINT:** When you revise for unnecessary colons, you can either omit any punctuation or add a word or phrase such as *the following* after the verb.
>
> The committee members who voted for the amendment were the following: Mia Lungren, Sam Heffelt, and Alexander Zubrev.

## Exercise 29.1: Proofreading Practice

*The following paragraph needs some colons and has some correct and incorrect colons. Add colons where they should be, and put an X under incorrect colons or other incorrect punctuation. If other punctuation is needed instead, put it above the incorrect punctuation. Underline colons that are added.*

When the Apollo astronauts brought back bags of moon rocks, it was expected that the rocks would provide some answers to a perennial question; the origin of the moon. Instead, the Apollo's moon rocks suggested a number of new theories. One that is gaining more supporters is called: the giant impact theory. Alan Smith, a lunar scientist, offers an explanation of the giant impact theory "Recently acquired evidence suggests that the moon was born of a monstrous collision between a primordial, just-formed Earth and a protoplanet the size of Mars." This evidence comes from modeling such a collision on powerful supercomputers. The theory proposes the following sequence of events (1) as Earth was forming, it was struck a glancing blow by a projectile the size of Mars; (2) a jet of vapor then spurted out, moving so fast that some of it escaped from Earth and the rest condensed into pebble-sized rock fragments; and (3) gravitational attraction fused this cloud of pebbles into the moon. There are several reasons that make some scientists favor this theory, for example it dovetails with what is known about the moon's chemistry and it explains why the moon's average composition resembles Earth's. Another lunar scientist says, "We may be close to tracking down the real answer."

## Exercise 29.2: Pattern Practice

*Using the patterns and examples given here, write your own sentences correctly punctuated with colons. Write one sentence for each pattern given.*

Pattern A: Sentence with a list following a colon

> The coffee shop offered samples of five new coffee flavors: mocha java, chocolate fudge, Swiss almond, cinnamon, and French roast.

Pattern B: Independent clause + colon + second independent clause that restates or explains the first clause

> That cat has only one problem: she thinks she is a human.

Pattern C: Sentence with a quotation not introduced by words such as *said, remarked,* or *stated*

> Jim clarified his views on marriage: "It should be a commitment for a lifetime, not a trial run for a relationship."

# 30 Quotation Marks (" ")

## 30a Quotation Marks with Direct and Indirect Quotations

Use quotation marks with direct quotations of prose, poetry, and dialogue.

## (1) Quotation Marks with Prose Quotations

Direct quotations are the exact words said by someone or the exact words you saw in print and are recopying. Use a set of quotation marks to enclose direct quotations included in your writing.

Indirect quotations are not the exact words said by someone else but the rephrasing or summarizing of someone else's words. Do not use quotation marks for indirect quotations. (For more information, see 44d.)

If the quotation extends more than four typed or handwritten lines on a page, set the quotation off by indenting ten spaces from the left margin and double-space the quotation. Do not use quotation marks for this indented material.

- Direct quotation of a whole sentence: Use a capital letter to start the first word of the quotation.

   Mr. and Mrs. Allen, owners of a 300-acre farm, said, "We refuse to use that pesticide because it might pollute the nearby wells."

- Direct quotation of part of a sentence: Do not use a capital letter to start the first word of the quotation.

   Mr. and Mrs. Allen stated that they "refuse to use that pesticide" because of possible water pollution.

- Indirect quotation:

   According to their statement to the local papers, the Allens will not use the pesticide because of potential water pollution.

- Quotation within a quotation: Use single quotation marks (' at the beginning and ' at the end) for a quotation enclosed inside another quotation.

   The agricultural reporter for the newspaper explained, "When I talked to the Allens last week, they said, 'We refuse to use that pesticide.' "

- If you leave some words out of a quotation, use an ellipsis mark (three spaced periods) to indicate omitted words. If you need to insert something within a quotation, use a pair of brackets [ ] to enclose the addition.

**Full Direct Quotation:**

The welfare agency representative said, "We are unable to help this family whom we would like to help because we don't have the funds to do so."

**Omitted Material with Ellipsis:**

> The welfare agency representative said, "We are unable to help this family . . . because we don't have the funds to do so."

**Added Material with Brackets:**

> The welfare agency representative explained that they are "unable to help this family whom [they] would like to help."

## (2) Quotation Marks in Poetry

When you quote a single line of poetry, write it like other short quotations. Two lines can be run into your text with a slash mark to indicate the end of the first line. Leave a space before and after the slash mark. If the quotation is three lines or longer, set it off like a longer quotation. (Some people prefer to set off two-line quotations for emphasis.) Quote the poem line by line as it appears on the original page, and do not use quotation marks. Indent ten spaces from the left margin. (For more information, see 33b.)

- Poetry quoted in your writing:

  > In his poem "Mending Wall," Robert Frost says: "Something there is that doesn't love a wall, / That sends the frozen-ground-swell under it."

- Longer quotation from a poem set off from the sentence:

  > In his poem "Mending Wall," Robert Frost questions the building of barriers and walls:
  >> Before I built a wall I'd ask to know
  >> What I was walling in or walling out,
  >> And to whom I was like to give offense.

## (3) Quotation Marks in Dialogue

Write each person's speech, however short, as a separate paragraph. Use commas to set off *he said* or *she said*. Closely related bits of narrative can be included in the paragraph. If one person's speech goes on for several paragraphs, use quotation marks at the beginning of each paragraph but not at the end of every paragraph before the last one. To signal the end of the person's speech, use quotation marks at the end of the last paragraph. (For more information, see 44d.)

> "May I help you?" the clerk asked as she approached the customer.
>
> "No, thanks," responded the woman in a quiet voice.
>
> "We have a special sale today on sweaters," persisted the salesperson. She continued to stand next to the customer, waiting for the woman to indicate why she was there.
>
> "How nice for you," the customer replied as she walked out, leaving a puzzled clerk wondering what she meant.

# 30b Quotation Marks for Minor Titles and Parts of Wholes

Use quotation marks for titles of parts of larger works (titles of book chapters, magazine articles, and episodes of television and radio series) and for short or minor works (songs, short stories, essays, short poems, one-act plays, and other literary works that are shorter than three-act plays or book length).

For larger, complete works, see Chapter 37 on italics. Neither quotation marks nor italics are used for referring to the Bible or legal documents.

Whenever he got involved with hard work in his garden, he'd hum his favorite song, "Old Man River."

Mark Twain's short story "The Celebrated Jumping Frog of Calaveras County" helped frog-jumping contests gain their great popularity.

She wanted to memorize the first eighteen chapters of Genesis.

# 30c Quotation Marks for Words

Use quotation marks for words that are used as words rather than for their meaning, and for words used in special ways, such as for irony (when the writer means the opposite of what is being said). Italics (underlining) can also be used.

Be consistent throughout your papers in choosing either quotation marks or italics.

Quotation marks can also be used to introduce unfamiliar or technical terms when they are used for the first time (and defined). No quotation marks are needed in later uses of the word after it has been introduced the first time.

"Neat" is a word I wish she'd omit from her vocabulary.

The three-year-old held up his "work of art" for the teacher to admire.

# 30d Use of Other Punctuation with Quotation Marks

Put commas and periods before the second set of quotation marks. When a reference follows the quotation, put the period after the reference. (For more information, see 44d.)

"The Politics of Hunger," a recent article in *Political Quarterly*, discussed the United Nations' use of military force to help victims of hunger.

He said, "I may forget your name, but I never remember a face."

Jenkins said, "Moshenberg's style of writing derives from his particular form of wit" (252).

Put the colon and semicolon after the quotation marks.

The critic called the movie "a potential Academy Award winner"; I thought it was a flop.

Put the dash, question mark, and exclamation point before the second set of quotation marks when these punctuation marks apply to the quotation and after the second set of quotation marks when the mark applies to the whole sentence.

He asked, "Do you need this book?"    [The quotation here is a question.]

Does Dr. Lim always say to her students, "You must work harder"?

[The quotation here is a statement, but it is included in a sentence that is a question.]

# 30e Unnecessary Quotation Marks

Don't put quotation marks around the titles of your essays (though someone else will use quotation marks if referring to your essay), and don't use quotation marks for common nicknames, bits of humor, technical terms, and trite or well-known expressions.

The crew rowed together like<sup>@</sup>a well-oiled machine.<sup>@</sup>

[No quotation marks needed.]

He decided to save his money until he could buy a<sup>@</sup>digital audio tape deck.<sup>@</sup>

[No quotation marks needed.]

## Exercise 30.1: Proofreading Practice

*Add quotation marks where they are needed in the following paragraph, and delete any quotation marks that are incorrect, unnecessary, or inappropriately placed. Place an X under the line where quotation marks are deleted.*

Remember Silverton wine coolers? Silverton, like hundreds of other products that appeared in the same year, was pulled from the shelf after it failed to gain a market. Silverton didn't seem to have any connotation as a cooler, explains G. F. Strousel, the company's vice-president in charge of sales. Every year new products appear briefly on the shelf and disappear, and established products that no longer have "customer appeal" are canceled as well. "Either way," experts say, "the signs that point to failure are the same." Companies looking to cut their losses pay attention to such signs. In a recent newspaper article titled *Over 75% of Business Ideas Are Flops*, T. M. Weir, a professor of marketing, explains that products that don't grow but maintain their percentage of the market are known as cash cows, and those that are declining in growth and in market share are called dipping dogs. Says Weir, "Marketers plot the growth and decline of products, especially of the dipping dogs, very closely." According to several sources at a New York research firm that studies new product development, "the final decision to stop making a product is a financial one." When the "red ink" flows, the product is pulled.

## Exercise 30.2: Pattern Practice

*Using the patterns and examples given here, write your own correctly punctuated sentences. Write two sentences for each pattern given.*

Pattern A: Direct quotation with a whole sentence being quoted

The president of the university stated, "It is my fervent hope that next year there will be no tuition increase."

Pattern B: Direct quotation with a part of a sentence being quoted

The president of the university vowed that next year "there will be no tuition increase."

Pattern C: A quotation within a quotation

The announcer said, "You heard it live on this station, Coach Williams predicting that his team 'will run away with the game tomorrow.' "

Pattern D: Dialogue between two speakers

"Can you help me with the chem lab report?" Ivan's roommate asked.
"I'll try, but my notes aren't very complete," Ivan said as he ambled off to turn up the stereo.
"That's OK. They have to be better than mine."

Pattern E: Quotation marks with a minor title or a title of a part of a whole work

In his autobiography Hsao titled his first chapter "In the Beginning."

Pattern F: Quotation marks with a word used as a word

I can't believe that any grown person really says "Golly, gee whiz."

# 31 Hyphens (hyph)

## 31a Hyphens to Divide Words

Use the hyphen to indicate that the last part of a word appears on the next line.

Be sure to divide words between syllables. Check your dictionary to see how words are split into syllables. When you split words, do so in a way that is most helpful to your reader. Follow these guidelines:

- Don't divide one-syllable words.
- Don't leave one or two letters at the end of the line.
- Don't put fewer than three letters on the next line.
- Don't divide the last word in a paragraph or the last word on a page.

**Wrong:** She took the big package a-
part very carefully.

[If there is no room for the word on the first line and the syllable to be left at the end of the line is only one letter, put the whole word on the next line.]

**Wrong:** Twila was so hungry she ordered panc-
akes, eggs, and sausage.

**Revised:** Twila was so hungry she ordered pan-
cakes, eggs, and sausage.

[If the first syllable contains two or more letters, it can be left at the end of the line.]

## 31b Hyphens to Form Compound Words

Use the hyphen to form compound words.

Hyphens are used in compounds of all kinds, including fractions and numbers that are spelled out, from twenty-one to ninety-nine. Because accepted usage and dictionaries vary, words forming compounds may be written separately, as one word, or connected by hyphens.

| | |
|---|---|
| mother-in-law | thirty-six |
| clear-cut | two-thirds |

For words in a series, use hyphens as follows:

mother-, father-, and sister-in-law

four-, five-, and six-page essays

# 31c Hyphens to Join Two-Word Units

Use the hyphen to join two or more words that work together and serve as a single descriptive word before a noun.

When the words come after the noun, they are usually not hyphenated. Don't use hyphens with *-ly* modifiers.

| | | |
|---|---|---|
| The office needed up-to-date scores. | (or) | The office needed scores that were up to date. |
| The repair involved a six-inch pipe. | (or) | The repair involved a pipe that was six inches long. |
| They brought along their nine-year-old son. | (or) | They brought along their son, who was nine years old. |

# 31d Hyphens to Join Prefixes, Suffixes, and Letters to a Word

Use hyphens between words and the prefixes *self-*, *all-*, and *ex-*.

For other prefixes, such as *anti-*, *non-*, *pro-*, and *co-*, use the dictionary as a guide. Use the hyphen when you add a prefix to a capitalized word (for example, *mid-August*) and when you add the suffix *-elect* to a word. In addition, use the hyphen to join single letters to words.

| | |
|---|---|
| co-author | self-supporting |
| anti-abortion | president-elect |
| pro-American | T-shirt |
| D-day | all-encompassing |

The hyphen is also used to avoid doubling vowels and tripling consonants:

anti-intellectual (not: antiintellectual)

bell-like (not: belllike)

# 31e Hyphens to Avoid Ambiguity

Use the hyphen to avoid confusion between words that are spelled alike but have different meanings.

| | | |
|---|---|---|
| re-creation (to make again) | vs. | recreation (fun) |
| re-cover (cover again) | vs. | recover (regain health) |
| co-op (something jointly owned) | vs. | coop (cage for fowls) |

## Exercise 31.1: Proofreading Exercise

*Add hyphens where they are needed in the following paragraph and delete any that are incorrect. Place an X under the line where a hyphen is deleted.*

For health conscious people who cringe at the thought of using a toothpaste with preservatives and dyes, there are now alternative tooth-pastes made entirely from plants. One brand of these new, all natural toothpastes advertises that its paste includes twenty nine different herbs, root and flower-extracts, and seaweed. Some of these toothpastes have a pleasant taste and appearance, but the owner of a San Francisco health food store decided not to carry one brand because it is a reddish-brown paste. "When squeezed from a tube, it resembles a fat earth-worm," she explained. She prefers a brand made of propolis, the sticky stuff bees use to line their hives, and myrrh. Another brand, a black paste made of charred eggplant powder, clay, and seaweed, is favored by the hard core macrobiotic crowd. This interest in natural toothpastes may be cyclical, explains the director of an oral health institute. He re-calls a gray striped, mint flavored paste from the Philippines that sought to capitalize on a spurt of interest several years ago. It was a big-seller for a few months and then disappeared.

## Exercise 31.2: Pattern Practice

*Using the patterns and examples given here, write your own correctly hyphenated sentences. Write one sentence for each pattern given.*

Pattern A: Hyphen that splits a word at the end of a line
Pattern B: Hyphen with at least two compound words

> Japanese-Americans in the area helped to elect more than twenty-seven delegates of Japanese descent to the convention.

Pattern C: Hyphen with two words serving as a single descriptive word in front of a noun (and, if possible, the same two words after the noun)

> The plastic-trimmed suitcase was promptly returned by unhappy customers who said the plastic trim fell off within several weeks.

Pattern D: Hyphen with prefixes or suffixes

The slogan on her T-shirt announced her pro-choice views.

# 32 End Punctuation

At the end of a sentence, use a period, a question mark, or an exclamation point.

## 32a Periods (.)

### (1) Periods at the End of a Sentence

Use the period to end sentences that are statements, mild commands, indirect questions, or polite questions where an answer is not really expected.

He's one of those people who doesn't like pets.    [statement]

Hand in your homework by noon tomorrow.    [mild command]

She asked how she could improve her golf game.    [indirect question]

Would you please let me know when the bus arrives.    [polite question]

### (2) Periods with Abbreviations

Use the period after most abbreviations.

| | | | |
|---|---|---|---|
| Mr. | Mrs. | etc. | 9 P.M. |
| Ms. | Ave. | A.D. | Ph.D. |
| R.S.V.P. | Inc. | U.S.A. | Dr. |

Don't use a second period if the abbreviation is at the end of the sentence.

She studied for her R.N.

Periods are not needed after certain common abbreviations, the names of well-known companies, agencies, organizations, and the state abbreviations used by the U.S. Postal Service.

| | | | |
|---|---|---|---|
| NATO | NBA | CIA | YMCA |
| TV | NFL | FBI | DNA |
| TX (and other state postal abbreviations) | | | |

## (3) Periods with Quotation Marks

Put periods that follow quotations inside the quotation marks.

As she said, "No one is too old to try something new."

However, if there is a reference to a source, put the period after the reference.

Hemmings states, "This is, by far, the best existing example of Renaissance art" (144).

## Exercise 32.1: Proofreading Practice

*Add periods where they are needed in the following paragraph. Take out any periods used incorrectly. Place an X under a line where a period is deleted.*

Several years ago the nation's print and broadcast media joined with advertising agencies to launch a massive media campaign against drugs. Some, like ABC-TV, announced that they would donate prime time T.V. spots, but CBS Inc, while agreeing to cooperate, announced its intention to continue to commit funds for campaigns for other public issues such as AIDS prevention. James R Daly, a spokesman for the anti-drug campaign, said, "We were glad to see other companies joining in to help the campaign". For example, the Kodak Co donated the film needed for TV spots, and in Washington, DC, a group of concerned parents volunteered to do additional fund raising. In the first two years of this media campaign, more than $500 million was raised Says Dr Harrison Rublin, a leading spokesperson for one of the fund-raising groups, "One effective thirty-second ad aired at 8 PM is ten times more effective than a hundred brochures on the subject".

## Exercise 32.2: Pattern Practice

*Using the patterns and examples given here, write your own correctly punctuated sentences. Write two sentences for each pattern given.*

Pattern A: Statement (with a period at the end)

Luis started guitar lessons at the age of six.

Pattern B: Mild command (with a period at the end)

Return that pencil to me when you are done.

Pattern C: Indirect quotation (with a period at the end)

Jennifer asked the gas station attendant whether he had a wrench.

Pattern D: Polite question (with a period at the end)

Would you please send the material I am requesting as soon as possible.

Pattern E: An abbreviation with periods

He couldn't decide whether to enroll for a B.S. or a B.A. degree.

Pattern F: An abbreviation without periods

The computer shop featured IBM and Apple computers.

Pattern G: With a quotation

His father announced, "If you use the car tonight, then you pay for the gas."

Pattern H: With a quotation and a reference

According to the article, "Smokers can no longer demand rights that violate the air space of others" (Heskett 27).

# 32b Question Marks (?)

## (1) Question Marks at the End of a Sentence

Use a question mark after direct quotations but not after indirect quotations.

**Direct Quotation:** "Do you have another copy of this book in stock?"

**Indirect Quotation:** She asked the salesperson if he had another copy of the book in stock.

Use the question mark in statements that contain direct quotations.

"Did Henry ever pay back that loan?" she wondered.

Enclose the question mark inside the quotation marks only if the question mark belongs to the quotation.

Alice said, "Who's that standing by the door?"

Did Alice really say, "Get lost"?

## (2) Question Marks in a Series

Question marks may be used between parts of a series.

Would you prefer to eat at a restaurant? go on a picnic? cook at home?

## (3) Question Marks to Indicate Doubt

Question marks can be used to indicate doubt about the correctness of the preceding word, figure, date, or other piece of information.

The city was founded about 1837 (?) but did not grow significantly until about fifty years later.

## (4) Unnecessary Question Marks

Don't use a question mark within parentheses to indicate sarcasm. Instead, rewrite the sentence so that the meaning is clear from the use of appropriate words.

**Unnecessary Question Mark:**  She was sure that it was her intelligence (?) that charmed him.

**Revised:**  Although she was sure that it was her intelligence that charmed him, she was greatly mistaken.

## Exercise 32.3: Proofreading Practice

*In the following paragraph, add question marks where they are needed and delete any incorrect, unnecessary, or inappropriate ones. Place an* X *under a line where a question mark is deleted.*

Oxford University has a chancellor, but members of the Oxford faculty wonder whether anyone in the general public knows who the chancellor is? As the principal of one of the colleges said, "Does anyone care"? The post of chancellor at Oxford is mostly ceremonial, carrying very few responsibilities. One previous chancellor, Lord Curzon, did try to get involved with running the university but was soon discouraged from such unseemly action. When Prime Minister Harold Macmillan was installed as chancellor, he delivered a speech in Latin saying that he was quite clear on the point that it was not one of his duties to run the university. He underscored his recognition of the heavy duties (?) of his new job by wearing his cap backward throughout the whole proceedings. Many old Oxonians fear that they'll never see his lackadaisical like again. Is there anyone who can be trusted to keep a campaign promise when he or she says, "If elected, I won't stir things up?"

## Exercise 32.4: Pattern Practice

*Using the patterns and examples given here, write your own correctly punctuated sentences. Write two sentences for each pattern given.*

Pattern A: Sentence with a question mark

Which way should I turn this knob?

Pattern B: Statement with a direct question

"Can you speak French?" he asked.

Pattern C: Quotation with question mark inside the quotation marks

> Jeff kept demanding, "Did she really ask my name?"

Pattern D: Quotation with the question mark outside the quotation marks

> Why did the coach say, "No more practice this week"?

Pattern E: Question mark to indicate doubt about a piece of information

> The cavalry unit had about 1,000 (?) horses before the battle.

# 32c Exclamation Points (!)

## (1) Exclamation Points at the End of a Sentence

Use an exclamation mark after strong commands; statements said with great emphasis; interjections; and sentences intended to express surprise, disbelief, or strong feeling.

> What a magnificent surprise!
>
> I am not guilty!
>
> Definitely!

Don't overuse the exclamation mark, and don't combine it with other end punctuation as shown here:

> Wow! What a party! There was even a live band!
>
> I won $500!
>
> Is he for real?!

## (2) Exclamation Points with Quotation Marks

Enclose the exclamation mark inside quotation marks only if it belongs to the quotation.

> He burst into the room and yelled, "We are surrounded!"
>
> In the middle of the meeting Maude quietly explained, "My committee has already vetoed this motion"!

## Exercise 32.5: Proofreading Practice

*Add exclamation marks where they are needed in the following paragraph, and delete any that are incorrect, unnecessary, or inappropriate. Place an X under a line where an exclamation mark is deleted.*

At the end of winter, when gardeners are depressed from the long months indoors, plant catalogs start flooding the mail! With their large type the catalogs blare out their news to hungry gardeners. "Amazing!!" "Fantastic!!!" "Incredible!!!!" The covers always belong to some enormous new strain of tomatoes. "Bigger than Beefsteaks" or "Too Big to Fit on This Page"! they yell. Even the blueberries are monsters. "Blueberries as big as quarters!" the catalogs promise. All you do, according to these enticing catalogs, is "Plant 'em and stand back!?!" On a gloomy February afternoon, many would-be gardeners are probably ready to believe that this year they too can have "asparagus thicker than a person's thumb"!!!

### Exercise 32.6: Pattern Practice

*Using the patterns and examples given here, write your own correctly punctuated sentences. Write one sentence for each pattern given.*

Pattern A: Sentence with an exclamation mark

This is the happiest day of my life!

Pattern B: Quotation with an exclamation mark enclosed

After the ballots were counted, Dan yelled, "I won!"

Pattern C: Quotation with an exclamation mark outside

Every time we try to study, Bob always says, "Let's go out instead"!

# 33 Other Punctuation

## 33a Dashes (dash)

Dashes, considered somewhat informal, can add emphasis and clarity. But they shouldn't be overused, especially as substitutes for commas or colons. When you are typing, use two hyphens to indicate the dash. Do not leave a space before or after the hyphens. For handwritten papers, draw a dash as an unbroken line, at least twice as long as a hyphen.

### (1) Dashes at the Beginning or End of a Sentence

Use the dash at the beginning or end of the sentence to set off added explanation or illustration and to add emphasis or clarity.

If the added explanation is of less importance than the rest of the sentence, use parentheses.

> Fame, fortune, and a Ferrari—these were his goals in life.

[When dashes are used this way at the beginning of a sentence, they tend to come after a series of items that are explained in the rest of the sentence, which usually then begins with *these, all,* or *none.*]

> Her acting gave an extra touch of humor to the play—an added sparkle.

## (2) Dashes to Mark an Interruption

Use the dash as an interrupter to mark a sudden break in thought, an abrupt change or surprise, or a deliberate pause and to show in a dialogue that the speaker has been interrupted.

> According to her way of looking at things—but not mine—this was a worthwhile cause.

> The small child stood there happily sniffing a handful of flowers—all the roses from my garden.

> Of course Everett was willing to work hard to get good grades—but not too hard.

> Sherri announced, "I'm going to clean up this room so that—"
> "Oh no, you don't," yelled her little brother.

## (3) Dashes to Set Off a Phrase or Clause with a Comma

When a phrase or clause already has commas within it, you can use dashes to set off the whole word group.

> Hildy always finds interesting little restaurants—such as Lettuce Eat, that health-food place, and Ho Ming's Pizza Parlor—to take us to after a concert.

## Exercise 33.1: Proofreading Practice

*Add dashes where they are needed in the following paragraph.*

Businesspeople, laborers, children, private clubs, and senior citizens these are some of the groups who sponsor floats in the New Orleans Mardi Gras parade. Every year more than fifty different parading organizations trundle their floats through the streets. All kinds of difficulties have to be anticipated, including rain, tipsy float riders who will fall off, and mechanical failures in the tractor engines pulling the floats, and have to be overcome. Rain can slow the parade but not stop it. Too much money, time, and dedication go into parade preparation to let anything prevent it or so the parade organizers say.

## Exercise 33.2: Pattern Practice

*Using the patterns and examples given here, write your own sentences with dashes. Write two sentences for each pattern given.*

Pattern A: At the beginning or end of the sentence for added explanation or illustration

> Those leather boots cost about $100—almost half a week's salary.

Pattern B: To mark an interruption or break in thought

> Rick is always borrowing—but not returning—everyone else's ballpoint pens.

Pattern C: To set off phrases and clauses with their own commas

> There were several exercise programs—including aerobic dancing, gymnastics, and aquatic exercises in the pool—to choose from in the students' recreational program at the gymnasium.

# 33b Slashes (/)

## (1) Slashes to Mark the End of a Line of Poetry

When you quote two or three lines of poetry within a paragraph, indicate the end of each line with a slash (with a space before and after the slash).

Don't use the slash mark when you indent and quote three or more lines of poetry.

> Andrew Marvell's poem "To His Coy Mistress" begins by reminding the lady that life is indeed short: "Had we but world enough, and time / This coyness, lady, were no crime." And as the poem progresses, the imagery of death reinforces this reminder of our brief moment of life:
>
>> But at my back I always hear
>> Time's winged chariot hurrying near;
>> And yonder all before us lie
>> Deserts of vast eternity.

## (2) Slashes to Indicate Acceptable Alternatives

Use the forward slash mark, with no space before or afterward, to indicate that either of two terms can apply. The forward slash mark on a typewriter or computer keyboard is the slanting line /.

> pass/fail        and/or        yes/no

## Exercise 33.3: Pattern Practice

*Using the patterns and examples given here, write your own sentences with slashes. Write one sentence for each pattern given.*

Pattern A: With poetry quoted within a sentence

> Whenever she was asked to discuss her ability to cope with great difficulties, she quoted John Milton: "The mind is its own place, and in itself / Can make a Heaven of Hell, a Hell of Heaven."

Pattern B: With two terms when either is acceptable

> Because the reading list for History 227 was so long, he decided to register for it on a pass/fail option.

# 33C Parentheses ( )

A dash gives emphasis to an element in the sentence, whereas a pair of parentheses indicates that the element enclosed is less important. *Parentheses* is the plural form of the word and indicates both the parenthesis at the beginning and the parenthesis at the end of the enclosed element.

## (1) Parentheses to Set Off Supplementary Matter

Use parentheses to enclose supplementary or less important material that you include as further explanation or as added detail or examples.

That added material does not need to be part of the grammatical structure of the sentence. If the material is inside the sentence, any punctuation needed for the rest of the sentence is outside the closing parentheses. If a whole sentence is enclosed with parentheses, put the end punctuation for that sentence inside.

> The officers of the fraternity (the ones elected last month) called a meeting just before the dance to remind everyone of the new alcohol regulations.

## (2) Parentheses to Enclose Figures or Letters

Use parentheses to enclose figures or letters that enumerate items in a series.

> The three major items on the agenda were as follows: (1) the budget review, (2) the new parking permits, and (3) the evaluation procedures.

## Exercise 33.4: Pattern Practice

*Using the patterns and examples given here, write your own sentences with parentheses. Write a sentence for each pattern given.*

Pattern A: To enclose less important material

> The sixth-grade teacher decided to offer his art class an opportunity to try out different drawing materials (such as pastel chalks and charcoal) that they hadn't used before.

Pattern B: To enclose figures and letters

> The job offer included some very important fringe benefits that similar positions in other companies did not include: (a) a day-care center in the building, (b) retirement benefits for the employee's spouse, and (c) an opportunity to buy company cars after they were used for a year or so.

# 33d Brackets [ ]

## (1) Brackets to Add Your Comments within a Quotation

When you are quoting material and have to add your own explanation, comment, or addition within the quotation, enclose your addition within brackets [ ].

The word *sic* in brackets means that you copied the original quotation exactly as it appeared, but you think that the word just before *sic* may be an error or a questionable form.

> After the town meeting, the newspaper's lead story reported the discussion: "The Town Board and the mayor met to discuss the mayor's proposal to raise parking meter rates. The discussion was long but not heated, and the exchange of views was fiendly [*sic*] despite some strong opposition."

> Everyone agreed with Phil Brown's claim that "this great team [the Chicago Bears] is destined for next year's Super Bowl."

## (2) Brackets to Replace Parentheses within Parentheses

When you need to enclose something already within parentheses, use brackets instead of a second set of parentheses.

> "Baby busters, the children born between 1965 and 1980, have more choices in the job market and better prospects for advancement than the

previous 'baby boom' generation," says John Sayers in his recent study of population trends (*The Changing Face of Our Population* [New York: Merian, 1994] 18).

## Exercise 33.5: Pattern Practice

*Using the patterns and examples given here, write your own sentences with brackets. Write one sentence for each pattern given.*

Pattern A: Brackets to add comments within a quotation

> The lab assistant explained that "everyone [who has finished the lab experiment] should hand in notebooks by Friday."

Pattern B: Brackets to replace parentheses within parentheses

> The new library guide (distributed by the Newcomers Council [a subcommittee of the Student Government Board] at no cost to students) is intended to help first-year composition students become acquainted with resources for researching term paper topics.

## Exercise 33.6: Proofreading Practice

*Add slashes, parentheses, and brackets where they are needed in the following paragraph. Correct any wrong punctuation.*

The last two lines of Archibald MacLeish's poem "Ars Poetica" (written in 1924 are often quoted as his theory of poetry. "A poem should not mean But be," he wrote. In his notebooks, he expanded on this statement: "The purpose of the expression of emotion in a poem is not to recreate the poet's emotion in someone else. . . . The poem itself is a finality, an end, a creation." G. T. Hardison, in his analysis of MacLeish's theory of poetry ("The Non-Meaning of Poetry," *Modern Poetics* 27 (1981): 45, explains that "when MacLeish says the poem 'is a finality, an ending *sic*,' he means that a good poem is self-sufficient; it is, it does not mean something else. One might as well ask the meaning of a friend or brother."

# 33e Omitted Words/Ellipsis  (. . .)

Use an ellipsis (a series of three spaced periods) to indicate that you are omitting words or a part of a sentence from material you are quoting.

**Original:**  "In 1891, when President Benjamin Harrison proclaimed the first forest reserves as government land, there were so many people opposed to the idea that his action was called undemocratic and un-American."

**Some Words Omitted:**   "In 1891, when President Benjamin Harrison proclaimed the first forest reserves . . . his action was
called undemocratic and un-American."

If you are omitting a whole sentence or paragraph, add a fourth period
with no space after the last word preceding the ellipsis:

"federal lands. . . . They were designated."

An ellipsis is not needed if the omission occurs at the beginning or end
of the sentence you are quoting. But if your sentence ends with quoted
words that are not the end of the original sentence, use an ellipsis mark.
Add your period (the fourth one) with no space after the last word if
there is no documentation included. If there is documentation, such as
a page number, add the last period after the parentheses.

"the National Forest System. . . ."
"the National Forest System . . ." (Smith 27).

If you omit words immediately after a punctuation mark in the original,
include that mark in your sentence.

"because of this use of forests for timbering, mining, and grazing, . . ."

In addition to indicating the omission of quoted words, three dots are
also used to show hesitation or an unfinished statement.

The lawyer asked: "Did you see the defendant leave the room?"
"Ah, I'm not sure . . . but he might have left," replied the witness.

# PART FIVE

## MECHANICS AND SPELLING

As we edit and proofread final drafts before handing them over to our readers, we need to attend to matters of correct visual presentation of our writing. Checking on these visual matters, the mechanics and spelling of our writing, is an important part of the final stage of the writing process.

### Part Five: Mechanics and Spelling

# 34 Capitals (caps)

Capitalize words that name one particular thing, most often a person or place rather than a general type or group of things.

Names that need capitals can be thought of as legal titles that identify a specific entity. For example, you can take a course in history (a word not capitalized because it is a general field of study), but the course is offered by a particular department with a specific name, such as History Department or Department of Historical Studies. The name of that specific department is capitalized. However, if you take a course in French, *French* is capitalized because it is the name of a specific language.

Listed here are categories of words that should be capitalized. If you are not sure about a particular word, check your dictionary.

- Persons

  Vincent Baglia        Rifka Kaplan                    Masuto Tatami

- Places, including geographical regions

  Indianapolis        Ontario                    Midwest

- Peoples and their languages

  Spanish        Dutch                    English

- Religions and their followers

  Buddhist        Judaism                    Christianity

- Members of national, political, racial, social, civic, and athletic groups

  Democrat        African-American              Chicago Bears
  Danes           Friends of the Library        Olympics Committee

- Institutions and organizations

  Supreme Court        Legal Aid Society                    Lions Club

- Historical documents

  The Declaration of Independence              Magna Carta

- Periods and events, but not century numbers

  Middle Ages        Boston Tea Party              eighteenth century

- Days, months, and holidays, but not seasons

  Monday              August        Thanksgiving        winter

- Trademarks

    Coca-Cola        Kodak                                Ford

- Holy books and words denoting the Supreme Being (including pronouns)

    Talmud          wonders of His creation          the Lord          the Bible

- Words and abbreviations derived from specific names, but not the names of things that have lost that specific association and now refer to the general type

    Stalinism        Freudian          NATO          CBS
    french fry       pasteurize        italics        panama hat

- Place words, such as *street, park,* and *city,* that are part of specific names

    New York City    Wall Street       Madison Avenue       Zion National Park

- Titles that precede people's names, but not titles that follow names

    Aunt Sylvia       Governor Lionel Washington       President Taft
    Sylvia, my aunt   Lionel Washington, governor

- Words that indicate family relationships when used as a substitute for a specific name

    Here is a gift for Mother.          Li Chen sent a gift to his mother.

- Titles of books, magazines, essays, movies, plays, and other works, but not articles (*a, an, the*), short prepositions (*to, by, on, in*), or short joining words (*and, but, or*) unless they are the first or last word. With hyphenated words, capitalize the first and other important words.

    *The Taming of the Shrew*              "The Sino-Soviet Conflict"
    *A Dialog Between Soul and Body*       "A Brother-in-Law's Lament"

    [For APA style, which has different rules, see 46c.]

- The pronoun *I* and the interjection *O,* but not the word *oh*

    "Sail on, sail on, O ship of state," I said as the canoe sank.

- The first word of every sentence and the first word of a comment in parentheses if the comment is a full sentence, but not for a series of questions in which the questions are not full sentences

    The American Olympic Ski Team (which receives very little government support) spent six months in training before the elimination trials while the German team trained for over two years. (Like most European nations, Germany provides financial support for all team members.)

    What did the settlers want from the natives? food? animal skins?

- The first word of directly quoted speech, but not for the second portion of interrupted direct quotations or quoted phrases or clauses integrated into the sentence

    She answered, "No one will understand."

    "No one," she answered, "will understand."

    When Hemmings declined the nomination, he explained that he "would try again another year."

- The first word in a list after a colon if each item in the list is a complete sentence

    The rule books were very clear: (1) No player could continue to play after committing two fouls. (2) Substitute players would be permitted only with the consent of the other team. (3) Every eligible player had to be designated before the game.

    (or)

    The rule books were very clear:
    1. No player could continue to play after committing two fouls.
    2. Substitute players would be permitted only with the consent of the other team.
    3. Every eligible player had to be designated before the game.

    The rise in popularity of walking as an alternative to jogging has already led to commercial successes of various kinds: (1) new designs for walking shoes, (2) an expanding market for walking sticks, and (3) a rapid growth in the number of manufacturers selling walking shoes.

    (or)

    The rise in popularity of walking as an alternative to jogging has already led to commercial successes of various kinds:
    1. new designs for walking shoes,
    2. an expanding market for walking sticks, and
    3. a rapid growth in the number of manufacturers selling walking shoes.

- Words placed after a prefix that are normally capitalized

    un-American                    anti-Semitic

## Exercise 34.1: Proofreading Practice

*In the following sentences there are some errors in capitalization. Revise the sentences so that the capitals are used correctly.*

1. Every Spring when the Madison avenue advertisers compete for Clio Awards for the best commercials, my Cousin Bert makes bets on who will win.
2. At the Dallas–fort Worth international airport, the Pan am plane landed with a cargo of dutch cigars and african diamonds.

3. When Marta signed up for an advanced course in Psychology, she was already familiar with Freudian Psychology and various Twentieth-Century views on dream interpretation.

4. Shanta Prabil, a Washington, D.C., Physician, has recently completed his study of the effects of Asthma as his contribution to a Task Force convened by the National Institutes of Health.

5. When Aleen drove South from Minnesota to Tennessee, she wondered whether "Every restaurant, including McDonald's, would serve grits."

## Exercise 34.2: Pattern Practice

*For each of the capitalization patterns listed here, write a sentence of your own that uses capitals correctly.*

Pattern A: A sentence with the name of a national, political, racial, social, civic, or athletic group; the name of a season of the year; and a person's name and title

> When Matthew Given, superintendent of the Monticello School Corporation, suggested a summer program for additional study, many parents vigorously supported his idea.

Pattern B: A sentence with a quotation interrupted by other words in the sentence

> "You know," said the customer to the salesclerk, "this is just what I was looking for."

Pattern C: Two place names and a holiday

> On the Fourth of July, Chicago hosts an art and food fair in Grant Park.

# 35 Abbreviations (ab)

In the fields of social science, science, and engineering, abbreviations are used frequently, but in other fields and in academic writing in the humanities, only a limited number of abbreviations are generally used.

## 35a Abbreviating Numbers

• Write out numbers that can be expressed in one or two words.

nine            twenty-seven            135

- The dollar sign abbreviation is generally acceptable when the whole phrase will be more than three words.

  $23 million        one million dollars

- For temperatures, use words if only a few temperatures are cited, but use figures if temperatures are cited frequently in a paper.

  ten degrees below zero, Fahrenheit        −10°F

# 35b Abbreviating Titles

- *Mr., Mrs.,* and *Ms.* are abbreviated when used as titles before the name.

  Mr. Tanato        Ms. Whitman        Mrs. Ojebwa

- *Dr.* and *St.* ("Saint") are abbreviated only when they immediately precede a name; they are written out when they appear after the name.

  Dr. Marlen Chaf        (but)        Marlen Chaf, doctor of internal medicine

- *Prof., Sen., Gen., Capt.,* and similar abbreviated titles can be used when they appear in front of a full name or before initials and a last name but are not abbreviated when they appear before the last name only.

  Gen. R. G. Fuller        (but)        General Fuller

- *Sr., Jr., J.D., Ph.D., M.F.A., C.P.A.,* and other abbreviated academic titles and professional degrees can be used after the name.

  Leslie Millen, Ph.D., . . .        Charleen Phipps, C.P.A.

- *Bros., Co.,* and similar abbreviations are used only if they are part of the exact name.

  Marshall Field & Co.        Brown Bros.

# 35c Abbreviating Places

In general, spell out names of states, countries, continents, streets, rivers, and so on.

Here are two exceptions:

- Use the abbreviation *D.C.* in Washington, D.C. Use *U.S.* only as an adjective, not as a noun.

  U.S. training bases        training bases in the United States

- If you include a full address in a sentence, citing the street, city, and state, you can use the postal abbreviation for the state.

> For further information, write to the company at 100 Peachtree Street, Atlanta, GA 30300 for a copy of their free catalog.
>
> The company's headquarters in Atlanta, Georgia, will soon be moved.

## 35d Abbreviating Measurements

Spell out units of measurement, such as acre, meter, foot, and percent, but use abbreviations in tables, graphs, and figures.

## 35e Abbreviating Dates

Spell out months and days of the week.

With dates and times, the following are acceptable:

> 57 B.C. (or) 57 B.C.E.    [the abbreviations B.C. and B.C.E. (Before the Common Era) are placed after the year.]
>
> A.D. 329    [The abbreviation A.D. is placed before the date.]
>
> a.m., p.m. (or) A.M., P.M.
>
> EST (or) E.S.T., est

## 35f Abbreviating Initials Used as Names

Use abbreviations for names of organizations, agencies, countries, and things usually referred to by their capitalized initials.

| | | |
|---|---|---|
| NASA | IBM | NAACP |
| UNICEF | USSR | VCR |

If you are using the initials for a term that may not be familiar to your readers, spell it out the first time and give the initials in parentheses. From then on, you can use the initials. (See 32a(2).)

> The study of children's long-term memory (LTM) has been a difficult one because of the lack of a universally accepted definition of LTM.

## 35g Abbreviating Latin Expressions

Some Latin expressions always appear as abbreviations.

| Abbreviation | Meaning | Abbreviation | Meaning |
|---|---|---|---|
| cf. | compare | i.e. | that is |
| e.g. | for example | n.b. | note carefully |
| et al. | and others | vs. (or) v. | versus |
| etc. | and so forth | | |

# 35h Abbreviating Documentation

Because the format for abbreviations may vary from one style manual to another, use the abbreviations listed in the particular style manual you are following. (See 45c and 46c.)

| Abbreviation | Meaning |
|---|---|
| abr. | abridged |
| anon. | anonymous |
| b. | born |
| c. (or) c | copyright |
| c. (or) ca. | about—used with dates |
| ch. (or) chap. | chapter |
| col., cols. | column, columns |
| d. | died |
| ed., eds. | editor, editors |
| esp. | especially |
| f., ff. | and the following page, pages |
| illus. | illustrated by |
| ms., mss. | manuscript, manuscripts |
| no. | number |
| n.d. | no date of publication given |
| n.p. | no place of publication given |
| n. pag. | no page number given |
| p., pp. | page, pages |
| trans. (or) tr. | translated by |
| vol., vols. | volume, volumes |

## Exercise 35.1: Proofreading Practice

*Proofread the following paragraph, and correct the errors in using abbreviations. Underline the words you correct.*

Some forms of illegal fishing are hard to define. For example, "noodling," the practice of catching fish by snagging them in the gills or flesh, is illegal in most places in the U.S. However, in a recent case, a man who had caught two fish, weighing 25 and 31 lbs., in a Texas lake argued that he wasn't noodling when he dived under water with a fishing pole & a very short line. This was not noodling, he claimed, because he poked his rod & baited hook into catfish nets instead of dragging his lines through the water to snag fish the way noodlers do. The local game warden charged the angler with noodling, a misdemeanor that carries a fine of up to $250. Residents of the area, near Cloud Creek Lake, TX, agreed that he was fishing illegally. But, after much debate, the man won his claim that although his unusual method was very close to noodling, he was innocent.

## Exercise 35.2: Pattern Practice

*Using the patterns listed here, write a sentence of your own that correctly uses abbreviations.*

Pattern A: A sentence that contains a number that can be written as one or two words, a name with a degree after it, and the names of a city and state

> When Cleon Martin, C.P.A., looked for office space in Rochester, New York, he found a somewhat expensive but convenient office on the thirty-sixth floor of a new high-rise office building near his home.

Pattern B: A sentence with the abbreviation for the United States used correctly and the names of a month and a day of the week

> Because of recent changes in the U.S. Post Office, many local post offices are now open on Saturday mornings, especially in December.

Pattern C: A sentence with a unit of measurement and a specific dollar amount

> The luxurious boat, more than sixty feet long, was purchased for $555,000.

# 36 Numbers (num)

Style manuals for different fields and companies vary. The suggestions for writing numbers given here are generally useful as a guide for academic writing.

- Spell out numbers that can be expressed in one or two words and use figures for other numbers.

| *Words* | *Figures* |
|---------|-----------|
| two pounds | 126 days |
| six million dollars | $31.50 |
| thirty-one years | 6,381 bushels |
| eighty-three people | 4.78 liters |

- Use a combination of figures and words for numbers when such a combination will keep your writing clear.

    The club celebrated the birthdays of six 90-year-olds who were born in the city.

1. Use figures for the following:

    - Days and years

        | | | |
        |---|---|---|
        | December 12, 1963 | (or) | 12 December 1963 |
        | A.D. 1066 | | |
        | in 1971–1972 | (or) | in 1971–72 |
        | the 1980s | (or) | the 1980's |

    - Time of day

        | | | |
        |---|---|---|
        | 8:00 A.M. (or) a.m. | (or) | eight o'clock in the morning |
        | 4:30 P.M. (or) p.m. | (or) | half past four in the afternoon |

    - Addresses

        15 Tenth Street
        350 West 114 Street   (or)   350 West 114th Street
        Prescott, AZ 86301

    - Identification numbers

        | | |
        |---|---|
        | Room 8 | Channel 18 |
        | Interstate 65 | Henry VIII |

    - Page and division of books and plays

        | | | |
        |---|---|---|
        | page 30 | | chapter 6 |
        | act 3, scene 2 | (or) | Act III, Scene ii |

    - Decimals and percentages

        | | |
        |---|---|
        | 2.7 average | 13 1/2 percent |
        | 0.037 metric ton | |

    - Numbers in series and statistics

        two apples, six oranges, and three bananas

        115 feet by 90 feet

        Be consistent, whichever form you choose.

    - Large round numbers

        | | | |
        |---|---|---|
        | four billion dollars | (or) | $4 billion |
        | 16,500,000 | (or) | 16.5 million |

- Repeated numbers (in legal or commercial writing)

  The bill will not exceed one hundred (100) dollars.

2. Do not use figures for the following:

- Numbers that can be expressed in one or two words

  the eighties          the twentieth century

- Dates when the year is omitted

  June sixth

- Numbers beginning sentences

  Ten percent of the year's crop was harvested.


## Exercise 36.1: Pattern Practice

*For each of the sentences given here, compose a sentence of your own using that model for writing numbers. The first sentence is done as an example.*

1. There was a 7.2 percent decrease in sales of cigarettes after the Surgeon General's speech.
   The study showed that 16.7 percent of the population in the country did not have running water.
2. The plane was due at 4:15 P.M. but arrived at 5:10 P.M.
3. That book was volume 23 in the series.
4. The astronomer calculated that the star is 18 million light-years from our planet.
5. In the sixties, during the height of the anti-war movement, the senator's political actions were not popular, but by the time of the 1972 election, more people agreed with him.
6. The television commercial warned buyers that there were only 123 days until Christmas.


# 37 Underlining/Italics (under)

When you are typing or writing by hand, use underlining (a printer's mark to indicate words to be set in italics). When you have italic lettering on a computer, you can use italics instead.

*970-850*

*3959,*

# 37a Underlining for Titles

Use underlining (or italics) for titles and names of books, magazines, newspapers, pamphlets, works of art, long works such as plays with three or more acts, movies, long musical works (operas, concertos, etc.), radio and television programs, and long poems.

For the use of quotation marks for titles of minor works and parts of whole works, see 30b.

Do not use underlining, italics, or quotation marks for references to the Bible or legal documents.

| **Underlining** | **(or)** | **Italics** |
|---|---|---|
| Catcher in the Rye | | *Catcher in the Rye* |
| U.S. News and World Report | | *U.S. News and World Report* |
| New York Times | | *New York Times* |

# 37b Other Uses of Underlining

**1.** Use underlining or italics for the following:

- Names of ships, airplanes, and trains

  Queen Mary        Concorde        Orient Express

- Foreign words and phrases and scientific names of plants and animals

  in vino veritas        Canis lupus

- Words used as words, or letters, numbers, and symbols used as examples or terms

  Some words, such as Kleenex, are brand names for products.

  In English the letters ph and f often have the same sound.

  The keys for 9 and & on that typewriter are broken.

- Words being emphasized

  It never snows here at this time of year.

  Use italics or underlining for emphasis only sparingly.

**2.** Do not use underlining or italics for the following:

- Words of foreign origin that are now part of English

| alumni | cliché | karate |
|--------|--------|--------|
| rouge  | genre  | hacienda |

- Titles of your own papers

## Exercise 37.1: Proofreading Practice

*Add underlining where it is needed in the following paragraph and delete any incorrect underlining or quotation marks.*

Because of her interest in the influence of the media on people's attitudes, Sarah chose as the topic for her research project the media's image of the Japanese during the last ten years. For source material Sarah began by reading newsmagazines such as Time and Newsweek, but she found them less likely to portray attitudes than features in magazines such as "People" and "Fortune," which have articles on sushi bars, Japanese electronics, and <u>karate</u>. The index to the New York Times also led her to articles such as <u>The Japanese Influence on American Business</u> and <u>Japanese Technology in America.</u> Sarah also read reviews of old television programs, including the short-lived series Ohara, which featured a Japanese-American detective, and old movies, such as The Karate Kid. Sarah rapidly found herself buried under mounds of notes and decided to limit her topic to one of the media, though she couldn't decide which one.

## Exercise 37.2: Pattern Practice

*Using the patterns and examples given here, write your own correctly italicized (or underlined) sentences. Write two sentences for each pattern given.*

Pattern A: Italics (or underlining) with titles of books, magazines, newspapers, and long works of art

> After surveying its recently checked out materials, the library concluded that the most popular items on the shelves were murder mysteries, such as Blodgen's <u>The Dead Hero</u>; current big city newspapers, such as the <u>New York Times</u>; and videotapes of old movies, such as <u>North by Northwest</u> and <u>Gone With the Wind</u>.

Pattern B: Italics (or underlining) with names of ships, airplanes, and trains

> When the old <u>Queen Mary</u> was no longer fit for sailing, it became a floating hotel.

Pattern C: Italics (or underlining) with foreign words or phrases and scientific names

> Dr. Galland diagnosed the cause of his illness: infection with a combination of <u>Candida albicans</u> and <u>Giardia lamblia</u>.

Pattern D: Italics (or underlining) with words used as words or figures used as examples

> If she would stop overusing empty words such as <u>great</u> or <u>nice</u> in her composition class papers, she would probably be able to get an <u>A.</u>

Pattern E: Italics (or underlining) for emphasis

> When Mike woke up, he couldn't believe that he felt so refreshed even though he had been asleep for <u>only</u> ten minutes.

# 38 Spelling (sp)

English spelling can be difficult because many words have been imported from other languages that have different spelling conventions. But despite the difficulty, it is important to spell correctly. Some misspelled words can cause confusion in the reader's mind, but any misspelled word can signal the reader that the writer is careless and not very knowledgeable. Since no writer wants to lose credibility, correct spelling is necessary. So it is wise to spend some time on spelling, doing one or more of the following:

- **Learn some spelling rules.**
- **Make up your own memory aids.**
- **Make up some rules or letter associations** that will help you remember particularly troublesome words. Example: If you have trouble choosing between *e*'s and *a*'s in *separate*, it may help to remember that there's a *pa* in se*pa*rate.
- **Learn your own misspelling patterns.**
- **Learn how to proofread.**

## 38a Proofreading

---

**Proofreading** means reading your final written work slowly and carefully to catch misspellings and typographical errors.

---

Proofreading is best done after you are finished writing and are preparing to turn your paper over to your readers. Some useful proofreading strategies:

- **Slow down.** Proofreading requires slowing down your reading rate so you will see all the letters in each word. In normal reading, your eyes skip across the line and you notice only groups of words.
- **Focus on each word.** One way to slow yourself down is to point a pencil or pen at each word as you say it aloud or to yourself.
- **Read backward.** Don't read left to right as you would normally do, or you will soon slip back into a more rapid reading rate. Instead, move backward through each line from right to left. In this way, you won't be listening for meaning or checking for grammatical correctness.
- **Cover up any distractions.** To focus on each word, hold a sheet of paper or a notecard under the line being read. This way you won't be distracted by other words on the page.
- **Watch for your patterns of misspellings.** Remember to look for those groups or patterns of misspellings that occur most frequently in your writing.
- **Read forward.** End-to-beginning proofreading will not catch problems with omitted words or sound-alike words. To check for those, do a second proofreading moving forward, from left to right, so that you can watch the meaning of your sentences. Listen for each word as you read aloud or to yourself.

## Exercise 38.1: Proofreading Practice

*Practice the proofreading strategies described in 38a by proofreading the following paragraph, which has a number of typos, misspellings, and omitted words. Underline each word that is spelled incorrectly, and correct the spelling. Write in above the line any word or words that are missing.*

3
sp

Turkish people do'nt think of St. Nicholas as having reindeer or elfs, living at North Pole, or climbing down chimneys with gifts on Christmass Eve. Accept for a twist of history, Santa Claus might well speak Turkish, ride a camel, dress for a warmmer climate, bring gifts of oranges and tomatoes, and appear on December 5 instead of Christmas Eve. According to the story of the Turkish church about his backround, Nicholas was the frist bishop of Myra, on the coast Turkey. Turkish scholars say he was known far and wide for his peity and charity. He was killed around A.D. 245, and after his martyrdom, on December 6, tails of his good deeds lived on. His faime was so great that in the eleventh centruy, when the Italian branch of the Catholic church began a drive to bring to Italy the remains of the most famous saints, theives stole most of Nicholas's bones from the church tomb in Turkey and took them to a town in southren Italy. Nicholas was abbreviated to Claus, and St. Nick became Santa. Since there are no dociuments or records of the original Nicholas of Myra, some sholars doubt his existance. But others are convinced there really was a St. Nicholas, even if he didn't have reindeer or live at North Pole.

# 38b Using Spell Checkers

Spell checkers on computers are a useful tool, but they can't catch all spelling errors. While different spell checking programs have different capabilities, they are not foolproof, and they do make mistakes. Most spell checkers will not locate or correct the following errors:

- **Omitted words**
- **Sound-alike words (homonyms)** Some words sound alike but are spelled differently (see 38e). The spell checker will not flag a word if it is a correctly spelled homonym of the one you want. For example, if you meant "*They're* going to the tennis match" but write "*Their* going to the tennis match," the spell checker recognizes *Their* as a word and will not highlight it for you.
- **Many proper nouns** Some well-known proper nouns, such as *Washington,* may be in the spell checker dictionary for your program, but many will not be there.
- **Misspelled words for which the spell checker can't find the appropriate word** Depending on the power of the spell checker and the way a word is misspelled, the program may not be able to provide the correct spelling. For example, if you meant to write *phenomena* but instead typed *phinomina,* spell checkers will highlight the word as not matching any word in their dictionary, but many won't be able to suggest the correct spelling.

# 38c Some Spelling Guidelines

### (1) *ie/ei*

> Write *i* before *e*
> Except after *c*
> Or when sounded like *ay*
> As in *neighbor* and *weigh.*

This rhyme reminds you to write *ie,* except under two conditions:

- When the two letters follow a *c*
- When the two letters sound like *ay* (as in *day*).

| Some ie words | | Some ei words | |
|---|---|---|---|
| believe | niece | ceiling | eight |
| chief | relief | conceit | receive |
| field | yield | deceive | vein |

The following common words are exceptions to this rule:

| | | |
|---|---|---|
| conscience | forfeit | seize |
| counterfeit | height | sheik |
| either | leisure | species |
| financier | neither | sufficient |
| foreign | science | weird |

## Exercise 38.2: Proofreading Practice

*Spell these words correctly by writing* ie *or* ei *in the blanks.*

1. There are _____ght candles on the cake.
2. I have not rec_____ved a letter from her.
3. Her n_____ce is coming to visit next week.
4. Drop that silver, you th_____f!
5. She is not a conc_____ted person, despite her beauty.
6. The ch_____f of the tribe led the dancing.
7. May I have a p_____ce of cheese?
8. The fr_____ght train woke the n_____ghbors.
9. He wanted n_____ther the pants nor the shirt the salesperson showed him.
10. I bel_____ve that I already returned the library book.
11. There was a spider web hanging from the c_____ling.
12. What did you w_____gh before your diet?
13. I'll need a rec_____pt for this purchase.
14. The f_____ld of wheat waved in the wind.
15. The dollar bill was obviously a counterf_____t.

## (2) Doubling Consonants

A few rules about doubling the last consonant of the base word will help you spell several thousand words correctly.

### One-Syllable Words

If the word ends in a consonant preceded by a single short vowel, double that last consonant when you are adding a suffix beginning with a vowel.

| | | | |
|---|---|---|---|
| drag | dragged | dragging | |
| flip | flipped | flipping | flipper |
| nap | napped | napping | |
| shop | shopped | shopping | shopper |
| slip | slipped | slipping | slipper |
| star | starred | starring | |
| tap | tapped | tapping | |
| wet | wetted | wetting | wettest |

**Two-Syllable Words**

For words with two or more syllables that end with a consonant preceded by a single vowel, double the consonant when both of the following conditions apply:

1. You are adding a suffix beginning with a vowel.
2. The last syllable of the base word is accented.

| | | | |
|---|---|---|---|
| begin | | beginning | beginner |
| occur | occurred | occurring | occurrence |
| omit | omitted | omitting | |
| prefer | preferred | preferring | |
| refer | referred | referring | |
| regret | regretted | regretting | regrettable |
| submit | submitted | submitting | |
| unwrap | unwrapped | unwrapping | |

## Exercise 38.3: Proofreading Practice

*Underline the words that are misspelled in the following paragraph, and write the correct spelling above the word.*

Last week Michael planed to have his bicycle repaired, though he admitted that he was hopping he had stopped the leak in the front tire with a patch. Even though he concealled the patch with some heavy tape, he found that he had to keep tapping the patch back on the tire. Yesterday, when Michael looked at the bicycle on the way to his first class, he could see that the front tire had become flatter than it should be because it was lossing air. With no time to spare, he jogged off to class, resolved that he would take the bicycle to a shop that afternoon.

## (3) Prefixes and Suffixes

---

A **prefix** is a group of letters added at the beginning of a base word. A **suffix** is a group of letters added to the end of the word.

---

The following prefixes are used in many English words:

| *Prefix* | *Meaning* | *Examples* |
|---|---|---|
| ante- | before | anteroom |
| anti- | against | antidote |
| auto- | self | automobile |
| bene- | good | benefit |
| bi- | two, twice | bicycle, biweekly |
| bio- | life | biography, biology |
| de- | away, down | depress |

| dis- | not, no longer, away | disappear |
| ex- | out, no longer | exclude, expel, ex-wife |
| inter- | between, among | interact, interstate |
| intra- | within, between members of the same group | intramural, intrastate |
| mis- | wrong, bad | misspell, misdeed |
| per- | entirely, through | perfect, pertain |
| post- | after | postgame, postdate |
| pre- | before | pregame, prefix |
| pro- | for, take place of | prohibit, pro-American, proclaim |
| re- | again, back | retell, redo, readmit |
| semi- | half, partially | semicircle, semiautomatic |
| un- | not, contrary to | unhappy, unable |

### The *-ly* Suffix

If a word ends in *-l,* don't drop the *-l* when adding the suffix *-ly.* But if the word already ends with two *-l's,* add only the *-y.*

| chill | chilly |
| formal | formally |
| hill | hilly |
| real | really |
| usual | usually |

### Suffixes with Words Ending in *-ic*

When a word ends in *-ic,* add a *-k* before suffixes starting with *-i, -e,* or *-y.* Some words that end in *-ic* add the suffix *ally,* not *-ly.*

| logic | logically |
| picnic | picnicking |
| politic | politicking |
| traffic | trafficking |
| tragic | tragically |

## Exercise 38.4: Pattern Practice

*Using your dictionary, look up three examples of words that include the prefixes listed here:*

| | | |
|---|---|---|
| **1.** ante- | **7.** dis- | **13.** post- |
| **2.** anti- | **8.** ex- | **14.** pre- |
| **3.** auto- | **9.** inter- | **15.** pro- |
| **4.** bene- | **10.** intra- | **16.** re- |
| **5.** bio- | **11.** mis- | **17.** semi- |
| **6.** de- | **12.** per- | **18.** un- |

## Exercise 38.5: Pattern Practice

*Using your dictionary to check the correct spelling, add the suffixes to the words listed here:*

**1.** -ing        rise, guide, come
**2.** -ly         like, sure, true
**3.** -ful        care, use, stress
**4.** -ous        continue, courage, nerve
**5.** -able       desire, notice, knowledge

## (4) *y* to *i*

When adding a suffix to words ending with *-y*, change the *-y* to an *-i*. But to avoid a double *i* in a word, keep the *-y* before the *-ing* suffix.

| apply | applies, applied | (but) applying |
| carry | carries, carried | (but) carrying |
| study | studies, studied | (but) studying |
| apology | apologies | |
| beauty | beautiful | |
| ceremony | ceremonious | |
| busy | busied, business | |
| easy | easily, easiness | |
| happy | happily, happiness | |

**Exception:** If there is a vowel before the final *-y*, keep the *-y* before adding *-s* or *-ed:*

| stay | stays, stayed |
| enjoy | enjoys, enjoyed |
| day | days |
| attorney | attorneys |
| key | keys |

## Exercise 38.6: Pattern Practice

*Using your dictionary to check the correct spelling, add the suffixes in parentheses to the words listed here:*

**1.** tray + (*-s*)
**2.** apology + (*-s*)
**3.** ally + (*-ed*)
**4.** steady + (*-ing*)
**5.** accompany + (*-ing*)
**6.** study + (*-ing*)
**7.** mercy + (*-ful*)
**8.** funny + (*-er*)
**9.** monkey + (*-s*)
**10.** bury + (*-al*)
**11.** likely + (*-er*)
**12.** story + (*-s*)
**13.** lonely + (*-ness*)
**14.** vary + (*-ed*)
**15.** ninety + (*-eth*)
**16.** study + (*-ous*)
**17.** pretty + (*-ness*)
**18.** employ + (*-er*)

# 38d Plurals

- Most plurals are formed by adding *-s*. Add *-es* when words end in *-s*, *-sh*, *-ch*, *-x*, or *-z* because another syllable is needed.

| | |
|---|---|
| one apple | two apples |
| one box | two boxes |
| a brush | many brushes |
| a buzz | six buzzes |
| the card | all those cards |
| the church | several churches |
| a loss | some losses |
| one wall | three walls |

- With phrases and hyphenated words, pluralize the last word unless another word is more important.

| | |
|---|---|
| one videocassette recorder | two videocassette recorders |
| one systems analyst | two systems analysts |
| one sister-in-law | two sisters-in-law |

- For some words that end in *-f* or *-fe*, change the *f* to *ve* and add *-s*. For other words that end in *-f*, add *-s* without any change in the base word.

| | |
|---|---|
| one thief | six thieves |
| a leaf | some leaves |
| a roof | two roofs |
| his belief | their beliefs |
| the chief | two chiefs |

- For words ending in a consonant plus *-y*, change the *y* to *i* and add *-es*. For words ending in a vowel plus *-y*, add an *-s*.

| | |
|---|---|
| one boy | several boys |
| one company | four companies |
| one candy | some candies |
| a monkey | two monkeys |

- For words ending in a vowel plus *-o*, add an *-s*. For words ending in a consonant plus *-o*, add an *-s*, *-es*, or either *-s* or *-es*.

| | |
|---|---|
| a radio | some radios |
| one patio | two patios |
| the auto | some autos |
| his hero | their heroes |
| one potato | bag of potatoes |
| one zero | two zeros (or) zeroes |
| the cargo | boats' cargos (or) cargoes |

- For some words, the plural is formed by changing the base word.

  one child            several children
  one woman            two women
  one goose            nine geese
  one mouse            some mice

- Some words have the same form for both singular and plural:

  deer            sheep            pliers

- Some words from other languages keep their original plural endings:

  for men: one alumnus       some alumni
  for women: one alumna      several alumnae
  one antenna                two antennae
  an appendix                three appendices
  a basis                    some bases
  a criterion                some criteria
  a crisis                   two crises
  one datum                  several pieces of data
  a medium                   all the media
  one memorandum             two memoranda
  a phenomenon               some phenomena
  one radius                 two radii
  a thesis                   several theses

  But some of these words are beginning to acquire an English plural,
  such as *antennas, appendixes,* and *memorandums.*

## Exercise 38.7: Proofreading Practice

*Which of the following words has an incorrectly spelled plural? Use your diction-
ary if needed.*

1. foxs
2. papers
3. companys
4. latchs
5. analyses

6. stereos
7. tariffs
8. brother-in-laws
9. bushes
10. windows

11. womans
12. freshmans
13. passer-bys
14. heroes
15. attorneys

# 38e Sound-Alike Words (Homonyms)

English has a number of words that sound alike but are spelled differently and have different meanings. These are called **homonyms.**

**accept/except**
*accept* (a verb meaning "to agree," "to receive"): She accepted the gift.
*except* (a preposition meaning "other than"): Everyone danced except
Tom.

**affect/effect**

*affect* (a verb meaning "to influence"): Lack of sleep affects his performance.

*effect* (a noun meaning "result," used in phrases such as *in effect, take effect,* and *to that effect,*): What effect does that medicine have?

*effect* (a verb meaning "to accomplish"): to effect a cure

**all ready/already**

*all ready* (an adjective expressing readiness): Finally, the family was all ready to leave.

*already* (an adverb expressing time): Everyone had already left.

**all together/altogether**

*all together* (an adverb meaning "in a group"): The students were all together in the cafeteria.

*altogether* (an adverb meaning "thoroughly"): Her actions were altogether unnecessary.

**any more/anymore**

*any more* (a phrase referring to one or more items): Are there any more potato chips?

*anymore* (an adverb meaning "now," "henceforth"): I don't want to see her anymore.

**any one/anyone**

*any one* (a phrase referring to a specific person or thing): Any one of those newspapers will have the story.

*anyone* (a pronoun meaning any person at all): Can anyone hear me?

**a while/awhile**

*a while* (an article and a noun meaning "a period of time"): It will take a while to finish this.

*awhile* (an adverb meaning "for a short while"): I can stay awhile.

**desert/dessert**

*desert* (a noun meaning "dry," "arid place"; a verb meaning "to abandon"): While exploring the Mojave Desert, they deserted their friends when danger appeared.

*dessert* (a noun meaning "sweet course at the end of a meal"): They ordered cherry pie for dessert.

**hear/here**

*hear* (a verb): Did you hear that?

*here* (indicates a place): Come over here.

**its/it's**

*its* (shows possession): We checked its oil and gas.

*it's* (a contraction = "it is"): It's hard to do that.

**quiet/quit/quite**

*quiet* (an adjective meaning "no sound or noise"): Mornings are a quiet time.

*quit* (a verb meaning "to give up," "abandon"): He quit working on it.

*quite* (an adverb meaning "very," "entirely"): That painting is quite nice.

**than/then**

*than* (a word used in comparisons): She is richer than I.

*then* (a time word): Then he went home.

**their/there/they're**

*their* (shows possession): They paid for their books.

*there* (indicates a place): Look over there.

*they're* (a contraction = "they are"): They're going to paint that house.

**to/too**

*to* (a preposition): Take this to the office.

*too* (adverb meaning "also," "very"): It is too bad that she is too tired to join us.

**were/we're/where**

*were* (verb): They were singing.

*we're* (contraction = "we are"): We are about to leave here.

*where* (in what place): Where is he?

**who's/whose**

*who's* (contraction = "who is"): Who's going to the game?

*whose* (shows possession): Whose book is this?

**your/you're**

*your* (shows possession): Your grades have improved.

*you're* (a contraction = "you are"): You're part of that group.

## Exercise 38.8: Proofreading Practice

*Select the correctly spelled word for each of the following sentences.*

1. The weather always (affects, effects) my moods.
2. She was (to, too) tired to join in.
3. It was a (quite, quiet) summer evening.
4. Would (anyone, any one) of these shirts be acceptable?
5. I need another (envelop, envelope) for these letters.
6. Her tardiness was an (every day, everyday) occurrence.
7. The coach offered some useful (advice, advise).
8. It seemed that (any way, anyway) he threw the hoop, it landed on the rung.
9. It is always cooler in the woods (than, then) in the city.
10. I often drive (by, buy) the Smiths' house.

11. When (it's, its) snowing, the street sounds seem muffled.
12. The table remained (stationary, stationery) when the wind shook the room.
13. When the teacher asked a question, the students answered (all together, altogether).
14. The dictionary (maybe, may be) helpful in deciding which word you want.
15. Whenever the train (passed, past) the station, the conductor waved to the stationmaster.
16. The salesclerk asked his supervisor for some (assistants, assistance) with the computer.
17. The committee agreed that it was (alright, all right) to table the motion being discussed.
18. The football game was nearing the end of the (forth, fourth) quarter.
19. The teacher asked everyone to (sight, cite, site) all the sources used in the term paper.
20. What does (there, their, they're) car horn sound like?

# PART SIX

## STYLE AND WORD CHOICE

This part reviews suggestions for choosing the right or most appropriate words and phrases. The word choices you make can affect the tone of a paper and can influence your readers' reaction to the writing, so your choices are important. The suggestions here will help you avoid sexist language and language that unnecessarily inflates your writing. You will also find help with choosing the most appropriate level of formality as well as choosing appropriate levels of specificity and concreteness.

# 39 Sexist Language (sxt)

In order to avoid language that either favors the male noun or pronoun or excludes females, consider the following guidelines and suggestions.

## 39a Alternatives to *Man*

*Man* originally referred in a general way to both males and females, but the word has become closely associated with adult males only. To avoid this use of *man*, use alternative terms.

| *Man* | *Alternative* |
|---|---|
| man | person, individual |
| mankind | people, human beings, humanity |
| man-made | machine-made, synthetic |
| the common man | the average (or ordinary) person |
| to man | to operate |

## 39b Alternative Job Titles

Many terms for jobs suggest that only men hold or can hold those jobs. To avoid this, try an alternative term.

| *Man* | *Alternative* |
|---|---|
| chairman | chairperson, chair, coordinator |
| mailman | letter carrier, postal worker |
| policeman | police officer |
| steward, stewardess | flight attendant |
| congressman | congressional representative |
| Dear Sir: | Dear Editor:    Dear Service Representative: |

## 39c Alternatives to the Masculine Pronoun

Use an alternative term when you want to convey a general meaning or refer to both sexes instead of using the masculine pronoun *he*.

- Use the plural instead.

   Give the customer his receipt with the change.

   **Revised:** Give customers their receipts with the change.

- Eliminate the male pronoun or reword to avoid unnecessary problems.

  The average citizen worries about his retirement benefits.

  **Revised:** The average citizen worries about retirement benefits.

  If the taxpayer has questions about the new form, he can call a government representative.

  **Revised:** The taxpayer with questions about the new form can call a government representative.

- Replace the male pronoun with *one, you, he or she,* or an article (*a, an, the*).

  The pet owner who can afford it takes his pet to a veterinarian.

  **Revised:** The pet owner who can afford it takes his or her pet to a veterinarian.

  (or)

  The pet owner who can afford it takes the pet to a veterinarian.

- Repeat a title rather than using a male pronoun.

  See your doctor first, and he will explain the prescription.

  **Revised:** See your doctor first, and the doctor will explain the prescription.

- Alternate male and female examples. (But be careful not to confuse your reader.)

  A young child is often persuaded by advertisements to buy what he sees on television. When a child goes shopping with a parent, she sees the product on the shelf, remembers it, and asks to have it.

- Address the reader directly in the second person.

  The applicant must mail his form by Thursday.

  **Revised:** Mail your form by Thursday.

For the indefinite pronouns *everybody, anybody, everyone,* and *anyone,* some people prefer to continue using the male pronoun (*everyone . . . he*). But the plural pronoun has also become acceptable (*everyone . . . they*).

## Exercise 39.1: Proofreading Practice

*In the following paragraph there is some language that could be deemed sexist. Revise the paragraph so that nonsexist language is used consistently.*

In the curricula of most business schools, the study of failure has not yet become an accepted subject. Yet the average business student needs to know what he should do when a business strategy fails and how he can learn from his mistakes. Even the chairman of one Fortune 500 company says that the average businessman can learn more from his mistakes than from his successes. Yet the concept of studying failure has been slow in catching on. However, a few business schools and even engineering management majors at one university in California now confront the question of how anyone can recover from his mistakes. Student papers analyze how a typical failed entrepreneur might have better managed his problems. Sometimes, a perceptive student can even relate the lessons to his own behavior. One of the typical problems that is studied is that of escalating commitment, the tendency of a manager to throw more and more of his financial resources and manpower into a project that is failing. Another is the tendency of the hapless executive not to see that his idea is a bomb. For this reason, computers are being enlisted to help him—and his superiors—make decisions about whether he should bail out or stay in. The study of failure clearly promises to breed success, at least for future businessmen now enrolled in business schools.

## Exercise 39.2: Pattern Practice

*Using the suggestions for avoiding sexist language offered in Section 39c, write a short paragraph about people in a particular profession or group. To gain practice in using various options for using nonsexist language, try to include a variety of suggestions from this section.*

# 40 Unnecessary Words

## 40a Conciseness (con)

Be concise when writing because you will be communicating to your reader more clearly and are more likely to keep your reader's interest. Many readers also don't have time for excess words.

To keep your paper concise, eliminate what your readers do not need to know, what they already know, and whatever doesn't further the purpose of your paper. That often means resisting the impulse to include everything you know about a subject. Suggestions for eliminating unnecessary words:

- Avoid repetition. Some phrases, such as the following, say the same thing twice:

| | |
|---|---|
| first beginning | 6 P.M. in the evening |
| final completion | beautiful and lovely |
| circular in shape | true facts |
| green in color | prove conclusively |
| really and truly | each and every |
| positive benefits | connected together |

- Avoid fillers. Some phrases, such as the following, say little or nothing:

| | |
|---|---|
| there is (or) that there is | there are |
| in view of the fact that | I am going to explain |
| I am going to discuss | |

❖ He said ~~that there is~~ a storm <sub>∧</sub> approaching.  *[is]*

❖ The mayor said that ~~in view of the fact that~~ the budget was overspent, no more projects could be started.  *[because]*

❖ ~~It seems to me that it~~ is getting dark out.  *[It]*

❖ ~~I am going to discuss artificial~~ intelligence, ~~which~~ is an exciting new field of research.  *[Artificial]*

- Combine sentences. When the same nouns or pronouns appear in two sentences, combine the two sentences into one.

❖ The data will be entered into the reports. ~~It will~~ also be included in the graphs.  *[and]*

- Eliminate *who, which,* and *that.*

❖ The book ~~that was~~ lying on the piano belongs to her.

- Turn phrases and clauses into adjectives and adverbs.

| | | |
|---|---|---|
| the player who was very tired | = | the tired player |
| all applicants who are interested | = | all interested applicants |
| touched in a hesitant manner | = | touched hesitantly |
| the piano built out of mahogany | = | the mahogany piano |

- Turn prepositional phrases into adjectives.

| | | |
|---|---|---|
| an employee with ambition | = | an ambitious employee |
| the entrance to the station | = | the station entrance |

- Use active rather than passive.

  ❖ The ~~figures were~~ *research department* checked ~~by the research department.~~ *the figures.*

- Remove excess nouns and change to verbs whenever possible.

  ❖ He ~~made the statement that he~~ agreed ~~with the concept~~ that inflation could be controlled.

  ❖ The ~~function of the~~ box ~~is the storage of~~ *stores* excess wire connectors.

- Replace jargon with clearer, shorter words.

| *Avoid* | *Use* |
|---|---|
| advantageous | beneficial |
| implement | carry out |
| procure | acquire |
| utilize | use |
| effectuate | carry out |
| ascertain | find out |

## Exercise 40.1: Proofreading Practice

*The following paragraph is very wordy. Eliminate as many words as you can without losing clarity. You may need to add a few words, too.*

It has recently been noted by researchers that there is a growing concern among psychologists that as more parents who are working entrust the responsibility for caring for their infants of a very young age to day care centers, some of these babies may face harm of a psychological nature. The research findings of the researchers in this field focus on children who are younger than eighteen months of age who are left in day care centers more than twenty hours a week. For children who are at that most formative age, say the researchers, day care seems to increase the feeling of insecurity. One of the foremost leading researchers in this field says that he isn't sure how the increase in the feeling of insecurity happens, but it is his guess that the stress that a child undergoes each and every day as a result of the separation from the parent can be a contributing causal factor here. Studies of the infants who are in day care for long periods of time each week have shown that more of these infants exhibit feelings of anxiousness and also of hyperactivity. These findings definitely and strongly challenge the older view that day care does not harm or hurt a young child.

## Exercise 40.2: Pattern Practice

*Listed here are some patterns for eliminating unnecessary words. Following the patterns and examples given here, make up a wordy sentence and then a more concise revision.*

**Pattern A:** Reducing a *who, which,* or *what* clause

**Wordy:** The cook who was flipping hamburgers . . .

**Revised:** The cook flipping hamburgers . . .

**Pattern B:** Eliminating fillers

**Wordy:** It is important that we agree that . . .

**Revised:** We must agree that . . .

**Pattern C:** Changing a passive verb to active

**Wordy:** The car was started by the driver.

**Revised:** The driver started the car.

**Pattern D:** Combining sentences

**Wordy:** The cereal box was decorated with pictures of famous athletes on one side. The box had recipes for candy and snacks on the other side.

**Revised:** The cereal box was decorated with pictures of famous athletes on one side and recipes for candy and snacks on the other side.

**Pattern E:** Turning a phrase or clause into an adjective or adverb

**Wordy:** The salesperson who sold used cars starred in the TV commercial.

**Revised:** The used-car salesperson starred in the TV commercial.

**Pattern F:** Eliminating repetition

**Wordy:** When she was first beginning to drive her car, she never drove more than thirty miles per hour.

**Revised:** When she began to drive her car, she never drove more than thirty miles per hour.

**Pattern G:** Turning a prepositional phrase into an adjective

**Wordy:** Use the paper with the red lines.

**Revised:** Use the red-lined paper.

# 40b Clichés (cl)

Clichés are overused, tired expressions that have lost their ability to communicate effectively.

When you read phrases such as "busy as a beaver" or "a crying shame," you are not likely to think about a beaver busily working or someone actually crying in shame. Avoid expressions such as the following, which are worn out from too much repetition and are no longer vivid:

| | |
|---|---|
| white as snow | rat race |
| beat around the bush | have a screw loose |
| suits me to a tee | add insult to injury |
| in a nutshell | calm before the storm |
| crack of dawn | better late than never |
| clear as mud | green with envy |
| playing with fire | stubborn as a mule |
| at the drop of a hat | sell like hotcakes |

## Exercise 40.3: Proofreading Practice

*Underline the clichés in the following paragraph.*

When learning good study habits, some students are sharp as a tack. They know how to make study sessions short and sweet by concentrating on only the most important material. First and foremost, they look at chapter headings and subheadings to get a fix on what the main ideas are. Getting down to business means getting in there and seeing the big picture. Once that is crystal clear, they review arguments or add details. Slowly but surely they go through the material, asking themselves questions that get down to the nitty-gritty. Climbing the ladder of success in college means putting your nose to the grindstone and working hard.

## Exercise 40.4: Revision Practice

*Revise the paragraph in Exercise 40.3 by using more precise language in place of the clichés.*

# 40c Pretentious Language (wc)

**Pretentious language** is language that is too showy; it calls attention to itself by the use of overly complex sentences and ornate, polysyllabic words used for their own sake.

The following sentence is an example of overblown, pompous language that makes the writer sound pretentious and affected. Plain English that communicates clearly is far better than such attempts at showing off.

**Pretentious:** The lucidity with which she formulated her questions as she interrogated the indigenous population of the rustic isle drew gasps of admiration from her cohorts.

**Revised:** Her friends admired her ability to clearly phrase the questions she asked the island's inhabitants.

# 41 Appropriate Words (wds)

Choosing among words is a matter of selecting the correct word, the word that is right in any writing situation. For example, whether an essay is formal or informal, you should always write "between you and *me*" (not "between you and *I*"). But other word choices are not so clear-cut. Instead, it is a question of which word is appropriate for the subject, audience, and purpose of a particular piece of writing.

## 41a Standard English

**Standard English** is the generally accepted language of educated people. It is "standard" because it conforms to established rules of grammar, sentence structure, punctuation, and spelling.

Standard English, the language used in magazines, newspapers, and books read by educated people, is the language you are expected to use in academic writing. If you are not sure a particular word is standard, check the dictionary. Nonstandard words such as *ain't* are labeled to indicate that they are not acceptable for standard usage.

## 41b Colloquialisms, Slang, and Regionalisms

**Colloquial words** are the language of casual conversation and informal writing.

kids (instead of *children*)
sci-fi (instead of *science fiction*)
flunk (instead of *fail*)

**Slang words** are terms that are made up (such as *barf* or *zonked out*) or are given new definitions (such as *pot* for marijuana or *pig* for police officer) in order to be novel or unconventional. (Distinguishing between colloquialisms and slang is often difficult, and experts who are consulted when dictionaries are compiled do not always agree.)

| to dis (to show disrespect) | get your act together |
|---|---|
| bad (in the sense of very good) | in your face |
| chill (in the sense of calm down) | hit on |

**Regional words** (also called *localisms* or *provincialisms*) are words and phrases more commonly used in one geographic area than in another.

| pail | (or) | bucket | | | | |
|---|---|---|---|---|---|---|
| bag | (or) | sack | (or) | poke | (or) | tote |
| porch | (or) | verandah | | | | |
| seesaw | (or) | teeter-totter | (or) | teeterboard | | |

Although colloquialisms, slang, and regionalisms are not substandard or illiterate, most readers consider them inappropriate for formal academic writing. Colloquial language is acceptable for informal writing and dialogue, but slang may be unfamiliar to some readers. Slang terms are appropriate for very informal conversations among a group familiar with the current meanings of the terms. After a period of usage, many slang terms become outdated and disappear (for example, *the cat's pajamas, twenty-three skiddoo,* or *a real cool cat*), but some, such as *mob, dropout, fan, job,* and *phone,* have become accepted as standard usage.

Some writers are able to make use of an occasional colloquialism or slang term for effect when the writing is not highly formal.

The arts and humanities should be paid for by the private sector, not by government grants. Freedom of artistic expression is in danger when government has its paws where they should not be.

The National Park Service is fighting back at people who say it doesn't know beans about keeping up the ecological health of our national parks. To stand up for its recent actions, the service has sent out some reports that show its policies have had beneficial effects.

## Exercise 41.1: Dictionary Practice

*Look up the following colloquialisms and slang terms in two or three different dictionaries. What labels and usage suggestions are given for these terms?*

1. cop (meaning: "police officer")
2. hot potato (meaning: "something likely to cause trouble")
3. schlock (meaning: "something of poor quality")
4. cool it (meaning: "calm down")
5. buddy (meaning: "a friend")
6. split (meaning: "leave")
7. flaky (meaning: "eccentric, strange")
8. uptight (meaning: "very nervous")
9. chicken (meaning: "coward")
10. rip off (meaning: "steal")

## Exercise 41.2: Writing Practice

*List five slang words that you know. Use the words in sentences, and then rewrite the sentence using a standard word with the same definition.*

**Example:** gross out

**Slang:** He was so grossed out by the biology experiment that he was unable to finish.

**Revised:** He was so disgusted by the biology experiment that he was unable to finish.

# 41c Levels of Formality

The level of formality is the **tone** in writing; it reflects the attitude of the writer toward the subject and audience. The tone may be highly formal or very informal or somewhere in between.

**Informal tone** uses words and sentence constructions close to ordinary speech and may include slang, colloquialisms, and regionalisms. Like everyday speech, informal writing tends not to have the most precise word choices. It uses contractions; it uses first and second person pronouns such as *I* and *you* (see 17b); it uses verbs such as *get, is,* and *have,* and it may include sentence fragments for effect. An informal tone is used by speakers and writers for everyday communication and is appropriate in informal writing.

**Informal:** He was *sort of* irritated because he could*n't* find his car keys and did*n't* have *a whole lot of* time to get to his office.

**Medium tone** is not too casual, not too scholarly. It uses standard vocabulary, conventional sentence structures, and few or no contractions, and it is often the level you'll be expected to use for papers.

**Medium:** He was *somewhat* irritated because he could *not* find his car keys and did *not* have *much* time to get to his office.

**Formal tone** is scholarly and uses sophisticated, multisyllabic words in complex sentence structures not likely to be used when speaking. It often uses the third person pronouns *he or she* or *one* (see 17b) instead of *I* or *you*. Formal writing is preferred by some readers, but others find that it is not as easy to read or understand. Many businesses as well as government and other public offices encourage employees to maintain a medium level of formality.

4
W

**Formal:** Unable to locate his car keys and lacking sufficient time to find alternative transportation to his office, he was agitated.

In the following example the same information is presented at several levels of formality.

**Informal:** Someone who wants to have a bill passed in this state should start the process by getting it presented in the General Assembly or the Senate. The next thing that happens is that there's a committee that looks at it. The committee meets to decide on changing, accepting, or killing the bill. Usually, there's a lot of discussion when the bill comes back to the General Assembly and Senate. Both places have to okay the bill. If they don't like it, then a committee gets together with people from both the General Assembly and the Senate. They pound out a version that will make both houses happy. When the bill gets passed in both houses, it gets to move on to the governor. If the governor signs the bill or just doesn't do anything, it becomes a law. If the governor says no, it either dies or goes back to the Senate and General Assembly. It's got to get a two-thirds vote in both houses to become a law.

**Medium:** For a bill to become a law in this state, the first step is to have it introduced in the General Assembly or the Senate. Next, the bill is sent to a committee that holds hearings to change, approve, or kill the bill. When the bill returns to the General Assembly and Senate, there is often a great deal of debate before a vote is taken. If both houses do not pass the bill, a joint committee is appointed, with representatives from both the General Assembly and the Senate. This committee then draws up a bill that is acceptable to both houses. When both houses approve and pass the bill, it moves to the governor's office. For the bill to become a law, the governor can either sign it or take no action. The governor may, however, veto the bill. In this case, it either dies or goes back to both houses where it must pass with a two-thirds majority. If so, it then becomes a law, despite the governor's veto.

**1c**
**ds**

**Formal:** The procedure for passage of legislation in this state originates in either the General Assembly or the Senate. From here the bill is forwarded to a committee where hearings are initiated to determine whether the bill will be endorsed, altered, or terminated. From there, the bill returns to the General Assembly and Senate where extensive debate occurs before voting is completed. If the bill fails to pass both houses, a joint committee is charged with formulating a compromise bill acceptable to both the Senate and General Assembly. Approval by both houses results in advancing the bill to the governor; the bill will then become law with the governor's signature or with no action being taken in the governor's office. Should the governor reject the bill with a veto, it is either no longer viable or can be resuscitated through a two-thirds favorable vote in both houses, which then constitutes passage into law.

Once you set the level of formality in an essay, keep it consistent. Mixing levels can be distracting and indicates that the writer doesn't have adequate control (see 10c).

❖ The economist offered the business executives a lengthy explanation for

the recent fluctuation in the stock market. But it was ~~pretty~~ *quite* obvious from

their questions afterward that they ~~didn't get~~ *did not understand* it.

For an example of a paragraph with an inconsistent level of formality, see Exercise 41.3.

## Exercise 41.3: Proofreading Practice

*The following paragraph is intended to be written in a medium to formal tone, but the writer lost control and slipped into some inappropriate choices of informal words and phrases. Rewrite the paragraph so that the wording is consistently at a medium to formal level.*

To eliminate sexual harassment in the workplace, companies should come up with clearly defined guidelines that help you figure out which actions to avoid. Merely telling people not to engage in sexual harassment doesn't do much to illustrate things to cut out. Therefore, to sensitize their personnel, some companies hold seminars in which employees who have complaints act out unpleasant or demeaning stuff directed at them by their bosses or fellow workers. Seeing such actions portrayed often helps the offender recognize how insulting some act was, even if the offending person didn't mean it like that. Discussions that get going later also help people realize how their actions affect those they work with, and further definitions or memos often aren't needed.

## Exercise 41.4: Pattern Practice

*The tone of the following sentences can be changed by changing some of the key terms. If the sentence is informal, change it to a more formal tone. Similarly, if the sentence is formal, change it to a more informal tone. A sample sentence has been changed from formal to informal.*

**Original:** Scientists are issuing warnings that one procedure for alleviating the menace of global warming is to reduce carbon dioxide emissions.

**Informal Tone:** Scientists warn that one way to reduce the threat of global warming is to cut down on carbon dioxide exhaust.

1. A step in the right direction would be to lean on automobile makers and make them raise the fuel efficiency of the gas-guzzling cars they are turning out.
2. But an even quicker way to drop fuel use would be to hike the gas tax.
3. Environmentalists are also requesting stricter limitations on smokestack emissions of sulfur dioxide, a major contributor to acid rain.
4. But states now producing high-sulfur coal aren't happy about the damage this will do to their economies.

# 41d Jargon and Technical Terms

**Jargon** (also called **technical terms**) is the specialized language of various trades, professions, and groups, such as lawyers, plumbers, electricians, biologists, horse racers, and pharmacists. These terms are used by specialists within a group to communicate with each other in a concise way when referring to various complex concepts, objects, techniques, and so on. Jargon is also a negative term that refers to the use of unnecessarily inflated expressions, including euphemisms, which are terms used to disguise unpleasant realities.

**Specialized Language:** subcutaneous hemorrhage, metabolic disorders, carburetors, fuel injectors, exhaust manifolds

**Inflated Expressions:** learning facilitator (teacher)
monetary remuneration (pay)

**Euphemisms:** revenue enhancement (taxes)
pre-owned (used)
nonmilitary collateral damage (dead citizens)

When you are writing about a specialized subject for a general audience and need to use a technical term, define the term in easily understandable language the first time it is used. You can then use the word later on and not lose the reader.

One of the great challenges for the future is the development of superconductors, metallic ceramics that when cooled below a certain critical temperature offer no resistance to the flow of an electric current. Presently, research on superconductors has not resulted in any major breakthroughs.

Unnecessary jargon indicates the writer's inability to write clearly. Note the wordiness and pompous tone of this example:

**Original:** Utilize this receptacle, which functions as a repository for matter to be disposed of.

**Revised:** Deposit litter here.

# 41e General and Specific Words

**General words** refer to whole categories or large classes of items. **Specific words** identify items in a group.

*Tree* is more general than *maple*, and *maple* is more general than *sugar maple*, a particular kind of maple tree.

| General | Specific | More specific |
|---------|----------|---------------|
| animal | dog | cocker spaniel |
| plant | flower | rose |
| clothing | shoes | loafers |

Sometimes, a general word is adequate or appropriate for the occasion. For example, *car* is a more general word than *Ford*, and it is more appropriate in the following brief account of a trip:

This year we visited several parts of the country that we had not seen before. Last fall, we flew to New Mexico for a week, and during spring vacation we traveled by car from New York to Chicago.

General terms are appropriate in some contexts, but specific words are often better choices because they are more precise and vivid and can help the reader's imagination in seeing, hearing, feeling, and smelling what is described (if that is the writer's purpose). Compare these examples.

**General:** He walked across the street to see the merchandise in the store window.

**More Specific:** He ambled across Lexington Avenue to see the velvet ties in the window at Bloomingdale's.

**General:** To help our economy, America needs to sell more products on the world market.

**More Specific:** To decrease our trade deficit, American industries should develop their best high-tech products, such as high-resolution television and communications satellites, to sell to growing markets in China and Europe.

Some general words are too vague to convey a writer's meaning:

bad child    [Is the child rude? evil? ungrateful?]

bad food    [Is the food contaminated? tasteless? unhealthy?]

## Exercise 41.5: Pattern Practice

*Listed next are some general terms. What are more specific words that could be used instead?*

| General | Specific | More Specific |
|---------|----------|---------------|
| food | vegetable | carrot |

**1.** music
**2.** book
**3.** animal
**4.** clothes

**5.** field of study
**6.** machine
**7.** car
**8.** food

**9.** place of business
**10.** athlete

# 41f Concrete and Abstract Words

**Concrete words** refer to people and things that can be perceived by the senses. We are able to form images in our minds of concrete terms: the *thick white foam in the glass, dog, garden gate, smoke.*

**Abstract words** refer to qualities, concepts, conditions, and ideas: *truth, economics, slow, happy, ethical.*

We need both abstract terms to communicate complex ideas and concrete words to convey what we see, hear, taste, touch, and feel. However, dull writing tends to be unnecessarily abstract and overuses words such as *aspects, factors, and means.*

**Abstract:** Rain forest trees constitute more than 20 percent of the industrial world's consumption of wood. The harvest from rain forest trees is a valuable crop because of the trees' resistance to disease and insect infestations. In addition, because wood from these trees has special properties, they are useful for particular types of structures. Their characteristic colors and growth patterns make rain forest trees well suited for use in furniture and other wooden products where color is a prized commodity. Thus, in recent years, global demand for tropical hardwoods has increased dramatically.

**Concrete:** More than 20 percent of the wood used throughout the world is cut from rain forests. The trees from these forests are valued for their ability to resist termites, fungi, and other common diseases of wood. In addition, rain forest hardwoods have qualities that make them especially useful for certain purposes. For example, teak resists water damage, so it is used on sailboats. The dark reddish color and interesting grain of rosewood are particularly attractive when made into chairs, tables, and beds; dark brown or black ebony wood is used in billiard balls and for the black keys of pianos. Thus, in the last five years, countries throughout the world have ordered and imported more tropical wood than they used in the last fifty years.

## Exercise 41.6: Revision Practice

*The following description in a travel magazine has some abstract and general terms that could be revised to be more specific and concrete. Rewrite the paragraph so that it is more specific and concrete.*

Traveling to the Bahamas, a group of islands fifty miles across the water from the United States, is an easy trip for private boats. Since gambling is a popular sport, people go on weekends to gamble and to enjoy other sports. Tourism is the nation's leading industry, and Bahamian planners predict a sharp rise in the future. Because of this expectation, developers are building more housing of different types. Nassau, which has suffered from increased crime, is no longer the primary location for tourist development, but boats continue to stop there to let people look around.

# 41g Denotation and Connotation

The **denotation** of a word is the dictionary meaning, the definition. The **connotation** is the group of ideas implied but not directly indicated by the word. The connotation conveys attitudes and emotional overtones, either positive or negative, beyond the direct definition. Although connotations may vary among individuals, there is also a large group of shared connotations.

A pig is an animal (the denotation), but there are also negative connotations of sloppiness, dirt, and fat associated with pigs. *Elected official* and *politician* have similar denotative meanings, but *politician* has a negative connotation, whereas *elected official* connotes a more positive quality. While *fat, plump,* and *obese* describe the same condition, *fat* has a more negative connotation than *plump,* and *obese,* a medical term, is generally considered to be a more neutral term.

41
WC

## Exercise 41.7: Pattern Practice

*The following groups of words have similar denotative meanings, but their connotations differ. Arrange each group so that the words go from most positive to most negative.*

| Most Positive | Neutral | Most Negative |
|---|---|---|
| slender | lean | scrawny |

1. canine, mutt, puppy
2. law-enforcement officer, police officer, cop
3. cheap, inexpensive, economical
4. ornate, embellished, garish
5. counterfeit, replica, copy
6. scholar, egghead, intellectual

7. determined, stubborn, uncompromising
8. scared, apprehensive, paranoid
9. explanation, excuse, reason
10. gabby, talkative, chatty

# PART SEVEN

## RESEARCH AND DOCUMENTATION

Other parts of this book discuss writing processes, matters of grammar and mechanics, and document design. These are concerns for all writing. This part, however, addresses the special concerns of writing research papers and documenting your sources. The process of writing research papers begins with the selection of a topic and then the formulation of a research question about this topic you want to answer. To find your answer you need to search out and evaluate information from a variety of sources, then organize that information and integrate it into your own writing. You also need to document your sources so that you give appropriate credit to the work of others and so that your readers will be able to identify and locate these sources when they, in turn, research the topic and use your writing as one of their resources. You'll find help with all of these aspects of writing research papers in this part of the book.

# 42 Finding a Topic (top)

Finding a topic for a research paper is a four-step process:

1. **Find** a general subject that interests you.
2. **Narrow** that subject into a topic to fit the assignment.
3. **Formulate** a research question about your topic.
4. **Formulate** a thesis statement that answers your research question.

## 42a Finding a General Subject

If you are not assigned a specific topic for a research paper, you can begin by looking for information about any subject that interests you. This can be an opportunity to learn about some aspect of your major field, about future careers, or about another subject that interests you. Do some explorative thinking about your hobbies, about the world around you, about interesting topics that have come up in conversation, or about something you're studying in a course. For example, have you recently heard something interesting about organic food? Teaching animals to communicate? The rapid growth of the electronic industry? The history of jazz? Earthquake predictions? The future of car design? The technology boom? The confusing options in health care insurance? Pollution in the ocean? America's changing preferences in sports? Fossil findings? What news items do you read or hear on television that you'd like more background on?

One way to locate an interesting subject is to browse through any book or catalog of subject headings. For example, the *Library of Congress Subject Headings* or the *Reader's Guide to Periodical Literature* are thick volumes of headings and subheadings. Another way to locate a fresh subject is to skim through the table of contents of a magazine you read regularly or a magazine in your library's collection.

## 42b Narrowing the Subject

Once you've identified a general subject, you will need to narrow it into a topic that is more specific and manageable. How much time will you have to do the research? How long will the paper be? The answers to these questions will determine how much you have to narrow your topic. A topic you can spend six to eight weeks researching can be larger or more complex than one you only have two weeks to investigate. Similarly, if you are expected to write a twenty-page paper, you will be able to cover more about a topic than if you are expected to write an eight-page paper.

To narrow your topic, begin by thinking of it as a tree with many branches or a blanket covering many subtopics or smaller aspects. What are some of those subtopics? Choose one and think of some of the aspects of that subtopic that might be topics in themselves. For example, suppose you had decided on the topic of changing preferences in sports in America. That topic could branch into sports that have declined in popularity as well as other sports that are becoming national pastimes. If you choose sports that have become more popular, you could focus on one of these sports, such as soccer. Now, if you need to narrow your topic even further, you might subdivide it into categories, such as the growing popularity of soccer as a school sport or as a national spectator sport in America, and choose only one of those. As you search for information, you may find the need to narrow even further.

## 42c Formulating a Research Question

After you have located a general topic and narrowed it sufficiently, you need to formulate a question your research is going to answer. This process will lead to your thesis, but before you formulate a thesis, collect your information and see what you find. The research question will help you decide what information is relevant. Suppose you are writing about the benefits to your community for recycling paper, glass, and aluminum. What will your research question be? Are you interested in knowing whether the local government saves money by recycling? Or are you interested in the effect recycling might have on the cost of dumping garbage? Or are you interested in the community's support for this program? You can also ask yourself the reporter's *who, what, why, how,* and *when* questions. It may help to formulate a thesis, a statement that you think might be true but that might also change as you do your research.

## 42d Formulating a Thesis

42 to

After completing your research and reviewing your information, you will be able to formulate a tentative thesis or main point that is the result of your investigation. This main point will answer your research question and will make a statement about one aspect of the general topic you started with. It may need to be revised as you write and revise the paper. The thesis is more than a summary of the information, however. It states your position or the point that you are arguing and should synthesize and bring together the information into a unified whole that conveys what you, the knowledgeable writer, have learned.

| | |
|---|---|
| <u>Subject</u> | Alternative health treatments, such as herbal therapies |
| <u>Topic</u> | Herbal medicines |
| <u>Original research question</u> (too broad and had to be narrowed) | What are herbal medicines being used for? |
| <u>Revised research question</u> | What herbal remedies are investigators learning about that fight colds? |
| <u>Thesis</u> | Investigators are finding that elderberry root shows promise of reducing or eliminating the growth of flu viruses. |

# 43 Searching for Information (info)

The information gathered for a research paper can come from a wide variety of sources. Writers need strategies to locate useful information and must use good judgment in selecting the most appropriate sources.

## 43a Locating Sources of Information

The two categories of information are primary and secondary sources:

- **Primary sources** are original or firsthand materials. If you read a novel or a poem by an author, you are reading the original or primary source; if you read a study or review of that writing, you are reading secondary material *about* that work of fiction or poetry, not the work itself. Primary sources include writings by the original author, such as novels or autobiographies (but not, for example, biographies *about* that person); surveys, studies, speeches, or interviews that you conduct; any creative work by the original author (poems, plays, art forms such as pictures and sculpture, etc.); and firsthand accounts of events.

  Primary sources may be more accurate because they have not been distorted by others, though they are not always available and may be difficult to access. That is, you might not be able to view an older movie no longer publicly available and may have to settle for a secondhand report of it. But the secondhand report will be filtered through someone else's mind or viewpoint, so whenever possible, use primary sources.

- **Secondary sources** are secondhand accounts, information, or reports *about* primary sources. Typical secondary sources include reviews, biographies about a person you are studying, documentaries, encyclopedia articles, and other material interpreted or studied by others. Although reading secondary sources may save time, remember that they are interpretations or analyses that may be biased, inaccurate, or incomplete. Because real research does not depend solely on the analyses or evaluations done by others, use secondary sources to support your own thinking.

It's important to remember that the same source can be both a primary source in one field of research and a secondary source for another. For example, a biography about President Nixon would be a secondary source if you are researching some aspect of his life. But if you are researching public opinion and reactions to President Nixon, that biography would be a primary source.

> **ESL HINT:** While some cultures place more value on student writing that primarily brings together or collects the thoughts of great scholars or experts, readers of research papers in American institutions value the writer's own interpretations and thinking about the subject .

Finding information is an art, not a science. Just as a good fisherman learns where the best fishing spots are located, a skilled researcher learns where the best sources are, depending on the kinds of information being sought. Some information is best found in print sources located through the library or online, but it might be supplemented by information you gather from knowledgeable people around you. For example, if you're interested in health care for the elderly, there are a variety of articles in printed sources, but don't overlook local hospitals and nursing home administrators or local government agencies that are designed to provide such health care. Perhaps there is a faculty member at your school who does research in this area.

Start by building a working bibliography of materials to read, that is, an initial list of sources that seem promising, even though some will not turn out to be helpful and will be dropped before you put together your final list of works cited. Build the working bibliography by consulting a variety of sources in your library, by accessing online information on the Internet, by consulting resources in your own community, by communicating with people who can add to your knowledge about the topic, and by doing field research to collect firsthand information. (See 43b(1).)

## (1) Libraries

Before you begin searching, spend some time learning about your library—what its resources are, where they're located, and how they're used. Libraries have various printed guides for users and an information desk where helpful librarians will answer your questions. Library catalogs, which list all the library's materials by author, title, and subject, may be available on cards, microfiche, or computers. Many library online catalogs are also connected to thousands of other library catalogs so that you can locate materials in other libraries and ask for an interlibrary loan. Libraries have a variety of sources to help you begin with general or broad surveys of a topic. That will help you gain an overview and provide suggestions for further reading before you go on to more specific sources. Libraries also have collections of pamphlets and brochures, audio and video materials, and interlibrary loan services. (To document your sources, including those found on CD-ROM, videos, etc., see 45b and 46b.)

## General Reference Sources

The library's reference section has encyclopedias such as *The New Encyclopaedia Britannica* and the *Encyclopedia Americana,* as well as encyclopedias for specific areas of study such as the *Encyclopedia of Anthropology, Encyclopedia of Computer Science and Technology, Harvard Guide to American History,* or *The Oxford Companion to American Literature.* Librarians can show you where to locate such books and direct you to encyclopedias relevant to your topic. Other general sources include collections of biographies such as *Current Biography* or *African American Biographies,* yearbooks and almanacs such as the *World Almanac and Book of Facts,* dictionaries, atlases, and government publications such as *Statistical Abstract of the United States.*

## Indexes, Catalogs, and Databases

Your library will have book indexes such as *Books in Print* and periodical indexes such as the *Reader's Guide to Periodical Literature.* If the library's catalog is computerized, you can also do online searches of the library's holdings by author, title, key word, and subject heading. When you request a *key word search,* the search tool will look for the word in any part of the entry in the catalog (title, subtitle, abstract, etc.), while the *subject heading* has to match word for word with the Library of Congress headings (listed in the *Library of Congress Subject Headings*). When doing a key word search, you can also try synonyms for your topic or broader terms that might include it. For example, when searching for information about electric cars, you can also try "battery-operated cars" or "alternative energy sources" as key words.

Library collections of CD-ROM databases permit you to search a great variety of sources. Many libraries also subscribe to one or more computerized bibliographic utilities such as *FirstSearch* (which accesses databases such as academic journals, corporations, congressional publications, and medical journals) or *Newsbank CD News* (which indexes articles from a variety of newspapers). Nexis/Lexis, a commercial service available online, has abstracts and full texts of magazines, newspapers, publications from industry and government, wire services, and other sources.

## (2) Online Sources

The Internet, an online network of networks, is a vast storehouse of information that can be searched in a variety of ways. (To document sources found online, see 45c and 46c.) Source material on the Internet includes documents and archives of government agencies, public interest groups, newsgroups with their archives and FAQ (frequently asked questions) lists, online publications, texts of published materials, and databases provided by commercial servers such as America Online, CompuServe, and Prodigy. Gopher servers and the World Wide Web are available to browse the noncommercial contents of the Internet. One way to begin your search for source material on the Internet is to conduct topic, subject, or word searches in one or more of the more powerful Internet search programs, often called *search engines*. (See 43b(3).)

### Gopher Servers

If you have access to a Gopher server, you can link to other Gopher servers all over the world and check the print menus for repositories of information, library catalogs, news bulletins, and so on. When you find something of interest, you can read online or send a copy to yourself via E-mail.

The most powerful programs that search Gopher sites are Veronica and Archie, and there are instructions online for using these. After you type in a word or words that describe your interest, Veronica constructs a Gopher menu that lists all the items in its database with this term. You can then browse through the contents of items in the menu just as you would in any other Gopher menu.

### World Wide Web

Growing faster than Gopher servers, the World Wide Web connects sites that show documents with formatted texts, pictures, and sounds. You can view photographs of art collections in museums, learn about Japanese pottery, hear recordings of speeches and radio programs, read the latest CIA bulletins on various countries, view current weather maps, read the texts of bills being introduced in Congress, and so on. You can view material online and print out copies of relevant material.

Some of the most popular search engines on the World Wide Web are Excite, Yahoo, Lycos, Open Text Web Index, WebCrawler, InfoSeek, and Web Index. Yahoo also has an extensive subject guide so that you can browse in subject areas such as the arts, business, education, entertainment, government, health, news, and society and culture.

**HINT: Useful Addresses on the World Wide Web**

**Yahoo: http://www.yahoo.com/**

This very popular site has both a search capability and links to resources in numerous fields, such as the arts, business and economics (including job listings), computers, the Internet, education, entertainment, government, health, news, recreation, reference, regional studies, science, and social science.

These resources contain subcategories such as the following:

- Health: Includes links to material on medicine, drugs, disease, fitness, and so on.
- Science: Includes links to material on acoustics, anthropology, astronomy, biology, computer science, ecology, energy, environment, oceanography, psychology, space, and so on.
- Social science: Includes links to material on African American studies, Asian studies, economics, history, Latin American studies, urban studies, women's studies, and so on.

**Library of Congress:  http://lcweb.loc.gov/homepage/lchp.html**

This site has links to Library of Congress publications, online services, and federal legislation. The "Government, Congress, and Law" section of this site (http://lcweb.loc.gov/homepage/govt.html) can search for topics involving federal legislation, the judicial branch of the government, the military, state and local governments, and foreign and international governments.

**WWW Virtual Library:**
**http://www.w3.org/hypertext/DataSources/**
**bySubject/Overview.html**

This is a huge list with links set up under topics such as education, literature, and movies.

**Galaxy: http://www.einet.net/galaxy.html**

This site has links to items listed by topic. It is heavily used for searching the Internet by the terms you enter.

**Lycos: http://lycos.cs.cmu.edu/**

This is a very heavily used site at Carnegie Mellon University for searching the Internet by terms you enter.

**Open Text Web Index**:
**http://www.opentext.com:8080/omw/f-omw.html**

This site is primarily for searching the Internet by terms you enter.

**WebCrawler: http://www.webcrawler.com**

This is another site that is primarily for searching the Internet by terms you enter.

**3a**
**fo**

## (3) Community Sources

Your community has a variety of resources that can be tapped. If you are seeking public records or other local government information, your city hall or county courthouse can be a good place to search. Other sources of information are community service workers, social service agencies, schoolteachers and school administrators, community leaders, and religious leaders and religious institutions, as well as coordinators in nonprofit groups. The local newspaper is another storehouse of useful information. If there is a Chamber of Commerce or Visitors and Convention Bureau nearby, their lists of local organizations may be helpful. Or you can check the phone book or the local public library for lists of community resources and people to contact. Local history can be studied at a historical museum or the local library, and the newspaper may have useful archives. Don't forget your campus as part of your community; faculty or administrators can be good sources of information.

### (4) Interviews and Surveys

You can do field research and seek information firsthand by interviewing people, sending e-mail messages, conducting surveys, and taking notes on your own observations. These forms of information gathering need to be undertaken thoughtfully. You need to be sure that you ask good questions and that you know how to collect information without distorting it. You should always be aware of your own filtering of material. Use these methods carefully.

# 43b Using Search Strategies

To search efficiently through the sources you've found, begin by drawing up a systematic plan and a schedule for finding the materials you want. Ask yourself the following questions:

- *Given the deadline I have, how much time can I devote to searching for materials?* Remember that you'll need time for reading, note taking, and organizing your material as well as for writing drafts of the paper. Allow for delays in getting resources, especially if you are requesting materials through interlibrary loan.
- *How current do the materials need to be?* Periodicals have more current materials than books do.
- *Does the assignment specify how many or what types of sources I should consult?*

### (1) Starting a Working Bibliography

Build a working bibliography, a list of all the sources you will read. Since you may not use all of these sources in your paper, the final list of sources you used will be shorter than your working bibliography. Use the suggestions in 43c to help evaluate the sources as you decide which you will read.

Consider making each bibliographic entry on a separate 3″ × 5″ card so that you can easily insert new entries in alphabetical order. Or, if you are using a computer, construct your list in a separate file from the paper. You can use the printout when you are not near your computer, and you won't need to retype your list of works cited, though you'll need to delete the entries that didn't provide material for the paper.

In each entry, include all the information you'll need in your references list (see 45c and 46c) to locate the source. You'll save time later by determining now what documentation style you will be using (for example, MLA or APA) and putting all your working bibliography references in that style.

For books:

- Library call number (or other information needed to locate the entry)
- Names of authors, editors, translators
- Title and subtitle of the book
- Edition
- Publishing information (city, publishing company name, date)

---

*329.54*
*Re7*
*1989*
*(library call number)*

*Marbell, Jaime. Route 66: The First American Transcontinental*
　　*(author)*　　　　　　　　　*(title and subtitle)*

*Highway. Rev. ed. San Francisco: Berham, 1989.*
　*(edition)*　　　*(publishing information)*

---

**Sample bibliography card in MLA documentation style for a book**

For articles:

- Names of author(s)
- Title and subtitle of the article
- Title of magazine, journal, newspaper
- Volume and issue numbers, if needed
- Date and page numbers

---

*Yang, James, Thomas Udervek, and Kulma Mahtar. "Credit Card*
　　　　　　　　　　*(authors)*

*Security Systems for the Internet." Business Week*
　　*(article title)*　　　　　　　*(magazine title)*

*14 Feb. 1995: 90-96.*
*(date and page numbers)*

---

**Sample bibliography card in MLA documentation style for an article**

## (2) Finding Useful Terms

The subject headings in the *Library of Congress Subject Headings* can be useful in suggesting terms or key words to use as well as additional terms that might not have occurred to you. Under most entries are alternative terms listed as BT (broader topic), RT (related topic), and NT (narrower topic). For example, if you look up global warming, you will find as a broader topic "global temperature changes" and as related topics "greenhouse effect, atmospheric changes." These are alternative terms you can use as you search for sources. Also, many databases have a thesaurus of key words, and you can consult a print thesaurus for other options. As you read your sources, other synonyms or relevant key words may occur to you.

## (3) Using Search Engines

Computer searches for library catalogs, online databases, and Internet search engines vary in the way you can use them. Some permit only the entry of key words or terms, but in others you can indicate logical relationships between terms, using words such as *and*, *or*, and *not* to help you either broaden or narrow the search. The following examples in parentheses assume you are looking for material on teen alcoholism but not its relationship to teen crime:

| | | |
|---|---|---|
| **and** | Use this to get listings that include two items. | |
| | A **and** B | [alcoholism *and* teens] |
| **or** | Use this to find items containing either term. | |
| | A **or** B | [teens *or* juveniles] |
| **not** | Use this to eliminate irrelevant items. | |
| | A **not** B | [alcoholism *not* crime] |
| **and not** | Use this to combine some related topics and eliminate others. | |
| | A **and** B **not** C | [teens *and* alcohol *not* drugs] |
| * | Use this to include various forms of a word. | |
| | alcohol* | [listing will include alcohol, alcoholism, alcoholics, etc.] |

# 43c Evaluating Information

As you search for information, you will have to select which sources you will locate and read, and after reading them, you will need to select which are appropriate to include in your paper. Consider the following criteria when you evaluate sources:

- **Relevance** How closely related is the material to your topic? Is it really relevant or merely related material? Too general? Too specific? Too technical? Too superficial?

- **Reliability** Is the source that includes the material generally trusted by the public? The *New York Times* is considered to be a credible newspaper, but the tabloids near the supermarket checkout lanes are not considered to be credible.

  Does the source undergo a review process or some check on what is included? For example, an article in a scholarly journal has been reviewed by knowledgeable people in the field. But the Internet is full of both useful information and misinformation because anyone can post material for public consumption. If someone posts to a newsgroup about a new flu epidemic, that person may be passing along personal perceptions or rumor. A report by the Centers for Disease Control and Prevention (also available on the Internet) is far more likely to be credible.

  Is the author an expert? What are that person's credentials for being considered knowledgeable about the subject? What is the author's professional affiliation? Is that person associated with an educational institution or some other place likely to employ reliable people? (Biographical indexes may help you establish an author's credibility.)
- **Timeliness** Is the information current or outdated? How necessary is timeliness for your topic?
- **Availability** Is the material easy to access? Will you be able to read it without delaying your work schedule?
- **Objectivity** Does the author or source have a bias or disregard for opposing views? Does the author or source have a point of view to promote? If you are reading an article in a magazine, look at the other articles in that issue. Do they seem to promote a particular viewpoint or perspective? This warning does not mean that you should disregard opposing views, only that you should be aware of the perspective or filter through which writers view their topics and the effects of this attitude on the reasons or arguments offered for proposing a viewpoint.
- **Quantity** Is the amount of material more than you can read in the given amount of time? A three-volume study of Arctic weather is probably more than you have time to read. Is the material so brief that it is not likely to be helpful? A half-page story in a newsmagazine on someone's trip to the Arctic to measure climate changes is probably not going to offer much helpful information.

# 44 Taking Notes (note)

## 44a Writing Notecards

When you've decided a source is likely to be useful, you can record information on notecards, using either 3″ × 5″ or 4″ × 6″ cards, to summarize (see 44b), paraphrase (see 44c), or record a quotation (see 44d). Use parentheses to include your own comments on the significance of a source and to record your thoughts as to how you can use this source in your paper. It is best to limit each notecard to one short aspect of a topic so that you can reorder the cards later as you organize the whole project. One way to limit the notecard is to decide what the heading or subheading for this notecard will be. You can use the headings and subheadings of your outline, and as you take more notes, new subheadings may occur to you.

For each notecard, record the last name of the author in the upper right-hand corner with a shortened form of the title. The heading for the card's topic can be written in the upper left-hand corner. As you write information on the card, include the exact page reference. If the note refers to more than one page in your source, indicate where the new page starts. For quotations, be sure that you've copied the original exactly. For short research projects, you can photocopy some material and highlight or write notes in the margin. Or you can type notes into a computer as you read and then print out your notes for reordering.

For information on how to document your sources for summaries, paraphrases, and quotations, see Chapters 45 and 46.

# 44b Summarizing

A **summary** is a brief restatement of the main ideas in a source, using your own words.

As you write, include summaries of other people's writing when you refer to the main idea but do not wish to quote that person. Good reasons for using summaries are that the source has unnecessary detail, that the writer's phrasing is not particularly memorable or worth quoting, or that you want to keep your writing concise. When you include a summary, you need to cite the source to give credit to the writer. (See Chapters 45 and 46 for information on how to cite your sources and 44e on avoiding plagiarism.) Unlike paraphrases (see 44c), summaries are shorter than the original source. They include only the main points and do not follow the organization of the source.

---

**HINT: Characteristics of Summaries**
- Summaries are written in your own words, not those of your source.
- Summaries include only the main points, omitting details, facts, examples, illustrations, direct quotations, and other specifics.
- Summaries use fewer words than the source being summarized.
- Summaries do not follow the organization of the source.
- Summaries are objective and do not include your own interpretation or reflect your slant on the material.

To write a summary, follow these steps:

- Read the original source carefully and thoughtfully.
- After the first reading, ask yourself what the author's major point is.
- Go back and reread the source, making a few notes in the margin.
- Look away from your source, and then, like a newscaster, panelist, or speaker reporting to a group, finish the sentence: "This person is saying that. . . ."
- Write down what you've just said.
- Go back and reread both the source and your notes in the margins to check that you've correctly remembered and included the main points.
- Revise your summary as needed.

### *Original Source:*

> As human beings have populated the lands of the earth, we have pushed out other forms of life. It seemed to some that our impact must stop at the ocean's edge, but that has not proved to be so. By overharvesting the living bounty of the sea and by flushing the wastes and by-products of our societies from the land into the ocean, we have managed to impoverish, if not destroy, living ecosystems there as well.

(Thorne-Miller, Boyce, and John G. Catena. *The Living Ocean: Understanding and Protecting Marine Biodiversity.* Washington: Island, 1991. 3–4.)

---

*Thorne-Miller, "Living Ocean"*

*People have destroyed numerous forms of life on land and are now doing the same with the oceans. Overfishing and dumping waste products into the waters have brought about the destruction of various forms of ocean life. (pp. 3–4)*

---

**Summary on a notecard**

# 44c Paraphrasing

A **paraphrase** restates information from a source, using your own words.

---

**HINT: Characteristics of Paraphrases**
- Paraphrases have approximately the same number of words as the source. (A summary, conversely, is much shorter.)
- Paraphrases use your own words, not those of the source.
- Paraphrases keep the same organization as the source.

- Paraphrases are more detailed than a summary.
- Paraphrases are objective and do not include your own interpretation or slant on the material.

Unlike summaries (see 44b), paraphrases are approximately the same
length as the source. They keep the same organization and are more detailed than a summary.

To write a paraphrase, follow these steps:

- Read the original passage as many times as is needed to understand
  its full meaning.
- As you read, take notes, using your own words, if that helps.
- Put the original source aside and write a draft of your paraphrase, using your notes if needed.
- Check your version against the original source by rereading the original to be sure you've included all the ideas and followed the same
  organization as the source.
- If you find a phrase worth quoting in your own writing, use quotation
  marks in the paraphrase to identify your borrowing, and note the
  page number.

### Original Source:

The automobile once promised a dazzling world of speed, freedom, and
convenience, magically conveying people wherever the road would take
them. Given these alluring qualities, it is not surprising that people around
the world enthusiastically embraced the dream of car ownership. But societies that have built their transport systems around the automobile are now
waking up to a much harsher reality. The problems created by overreliance
on the car are outweighing its benefits.

(Lowe, Marcia D. "Rethinking Urban Transport." *State of the World 1991.* New
York: Norton, 1991. 56.)

---

*Lowe, "Rethinking"*

*Automobiles, which offered swift, easy, and independent trans-
portation, allowed people to travel wherever there were roads.
Owning a car became everyone's dream, a result that is not surprising, given the benefits of car travel. Nations built their transportation systems on the car, but despite its advantages, societies
that rely heavily on cars are beginning to recognize that they cause
severe problems as well. Heavy dependence on automobiles creates
problems that offset their advantages (p. 56).*

**Paraphrase on a notecard**

## Exercise 44.1: Writing Practice

*A. To practice summarizing and paraphrasing, rewrite both of the following quotations, first as a summary of the contents and then as a paraphrase. These quotations are not from any real source, but when you cite them in the second part of this exercise, create a fictitious source to cite.*

1. The National Rifle Association (NRA), which was founded in 1871 to teach safety and marksmanship to gun owners, has become the nation's most powerful lobbying group in the bitter fight against gun-control laws. Arguing that the Second Amendment to the Constitution guarantees the rights of citizens to own guns, the NRA promotes people's right to protect themselves and their property. Most gun owners, claims the NRA, are law-abiding people who use guns for sport or for self-defense. While the NRA acknowledges the widespread use of guns by criminals and the ever-increasing numbers of innocent children killed by guns, NRA officials also point out that criminals are the ones who kill, not guns. Stricter laws and law enforcement, argues the NRA, can reduce crime, not gun-control laws. No matter how strict the laws become for the purchase of guns, those bent on illegally owning a gun can find ways to get one if they have the money.

2. Gun-control supporters, who lobby for stricter ownership laws and against the National Rifle Association (NRA), argue that guns are not useful for self-defense and do not inhibit crime. Various groups calling for stronger legislation against gun ownership point out that guns promote killing. When a gun is present, they note, the level of violence can increase rapidly. Research shows that a gun kept for protection is far more likely to be used to kill someone the gun owner knows than to be used to kill a thief. Moreover, guns in the home result in accidents in which children are killed. Opponents of the NRA answer the charge that they are ignoring the Second Amendment by citing the First Amendment, which guarantees the right to hold public meetings and parades. Although Americans have the right to hold parades, they point out, people have to get a permit to do so, and gun permits are no more of an infringement on the rights of Americans than are parade permits.

*B. To practice incorporating summaries and paraphrases into your own writing, write a paragraph either for or against stronger gun-control laws, and make use of the sources you have just summarized and paraphrased. Remember to cite the made-up source you create. For help with citing sources, see 44d.*

# 44d Quoting

A **quotation** is the record of the exact words of a written or spoken source and is set off by quotation marks. All quotations should have an accompanying citation to the source of the quotation.

Follow these guidelines for using quotations effectively:

- Use quotations as evidence, as support, or as further explanation of what you have written. Quotations are not substitutes for stating your point in your own words.
- Use quotations sparingly. Too many quotations strung together with very little of your own writing makes a paper look like a scrapbook of pasted-together sources, not a thoughtful integration of what is known about a subject. (See 44f on integrating your sources into your writing.)
- Use quotations that illustrate the author's own viewpoint or style, or quote excerpts that would not be as effective if rewritten in different words. Effective quotations are succinct or particularly well phrased.
- Introduce quotations with words that signal the relationship of the quotation to the rest of your discussion (see 44f).

> **HINT: When should you quote a source?**
> - Quote when the writer's words are especially vivid, memorable, or expressive.
> - Quote when an expert explains so clearly and concisely that a paraphrase would be less clear and would contain more words.
> - Quote when the words the source uses are important to the discussion.

### Original Source 1:

When asked to comment on the recent investigations of government fraud, Senator Smith said to a *New York Times* reporter, "Their ability to undermine our economy is exceeded only by their stupidity in thinking that they wouldn't get caught."

("Fraud Hearings." *New York Times* 18 Nov. 1995, late ed.: A4.)

[This statement is worth quoting because restating it in different words would probably take more words and have less punch.]

### Original Source 2:

When asked in a televsion interview to comment on the recent investigations of government fraud, Senator Smith said "These huge payments for materials that should have cost less will now cost the government money because they will increase our budget deficit more than we anticipated."

(Smith, Saul. Interview with Nina Totenberg. *Nightline*. ABC. WILI, Chicago. 23 Nov. 1995.)

[This statement is a good candidate for paraphrasing, with a reference to Senator Smith, because the statement is not particularly concise, well phrased, or characteristic of a particular person's way of saying something.]

### *Paraphrase of Source 2 (using the same source):*

During a televised interview Senator Smith responded to a question about investigations of government fraud by noting that overpayments on materials will cause an unexpected increase in the budget deficit.

## (1) Types of Quotations

### Quoting Prose

If your quotation is no more than four lines (either handwritten or typed), include the quotation in your paragraph and use quotation marks (see 30a).

During the summer of 1974, at a crucial stage of development in the Apollo program, national interest in NASA was sharply diverted by the Watergate affair. As Joseph Trento, an investigative reporter, explains in his book on the Apollo program: "The nation was sitting on the edge of its collective seat wondering if Richard Nixon would leave us in peace or pull the whole system down with him" (142).

(Trento, Joseph. *Prescription for Disaster*. New York: Crown, 1987.)

If the quotation is more than four handwritten or typed lines, set it off by indenting ten spaces from the left margin. Double-space the quotation, and do not use quotation marks. If the first line of the quotation is the beginning of the paragraph in the source, indent that line an additional five spaces.

In his book on the Apollo and space shuttle programs, Joseph Trento reports on the final mission in the Apollo program:

The last mission involving the Apollo hardware nearly ended in tragedy for the American crew. After reentry the crew opened a pressure release valve to equalize the command module atmosphere with the earth's atmosphere. But the reaction control rockets failed to shut down and deadly nitrogen tetroxide oxydizer gas entered the cabin's breathing air. The crew survived the incident, but some at Houston and in Washington wondered if the layoff from manned flight hadn't put the crew at risk. (144)

(Trento, Joseph. *Prescription for Disaster.* New York: Crown, 1987.)

**Quoting Poetry**

If you are quoting a line of poetry, see 30a(2).

**Quoting Dialogue**

If you are quoting the speech of two or more people who are talking, see 30a(3).

## (2) Capitalization of Quotations

Capitalize the first word of directly quoted speech in the following situations:

- When the first quoted word begins a sentence

  She said, "He likes to talk about football, especially when the Super Bowl is coming up."

- When the first word in the dialogue is a fragment

  "He likes to talk about football," she said. "Especially when the Super Bowl is coming up."

Do not capitalize quoted speech in the following situations:

- When the first quoted word is not the beginning of a sentence

  She said that he likes talking about football, "especially when the Super Bowl is coming up."

- When the quotation is interrupted and then continues on in the same sentence

  "He likes to talk about football," she said, "especially when the Super Bowl is coming up."

## (3) Punctuation of Quotations

### Commas

When you introduce quotations, use the comma to set off less formal expressions such as *he said, she asked,* or *Brady stated.*

  As R. F. Notel explains, "The gestures people use to greet each other differ greatly from one culture to another."

But when the quotation follows *that,* do not use a comma and do not capitalize the first letter of the first word in the quotation.

> The public relations director noted that "newsletters to alumni are the best source of good publicity—and donations."

## Colon

Use the colon to introduce formal quotations and quotations that have two or more sentences.

> The selection of juries has become a very complex and closely researched process: "In addition to employing social scientists, some lawyers now practice beforehand with 'shadow juries,' groups of twelve people demographically similar to an actual jury."

## End Punctuation

Put periods before the second quotation mark. If the quotation has an exclamation mark or question mark, include that before the second quotation mark. But if the exclamation mark or question mark is part of the sentence but not the quotation, put the mark after the second quotation mark.

> The stage director issued his usual command to the actor: "Work with me!"

> Did she really say "I quit"?

## Brackets

Occasionally, you may need to add some information within a quotation, insert words to make the quotation fit your sentence, or indicate with *sic* that you are quoting your source exactly even though you recognize an error there. When you insert any words within the quotation, set off your words with brackets. (See 33d for more on brackets.)

> "During President Carter's administration, Press [Frank Press, Carter's science adviser] indicated his strong bias against funding applied research."

## Ellipsis (for omitted words)

When you omit words from a quotation, use an ellipsis (three spaced dots) to indicate that material has been left out. (See 33e for more information on ellipsis.)

### *Original Source:*

> "Contributing editors are people whose names are listed on the masthead of a magazine, but who are usually not on the staff. Basically, they're freelance writers with a good track record of producing ideas and articles prolifically."

*Use of Quotation:*

> Not all the names listed on the masthead of a magazine are regular staff members. Some are "freelance writers [who have] . . . a good track record of producing ideas and articles prolifically."

## Single Quotation Marks

When you are enclosing a quotation within a quotation, use a single quotation mark (the apostrophe mark on a typewriter).

> In his book on the history of the atomic bomb, Richard Rhodes describes Enrico Fermi, one of the creators of the first atomic bomb, as he stood at his window in the physics tower at Columbia University and gazed out over New York City: "He cupped his hands as if he were holding a ball. 'A little bomb like that,' he said simply, for once not lightly, 'and it would all disappear' " (275).

(Rhodes, Richard. *The Making of the Atomic Bomb.* New York, Simon, 1986.)

(For more information on the use of punctuation with quotation marks, see 30d.)

# 44e Avoiding Plagiarism

**Plagiarism** results when writers fail to document a source so that the words and ideas of someone else are presented as the writer's own work.

## (1) Information that Requires Documentation

When we use the ideas, findings, data, conclusions, arguments, and words of others, we need to acknowledge that we are borrowing their work and inserting it in our own by documenting it. Consciously or unconsciously passing off the work of others as our own results in the very serious form of stealing known as plagiarism, an act that can cause the writer to fail a course or even be expelled from a school. Summarizing or paraphrasing that follows the wording of a source too closely is one form of unconscious plagiarism; depending too heavily on quotations from a source is another form of plagiarism.

> **ESL HINT:** In some cultures educated writers are expected to know and incorporate the thinking of great scholars, and it may be considered an insult to the reader to mention the names of scholars, implying that the reader is not acquainted with these scholarly works. However, in American writing this is not the case, and writers are always expected to acknowledge their sources and give public credit to the appropriate person or group.

## (2) Information that Does Not Require Documentation

Common knowledge, that body of general ideas we share with our readers, does not have to be documented. Common knowledge consists of standard information on a subject that people know, information that is widely shared and can be found in numerous sources without reference to any source. For example, if your audience is American educators, it is common knowledge among this group that American schoolchildren are not well acquainted with geography. However, if you cite test results proving the extent of the problem or use the words and ideas of a knowledgeable person about the causes of the problem, that is not common knowledge and needs documentation. Similarly, it is common knowledge among most Americans aware of current energy problems that solar power is one answer to future energy needs. But forecasts about how widely solar power may be used twenty years from now would be the work of some person or group studying the subject, and documentation would be needed. Common knowledge also consists of facts widely available in a variety of standard reference books. Field research you conduct also does not need to be documented, though you should indicate that you are reporting your own findings.

---

**HINT:** To avoid plagiarism, read over your paper and ask yourself whether your readers can properly identify which ideas and words are yours and which are from the sources you cite. If that is clear, if you have not let your paper become merely a string of quotations from sources, and if the paper predominantly reflects your words, phrases, and integration of ideas, then you are not plagiarizing.

---

### Original Source:

One of the most obvious—and most important—approaches to saving rainforests is to protect them in national parks, the same way that industrialized nations such as the United States and Canada safeguard their tropical wonders. Yet so far fewer than 5% of the world's tropical forests are included in parks or other kinds of protected areas. Most of the developing countries that house these forests simply do not have enough money to buy land and set up park systems. And many of the nations that do establish parks are then unable to pay park rangers to protect the land. These unprotected parks routinely are invaded by poor, local people who desperately need the forest's wood, food, land, or products to sell. The areas are often called 'paper parks' because they exist on paper but not in reality (105–106).

(Tangley, Laura. *The Rainforest: Earth at Risk.* New York: Chelsea, 1992.)

*Accidental Plagiarism:*

[In this paragraph the words, phrases, and ideas from the original source are underlined. Note how much of this paraphrase comes from the original source and how the author has neglected to signal to the reader that this material comes from another source.]

The problem of saving the world's rainforests has become a matter of great public concern. There are a number of solutions being offered, <u>but the most obvious and most important approach is to protect them in national parks</u>. This is <u>the same way that industrialized nations such as the United States and Canada safeguard their natural wonders</u>. In poorer nations this does not work because they <u>do not have enough money to buy land and set up park systems</u>. What happens is that when they don't have money, <u>they are unable to pay park rangers to protect the land</u>. Without any protection from rangers, poor people come in and invade because they <u>desperately need the forest's wood, food, land, or products to sell</u>. These parks then don't really exist as parks.

*Acceptable Paraphrase:*

The problem of saving the world's rain forests has become a matter of great public concern. Of the approaches being considered, Laura Tangley, in *The Rainforest,* considers one of the most important solutions to be turning rainforests into national parks. Tangley points out, however, that this is only a solution for industrialized nations such as the United States and Canada because they have the funding to keep national parks protected from poachers. In developing nations which cannot afford park rangers, the local populations are not prevented from taking wood, food, land, or forest products that they can sell. Tangley states that such forests, because they are not protected from human destruction, "exist on paper but not in reality" (105–06).

## Exercise 44.2: Writing Practice

*To practice citing sources and avoiding plagiarism, add citations in MLA format to the following paragraph, which incorporates material from the two sources listed here. For information on parenthetical references and citations in MLA format, see 45a and 45b.*

**A.** The quotations included here are from the following source:
Lowe, Marcia D. "Rethinking Urban Transport." *State of the World 1991.* New York: Norton, 1991.

- "Cities with streets designed for cars instead of people are increasingly unlivable" (56).
- "Traffic congestion, now a fact of life in major cities, has stretched daily rush hours to 12 hours or longer in Seoul and 14 in Rio de

Janeiro. In 1989, London traffic broke a record with a 53-kilometer backup of cars at a near standstill" (57).

- "Roaring engines and blaring horns cause distress and hypertension, as in downtown Cairo, where noise levels are 10 times the limit set by health and safety standards" (57).

**B.** The quotations here are from the following source:

Lipperman, Irwin. *Planning for a Livable Tomorrow.* New York: Nathanson, 1992.

- "City space is rapidly being eaten up by automobiles. Parking in a city center can use up to 20 or 30% of the available space, and suburban malls often have parking lots bigger than the malls themselves" (99).
- "Automobile pollutants in the air inhaled by urbanites increase the likelihood of lung disorders and make bronchial problems more severe, especially among the elderly" (108).

*The following paragraph is part of a research paper on the topic of city planning:*

Another important concern in city planning is to formulate proposals to eliminate or reduce problems caused by automobiles. Cities with streets designed for cars instead of people are increasingly unlivable, for cars cause congestion, pollution, and noise. Providing more public transportation can reduce these problems, but it is not likely that city dwellers will give up owning cars. Therefore, solutions are needed for parking, which already uses up as much as 20 to 30 percent of the space available in downtown areas, and for rush hour traffic, which now extends to more than twelve hours in Seoul and to fourteen hours in Rio de Janeiro. Pollution, another urban problem caused partly by cars, needs to be controlled. Automobile emissions cause lung disorders and aggravate bronchial problems. In addition, noise from automobiles must be curbed. Noise has already become a health problem in cities such as Cairo, where noise levels are already ten times the acceptable standard for human health.

# 44f Integrating Quotations

As you include summaries, paraphrases, and quotations in your own writing, you need to integrate them smoothly so that there is not a sudden jump or break between the flow of your words and the source material. Use the following strategies to prepare your reader and to create a smooth transition into the inserted material:

- **Use signal phrases.** Signal phrases are words that let the reader know a quotation will follow. The phrase you choose should be appropriate to the quotation and its relationship to the ideas being discussed. The following list includes common signal words:

| | | |
|---|---|---|
| according to | condemns | observes |
| acknowledges | considers | points out |
| adds | contends | predicts |

| admits | denies | proposes |
| agrees | describes | rejects |
| argues | disagrees | reports |
| as (name) explains | emphasizes | responds |
| asks | explains | reveals |
| asserts | finds | says |
| believes | has found that | shows |
| claims | holds that | speculates |
| comments | illustrates | suggests |
| complains | insists | thinks |
| concedes | maintains | warns |
| concludes | notes | writes |

### *Examples:*

Although it is hard to predict the future of the toy industry, Robert Lillo, a senior analyist at The American Economics Institute, warns that "the bottom may fall out of the electronic game industry as CD-ROMs gobble up that market with cheaper, more elaborate products with better graphics" (21).

(Lillo, Robert. "The Electronic Industry Braces for Hard Times." *Business Weekly* 14 Feb. 1996: 18–23.)

In 1990 when the United Nations International Human Rights Commission predicted "there will be an outburst of major violations of human rights in Yugoslavia within the next few years" (14), few people in Europe or the United States paid attention to the warning.

(United Nations. International Human Rights Commission. *The Future of Human Rights in Eastern Europe.* New York: United Nations, 1990.)

- **Explain the connection.** Always explain the connection between a quotation you use and the point you are making. Show the logical link, or add a follow-up comment that integrates the quotation into your paragraph.

### *Quotation not integrated into the paragraph:*

Modern farming techniques are different from those used twenty years ago. John Hession, an Iowa soybean grower, says, "Without a computer program to plan my crop allotments or to record my expenses, I'd be back in the dark ages of guessing what to do." New computer software programs are being developed commercially and are selling well.

(Hession, John. Personal interview. 27 July 1995.)

[The quotation here is abruptly dropped into the paragraph, without an introduction and without a clear indication from the writer as to how Mr. Hession's statement fits into the ideas being discussed.]

### Revised:

Modern farming techniques differ from those of twenty years ago, particularly in the use of computer programs for planning and budgeting. John Hession, an Iowa soybean grower who relies heavily on computers, explains, "Without a computer program to plan my crop allotments or to record my expenses, I'd be back in the dark ages of guessing what to do." Commercial software programs such as those used by Mr. Hession, for crop allotments and budgeting, are being developed and are selling well.

[This revision explains how Mr. Hession's statement confirms the point being made.]

## Exercise 44.3: Writing Practice

*Assume that you are writing a paper on the topics listed here and want to quote from the source given for each topic. Using the information in 44d, write a paragraph that quotes the source directly. Include some summarizing and paraphrasing (see 44b and 44c).*

1. Possible topics: The history of racing cars, aerodynamics in car design, famous old racing cars

> In the Fifties, Grand Prix teams like Vanwall, Mercedes and Maserati experimented with wind-cheating bodywork, but abandoned the endeavor. Racing teams then didn't have the resources to study the entire aero package—lift, drag, driver cooling, etc.—and there were tragic reminders, such as Bernd Rosemeyer's death in an Auto Union record car, that the black art could also be deadly.
> Ettore Bugatti had made an early unsuccessful attempt at racing car aerodynamics with "Tank" bodies on Type 32s in 1923. But there was another Bugatti Tank, built in the next decade, that became an example of how effective an aero body could be. In 1937 a supercharged Bugatti Type 57 with an all-enveloping body was driven by those two wonderful French drivers Robert Benoist and Jean-Pierre Wimille in the 24 hours of Le Mans. The car won the race at an average 85.13 mph, nearly 4 mph better than the old record. It was the first to travel more than 2000 miles during the 24-hour event (126).

(Hill, Phil. "Salon: Bugatti 57G." *Road and Track* July 1987: 126–32.)

2. Possible topics: George Gershwin, American musicals, history of musical theater, popular music

> Among the songwriters Americans love best Gershwin ranks very high. His success went beyond the realm of popular music, however, to the concert hall and opera house, and he may well be the greatest composer the United States has ever produced.
> The best of his so-called serious works—*Rhapsody in Blue, An American in Paris,* and *Porgy and Bess*—have grown in stature since

his death, as have such songs as "Embraceable You," "The Man I Love," and "Fascinating Rhythm." Writing of his songs in the book *The Gershwin Years,* Edward Jablonski and Robert D. Lawrence said: "Each year since 1937 we hear them more delightedly and gratefully than ever before—ever discovering in them a resilient charm, a durable brilliance, a permanent beauty" (63).

(Livingstone, William, "Gershwin." *Stereo Review* Aug. 1987: 63–66.)

**3.** Possible topics: Coping at college, verbal self-defense

Sometimes, in spite of all your best intentions, you find yourself in a situation where you have really fouled it up. You are 100 percent in the wrong, you have no excuse for what you've done, and disaster approaches. Let us say, for example, that you enrolled in a class, went to it three or four times, did none of the work, forgot to drop it before the deadline, and are going to flunk. Or let's say that you challenged an instructor on some information and got nowhere trying to convince him or her that you were right; then you talked to a counselor, who got nowhere trying to convince you that you were wrong; next you spent quite a lot of time doing your duty to the other students in the class by telling them individually that the instructor is completely confused; and how, much too late, you have discovered that it is you who are in error. Either of these will do as a standard example of impending academic doom.

In such a case, there's only one thing you can do, and you're not going to like it. Go to the instructor's office hour, sit down, and level. Say that you are there because you've done whatever ridiculous thing you have done, that you already know you have no excuse for it, and that you have come in to clear it up as best you can. Do not rationalize; do not talk about how this would never have happened if it hadn't been for some other instructor's behavior; do not mention something the instructor you are talking to should have done to ward this off; do not, in other words, try to spread your guilt around. Level and be done with it (260–61).

(Elgin, Suzette Haden. *The Gentle Art of Verbal Self-Defense.* New York: Dorset, 1988.)

# 45 Documenting in MLA Style (MLA)

**Modern Language Association (MLA)** format is used to document papers in the arts and humanities.

As you research your topic, you will be building on the work of others. Your work can, in turn, contribute to the pool of knowledge about the topic for others who will read and depend on your research. The process of documentation requires that you acknowledge those whose work you have summarized, paraphrased, and quoted in your research paper so that readers of your work can find the sources you have used.

Documentation formats can vary, depending on the field of study. For research papers in the arts and humanities, use the format of the Modern Language Association (MLA):

```
Gibaldi, Joseph. MLA Handbook for Writers of

          Research Papers. 4th ed. New York: MLA, 1995.
```

For the social sciences, use the format of the American Psychological Association (APA) (see Chapter 46):

```
American Psychological Association (1994).

          Publication manual of the American Psychological

          Association. 4th ed. Washington, D.C.: Author.
```

The MLA and APA styles are explained here, and your library will have manuals for other fields as well. For example, two other widely used formats are found in the *CBE Style Manual: A Guide for Authors, Editors, and Publishers in the Biological Sciences* (6th ed., Bethesda: Council of Biology Editors, 1983) and *The Chicago Manual of Style* (14th ed., Chicago: University of Chicago Press, 1993). Newspapers and other publishing companies, businesses, and large organizations often have their own formats, which are explained in their own style manuals.

Some of the major features of MLA style are as follows:

- In in-text citations, give the author's last name and the page number of the source, preferably within the sentence rather than after it.
- Use full first and last names and middle initials of authors.
- Capitalize all major words in titles, and underline titles or put them in italics. Enclose article titles in quotation marks.
- In a list of works cited at the end of the paper, give full publication information, alphabetized by author.

When you document sources using MLA format, there are three aspects to consider:

- **In-text citations**
  In your paper you need parenthetical references to your sources to acknowledge wherever you use the words, ideas, and facts you've taken from your sources.
- **Endnotes**
  If you need to add material that would disrupt your paper if it were included in the text, include such notes at the end of the paper.
- **Works cited**
  At the end of your paper, include a list of the sources from which you have quoted, summarized, or paraphrased.

**Example of MLA format**

In the late 1950s the United States plunged
enthusiastically into the exploration of space.
After years of real successes, though, it all
slowed down. The reason for the failure of the
grand dream, says Kevin Doobe, a design engineer
for the National Aeronautics and Space
Administration (NASA), was that "the exorbitant
bills drained our budgets and cooled our
excitement" (42). But space technology will
continue to be developed for practical purposes,
and the projects will be greatly scaled down to
fit smaller budgets (Dyson 36).

Industry planners interested in bidding for
government contracts for these future projects
have turned to a variety of sources and are
coming up with answers as to where the
technology is heading. Freeman Dyson, professor
of physics at the Institute for Advanced Study
in Princeton, New Jersey, notes that presently
enough is known about the laws of physics to
set limits about what can and cannot be
accomplished with the technology we have for
space exploration. He concludes that solar-
electric propulsion will be the cheapest, most
efficient way to power equipment in space

*continued on next page*

*continued from previous page*

("21st-Century" 116). A United States

Department of Energy report notes that solar

sails are also worth investigating because,

although not as efficient as other means, they

are inexpensive (27). Dyson, considered a

leading figure in the field of space

exploration, has expressed some doubts about

the durability of solar sails ("Science" 32).

Works Cited

Doobe, Kevin. Space at a Crossroads. Prod. Science

Today, Institute for Science Education.

Videocassette. Technicon Video, 1995.

Dyson, Freeman. "Science and Space." The First

25 Years in Space. Ed. Allan Needell.

Washington: Smithsonian, 1983. 22-37.

---. "21st-Century Spacecraft." Scientific

American Sept. 1995: 114-116A.

United States. Dept. of Energy. Report on the

Future of Solar Energy. Washington: GPO,

1994.

Sa
A

For other sample pages from a paper using MLA documentation, see
45d. Parenthetical citations, endnotes, and works cited are formatted as
illustrated in the following sections.

# 45a In-Text Citations

The purpose of in-text citations is to help your reader find the appropriate reference in the list of works cited at the end of the paper. You may have previously used footnotes to indicate each source as you used it, but the current MLA format recommends parenthetical references, depending on how much information you include in your sentence or in your introduction to a quotation. Try to be brief, but not at the expense of clarity, and remember to use signal words and phrases (see 44f).

---

**EXAMPLES OF MLA IN-TEXT CITATIONS**

1. Author's Name Not Given in the Text
2. Author's Name Given in the Text
3. Two or More Works by the Same Author
4. Two or Three Authors
5. More than Three Authors
6. Unknown Author
7. Corporate Author or Government Document
8. An Entire Work
9. A Literary Work
10. A Multivolume Work
11. Indirect Source
12. Two or More Sources

---

**1. Author's Name Not Given in the Text**    If the author's name is not in your sentence, put the last name in parentheses, leave a space with no punctuation, and then put the page number.

```
Recent research on sleep and dreaming indicates that

dreams move backward in time as the night progresses

(Dement 72).
```

**2. Author's Name Given in the Text**    If you include the author's name in the sentence, only the page number is needed in parentheses.

```
Freud states that "a dream is the fulfillment of a

wish" (154).
```

**3. Two or More Works by the Same Author**    If you used two or more different sources by the same author, put a comma after the author's last name and include a shortened version of the title and the page reference. If the author's name is in the text, include only the title and page reference.

```
One current theory emphasizes the principle that

dreams express "profound aspects of personality"

(Foulkes, Sleep 144).
```

```
Foulkes' investigation shows that young children's

dreams are "rather simple and unemotional"

(Children's Dreams 90).
```

**4. Two or Three Authors**    If your source has two or three authors, either name them in your sentence or include the names in parentheses.

Jeffrey and Milanovitch argue that the recently

reported statistics for teen pregnancies are

inaccurate (112).

The recently reported statistics for teen-age

pregnancies are said to be inaccurate (Jeffrey and

Milanovitch 112).

**5. More than Three Authors**    If your source has more than three authors, either use the first author's last name followed by *et al.* (which means "and others") or list all the last names.

The conclusion drawn from a survey on the growth of

the Internet, conducted by Martin et al., is that

global usage will double within two years (36).

Recent figures on the growth of the Internet

indicate that global usage will double within two

years (Martin, Ober, Mancuso, and Blum 36).

**6. Unknown Author**    If the author is unknown, use a shortened form of the title in your citation.

More detailed nutritional information in food labels

is proving to be a great advantage to diabetics

("New Labeling Laws" 3).

**7. Corporate Author or Government Document**    Use the name of the corporation or government agency, shortened or in full. Try to include long names in your sentence to avoid extending the parenthetical reference.

The United Nations Regional Flood Containment

Commission has been studying weather patterns that

contribute to flooding in Africa (4).

**8. An Entire Work**    If you cite an entire work, it is preferable to include the author's name in the text.

```
Lafmun was the first to argue that small infants
respond to music.
```

**9. A Literary Work**   If you refer to classic prose works, such as novels or plays, that are available in several editions, it is helpful to provide more information than just a page reference to the edition you used. A chapter number, for example, might help readers locate the reference in any copy they find. In such a reference, give the page number first, add a semicolon, and then give other identifying information.

```
In The Prince, Machiavelli reminds us that while
some manage to jump from humble origins to great
power, such people find their greatest challenge to
be staying in power: "Those who rise from private
citizens to be princes merely by fortune have
little trouble in rising but very much trouble in
maintaining their position" (23; ch. 7).
```

For verse plays and poems, omit page numbers and use act, scene, canto, and line numbers separated by periods. For lines, use the word *line* or *lines* in the first reference, and then afterwards give only the numbers.

```
Eliot again reminds us of society's superficiality
in "The Love Song of J. Alfred Prufrock": "There
will be time, there will be time / To prepare a face
to meet the faces that you meet" (lines 26-27).
```

**10. A Multivolume Work**   When you cite a volume number as well as a page reference for a multivolume work, separate the two by a colon and a space. Do not use the words *volume* or *page*.

```
In his History of the Civil War, Jimmersen traces
the economic influences that contributed to the
decisions of several states to stay in the Union
(3:798-823).
```

**11. Indirect Source**   If you have to rely on a secondhand source in which someone's quoted words appear in a source written by someone else, start the citation with the abbreviation *qtd. in.*

```
Although Newman has established a high degree of
accuracy for such tests, he reminds us that "no
test like this is ever completely and totally
accurate" (qtd. in Mazor 33).
```

**12. Two or More Sources**    If you cite more than one work in your parenthetical reference, separate the references by a semicolon.

```
Recent attempts to control the rapid destruction of
the rain forests in Central America have met with
little success (Costanza 22; Kinderman 94).
```

# 45b Endnotes

When you have additional comments or information that would disrupt the paper, cite the information in endnotes numbered consecutively through the paper. Put the number at the end of the phrase, clause, or sentence containing the material you are referring to, after the punctuation. Raise the number above the line, with no punctuation. Leave no extra space before the number and one extra space after if the reference is in the middle of the sentence and two extra spaces when the reference number is at the end of the sentence.

```
The treasure hunt for sixteenth-century pirate loot
buried in Nova Scotia began in 1927,³ but hunting
was discontinued when the treasure seekers found
the site flooded at high tide.⁴
```

At the end of your paper, begin a new sheet with the heading "Notes," but do not underline or put the heading in quotation marks. Leave a one-inch margin at the top, center the heading, double-space, and then begin listing your notes. For each note, indent five spaces, raise the number above the line, and begin the note. Double-space, and if the note continues on the next line, begin that line at the left-hand margin. The format is slightly different from that used in the works cited section in that the author's name appears in normal order, followed by a comma, the title, the publisher, the date in parentheses, and a page reference.

```
    ³Some historians argue that this widely
accepted date is inaccurate. See Jerome Flynn,
Buried Treasures (New York: Newport, 1978): 29-43.
```

⁴Avery Jones and Jessica Lund, "The Nova Scotia Mystery Treasure," *Contemporary History* 9 (1985): 81-83.

If you are asked to use footnotes instead of endnotes, place them at the bottoms of pages, beginning four lines (two double spaces) below the text. Single-space footnotes, but double-space between them. Number them consecutively through the paper.

# 45c Works Cited List

The list of works cited lists all the sources you cite in your paper. Do not include other materials you read but didn't refer to in your paper. Arrange the list alphabetically by the last name of the author: if there is no author, alphabetize by the first word of the title (but not the articles *a, an,* or *the*).

For the Works Cited section, begin a new sheet of paper, leave a one-inch margin at the top, center the heading "Works Cited" (with no underlining or quotation marks), and then double-space before the first entry. For each entry, begin at the left-hand margin for the first line, and indent five spaces (or one-half inch) for additional lines in the entry. Double-space throughout. Place the Works Cited list at the end of your paper after the notes, if you have any.

There are three parts to each reference: (1) author, (2) title, and (3) publishing information. Each part is followed by a period and one space.

**Books**

*(indent 5 spaces)*

**Articles in Periodicals**

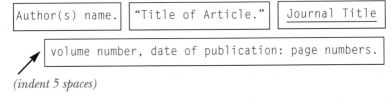

*(indent 5 spaces)*

## EXAMPLES OF MLA WORKS CITED

### Books

1. One Author
2. Two or Three Authors
3. More than Three Authors
4. More than One Work by the Same Author
5. A Work that Names an Editor
6. A Work with an Author and an Editor
7. A Work that Names a Translator
8. A Work by a Corporate Author
9. A Work by an Unknown Author
10. A Work that Has More than One Volume
11. A Work in an Anthology
12. Two or More Works in the Same Anthology
13. An Article in a Reference Book
14. Introduction, Foreword, Preface, or Afterword
15. A Work with a Title within a Title
16. Second or Later Edition
17. Modern Reprint
18. A Work in a Series
19. A Work with a Publisher's Imprint
20. Government Publication
21. Proceedings of a Conference

### Articles in Periodicals

22. Scholarly Journal with Continuous Paging
23. Scholarly Journal that Pages Each Issue Separately
24. Monthly or Bimonthly Magazine Article
25. Weekly or Biweekly Magazine Article
26. Newspaper Article
27. Unsigned Article
28. Editorial or Letter to the Editor
29. Review of a Work
30. Article in Microform Collection of Articles

### Electronic Sources

*CD-ROMs and Other Portable Databases*
31. Material Accessed from a Periodically Published Database on CD-ROM
32. Publication on CD-ROM
33. Publication on Diskette
34. Publication on Magnetic Tape
35. Work in More than One Published Medium

*Online Databases*
**36.** Material Accessed through a Computer Service
**37.** Material Accessed through a Computer Network

**Other Sources**

**38.** Computer Software
**39.** Television or Radio Program
**40.** Record, Tape Cassette, or CD
**41.** Film or Video Recording
**42.** Live Performance of a Play
**43.** Musical Composition
**44.** Work of Art
**45.** Letter, Memo, E-mail Communication, or Public Online Posting
**46.** Personal Interview
**47.** Published Interview
**48.** Radio or Television Interview
**49.** Map or Chart
**50.** Cartoon
**51.** Advertisement
**52.** Lecture, Speech, or an Address
**53.** Pamphlet
**54.** Published Dissertation
**55.** Abstract of a Dissertation
**56.** Unpublished Dissertation

## Books

### 1. One Author

Joos, Martin. The Five Clocks. New York: Harcourt,
    Brace, and World, 1962.

### 2. Two or Three Authors   Reverse name of first author only.

Duggan, Stephen, and Betty Drury. The Rescue of
    Science and Learning. New York: Macmillan, 1948.

Mellerman, Sidney, John Scarcini, and Leslie
    Karlin. Human Development: An Introduction to
    Cognitive Growth. New York: Harper, 1981.

**3. More than Three Authors**    For more than three authors, you may name only the first and add *et al.* (for "and others") or you may give all names in full in the order in which they appear on the title page.

```
Spiller, Robert, et al. Literary History of the
    United States. New York: Macmillan, 1960.
    (or)
Spiller, Robert, Harlan Minton, Michael Upta, and
    Gretchen Kielstra. Literary History of the
    United States. New York: Macmillan, 1960.
```

**4. More than One Work by the Same Author**    Use the author's name in the first entry only. From then on, type three hyphens and a period and then begin the next title. Alphabetize by title. If the person edited or translated another work in your list, use a comma and *ed.* or *trans.* after the three hyphens.

```
Newman, Edwin. A Civil Tongue. Indianapolis: Bobbs-
    Merrill, 1966.
---. Strictly Speaking. New York: Warner Books, 1974.
```

**5. A Work that Names an Editor**    Use the abbreviation *ed.* for one editor (for "edited by") and *eds.* for more than one editor.

```
Kinkead, Joyce A., and Jeanette Harris, eds.
    Writing Centers in Context: Twelve Case
    Studies. Urbana: NCTE, 1993.
```

**6. A Work with an Author and an Editor**    If there is an editor in addition to an author, give the editor's name after the title. Before the editor's name, put the abbreviation *Ed.* (for "Edited by") or *Eds.* if there is more than one editor.

```
Frankfurter, Felix. The Diaries of Felix Frankfurter.
    Ed. Thomas Sayres. Boston: Norton, 1975.
```

**7. A Work that Names a Translator**    Use the abbreviation *Trans.* (for "Translated by").

```
Sastre, Alfonso. Sad Are the Eyes of William Tell.
    Trans. Leonard Pronko. Ed. George Wellwarth.
    New York: New York UP, 1970.
```

**8. A Work by a Corporate Author**

United States Capitol Society. <u>We, the People:</u>
<u>The Story of the United States Capitol</u>.
Washington, National Geographic Soc.,
1964.

**9. A Work by an Unknown Author**

<u>Report of the Commission on Tests</u>. New York:
College Entrance Examination Board, 1970.

**10. A Work that Has More than One Volume**    If you are citing two or more volumes of a work in your paper, put references to volume and page numbers in the parenthetical references. If you are citing only one of the volumes in your paper, state the number of that volume in the works cited list and give publication information for that volume alone.

Esler, Anthony. <u>The Human Venture</u>. 3rd ed. Vol. 1.
Upper Saddle River, NJ: Prentice, 1996.

Rutherford, Ernest. <u>The Collected Papers</u>. 3 vols.
Philadelphia: Allen, 1962.

**11. A Work in an Anthology**    State the author and title of the work first, and then give the title and other information about the anthology, including page numbers on which the selection appears. Use the abbreviation *Comp.* (for "Compiled by"). If a selection has been published before, give that information, then use *Rpt.* (for "Reprinted in") with the anthology information.

Dymvok, George E., Jr. "Vengeance." <u>Poetry in the</u>
<u>Modern Age</u>. Comp. and ed. Jason Metier. San
Francisco: New Horizons. 1994. 54.

Licouktis, Michelle. "From Slavery to Freedom." <u>New</u>
<u>South Quarterly</u> 29 (1962): 87-98. Rpt. in <u>Voices</u>
<u>of the Sixties: Selected Essays</u>. Ed. Myrabelle
McConn. Atlanta: Horizons, 1995. 12-19.

**12. Two or More Works in the Same Anthology**    If you cite two or more works from the same collection and wish to avoid unnecessary repetition, you may include a complete entry for the collection and then cross-reference the works to that collection. In the cross-reference include the author and title of the work, the last name of the editor of the collection, and the inclusive page numbers.

```
Batu, Marda, and Hillary Matthews, eds. Voices of
    American Women. New York: Littlefield, 1995.
Jamba, Shawleen. "My Mother's Not Going Home." Batu
    and Matthews 423-31.
Little River, Lillian. "Listening to the World."
    Batu and Matthews 234-45.
```

**13. An Article in a Reference Book**    Treat an encyclopedia article or a dictionary entry like a piece in an anthology, but do not cite the editor of the reference work. If the article is signed, give the author first. If it is unsigned, give the title first. If articles are arranged alphabetically, omit volume and page numbers. When citing familiar reference books, list only the edition and year of publication.

```
"Bioluminescence." The Concise Columbia Encyclopedia.
    1983 ed.
```

**14. Introduction, Foreword, Preface, or Afterword**    Start the entry with the author of the part you are citing. Then add the information about the book, followed by the page numbers where that part appears. If the author of the part is not the author of the book, use the word *By* and give the book author's full name. If the author of the part and the book are the same, use *By* and the author's last name only.

```
Asimov, Isaac. Foreword. Issac Asimov's Book of
    Facts. By Asimov. New York: Bell, 1979. vii.
Bruner, Jerome. Introduction. Thought and Language.
    By Lev Vygotsky. Cambridge: MITP, 1962. v-xiii.
```

**15. A Work with a Title within a Title**    If a title that is normally underlined appears within another title, do not underline it or put it inside quotation marks.

```
Lillo, Alphonso. Re-Reading Shakespeare's Hamlet
    from the Outside. Boston: Martinson, 1995.
```

**16. Second or Later Edition**

```
Ornstein, Robert E. The Psychology of Consciousness.
    2nd ed. New York: Harcourt, 1977.
```

**17. Modern Reprint**    State the original publication date after the title of the book. In the publication information that follows, put the date of publication for the reprint.

> Weston, Jessie L. From Ritual to Romance. 1920.
>> Garden City: Anchor-Doubleday, 1957.

**18. A Work in a Series**    If the title page or preceding page of the book you are citing indicates that it is part of a series, include the series name, without underlining or quotation marks, and the series number, followed by a period, before the publication information. Use common abbreviations for words in the series name.

> Waldheim, Isaac. Revisiting the Bill of Rights.
>> Studies of Amer. Constitutional Hist. 18. New
>> York: Waterman, 1991.

**19. A Work with a Publisher's Imprint**    Publishers sometimes put some of their books under imprints or special names that usually appear with the publisher's name on the title page. Include the imprint name, a hyphen, and the name of the publisher.

> Tamataru, Ishiko. Sunlight and Strength. New York:
>> Anchor-Doubleday, 1992.

**20. Government Publication**    Use the abbreviation *GPO* for publications from the Government Printing Office.

> United States. Office of Education. Tutor-Trainer's
>> Resource Handbook. Washington: GPO, 1973.

**21. Proceedings of a Conference**    If the proceedings of a conference are published, treat the entry like a book and include information about the conference if such information isn't included in the title.

> Esquino, Luis. Second Language Acquisition in the
>> Classroom. Proc. of the Soc. for Second
>> Language Acquisition Conference, Nov. 1994,
>> U of Texas. Dallas: Midlands, 1995.
> Standino, Alexander, ed. Proceedings of the Fifteenth
>> Annual Meeting of the Native American Folklore
>> Society, March 15-17, 1991. Albuquerque: Native
>> American Folklore Soc., 1991.

## Articles in Periodicals

**22. Scholarly Journal with Continuous Paging**    Most scholarly journals have continuous pagination throughout the whole volume for the year. Then, at the end of the year, all issues in that volume are bound together and ordered on shelves by the year of the volume. To find a particular issue on the shelf, you need only the volume number and the page, not the issue number.

```
Delbrück, Max. "Mind from Matter." American Scholar
     47 (1978): 339-53.
```

**23. Scholarly Journal that Pages Each Issue Separately**    If each issue of the journal starts with page 1, then include the issue number.

```
Barthla, Frederick, and Joseph Murphy. "Alcoholism in
     Fiction." Kansas Quarterly 17.2 (1981): 77-80.
```

**24. Monthly or Bimonthly Magazine Article**    If the article is not printed on consecutive pages, give only the first page number followed by a plus sign.

```
Diamond, Jared. "The Worst Mistake in Human
     History." Discover May 1987: 64+.
Lillio, Debra. "New Cures for Migraine Headaches."
     Health Digest Oct. 1995: 14-18.
```

**25. Weekly or Biweekly Magazine Article**    For a magazine published every week or every two weeks, give the complete date beginning with the day and abbreviating the month. Do not give the volume and issue numbers even if they are listed.

```
Isaacson, Walter. "Will the Cold War Fade Away?"
     Time 27 Feb. 1987: 40-45.
```

**26. Newspaper Article**    Provide the author's name and the title of the article, then the name of the newspaper as it appears on the masthead, omitting any introductory article such as *The*. If the city of publication is not included in the name, add the city in square brackets after the name: Journal-Courier [Trenton]. If the paper is nationally published, such as the Wall Street Journal, do not add the city of publication. Abbreviate all months except for May, June, and July. Give any information about edition, and follow it with a colon and page numbers.

```
Strout, Richard L. "Another Bicentennial." New York
     Times 10 Nov. 1994, late ed.: A9+.
```

**27. Unsigned Article**

"Trading Lives." <u>Newsweek</u> 21 Apr. 1993: 87-89.

**28. Editorial or Letter to the Editor**    If you are citing an editorial, add the word *Editorial* after the title of the editorial. Use the word *Letter* after the author of a letter to the editor.

"Watching Hillary's Defense Team at Play." Editorial.

<u>Washington Times</u> 5 Jan. 1996, late ed.: A18.

Berwitz, Ken. Letter. <u>New York Times</u> 14 Feb. 1996,

late ed.: A20.

**29. Review of a Work**    Include the reviewer's name and title of the review, if any, followed by the words *Rev. of* (for "Review of"), the title of the work being reviewed, a comma, the word *by,* and then the author's name. If the work has no title and is not signed, begin the entry with *Rev. of* and in your list of works cited alphabetize under the title of the work being reviewed.

Kauffmann, Stanley. "Cast of Character." Rev. of

<u>Nixon</u>, dir. Oliver Stone. <u>New Republic</u> 22 Jan.

1996: 26-27.

Rev. of <u>The Beak of the Finch</u>, by Jonathan Weiner.

<u>Science Weekly</u> 12 Dec. 1995: 36.

**30. Article in Microform Collection of Articles**

Gilman, Elias. "New Programs for School Reform."

<u>Charleston Herald</u> 18 Jan. 1991: 14. <u>Newsbank:

School Reform</u> 14 (1991): fiche 1, grids A7-12.

## Electronic Sources

### CD-ROMs and Other Portable Databases

Sources in electronic form that are stored on CD-ROMs, diskettes, and magnetic tapes and have to be read on computers are portable databases (that is, they can be carried around, unlike online databases, which are explained in entries 36 and 37). When citing these sources, state the medium of publication (such as CD-ROM or diskette), the vendor's name, and the date of electronic publication.

**31. Material Accessed from a Periodically Published Database on CD-ROM**    If no printed source is indicated, include author, title of material (in quotation marks), date of material (if given), title of database (under-lined), publication medium, name of vendor, and electronic publication date.

> Anstor, Marylee. "Nutrition for Pregnant Women." New
>> York Times 12 Apr. 1994, late ed.: C1. New York
>> Times Ondisc. CD-ROM. UMI-Proquest. Oct. 1994.
>
> Institute for Virus Research. "Coenzyme-Cell Wall
>> Interaction." 14 Feb. 1995. Institutes for
>> Health Research. CD-ROM. Health Studies Source
>> Search. June 1995.

**32. Publication on CD-ROM**   Many CD-ROM publications are pub-lished, like books, without updates or regular revisions. Cite these like books, but add a description of the medium of publication.

> Mattmer, Tobias. "Discovering Jane Austen."
>> Discovering Authors. Vers. 1.0. CD-ROM.
>> Detroit: Gale, 1992.
>
> All-Movie Guide. CD-ROM. Ottawa: Corel, 1996.

**33. Publication on Diskette**   Diskette publications are cited like books, with an added description of the medium of publication.

> Lehmo, Jarred. Ethnicity in Dance. Diskette.
>> Chicago: U of Chicago P, 1995.

**34. Publication on Magnetic Tape**   Magnetic tape publications are cited like books, with an added description of the medium of publication.

> "Television Advertising." Encyclopedia of Modern
>> Advertising. Magnetic tape. Detroit: Giley, 1994.

**35. Work in More than One Published Medium**   Some electronic pub-lications appear as packages of materials in different publication media. For example, a CD-ROM may be packaged with a diskette. Cite such publication packages as you would a CD-ROM product (see entry 32), specifying the media in the package.

> History of Stage Costuming In Europe. CD-ROM,
>> videodisc. Philadelphia: Michelson, 1995.

**Online Databases**

Online databases are those that are not bought in stores and cannot be carried around. They can be accessed only online and may be continually updated or revised. Some additional elements to be included in the citation are the publication medium (that is, *Online*), the name of the computer service or computer network through which the database is accessed, and the date of access.

**36. Material Accessed through a Computer Service**   There are two groups of such materials:

1. **Materials with a Print Source:** For materials that include publication information for a source that was or is available in print, include the print information first (including title and date of print publication), then the title of the database (underlined), the publication medium (*Online*), the name of the computer service, and the date of access.

2. **Materials with No Print Source:** For materials that do not indicate a printed source, include the author, the title of material (in quotation marks), the date (if given), the title of the database (underlined), the publication medium (*Online*), the name of the computer service, and the date of access.

Meharry, William. "Beta-Carotene May be Dangerous to

   Your Health." <u>New York Times</u> 24 January 1996,

   late ed.: B3. <u>New York Times Online</u>. Online.

   Nexis. 15 August 1996.

Sapir, Mortimer. "Dangers of Anesthesia." <u>American</u>

   <u>Medical Encyclopedia</u>. Online. Prodigy. 9 Aug.

   1995.

MLA offers no specific format for documenting World Wide Web pages with no print versions, but the following is a suggestion for adapting the format in entry 36.2 (Materials with No Print Source). Include the author (if available), the title of the page (in quotation marks), the title of the site (underlined), the publication medium (*Online*), the date of access, and the electronic address.

"Virtual Antarctica: Ship's Log." <u>Terraquest:</u>

   <u>Virtual Expeditions on the World Wide Web</u>.

   Online. 28 April 1996. http://www.terraquest.

   com/va/shipslog/shipslog.html

```
"Progress Uneven for Women and Minorities in
       Science." Frontiers: Newsletter of the National
       Science Foundation. Online. 28 April 1996.
       http://stis.nsf.gov/nsf/homepage/frontier/may
       95/may 1995.htm#progress
```

**37. Material Accessed through a Computer Network**    There are two categories of sources:

1. **Electronic Journals, Electronic Newsletters, and Electronic Conferences (such as discussion lists).** These should be similar to references to articles in print periodicals. Include the name of the author; the title of the document (in quotation marks), the title of the journal, newsletter, or conference (underlined); the volume or other identifying number, the year or date of publication (in parentheses); the number of pages or paragraphs (if given) or *n. pag.* (for "no pagination"); the publication medium (*Online*); the name of the computer network; and the date of access. At the end of the entry, the electronic address used to access the document, preceded by the word *Available,* may be added.

2. **Electronic Texts:** If you use a text or document available through a computer network, include the author's name, the title of the text (underlined), publication information for the printed source, the publication medium (*Online*), the name of the repository of the electronic text, the name of the computer network, and the date of access.

```
Moultrip, Lisa. "Using LANs in the Classroom."
       Computers in Composition Newsletter 2.3 (Nov.
       1995): n. pag. Online. Internet. 24 December
       1995.

Shakespeare, William. Hamlet. Ed. Arthur H. Bullen.
       Stratford Town Ed. Stratford-on-Avon:
       Shakespeare Head, 1911. Online. Dartmouth
       Coll. Lib. Internet. 15 April 1995. Available:
       FTP:shtxt.dartmouth.edu
```

## Other Sources

**38. Computer Software**    References to computer software are similar to references to CD-ROM or diskette materials (see entries 32 and 33).

```
McProof. Vers. 3.2.1. Diskette. Salt Lake City:
     Lexpertise, 1987.
```

**39. Television or Radio Program**   Include the title of the episode (in quotation marks), the title of the program (underlined), the title of the series (with no underlining or quotation marks), the name of the network, the call letters and city of the local station, and the broadcast date. If pertinent, add information such as the names of the performers, director, or narrator.

```
"Tall Tales from the West." American Folklore.
     Narr. Hugh McKenna. Writ. Carl Tannenberg.
     PBS. WFYI, Indianapolis. 14 Mar. 1995.
```

**40. Record, Tape Cassette, or CD-ROM**   Depending on which you want to emphasize, cite the composer, conductor, or performer first. Then list the title (underlined); artist, medium, if not a compact disc (no underlining or quotation marks); manufacturer; and year of issue (if unknown, include *n.d.* for "no date"). Place a comma between manufacturer and date, with periods following all other items.

```
Perlman, Itzhak. Mozart Violin Concertos Nos. 3 &
     5. Weiner Philarmoniker Orch. Cond. James
     Levine. Deutsche Grammophon, 1983.
Schiff, Heinrich. Five Cello Concertos. By Antonio
     Vivaldi. Academy of St. Martin-in-the-Fields.
     Dir. Iona Brown. Audiocassette. Philips, 1984.
```

**41. Film or Video Recording**   Begin a reference to a film with the title (underlined), and include the director, distributor, and year. You also may include the names of the writer, performers, and producer. Treat a videocassette, videodisc, slide program, or filmstrip like a film, and give the original release date and the medium before the name of the distributor.

```
Richard III. By William Shakespeare. Dir. Ian
     McKellen and Richard Loncrain. Perf. Ian
     McKellen, Annette Bening, Jim Broadbent, and
     Robert Downey, Jr. MGM/UA, 1995.
Renoir, Jean, dir. The Rules of the Game [Le Regle
     du Jeu]. Perf. Marcel Dalio and Nora Gregor.
     1937. Videocassette. Video Images, 1981.
```

**42. Live Performance of a Play**   Like a reference to a film (see entry 41), references to performances usually begin with the title and include similar information. Include the theater and city where the performance was given, separated by a comma and followed by a period, and the date of the performance.

> Inherit the Wind. By Jerome Lawrence and Robert E.
>> Lee. Dir. John Tillinger. Perf. George C.
>> Scott and Charles Durning. Royale Theatre, New
>> York. 23 January 1996.

**43. Musical Composition**   Begin with the composer's name. Underline the title of an opera, ballet, or a piece of music with a name, and put quotation marks around the name of a song. If the composition is known only by number, form, or key, do not underline or use quotation marks. If the score is published, cite it like a book and capitalize abbreviations such as *no.* and *op.* You may include the date after the title.

> Bach, Johann Sebastian. Brandenburg Concertos.
> Bach, Johann Sebastian. Orchestral Suite no. 1 in C
>> major.

**44. Work of Art**   Begin with the artist's name; underline the title of the work; and include the institution that houses the work or the person who owns it, followed by a comma and the city. If you include the date the work was created, add that after the title. If you use a photograph of the work, include the publication information for your source, including the page, slide, figure, or plate number.

> Manet, Edouard. The Balcony. Jeu de Paume, Paris.
> Monet, Claude. Rouen Cathedral. Metropolitan Museum
>> of Art, New York. Masterpieces of Fifty
>> Centuries. New York: Dutton, 1970. 316.

**45. Letter, Memo, E-Mail Communication, or Public Online Posting**

> Blumen, Lado. Letter to Lui Han. 14 Oct. 1990. Lado
>> Blumen Papers. Minneapolis Museum of Art Lib.,
>> Minneapolis.
> Milan, Theresa. E-mail to Simon Mahr. 18 Sept. 1995.
> Terwin, Isaac. "Re: Mechanical Realignment." 6 July

1994. Online posting. Newsgroup eng.edu.
transportation.robot. Usenet. 18 July
1994.

## 46. Personal Interview

Kochem, Prof. Alexander, Personal interview. 18
Apr. 1995.

## 47. Published Interview

Goran, Nadya. "A Poet's Reflections on the End of
the Cold War." By Leonid Tuzman. International
Literary Times 18 Nov. 1995: 41-44.

## 48. Radio or Television Interview

Netanyahu, Benjamin. Interview with Ted Koppel.
Nightline. ABC. WABC, New York. 18 Aug. 1995.

**49. Map or Chart**    Treat a map or chart like a book without an author (see entry 9), but add the descriptive label (*Map* or *Chart*).

New York. Map. Chicago: Rand, 1995.

**50. Cartoon**    Begin with the cartoonist's name, followed by the title of the cartoon (if any) in quotation marks and the descriptive label *Cartoon,* and conclude with the usual publication information.

Adams, Scott. "Dilbert." Cartoon. Journal and
Courier [Lafayette] 20 Jan. 1996: B7.

**51. Advertisement**    Begin with the name of the product, company, or institution that is the subject of the advertisement, followed by the descriptive label *Advertisement,* and conclude with the usual publication information.

Apple Computer. Advertisement. GQ, Dec. 1994: 145-46.

**52. Lecture, Speech, or an Address**    Begin with the speaker's name, the title of the presentation in quotation marks, the meeting and sponsoring organization, location, and date. Use a descriptive label such as *Address* or *Reading* if there is no title.

Lihandro, Alexandra. "Writing to Learn." Conf. on
Coll. Composition and Communication Convention.
Palmer House, Chicago. 23 Mar. 1990.

```
Trapun, Millicent. Address. Loeb Theater.
        Indianapolis. 16 Mar. 1995.
```

**53. Pamphlet**    Cite a pamphlet like a book.

```
Thirty Foods for Your Health. New York: Consumers
        Health Soc., 1996.
```

**54. Published Dissertation**    Treat a published dissertation like a book, but include dissertation information before the publication information. You may add the University Microfilms International (UMI) order number after the date if they published the work.

```
Blalock, Mary Jo. Consumer Awareness of Food
        Additives in Products Offered as Organic.
        Diss. U Plainfield, 1994. Ann Arbor: UMI,
        1995. 10325891.
```

**55. Abstract of a Dissertation**    Begin with the publication information for the original work, and then add the information for the journal in which the abstract appears.

```
McGuy, Timothy. "Campaign Rhetoric of Conservatives
        in the 1994 Congressional Elections." Diss.
        Johns Hopkins U, 1995. DAI 56 (1996): 1402A.
```

**56. Unpublished Dissertation**    Put the title of an unpublished dissertation in quotation marks and include the descriptive label *Diss.*, followed by the name of the university granting the degree, a comma, and the year.

```
Tibbur, Matthew. "Computer-Mediated Intervention
        in Early Childhood Stuttering." Diss. Stanford
        U, 1991.
```

# 45d Sample Pages from an MLA-Style Research Paper

Included here are a sample page for a title page, a first page for a paper that does not have a title page, and a first page for the works cited list. Research papers that follow MLA style generally do not need a title page, but if you are asked to include one, follow the format shown here.

## (1) Title Page Following MLA Style

A Miracle Drug to Keep Us Young    *center title*
*one-third*
or Another False Hope?    *down page*


Michael G. Mitun    *name*


Professor Jomale    *instructor*

English 102, Section 59    *course*

18 November 1995    *date*

## (2) First Page Following MLA Style

1"

1/2"

Mitun 1

Michael G. Mitun

Professor Jomale        *} double space*

English 102

18 November 1995

*} double space*

A Miracle Drug to Keep Us Young

or Another False Hope?

*} double space*

Even before Ponce de Leon landed in
Florida in 1513, searching for a fountain of
youth, people looked for ways to resist the
aging process. Among the unsuccessful cures
that we find in history records are ice baths,
gold elixirs, and holding one's breath. But now
modern medicine is opening the door to new
therapies that might work, pills based on
hormones that our bodies produce when we're
young but that decrease as we grow old. At the
moment, the most promising of these hormones is
DHEA, the subject of magazine articles and a
television newsmagazine program ("Natures"; <u>Eye
to Eye</u>). As medical evidence continues to
appear, the number of believers is increasing.

1"

1"

1"

## (3) Works Cited Page Following MLA Style

Mitun 14

Works Cited

Ames, Donna Spahn. "The Effects of Chronic
    Endurance Training on DHEA and DHEA-S
    Levels in Middle-Aged Men." Diss. U. of
    New Hampshire, 1991.

Bilger, Burkhard. "Forever Young." The Sciences
    Sept./Oct. 1995: 26-30.

Eye to Eye. CBS. WCBS, New York. 15 June 1995.

Fahey, Thomas D. "DHEA." Joe Weider's Muscle
    and Fitness Aug. 1995: 94-97.

Garcia, Homer. "Effects of
    Dehydroepiandrosterone (DHEA) on Brain
    Tissue." DHEA Transformations in Target
    Tissue. Ed. Milan Zucheffa. London: Binn,
    1994: 36-45.

---. "Estrogens in Target Tissues."
    Endocrinology 136 (1995): 3247-56.

Jaroff, Leon. "New Age Therapy." Time 23 Jan.
    1995: 52.

Health and Aging. Prod. Hormone Therapy
    Project, Middleton Medical School.
    Videodisc. Middleton, 1994.

Li, Min Zhen, ed. The Biologic Role of
    Dehydroepiandrosterone (DHEA). Berlin: de
    Gruyter, 1990.

# 46 Documenting in APA Style (APA)

**American Psychological Association (APA)** format is used to document papers in the behavioral and social sciences.

If you are asked to use APA format, consult the *Publication Manual of the American Psychological Association* (4th ed., Washington, D.C.: American Psychological Association, 1994).

APA style is like MLA style (see Chapter 45) in that you have parenthetical citations in your paper to refer readers to the list at the end of the paper; numbered notes that are to be used only to include information that would disrupt the writing if included there; and at the end of the paper, a Reference list of works cited.* References in this list include only the sources used in the research and preparation of your paper. However, because of the greater emphasis in the social sciences on how current the source is, APA style includes the date of publication in parenthetical citations, and the date appears after the author's name in the reference list. In addition, authors' first and middle names are indicated by initials only. Capitalization and use of quotation marks and underlines also differ in APA style.

Some features of APA style are as follows:

- In in-text citations, give the author's last name and the publication year of the source.
- In quotations, put signal words (see 44f) in past tense (such as "Smith reported") or present perfect tense (such as "as Smith has reported").
- Use full last names and initials of first and middle names of authors.
- Capitalize only the first word and proper names in book and article titles, but capitalize all major words in journal titles. Underline titles of books and journals; do not put article titles in quotation marks.
- In your References list at the end of the paper, give full publication information, alphabetized by author.

## 46a In-Text Citations

When you use APA format and refer to sources in your text, include the author's name and date of publication. For direct quotations, include the page number also.

*Ask your instructor which of APA's two recommended formats you should use for Reference list entries: (1) first line indented five spaces, subsequent lines full measure (as shown in this book), or (2) first line full measure, subsequent lines indented five spaces.

**EXAMPLES OF APA IN-TEXT CITATIONS**

1. Direct Quotations
2. Author's Name Given in the Text
3. Author's Name Not Given in the Text
4. Work by Multiple Authors
5. Group as Author
6. Work with Unknown Author
7. Authors with the Same Last Name
8. Two or More Works in the Same Parentheses
9. Classical Works
10. Specific Parts of a Source
11. Personal Communications

**1. Direct Quotations**    When you quote a source, end with quotation marks and give the author, year, and page number in parentheses.

```
Many others agree with the assessment that "this is a
seriously flawed study" (Methasa, 1994, p. 22) and do
not include its data in their own work.
```

**2. Author's Name Given in the Text**    Cite only the year of publication in parentheses. If the year also appears in the sentence, do not add parenthetical information. If you refer to the same study again in the paragraph, with the source's name, you do not have to cite the year again if it is clear that the same study is being referred to.

```
When Millard (1970) compared reaction times among the
participants, he noticed an increase in errors.

In 1994 Pradha found improvement in short-term
memory with accompanying practice.
```

**3. Author's Name Not Given in the Text**    Cite the name and year, separated by a comma.

```
In a recent study of reaction times (Millard, 1970)
no change was noticed.
```

**4. Work by Multiple Authors**    For two authors, cite both names every time you refer to the source. Use *and* in the text, but an ampersand (&) in parenthetical material, tables, captions, and the Reference list.

```
When Glick and Metah (1991) reported on their
findings, they were unaware of a similar study
(Grimm & Tolman, 1991) with contradictory data.
```

For three, four, or five authors, include all authors (and date) the first time you cite the source. For additional references, include only the first author's name and *et al.* (for "and others"), with no underlining or italics.

```
Ellison, Mayer, Brunerd, and Keif (1987) studied
supervisors who were given no training. Later, when
Ellison et al. (1987) continued to study these same
supervisors, they added a one-week training program.
```

For six or more authors, cite only the first author and *et al.* and the year for all references.

```
Mokach et al. (1989) noted no improvement in norms
for participant scores.
```

**5. Group as Author**    The name of the group that serves as the author (for example, a government agency or a corporation) is usually spelled out every time it appears in a citation. If the name is long but easily identified by its abbreviation and you want to switch to the abbreviation, give the abbreviation in parentheses when the entire name first appears.

```
In 1992 when the National Institute of Mental
Health (NIMH) prepared its report, no field data
on this epidemic were available. However, NIMH
agreed that future reports would correct this.
```

**6. Work with Unknown Author**    When a work has no author, cite the first few words of the reference list entry and the year.

```
One newspaper article ("When South Americans," 1987)
indicated the rapid growth of this phenomenon.
```

**7. Authors with the Same Last Name**    If two or more authors who appear in your reference list have the same last name, include their initials in all text citations.

```
Until T. A. Wilman (1994) studied the initial survey
(M. R. Wilman, 1993), no reports were issued.
```

**8. Two or More Works in the Same Parentheses**    When two or more works are cited within the same parentheses, arrange them in the order they appear in the Reference list, and separate them with semicolons.

```
Several studies (Canin, 1989; Duniere, 1987;
Pferman & Chu, 1991) reported similar behavior
patterns in such cases.
```

**9. Classical Works**    Reference entries are not necessary for major classical works such as ancient Greek and Roman works and the Bible, but identify the version you used in the first citation in your text. If appropriate, in each citation, include the part (book, chapter, lines).

```
This was known (Aristotle, trans. 1931) to be
prevalent among young men with these symptoms.
```

**10. Specific Parts of a Source**    To cite a specific part of a source, include the page, chapter, figure, or table, and use the abbreviations *p.* (for "page") and *chap.* (for "chapter").

```
No work was done on interaction of long-term memory
and computer programming (Sitwa & Shiu, 1993, p. 224),
but recently (Takamuru, 1996, chap. 6) reported
studies that have considered this interaction.
```

**11. Personal Communications**    Personal communications include letters, memos, telephone conversations, and electronic communications such as e-mail, discussion groups, and messages on electronic bulletin boards. Because the data cannot be recovered, these are included only in the text and not in the Reference list. Include the initials and last name of the communicator and as exact a date as possible. (For electronic sources that can be documented, see 46c.)

```
According to I. M. Boza (personal communication,
June 18, 1995), no population studies of the
problem were done before 1993.
```

# 46b Footnotes

In the paper you may need footnotes for content and for copyright permission. Content footnotes add important information that cannot be integrated into the text, but they are distracting and should be used only if they strengthen the discussion. Copyright permission footnotes acknowledge the source of quotations that are copyrighted. Number the footnotes consecutively with superscript arabic numerals and include the footnotes on a separate page after the reference list.

# 46c Reference List

Arrange all entries in alphabetical order by the author's last name, and for several works by one author, arrange by year of publication with the earliest one first. For authors' names, give all surnames first and then the initials. Use commas to separate a list of two or more names, and use an ampersand (&) before the last name in the list. Capitalize only the first word of the title and the subtitle (and any proper names) of a book or article, but capitalize the name of the journal. Underline (or italicize) book titles, names of journals, and the volume number of the journal.

Start the reference list on a new page, with the word *References* centered at the top of the page, and double space all entries. Indent the first line of each entry five to seven spaces, the same as a paragraph in the text.

---

**EXAMPLES OF APA REFERENCES**

**Books**

1. One Author
2. Two or More Works by the Same Author
3. Two or More Authors
4. Group or Corporate Author
5. Unknown Author
6. Edited Volume
7. Translation
8. Article or Chapter in an Edited Book
9. Article in a Reference Book
10. Revised Edition
11. Multivolume Work
12. Technical and Research Report
13. Report from a University

**Articles in Periodicals**

14. Article in a Journal Paged Continuously
15. Article in a Journal Paged Separately by Issue
16. Article in a Magazine
17. Article in a Newspaper
18. Unsigned Article
19. Monograph
20. Review of a Book, Film, or Video

**Electronic Sources**

21. Online Abstract
22. Online Journal, Subscriber Based
23. Online Journal, General Access

**24.** Electronic Database
**25.** CD-ROM
**26.** Computer Program or Software

**Other Sources**

**27.** Information Service
**28.** Dissertation Abstract
**29.** Government Document
**30.** Conference Proceedings
**31.** Interview
**32.** Film, Videotape, Performance, or Artwork
**33.** Recording
**34.** Cassette Recording
**35.** Television Broadcast, Series, and Single Episode from a Series
**36.** Unpublished Paper Presented at a Meeting

## Books

**1. One Author**

> Rico, G. L. (1983). Writing the natural way.
Los Angeles: Tarcher.

**2. Two or More Works by the Same Author**   Include the author's name in all references and arrange by year of publication, the earliest first.

> Kilmonto, R. J. (1983). Culture and ethnicity.
Washington, DC: American Psychiatric Press.

> Kilmonto, R. J. (1989). Comparisons of cultural
adaptations. Modern Cultural Studies, 27, 237-243.

**3. Two or More Authors**

> Strunk, W., Jr., & White, E. B. (1979). The
elements of style (3rd ed.). New York: Macmillan.

**4. Group or Corporate Author**   If the publication is a brochure, list this in brackets.

> Mental Health Technical Training Support Center.
(1994). Guidelines for mental health nonprofit agency
staffs (2nd ed.) [Brochure]. Manhattan, KS: Author.

**5. Unknown Author**

Americana collegiate dictionary (4th ed.).
(1995). Indianapolis: Huntsfield.

**6. Edited Volume**

Griffith, J. W., & Frey, C. H. (Eds.). (1996).
Classics of children's literature (4th ed.) Upper
Saddle River, NJ: Prentice Hall.

**7. Translation**

Lefranc, J. R. (1976). A Treatise on
probability (R. W. Mateau & D. Trilling, Trans.).
New York: Macmillan. (Original work published 1952)

**8. Article or Chapter in an Edited Book**

Riesen, A. H. (1991). Sensory deprivation. In
E. Stellar & J. M. Sprague (Eds.), Progress in
physiological psychology (pp. 24-54). New York:
Academic Press.

**9. Article in a Reference Book**

Terusami, H. T. (1993). Relativity. In The new
handbook of science (Vol. 12, pp. 247-249). Chicago:
Modern Science Encyclopedia.

**10. Revised Edition**

Telphafi, J. (1989). Diagnostic techniques
(Rev. ed.). Newbury Park, CA: Pine.

**11. Multivolume Work**

Donovan, W. (Ed.). (1979-1986). Social sciences:
A history (Vols. 1-5). New York: Hollins.

**12. Technical and Research Report**

Birney, A. F., & Hall, M. M. (1981). Early
identification of children with written language

disabilities (Report No. 81-502). Washington, DC:
National Education Association.

### 13. Report from a University

Lundersen, P. S., McIver, R. L., & Yepperman,
B. B. (1990). Sexual harassment policies and the
law (Tech. Rep. No. 9). Springfield, IN:
University of Central Indiana, Faculty Affairs
Research Center.

## Articles in Periodicals

### 14. Article in a Journal Paged Continuously

Schaubroeck, J., Sime, W. E., & Mayes, B. T.
(1991). The nomological validity of the type A
personality. Journal of Applied Psychology, 76,
143-168.

### 15. Article in a Journal Paged Separately by Issue

Timmo, L. A., & Kikovio, R. (1994). Young
children's attempts at deception. Research in Early
Childhood Learning, 53(2), 49-67.

### 16. Article in a Magazine

Simmons, H. (1995, November 29). Changing our
buying habits. American Consumer, 21, 29-36.

### 17. Article in a Newspaper    For newspaper articles, use *p.* or *pp.* before the page numbers.

Leftlow, B. S. (1993, December 18). Corporate
take-overs confuse stockmarket predictions. Wall
Street Journal, pp. A1, A14.

### 18. Unsigned Article

New study promises age-defying pills. (1995,
July 27). The Washington Post, p. B21.

## 19. Monograph

Rotter, P. B., & Stolz, G. (1966). Generalized
expectancies of early childhood speech patterns.
Monographs of the Childhood Education Society, 36
(2, Serial No. 181).

**20. Review of a Book, Film, or Video**    If the review is untitled, use the material in brackets as the title and indicate if the review is of a book, film, or video; the brackets indicate the material is a description of form and content, not a title.

Carmody, T. P. (1982). A new look at medicine
from the social perspective [Review of the book
Social contexts of health, illness, and patient
care]. Contemporary Psychology, 27, 208-209.

## Electronic Sources

At the time of publication of the most recent *Publication Manual of the American Psychological Association* (4th edition), a standard had not yet emerged for referencing on line information. The goal of references remains the same—to credit the author and to help your reader find the material. Electronic correspondence (E-mail messages, electronic discussion groups, and so on) is cited as personal communication in your text but does not need to be included in your reference list (see 46a).

**21. Online Abstract**

Brindelstein, C., & Chen, S. (1993). The social
interaction of small children in task-differentiated
groups. [On-line]. Childhood Socializing, 14, 234-241.
Abstract from: DIALOG File: PsycINFO Item: 46-12144

**22. Online Journal, Subscriber Based**

Cross-Cultural Speech Interference Study Group.
(1995, October 21). Signaling affirmation in informal
conversation: Contrasting behaviors of Hispanics and
African-Americans [720 paragraphs]. Online Journal of
Contrastive Cultural Behaviors [On-line serial].
Available: Doc. No. 99

**23. Online Journal, General Access**    The example here is for e-mail retrieval. For FTP or other access, cite that path to retrieve the material.

> Totukeen, L. (1995, April). Responses to gender discrimination in on-line communication [27 paragraphs]. Internet Communication [On-line serial], 2 (14). Available E-mail: intercom@usn.edu Message: send intercom 47-118.

**24. Electronic Database**

> Survey of Public Response to Terrorism Abroad: 1992-93. [Electronic database]. (1994). Washington, DC: Center for Public Policy Study [Producer and Distributor].

**25. CD-ROM**

> Culrose, P., Trimmer, N., & Debruikker, K. (1996). Gender differentiation in fear responses [CD-ROM]. Emotion and Behavior, 27, 914-937. Abstract from: FirstSearch: PsycLIT Item: 900312

**26. Computer Program or Software**

> Gangnopahdhav, A. (1994). Data analyzer for E-mail usage [Computer software]. Princeton, NJ: MasterMinders.

## Other Sources

**27. Information Service**

> Mead, J. V. (1992). Looking at old photographs: Investigating the teacher tales that novice teachers bring with them (Report No. NCRTL-RR-92-4). East Lansing, MI: National Center for Research on Teacher Learning. (ERIC Document Reproduction Service No. ED 346 082)

**28. Dissertation Abstract**

>    Rosen, P. R. (1994). Learning to cope with family crises through counsellor mediation (Doctoral dissertation, Claremont University, 1994). Dissertation Abstracts International, 53, Z6812.

**29. Government Document**

>    United States Bureau of Statistics. (1994) Population density in the contiguous United States (No. A1994-2306). Washington, DC: U.S. Government Printing Office.

**30. Conference Proceedings**

>    Cordulla, F. M., Teitelman, P. J., & Preba, E. E. (1995). Bio-feedback in muscle relaxation. Proceedings of the National Academy of Biological Sciences, USA, 96, 1271-1342.

**31. Interview**    Personal interviews are not included in the reference list. Instead use a parenthetical citation in the text. List published interviews under the interviewer's name.

>    Daly, C. C. (1995, July 14). [Interview with Malcolm Forbes]. International Business Weekly, 37, 34-35.

**32. Film, Videotape, Performance, or Artwork**    Start with the name and, in parentheses, functions of the originators or primary contributors. Put the medium, such as film, videotape, slides, and so on, in brackets after the title. Give the name and location of the distributor, and if the company is not well known, include the address.

>    Weiss, I. (Producer), & Terris, A. (Director). (1992). Infant babbling and speech production [Film]. (Available from Childhood Research Foundation, 125 Marchmont Avenue, Suite 224, New York, NY 10022)

**33. Recording**

      Totonn, R. (1993). When I wander [Recorded by A. Lopper, T. Seagrim, & E. Post]. On <u>Songs of our age</u> [CD]. Wilmington, ME: Folk Heritage Records.

**34. Cassette Recording**

      Trussler, R. W., Jr. (Speaker). (1989). <u>Validity of mental measurements with young children</u> (Cassette Recording No. 21-47B). Washington, DC: American Psychological Measurements Society.

**35. Television Broadcast, Series, and Single Episode from a Series**

      Widener, I. (Executive Producer). (1995, October 21). <u>Window on the world.</u> New York: Public Policy Broadcasting.

      Biaccio, R. (Producer). (1994). <u>The mind of man.</u> New York: WNET.

      Nostanci, L. (1994). The human sense of curiosity (R. Mindlin, Director). In R. Biaccio (Producer), <u>The mind of man.</u> New York: WNET.

**36. Unpublished Paper Presented at a Meeting**

      Lillestein, M. A. (1994, January). <u>Notes on inter-racial conflict in college settings.</u> Paper presented at the meeting of the American Cultural Studies Society, San Antonio, TX.

## 46d Sample Pages from an APA-Style Research Paper

If you are using APA style and are asked to include a title page, follow the format shown here. Included also are a first page for a paper that does not also have a title page and a first page for the reference list. For all pages, leave a margin of at least one inch on all sides.

## (1) Title Page Following APA Style

*1 in.*

Militia Organizations    1
*abbreviated title*

*page numbering begins
on first page*

*center
and
double space*

Militia Organizations:    *title*

Their Attractions and Appeal

Leila Koach    *writer*

Prof. McIver    *instructor*

Humanities 204    *course*

March 22, 1996    *date*

**6d
PA**

## (2) First Page Following APA Style

1"

Militia Organizations      1

Militia Organizations: Their Attractions and

Appeal      *} double space*

1"      As the number of militia organizations continues to increase (Billman, 1995), their members are being studied to learn more about the attraction of such groups. A number of factors have surfaced in such interviews. Rudner (1994) finds that the publicity surrounding such groups gives meaning to the lives of the members. Other studies (Mukiyama, 1993; Tobias & Klein, 1994; Wormer, Melson, & Audati, 1994) focus on the feelings of frustration expressed by militia members, who typically work in jobs that keep them in lower socioeconomic groups. The research project completed by Mintz and Prumanyhuma (1995) indicates that a major attraction of militia groups is their ability to provide members with a strong sense of belonging. A discussion of these study results will provide a profile of typical members and their reasons for joining.      1"

1"

## (3) References Page Following APA Style

1 ″

Militia Organizations    21

References

Billman, R. T. (1995, April 14).
Paramilitary groups on the increase. American
Public Policy, 21, 47-53.

Calmanov, K., Messer, P. B., & Nocatio, L.
(1993). Public Response to Terrorism: 1992-93.
[Electronic database]. (1994). Washington, DC:
Center for Public Policy Study [Producer and
Distributor].

Defense responses of paramilitary groups.
(1991). (Report No. 27). Washington, DC:
National Crime Prevention Research Project.

Gumper, M., & Stark, P. T. (1993). The
warrior in postwar culture. New York: Mayfair.

Jukan, P. (1995). Factors contributing to
anti-government organizations' threats of violence. Journal of Culture and Contemporary
Society, 23, 78-103.

Liftner, B. (1994). Report on terrorism
and weapon use: 1992-1993. (U.S. Senate Task
Force on Terrorism Publication No. 7).
Washington, DC: Government Printing Office.

1 ″

1″        1″

# PART EIGHT

## ESL CONCERNS

The topics discussed in other parts of this book are matters of concern for all writers. But there are also aspects of English that may be confusing for writers learning English as an additional language. This confusion is normal as we learn another language, and if you are an ESL (English as a second language) student, you will find some of these matters—such as prepositions or the articles *a, an,* and *the*—are not mastered quickly or easily because there are long lists of examples and many exceptions. No grammar book can offer complete guidance, so as you write, consult a good dictionary intended especially for ESL students. Sometimes you may need to ask a native speaker of English for help.

Other areas that ESL students often need assistance with are culturally based conventions of writing. Many of the suggestions in this book will help to define those conventions. For example, in Part Two, the discussions of sentence clarity and variety will help to define characteristics of well written sentences in English, and Part Six offers help with matters of style and word choice. Part Seven should be particularly helpful in learning more about the need for citing sources and for being more aware of how plagiarism is defined.

# 47 Verbs

Verbs are very important parts of English sentences because they indicate time and person as well as other information explained in Chapter 16. This chapter provides additional information needed by writers learning English as an additional language.

## 47a  Helping Verbs with Main Verbs

**Helping (or auxiliary) verbs** combine with other verbs to form all the tenses except the simple present and simple past.

The following chart shows the forms of major helping verbs:

| FORMS OF HELPING VERBS | | |
|---|---|---|
| **be** | be  am  is  are  was  were + *-ing* form:<br>with modal first:<br>passive (with past participle): | I am going.<br>I may be going.<br>I was given the title. |
| **have** | have  has  had | I have started.<br>He had started. |
| **do** | do  does  did + base form | Did she buy that? |

7a
SL

## (1) Modals

**Modal verbs** are helping verbs with a variety of meanings. After a modal, use the base form.

| can | may | must | should | would |
|-----|-----|------|--------|-------|
| could | might | shall | will | ought to |

**Permission:** May I take this?    [Is it all right if I take this?]

**Advisability:** I ought to take this.    [It's a good idea to take this.]

**Necessity:**  Must I take this?    [Am I required to take this?]

**Ability:**     Can I take this?    [Am I able to take this?]

**Uncertainty:** Should I take this?

[I'm not certain if I should take this.]

**Possibility:**  Even an expert can make mistakes.
Even an expert might make a mistake.

[It is possible for experts to make a mistake.]

## (2)  Conditionals

In conditional sentences, clauses after *if, when,* and *unless* show whether the result is possible or real, depending on other circumstances.

• **Prediction:** Predicts something based on some condition.

| *Present* | *Future (Usually Modal + Base Form)* |
|-----------|--------------------------------------|
| If you eat more fresh fruit, | you will be healthier. |
| Unless she arrives soon, | we will be late for the concert. |

• **Fact:** Something usually happens when something else happens.

| *Present* | *Present* |
|-----------|-----------|
| When that dog barks at night, | he wakes us up. |

| *Past* | *Past* |
|--------|--------|
| When that dog barked at night, | he woke us up. |

• **Not real:** Use *would* in the result clause to show that the result is impossible, did not happen, or is unlikely to happen.

| *Past* | *Would + Base Form* |
|--------|---------------------|
| If she drove more slowly, | she would get fewer speeding tickets. |

To show that something is not reality in the past, use *were* instead of *was*.

| If I were rich, | I would travel to Tahiti. |
|-----------------|---------------------------|

4
E

- **Speculative:** To show that something is possible but unlikely, use *were* instead of *was*:

| Past | Would, Could, Might + Base Form |
|------|--------------------------------|
| If he had a car, | he could drive us to the restaurant. |
| If you were prepared, | you might understand the problem. |

> **HINT:** When *would, could,* and *might* are used with the base form, *-s* is not added to the base form for third person singular present.
>
> *drive*
> ❖ If he had a car, he could ~~drives~~ us to the restaurant.

# 47b Two-Word (Phrasal) Verbs

**Two-word (phrasal) verbs** have two (or sometimes three) words (particles) following the verb that help to indicate the meaning. Because the additional word or words often change the meaning, these verbs are idioms (see Chapter 53).

| | |
|---|---|
| look over (examine) | She looked over the terms of the contract. |
| look up (search) | I need to look up that phone number. |

In some cases, a noun or pronoun can be inserted so that the verb is separated from its additional word or words. In other cases, there can be no separation.

**Separable:** count in (include)

> Manuel told the team to count **him** in.
> *(inserted pronoun)*

**Inseparable:** count on (rely)

> The team could count on **him** to help.
> *(pronoun not inserted)*

### Some Common Two-Word Verbs

If the second word can be separated from the verb, a pronoun is included in parentheses.

| | | |
|---|---|---|
| add (it) up | cut (it)up | look like |
| back out of | drop (it) off | look out for |
| bring (it) on | fall behind | pass out |
| bring (it) up | get around | put (it) off |
| burn (it) down | get by | put (it) on |
| burn (it) up | get out of | run across |
| call for | get through | run into |

| | | |
|---|---|---|
| call (it) off | give (it) away | show off |
| call (her) up | go over | show up |
| carry (it) out | hand (it) in | stay up |
| clean (it) up | keep on | take (it) off |
| come across | keep (it) up | take (it) up |
| cross (it) out | leave (it) out | try (it) out |
| cut (it) off | look ahead | turn up |
| cut (it) out | look into | use (it) up |

# 47C Verbs with -ing and to + Verb Forms

Some verbs combine only with the *-ing* form of the verb (gerund); some combine only with the *to* + verb form (infinitive); some verbs can be followed by either form.

- Verbs followed only by *-ing* forms (gerunds):

| | | |
|---|---|---|
| admit | enjoy | practice |
| appreciate | finish | recall |
| avoid | fond of | regret |
| consider | keep | risk |
| deny | keep on | stop |
| dislike | postpone | suggest |

He <u>admits</u> <u>spending</u> that money.
  *(verb)* + *(gerund)*

> *reading*
> ❖ I recall ~~to read~~ that book.

- Verbs followed only by *to* + verb forms (infinitives):

| | | |
|---|---|---|
| agree | have | offer |
| ask | hope | plan |
| claim | manage | promise |
| decide | mean | wait |
| expect | need | want |

We <u>agree</u> <u>to send</u> an answer soon.
  *(verb)* + *(infinitive)*

> *to go*
> ❖ They planned ~~going~~ on vacation.

- Verbs that can be followed by either form:

| | | |
|---|---|---|
| begin | intend | prefer |
| continue | like | start |
| hate | love | try |

They begin to sing.    (or)    They begin singing.

4
E

Some verbs that can be followed by either form change meaning:

forget          remember          stop          try

She stopped talking.    [She ceased and did not talk.]

She stopped to talk.    [She paused while going somewhere in order to talk.]

## Exercise 47.1 Proofreading Practice

*In the following paragraph there are some errors in the verbs. Underline the errors, and write your corrections above the words underlined.*

(1) When people from other countries will visit the United States, they find a bewildering variety of words that can be used for the same thing. (2) In some parts of the United States, a salesperson will asked the customer if she would want the item in a "sack." (3) In other places, the salesperson might ask, "Did you wanted this in a 'bag'?" (4) It is hard for tourists who don't understand to bring up it when they don't know if there is a difference. (5) Or a tourist may ask, "May I take this metro to First Avenue?" in a city where the underground train is called "the subway." (6) If I was one of those tourists, I could always keep a dictionary in my pocket to use when the situation calls it for.

## Exercise 47.2: Pattern Practice

*In the following paragraph there are choices between verb forms. Underline the correct form of the verb that is needed.*

In schools in the United States, teachers hope (1. to encourage, encouraging) students to ask questions. They think that if students (2. talk, will talk) about a subject and ask questions, they (3. will learn, learn) more about the subject. In some other countries, students avoid (4. to ask, asking) questions because that may be a sign of rudeness in their country. The culture of the country has a very important influence on how teachers want (5.talking, to talk) to the class and how the class continues (6. to respond, responding) to the teacher. In the United States, some teachers like (7. to have, having) their students call them by their first name. This often surprises students from other countries where they (8. might be, must be) very formal with their teachers in order to show respect.

**7c**
**SL**

## Exercise 47.3: Pattern Practice

*Use the following verb forms in sentences of your own.*

1. may + verb
2. can + verb
3. If she were
4. hand (it) in

5. look like
6. hope + verb
7. try (it) out
8. forget + verb

9. begin + verb
10. do + verb
11. could + verb
12. have + verb

# 48 Omitted Words

## 48a Verbs

Verbs are necessary parts of English sentences and must be included. Verbs such as *is/are* or other helping verbs can be omitted in other languages, but not in English.

❖ Liu ᵪ *is* studying to be a computer programmer.

❖ She ᵪ *has* been studying ancient Mayan ruins in Mexico for many summers.

❖ It ᵪ *might* be a good idea to bring some water when we hike.

## 48b Subjects and *There/It*

In some languages the subject can be omitted, but in English the subject is left out only when expressing a command ("Put that box here, please.")

❖ All the children laughed when ᵪ *they* were watching the cartoon.

❖ The hockey player ᵪ *who* was guarding the goal got hurt in the game.

Particularly troublesome are *there* and *it* as subjects. Even when *there* is the subject word and the real subject is elsewhere in the sentence, *there* must be included. *It* is sometimes needed as a subject in sentences about the weather, distance, time, and other aspects of the world around us.

❖ Certainly, ᵪ *there* are many confusing rules in English spelling.

❖ I think ᵪ *it* is about ten miles from here to the shopping mall.

**48
ES**

# 49 Repeated Words

## 49a Subjects

In some languages, the subject can be repeated as a pronoun before the verb. In English, the subject is included only once.

Bones in the body ~~they~~ become brittle when people grow older.

[In this sentence both *bones* and *they* are the subject of the verb *brittle*.]

The plane that was ready for takeoff ~~it~~ stopped on the runway.

[In this sentence both *plane* and *it* are the subject of the verb *stopped*.]

## 49b Pronouns and Adverbs

When relative pronouns such as *who, which,* and *that* or relative adverbs such as *where* or *when* introduce clauses (see Chapter 23), they are the object of the verb or prepositional phrase, so no additional word is needed.

The woman tried on the hat that I left ~~it~~ on the seat.

[*That* is the object of the verb *left,* and *it* is unnecessary repetition.]

The city where I live ~~there~~ has two soccer fields.

[*Where* is the object of the verb *live,* and *there* is unnecessary repetition.]

### Exercise 49.1: Proofreading Practice

*The following paragraph has omitted words. Add the missing words. Where words are unnecessarily repeated, draw a line through them.*

(1) When students looking for part-time work, one difficulty is that they want the job to be after class hours. (2) Another difficulty for students is that want the job to be near their school so that don't have far to travel. (3) But that means are many students who want to work at the same time and in the same area of town. (4) The competition for the jobs that exist it causes too many students to be unable to find work. (5) Some counselors they tell their students to try looking for jobs that have flexible hours or for work that it can be done at home. (6) Is also worth trying to look farther away from the campus.

# 50 Count and Noncount Nouns

Nouns are either proper nouns that name specific things and begin with capital letters or common nouns (see Chapter 34). There are two kinds of common nouns, count and noncount nouns:

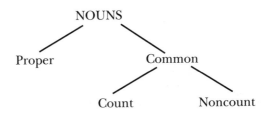

A **count noun** names something that can be counted because it can be divided into separate and distinct units. Count nouns have plurals (see 17a) and usually refer to things that can be seen, heard, touched, tasted, or smelled.

A **noncount noun** names something that cannot be counted because it is an abstraction (a substance that is thought of as a whole) or something that cannot be cut into parts. Noncount nouns do not have plurals and may have a collective meaning.

### Count Nouns

| | |
|---|---|
| apple | (one apple, two apples) |
| chair | (a chair, several chairs) |
| child | (the child, six children) |

### Noncount Nouns

| | | |
|---|---|---|
| air | humor | oil |
| furniture | milk | weather |

The names of many foods are noncount nouns:

| | | |
|---|---|---|
| bread | corn | spinach |
| coffee | spaghetti | tofu |

To indicate the amount for a noncount noun, use a count noun first:

| | |
|---|---|
| a pound of coffee | a loaf of bread |
| an ear of corn | a gallon of oil |

5
E

*Nouns that Can Be Both Count and Noncount Nouns*

Some nouns in English have both a count and a noncount meaning, depending on the context in which the noun is used. The count meaning is specific, and the noncount meaning is abstract.

**Count:**    The **exercises** were difficult to do.
**Noncount:** **Exercise** is good for our health.

**Count:**    There were bright **lights** in the sky.
**Noncount:** Those plants need more **light**.

**Count:**    She ate five **chocolates** from the box.
**Noncount:** **Chocolate** is fattening.

---

**HINT:** Knowing whether a noun is a count or noncount noun is important in determining whether or not to use *a, an,* or *the* (see 51c).

Singular count nouns need an article:    She returned **the** book.

Noncount nouns usually do not
need an article:    Plants enjoy water.

---

## Exercise 50.1: Proofreading Practice

*In the parentheses in the following paragraph, underline the correct choice between count and noncount nouns.*

(1. American, Americans) have always enjoyed drinking (2. coffee, coffees). Now there is a new trend as (3. restaurant, restaurants) and (4. store, stores) are beginning to sell many specialty (5. coffee, coffees) with (6. flavor, flavors) such as chocolate, cinnamon, and almond. Americans, who are used to eating (7. dozen, dozens) of different flavors of (8. ice cream, ice creams), can now decide between different types of coffee with (9. milk, milks) or with whipped (10. cream, creams). This can cause (11. problem, problems) because customers need more (12. information, informations) in order to choose between flavors and types of coffee they have never tried before. (13. Advertising, Advertisings) will surely help American coffee (14. drinker, drinkers) to become more familiar with specialty coffees.

## Exercise 50.2: Pattern Practice

*Make up sentences of your own, using the underlined count and noncount nouns in the following sentences:*

1. The insect had four <u>wings</u>.
2. They walked down many <u>streets</u> to the river.
3. Some <u>bones</u> in the skeleton were broken, but the museum had no <u>bone</u> to use in repairing the exhibit.

4. The coat was made of <u>cotton</u>.
5. She picked some <u>roses</u> from the garden.
6. He knew six <u>languages</u> and wanted to learn another one because <u>language</u> is a fascinating thing to study.
7. She likes to eat <u>rice</u> with a lot of <u>sugar</u> on it.
8. The <u>rain</u> caused some <u>mud</u> to splash on my car.
9. The <u>clothing</u> was on sale in the store.
10. After the <u>snow</u> melted and froze again, the street was like a sheet of <u>ice</u>.

# 51 Adjectives and Adverbs

## 51a Placement

The ordering of adjectives and adverbs in English is as follows:

*Adverb* ⟶ *Adjective* ⟶ *Noun*
very            large          gate

Adverbs are placed first because they describe adjectives. Then, adjectives are placed next because they describe nouns.

Adverbs that describe verbs can move around in the sentence and appear in the following places:

- At the beginning of the sentence

  <u>Sometimes</u>, Noah can find great bargains.

- At the end of the sentence

  Noah can find great bargains <u>sometimes</u>.

- Before the verb

  Noah <u>sometimes</u> can find great bargains.

- After the verb

  Jana types <u>quickly</u> on her laptop computer.

- Between the helping and main verb

  Noah can <u>sometimes</u> find great bargains.

Do not place adverbs between verbs and objects:

**Wrong:** She picks quickly the fruit.

**Revised:** She quickly picks the fruit.

# 51b Order

Putting adjectives in the accepted English order can be confusing to speakers of other languages. Follow the order of these categories, but it is best not to pile up more than two or three adjectives between the article (or other determiner) and the noun.

| | | Physical Description | | | | | | | |
|---|---|---|---|---|---|---|---|---|---|
| *Determiner* | *Evaluation or Opinion* | *Size* | *Shape* | *Age* | *Color* | *Nationality* | *Religion* | *Material* | *Noun* |
| a, three, her | lovely | big | round | old | green | English | Catholic | silk | purse |

**ORDER OF ADJECTIVES**

the quiet Japanese rock garden
a square blue cotton handkerchief
my lazy old Siamese cat

six excellent new movies
many difficult physics problems
every big green plant

## 51.1: Pattern Practice

*Reorder the adjectives and nouns in these clusters, and write your own sentences.*

1. old    famous    six    sports stars
2. Hispanic    favorite    her    song    old
3. steel    German    new    a    knife
4. square    small    strange    a    box
5. large    nine    balls    yellow

# 51c A/An/The

**A** and **an** identify nouns in a general or indefinite way and refer to any member of a group. *A* and *an*, which mean "one among many," are generally used with singular count nouns. (See Chapter 50 on count nouns.)

She likes to read **a** book before going to sleep.

[This sentence does not specify which book, just any book. *Book* is a singular count noun.]

*The* identifies a particular or specific noun in a group or a noun already identified in a previous phrase or sentence. *The* may be used with singular or plural nouns.

She read **the** book. [This sentence identifies a specific book.]

Give the coins to **the** boys. [This sentence identifies a specific group.]

**A** new model of computer was introduced yesterday. **The** model will cost much less than **the** older model.

[*A* introduces the noun the first time it is mentioned, and then *the* is used afterwards whenever the noun is mentioned.]

### *A, An,* and *The* with Proper Nouns
- **Singular:** Usually no article    Mrs. Samosa
- **Plural:** Usually use *the*    **the** United States

### *A, An,* and *The* with Common Nouns
- **Count nouns:**
  **Singular:** Use an article or pronoun for singular count nouns.
  **a** tree, **her** wrist

  **Plural:** Use *the* when naming a specific representative of a category.
  **the** committee

  Do not use *the* when the meaning is "all" or "in general"
  Chairs were provided.    People are creatures of habit.

- **Noncount nouns:** Never use *a* or *an* with noncount nouns.

### Other Uses of *The*
- Use *the* when an essential phrase or clause follows the noun (see Chapter 24).

  **The** man who is standing at the door is my cousin.

- Use *the* when the noun refers to a class as a whole.

  **The** ferret is a popular pet.

- Use *the* with names composed partly of common nouns.

  **the** British Commonwealth    **the** Sahara Desert

- Use *the* with names composed of common nouns plus proper names.

  **the** Province of Quebec    **the** University of Illinois

- Use *the* when names are plurals.

    **the** Netherlands                **the** Balkans

- Use *the* with names that refer to rivers, oceans, seas, points on the globe, deserts, forests, gulfs, and peninsulas.

    **the** Nile          **the** Pacific Ocean          **the** Persian Gulf

- Use *the* when points of the compass are used as names.

    **the** South          **the** Midwest

- Use *the* when points of time are indicated.

    **the** beginning          **the** present          **the** afternoon

- Use *the* with superlatives.

    **the** best reporter          **the** most expensive car

- Use *the* with adjectives used as nouns.

    **The** homeless are in need of health care.

- Use *the* with gerunds or abstract nouns followed by *of* phrases.

    **The** meaning of that word is not clear.

### No Articles

Articles are not used with names of streets, cities, states, countries, continents, lakes, parks, mountains, names of languages, sports, holidays, universities, and colleges without *of* in the name, and academic subjects.

| | |
|---|---|
| He traveled to Africa. | She is studying Chinese. |
| That shop is on Fifth Avenue. | Pollution in Lake Erie has been reduced. |
| He prefers to watch volleyball. | My major is political science. |
| They celebrated Thanksgiving. | She applied to Brandeis University. |

The following chart summarizes the most frequent uses of *a, an,* and *the:*

---

## USES OF A, AN, AND THE

### *A/An*

- Unspecified singular count nouns

    **A** computer is **a** useful tool.

### *The*

- Particular or specific singular count nouns and specific plural count nouns

  I ate **the** pizza, but she wanted **the** pretzels.

- Noncount nouns that are specific members of a general group

  **The** sunlight in the late afternoon sky cast interesting shadows.

- Plural proper nouns

  They sailed to **the** Virgin Islands.

### *No articles*

- Singular proper nouns

  He moved to Salt Lake City.

- Unspecified plural count nouns meaning "all" or "in general"

  Bats are night feeders.

- Noncount nouns

  Trina does not like beer.

## Exercise 51.2: Proofreading Practice

*In the following paragraph, add* a, an, *or* the *where needed.*

One of most interesting physicists of this century was Richard Feynman. He wrote best-selling book about his own life, but he became even more famous on television as man who was member of team that investigated after accident happened to Challenger, space shuttle that crashed in 1986. People watched on television as he demonstrated that faulty part in space shuttle probably caused accident. Feynman's greatest achievement in science was theory of quantum electrodynamics, which described behavior of subatomic particles, atoms, light, electricity, and magnetism. Field of computer science also owes much to work of Feynman. Many scientists consider Feynman to be one of geniuses of twentieth century.

# 51d *Some/Any, Much/Many, Little/Few, Less/Fewer, Enough, No*

### Some/Any/Enough/No

- These words modify count and noncount nouns (see Chapter 50).

  | | |
  |---|---|
  | She brought **some** fresh flowers. | There is **some** water on the floor. |
  | Do you have **any** erasers? | Do you have **any** food? |
  | I have **enough** glasses for everyone. | There is **enough** money to buy a car. |
  | There are **no** squirrels in the park. | There is **no** time to finish now. |

- *Some* is used in positive statements.

      They ate **some** fruit.

- *Any* is used in negative statements and in questions.

  | | |
  |---|---|
  | They did not eat **any** fruit. | Did they eat **any** fruit? |

| *With Noncount Nouns* | *With Count Nouns* |
|---|---|
| (not) much | (not) many |
| little | few |
| less | fewer |

| | |
|---|---|
| They have **much** money in the bank. | **Many** Americans travel to Europe. |
| He had **little** food in the house. | There are a **few** doctors here. |
| Use **less** oil in the mixture. | We ordered **fewer** books. |

# 52 Prepositions

For a list of idiomatic prepositions, see 20b. The following guide will help you choose among *on, at, in, of,* and *for* to indicate time, place, and logical relationships.

### Prepositions of Time

**On**  Use with days (**on** Monday).
**At**  Use with hours of the day (**at** 9 P.M.) and with noon, night, midnight, and dawn (**at** midnight).

**In**   Use with other parts of the day: morning, afternoon, evening (**in** the morning); use with months, years, seasons (**in** the winter).

They are getting married **on** Sunday **at** four o'clock **in** the afternoon.

## Prepositions of Place:

**On**   Indicates a surface on which something rests.

The car is **on** the street.
She put curtains **on** the windows.

**At**   Indicates a point in relation to another object.

My sister is **at** home.
I'll meet you **at** Second Avenue and Main Street.

**In**   Indicates an object is inside the boundaries of an area or volume.

The sample is **in** the bottle.
She is **in** the bank.

## Prepositions to Show Logical Relationships

**Of**   Shows relationship between a part (or parts) and the whole.

One **of** her teachers gave a quiz.

Shows material or content.

They gave me a basket **of** food.

**For**   Shows purpose.

We bought a new hose **for** our garden.

## Exercise 52.1: Proofreading Practice

*In the following paragraph, there are some errors in the use of prepositions in, on, and at and some errors in the use of* some/any/much/many/little/few. *Underline the errors, and write your corrections above the words.*

(1) Table Tennis used to be a minor pastime at America, but a little years ago it began to develop into an important sport. (2) Newcomers to the United States from countries such as Nigeria, Korea, and China, where table tennis is a major sport, have helped the United States become a respectable contender at world competition. (3) Much new residents who are very good in this sport have brought their skills to this country. (4) Now there are specialized table tennis parlors where players play in tables with special hard surfaces. (5) Players no longer use some sandpaper paddles. (6) Instead, much paddles are made of carbon fiber and have special coatings in the hitting surface. (7) At the past, America was

often on last place in international competitions. (8) But now, with many strong players, often born at China, the United States is beginning to win.

## Exercise 52.2: Pattern Practice

*Make up sentences of your own which use the following words:*

1. some
2. any
3. few
4. less
5. many

6. in (with a time expression)
7. on (a place)
8. in (a place)
9. of (showing a relationship)
10. at (a place)

# 53 Idioms

An **idiom** is an expression that means something beyond the simple definition or literal translation into another language. An idiom such as "kick the bucket" (meaning "die") is not understandable from the meanings of the individual words.

| | |
|---|---|
| par for the course | under the table |
| live high on the hog | the bottom line |
| the old college try | bats in his belfrey |
| by and large | on the ball |

For a list of idiomatic prepositions that follow certain words, see 20b. Because the meaning of two-word (phrasal) verbs (see 47b) is not the same as the literal meaning of each of the words, these verbs are also idioms.

# Appendices

a

# A Argument (arg)

Reading and writing persuasive arguments is very likely to be part of your everyday life. For example, you may have written letters to potential employers to persuade them to hire you. Perhaps you have written a business proposal to persuade your boss to implement a plan, or you've written an application to persuade some group to grant you admission to a program or give you funding. You've probably read advertisements in magazines that attempt to persuade you to buy certain products. Or maybe you have read letters from charitable organizations or political candidates persuading you to donate time or money to their causes. Even college brochures are written partly to persuade you to apply to that institution. The use of reasons as well as emotional appeals to persuade an audience is part of normal interaction with the world. People actively persuade you to believe, act on, or accept their claims, just as you want others to accept or act on your claims.

However, persuasion is not the only purpose for writing an effective argument. You might argue to justify to yourself and others what you believe and why you hold those positions. You also formulate arguments to solve problems and make decisions. The ability to argue effectively is clearly a skill everyone needs. Because argumentation is a process of researching to find support for your claims as well as a process of reasoning to explain and defend actions, beliefs, and ideas, you need to think about finding that information (see Part Seven of this book). You also need to consider how you present yourself as a writer to your audience, how your audience will respond to you, how you select topics to write about, and how you develop and organize your material into persuasive papers. These topics will be discussed in the following sections.

## A1 Writing and Reading Arguments

As a writer, you have to get your readers to commit themselves to listening to you and to letting you make your case. In order to gain your reader's trust and respect, your writing should indicate that you know what you are talking about, that you are truthful, and that you are reasonable enough to consider other sides of the argument. As the reader of an argument, you need to consider the writer's credibility. For example, if you were to read an article that claims cigarette smoking is not harmful to our health and then discover that the writer works in the tobacco industry, you would question the writer's credibility. Similarly, you need to establish your own credibility with your audiences.

> **HINT:** The following suggestions will help you establish your credibility with your audience:
>
> - **Show that your motives are reasonable and worthwhile.** Give your audience some reasonable assurance that you are arguing for a claim that is recognized as being for the general good or that shares the audience's motives. For example, are you writing an argument to a group of fellow students for more on-campus parking because you personally are having a parking problem or because you recognize that this is a problem many students are having? If you want action to solve your personal problem, you are not likely to get an attentive hearing. Why should others care about your problem? But if you help other students see that this is a widespread problem that they may have too, you are indicating that you share their motives and that you are arguing for a general good that concerns them too.
> - **Avoid vague and ambiguous terms and exaggerated claims.** Vague arguments such as "everyone says" (who is "everyone"?) or "it's a huge problem" (how big is "huge"?) raise doubts about the writer's knowledge and ability to write authoritatively. Exaggerations such as "Commercialism has destroyed the meaning of Christmas" or "No one cares about the farmer's problems any more" are highly inflated opinions that weaken the writer's credibility.

# A2 Considering the Audience

## (a) Types of Appeals

You need to formulate in your mind the audience for a particular piece of persuasive writing. If you are writing to an audience that already agrees with you, you need to decide what your purpose will be. What would be accomplished if your readers already agree with you? If your audience is likely to disagree, you need to think about how to acknowledge and address  reasons for disagreeing. You can use three different kinds of appeals to make your case:

- **Logical appeals** Logical reasoning is grounded in sound principles of inductive and deductive reasoning. It avoids logical fallacies and bases proofs on reality—that is, factual evidence gathered from data and events—as well as deduction, definitions, and analogies. Logical proof appeals to people's reason, understanding, and common sense.

For example, for a paper attempting to persuade readers that a particular job training program has worked and should therefore continue to be funded, logical arguments could include data showing the number of people in the program and the success rate of their employment after being in the program. The paper could then compare those figures to data on a similar group of people who did not take part in the program.

- **Emotional appeals** Emotional appeals arouse the audience's emotions, such as their sympathy, patriotism, pride, and other feelings based on values, beliefs, and motives. Appeals to emotions may include examples, description, and narratives.

    For example, for the paper on job training programs, an effective example might be the story of a woman who was previously unemployed for a long period of time, despite intensive job seeking, but who found a good job after acquiring new skills in the program. Her testimony would appeal to the audience's sympathy and to the belief that most people want to work and will be able to do so if they could just get some help in upgrading their skills.

- **Ethical appeals** Ethical proof appeals to the audience's impressions, opinions, and judgments about the person making the argument. That is, these appeals establish the credibility of the writer. The audience should be given proof that the writer is knowledgeable, does not distort evidence, and has some authority on the subject. To establish credibility, writers can draw on personal experience, explain their credentials for discussing the topic, and show that they are using their logical proofs appropriately.

    For example, for the job training paper, the author might draw on her experience working for the program or explain that the data she is presenting comes from a highly credible source such as county or state records.

    When writing arguments, consider what your audience is likely to value as evidence. You can use statistics, your experience, and research. How informed is your audience? What are the likely bases for readers' views and beliefs? What common ground can you establish with your readers so they will listen to you?

## (b) Common Ground

An important step in gaining a hearing from your audience is to identify the common ground you share with readers—the values, beliefs, common interests, motives, or goals where there is overlap between you and those likely to disagree with you. Without some common ground between you and the audience, there is no argument, no way to get that audience to listen to you or understand you. Think, for example, of some strong conviction you hold. If someone with an equally strong stand on the opposite side started arguing for that opposing position, are you immediately likely to listen attentively? Or would you instead start marshaling arguments for your side? For example, for a writer who firmly believes in everyone's right to own a gun, there is no common ground with equally firm advocates of gun control. Neither side is really likely to listen to the other. On the other hand, if you and your audience are in total agreement, there also is no argument. If someone who believes that higher education needs adequate funding talks to a group of faculty at his or her college, there are no points to argue. An appropriate topic for a persuasive paper will fall between these extremes and will have opposing views to consider and common ground to find.

Because the search for common ground is so important, let's examine how it might be discovered. Suppose a legislator wants to introduce a bill requiring motorcyclists to wear helmets, but the legislator knows she will be voted down because many other legislators oppose such laws that restrict people's freedom to decide these matters. One place to find some overlap would be to establish that everyone has a concern for the safety of bikers. It's also likely that everyone in the legislature will agree that bikers have a right to be on the road and that motorists often aren't sufficiently careful about avoiding them. Thus, there is general agreement (or common ground) that bikers are subject to some major hazards on the road and that everyone should be concerned about their welfare. When the legislator identifies to her audience that they share this much common ground, she is likely to get a hearing for her reasons why she wants her bill to pass.

One more example might help you to see where and how that very important common ground can be found. Suppose you are writing a proposal to the city council to spend funds beautifying one of the public playgrounds. If you believe the council is likely to turn down your proposal, you need to think about the council members' possible reasons for rejecting it. Is the city budget so tight that the council is reluctant to spend money on any projects that aren't absolutely necessary? If so, what appeals could you make in your proposal? Your opening argument could be a logical appeal, including some facts about the low cost of the beautification project. Or perhaps you could begin with an emotional appeal about the children who use the playground. What common ground do you share with the council? You and they want a well-run city that doesn't go into debt. If you acknowledge that you share those concerns and that you too don't want to put the city budget in the red, you will be more likely to get the council to listen to your proposal.

Getting ready to write a persuasive paper clearly requires thinking about yourself as the writer and about your audience who will read your arguments. But there are other considerations as you move through this writing process. How do you find a topic? How do you find the material you want to use in the development of your arguments? How do you build sound arguments? How do you organize all this information into a paper? The following sections offer help with these important parts of the process.

# A3 Finding a Topic

## (a) Arguable Topics

Topics for persuasion are always those that can be argued, that have two or more sides that can be claimed as worth agreeing upon. For example, no one can argue that the total number of reported rapes has not increased nationally in the last fifty years, so a claim that reported rapes have gone up would not be a topic for a persuasive paper. It is simply a fact that can be checked in lists of national crime statistics. But there are multiple sides to other issues about rape. Are those numbers higher because the population has grown, because of more accurate reporting, because more rapes are being committed, or because women are more inclined to actually report such attacks? So, a persuasive paper might take a stand about the causes of the increase in reported rapes.

## (b) Interesting Topics

When preparing to write a persuasive paper on a topic you are free to choose, think about the wide range of matters that interest you or that are part of your life. What do you and your friends talk about? What have you been reading lately in the newspaper or in magazines? What topics have you heard about on television? What are some ongoing situations around you, that is, events that are happening or about to happen? What unresolved public or family issues concern you? What topics have you been discussing or reading about in your classes? What matters concerning yourself are unresolved and need further consideration? What event happened to you that made you stop and think? Or get mad? Or cheer?

## (c) Local and General Topics

If you start with a subject that answers any of the questions asked above, you can begin to build a paper topic either by thinking it through on a local or personal level or by enlarging your perspective beyond your local setting. For example, you might start with some new rule, guideline, or restriction on your campus, such as a new electronic device that searched you as you left the library to see if you had a book you hadn't checked out. Is that something that bothers you? Do you see it as an invasion of student privacy? Or as a waste of the school's money? Or as a way, finally, to stop all the library theft you know is going on in your school? These are local views of the matter, and any one might be a springboard for a paper topic in which you argue that the antitheft system is or is not a beneficial addition to the library. Or, you could move to a larger view beyond your own library or campus or city. Is this instance part of a larger issue of new technology that implies everyone should be checked for dishonest behavior? Should we accept that new library device or airport scanners as a means to safeguard our security and well-being?

# A4 Developing Your Arguments

## (a) Claims, Support, and Warrants

To develop your arguments you need to clarify what your main point or claim is, what support you are going to offer for that claim, and what warrants or unspoken assumptions are present in the argument. This system for arguments was developed by Stephen Toulmin, a modern philosopher.

**Claim**

A *claim* is the proposition, the assertion or thesis that is to be proved. There are three types of claims: of fact, of value, and of policy. We can find these types of claims by asking questions that identify what an argument is trying to prove:

- Is there a **fact** the argument is trying to prove?

  Did the accused person really commit that theft?
  Is your college providing access for students in wheelchairs?
  Is the amount of television advertising increasing in relation to the amount of programming?

- Is there an issue of **values** in the argument?

  Should schools provide sex education for children?
  Should scientists be permitted total freedom to experiment with artificial insemination?
  Should the beliefs of major religions be taught in school?

- Is there an issue of **policy** in the argument?

  Should legislators be allowed to hold office for an unlimited number of terms?
  Should your college provide free parking for students?
  Should smokers be permitted to smoke in restaurants?

## Support

The *support* for an argument is the material or evidence used to convince the audience. Such support or proof may include evidence such as facts, data, examples, statistics, and the testimony of experts. Support may also include appeals to our emotions. If a claim is made that baseball is no longer the nation's favorite summer sport, then facts or data or statistics are needed to show that it once was the nation's favorite summer sport and that it has declined in popularity. If a claim is made that the U.S. Postal Service should issue commemorative stamps honoring famous American heroes of World War II, the argument might use an emotional appeal to our patriotism, asking us to remember these great people who served our country so bravely.

## Warrant

The *warrant* is an underlying assumption, belief, or principle in an argument. Some warrants are made explicit, while others are left unstated. Whether or not your audience shares your assumption determines if they will accept or reject your argument. If you hear someone say that she didn't learn a thing in her history class because her teacher was dull, an unstated warrant is that the teacher is solely responsible for what students learn or that dull teachers cannot help students gain knowledge. In this brief argument, it may be easy to spot the warrant, but other arguments have warrants that are not as obvious. If someone argues that more police are needed to patrol the streets of inner-city neighborhoods in order to reduce illegal drug traffic, what is the warrant here? Is there more than one warrant? One assumption, or warrant, is that patrolling police are able to find and arrest drug dealers. Another assumption is that by arresting drug dealers, police can cut down the incidence of such crime. This, in turn, assumes that when some drug dealers are taken off the streets, more will not appear on the scene to take their place.

As writers develop their arguments, they have to be aware both of what warrants exist in their arguments and of what warrants exist in the audience's minds. If an audience shares the writer's warrants, the argument is likely to be more effective and convincing. If the audience does not share the writer's warrants, it will be hard to persuade the audience because the warrant is the link that connects the claim to the support and leads the audience to accept the claim. When you see a commercial that shows a well-known athlete endorsing some new pizza chain, there are several warrants or unspoken assumptions operating behind the claim that this company has good pizza and the support that the pizza is good because the athlete said so. One warrant is that this athlete is not just making a statement because she has been paid to do so. Another is that this athlete really knows what good pizza is or that her standards and tastes in pizza are the same as yours. If you accept such warrants, you are likely to be convinced that the pizza is good. The support was adequate for the argument. If not, then the athlete's statement was not adequate support, and you are not likely to be enticed to try the pizza.

Similarly, for the argument you build, you should also examine the warrants in the opposing arguments. What assumptions are left unsaid in the case made by the opposing side? Does the opposing argument rest on underlying assumptions or accepted beliefs which your readers ought to know about because they might not accept those warrants? For example, if you oppose physician-assisted suicide for the terminally ill, the opposing side may not have presented any evidence that shows that doctors always know when a patient is terminally ill. This might be a warrant in their case that doctors should be allowed to make such judgments. Would your audience accept that warrant? If not, then you make your argument stronger by calling attention to the warrant.

## (b) Logical Arguments

Another consideration as you build your argument is the logical direction of the argument. For the claim you make, is it appropriate to move from a statement of a general principle to logical arguments that support that generalization? If so, your argument will develop deductively. Or is it more appropriate to construct your case from particular instances or examples that build to a conclusion? If so, your argument is an inductive one.

### Deductive Reasoning

When you reason deductively, you draw a conclusion from assertions (or premises). You start with a generalization or major premise and reason logically to a conclusion. The conclusion is *true* when the premises are true and is *valid* when the conclusion follows necessarily from the premises. For example, if you read an argument that starts with the generalization that all politicians spend their time seeking reelection, any conclusion that is drawn will not be true because the generalization is not universally true. An example of *invalid* deductive reasoning is the argument which proceeds to the following conclusion:

**Premise:** Lack of exercise causes people to be overweight.

**Premise:** Jillian is overweight.

**Conclusion:** Therefore, Jillian doesn't exercise.

In this example, it is possible that Jillian does exercise but eats fattening food that causes her to remain overweight. Thus, this is not a valid argument because the conclusion does not necessarily follow from the premise.

## Inductive Reasoning

When you reason inductively, you come to conclusions on the basis of observing a number of particular instances. Using the examples you observe, you arrive at a statement of what is generally true of something or of a whole group of things. For example, if you try a certain medication a few times and find that each time you take it, it upsets your stomach, you conclude that this medication bothers you. Inductive conclusions are, however, only probable at best. A new example might prove the conclusion false, or the number of examples may not have been large enough for a reasonable conclusion to be drawn. Or, the quality of the examples might be questionable. Suppose, for example, you want to find out the most popular major on your campus, and you decide to stand outside the engineering building. You ask each student entering and leaving the building what his or her major is, and the vast majority of the students say that they are majoring in engineering. The conclusion that engineering is the most popular major on campus is not reliable because the sample does not represent the whole campus. If you moved to the agriculture building and stood there and asked the same question, it's likely you would find agriculture to be the most popular major.

## (c) Logical Fallacies

Letters to the editor in a newspaper, advertisements, political campaign speeches, and courtroom battles are apt to offer proofs that have not been carefully thought through. As you develop your own arguments and read the arguments of others, you need to check for mistakes in the reasoning and to see whether opposing views present support that might have errors in reasoning. It is unfortunately very easy to fall into a number of traps in thinking, some of which are described here.

---

### HINT:  Recognizing and Avoiding Fallacies

- **Hasty generalization:** A conclusion reached with too few examples—or examples that are not representative.

  *Example:* Your friend complains that the phone company is a bunch of bumblers because they never send a bill that is correct.

  *To Avoid:* Many hasty generalizations contain words such as *all*, *never*, and *every*. You can correct them by substituting words such as *some* and *sometimes*.

- **Begging the question (circular reasoning):** An argument that goes round in circles, assuming that what has to be proved has already been proved.

  *Example:* When a salesperson points out that the product she is selling is "environmentally friendly," you ask why. Her reply is that it doesn't pollute the atmosphere. Why doesn't it pollute the atmosphere? Because, she explains, it's environmentally friendly.

*To Avoid:* Check to see if there is no new information in the development of the argument. If the arguments go round in circles, look for some outside proof or reasoning.

- **Doubtful cause** *(post hoc, ergo propter hoc)*: A mistake in reasoning that occurs when one event happens and then another event happens. As a result, people mistakenly reason that there is a cause and effect relationship when no such relationship exists. (The Latin phrase *post hoc, ergo propter hoc* means "after this, therefore because of this.")

  *Example:* If a school institutes a dress code and vandalism decreases the next week, it is tempting to reason that the dress code caused a decrease in vandalism, but this sequence does not prove a cause-and-effect relationship. Other factors may be at work, or incidents of vandalism might increase the next month. More conclusive evidence is needed.

  *To Avoid:* Do not automatically assume that because one event follows another, the second event was caused by the first event. Check for a real cause-and-effect relationship, an effect that can be continually repeated with the same results.

- **Using irrelevant proof to support a claim** *(non sequitur)*: Describes a line of reasoning in which the conclusion is not a logical result of the premises. (The Latin phrase *non sequitur* means "it does not follow.")

  *Example:* That movie was superb because it cost so much to produce.

  *To Avoid:* The proof of a statement must be a logical step in reasoning with logical connections. In the example given here, the amount of money spent on filming a movie is not necessarily related to the movie's quality and is therefore an irrelevant proof.

- **False analogy:** Assumes without proof that if objects or processes are similar in some ways, they are similar in other ways.

  *Example:* If engineers can design those black boxes that survive plane crashes, they should be able to build the whole plane from that same material.

  *To Avoid:* Check whether other major aspects of the objects or processes being compared are not similar. In the example above, the construction materials used in a huge and complex plane cannot be not the same as those for the little black boxes.

*continued on next page*

*continued from previous page*

- **Attack the person** *(ad hominem)*: Refers to a personal attack on someone that is intended to overthrow or dismiss the argument. (The Latin phrase *ad hominem* means "against the man.")

  *Example:* If an economist proposes a plan for helping impoverished people, her opponent might dismiss her plan by pointing out that she's never been poor.

  *To Avoid:* Avoid reasoning that diverts our attention from the quality of the argument to the person offering it.

- **Either . . . or:** Establishes a false *either/or* situation and does not allow for other possibilities or choices that may exist.

  *Example:* Either America balances the budget, or the country will slide into another Great Depression.

  *To Avoid:* When offered only two alternatives, look for others as well.

- **Bandwagon:** An argument that claims to be sound because a large number of people approve of it.

  *Example:* In a political campaign, we might hear that we should vote for someone because many other people have decided this person is the best candidate.

  *To Avoid:* Do not accept an argument just because some or even many others support it.

# A5 Organizing Your Arguments

The organization of an argument depends in part on how you analyze your audience. One way to begin is with the common ground you share with the audience so that your readers will be more likely to pay attention to your argument. You may wish to bring up points that favor your opponents' side of the argument early in the paper and discuss the merits of these points, or you may decide that it would be more effective to do this near the end of the paper. You can also consider other organizational patterns, such as starting with the claim followed by a discussion of the reasons. You may find a problem-and-solution pattern more appropriate. Cause and effect is yet another pattern to consider. You can either start with the cause and then trace the effects or begin with the effects and work back to the cause. You can also build your argument by establishing the criteria or standards by which to judge a claim and then showing how your claim meets these criteria. If your conclusion is one that an audience is not likely to be receptive to at first, a better organization might be to move through your points and then announce your thesis or claim after you have built some acceptance for your arguments.

# B Document Design (doc)

## B1 Titles

An essay's title serves several purposes. It indicates to readers what they can expect as to the topic and the author's perspective in the essay. Some titles state in a straightforward manner what the essay will be about; for example, the title "Nutritional Benefits of High-Fiber Foods" is a clear indication of the content and the author's intention to address it directly, in a formal manner. Other titles, particularly of personal essays, may offer the reader only a hint about the topic—a hint that becomes clearer after reading the essay. "At Sea over the Ocean" might be the title for an essay describing a frightening trip in a hot-air balloon or a humorous experience in an airplane.

### Choosing a Title

A title helps the writer organize a topic and select the emphasis for a particular essay. Writers who select the title before or during the early stages of writing may need to check at a later stage to see that the title still relates to the essay as it evolves and develops.

- **Good titles are clear and specific.** An example of an overly general title for a short essay would be "Divorce" because it does not indicate what aspect of divorce will be discussed. Even a title such as "Recent Trends in Automotive Design" is too general for a short essay because so much material could be discussed under this heading.
- **Good titles are brief.** Most titles are no more than six or seven words.

A title should stand alone. The title should not be part of the first sentence, and it should not be referred to by a pronoun in the first sentence. For example, in a research paper titled "The Influence of Television Advertisements in Presidential Elections," the first sentence should not read as follows:

**Incorrect Opening Sentence:** This is a topic of great concern both to politicians and to those who think that these elections have become popularity contests.

**Revised:** The degree to which television advertisements influence voters' choices in presidential elections worries politicians and others who think that national elections have become popularity contests.

## Capitalizing a Title

Capitalize the first and last words of a title, plus all other words except articles (*a, an, the*), short prepositions (*by, for, in, to, on,* etc.), and short joining words (*but, and, or,* etc.). Capitalize both words of a hyphenated word, and the first word of a subtitle that appears after a colon. (For more on capitalization, see Chapter 34.)

| | |
|---|---|
| Choosing a Career in Retailing | Short but Sweet |
| A History of Anti-Imperialism | Myths Through the Ages |
| My Childhood: The Plight of Growing Up Black | The Last Straw |

## Punctuating a Title

For your own essays, do not put the title in quotation marks, and do not use a period after the title. (For more information on using quotations marks and underlining, see Chapters 30 and 37.)

## Spacing a Title on the Page

- **For Typed Pages** If you have a cover page for research papers and reports and are using MLA format, see the sample pages in 45d. For APA format, see the sample pages in 46d. If you do not have a cover page, leave a one-inch margin at the top and then write your name, your instructor's name, the course and section number, and date submitted at the left-hand margin. Double-space this information. Then double-space and type the title, centered on the page. If you need more than one line for the title, double-space between these lines. Then double-space between the title and the first line of text.
- **For Handwritten Papers** Follow the format for typed papers by leaving a one-inch margin at the top and writing your name, your instructor's name, the course and section number, and date submitted at the left-hand margin. Put the title on the first ruled line of the page, skip a line, and then begin writing your paper, skipping every other ruled line.

# B2  Headings and Subheadings

Headings are the short titles that define sections and subsections in long reports and papers. Headings provide visual emphasis by breaking the paper into manageable portions that are easily seen and identified. Headings with numbers also indicate relationships because the numbers tell the reader which parts are segments of a larger part, which are equal, and which are of less importance. Subheadings are the headings of less importance within a series of headings. While headings and subheadings don't substitute for the transitions you provide for your readers, they help your readers see the organization of the paper and locate material more easily.

Headings for tables of contents, outlines, and most reports are numbered, either in the decimal system or with Roman numerals. While the decimal system is used more often in technical and professional fields than Roman numerals, some of these fields still follow traditional use of Roman numerals. Decimals can also be combined with letters.

| *Decimal numbers* | *Roman numerals* |
|---|---|
| 1.0 | I. |
|     1.1  (or)  1.a.  (or)  1a |     A. |
|     1.2  (or)  1.b.  (or)  1b |       1. |
|       1.2.1  (or)  1.a.1. |       2. |
|       1.2.2  (or)  1.a.2. |     B. |
|         1.2.2.1 |       1. |
| 2.0 |         a. |
|     2.1  (or)  2.a |           1) |
| |             a) |
| |       2. |
| | II. |

For all headings and subheadings, be sure to use the same grammatical form to start each phrase. (See Chapter 9 on parallelism.)

### Not Parallel

A. For Preliminary Planning
B. The Rough Draft
C. Polishing the Draft

### Revised

| A. Planning the Paper | | A. The Preliminary Draft |
|---|---|---|
| B. Writing the Rough Draft | (or) | B. The Rough Draft |
| C. Polishing the Draft | | C. The Polished Draft |

# B3  Page Preparation

- **Paper** Use 8 1/2″ × 11″ white, unlined paper for typing and printing, and use lined sheets for handwritten papers. Do not use thin or erasable paper. For handwritten, typed, and printed papers, use only one side of each sheet. For computer printout on continuous-sheet paper, tear off the edging of the paper, and separate the sheets.
- **Line spacing** Double-space typewritten and printed papers, and write on every other line for handwritten papers, including quotations, notes, and the list of works cited. Writing on every other line allows you room for making corrections and gives your instructor space in which to write comments.

- **Ink** Use black ribbon for typewritten papers and black or blue ink for handwritten papers. Do not use pencil.
- **Margins** Except for page numbers, leave margins of one inch at top and bottom and at both sides of the page.
- **Indentations** Indent the first word of each paragraph one-half inch or five spaces from the left-hand margin. For long quotations within paragraphs, indent one inch or ten spaces from the left-hand margin.
- **Page numbers** Use Arabic numerals (1, 2, 3, and so on), and place them in the upper right-hand corner, one-half inch from the top of the page and flush with the right-hand margin. Include your last name before the page number (to prevent confusion if pages are misplaced), and do not use the abbreviation *p.* before the page number. Do not use any punctuation in page numbers.

# B4 Spacing for Punctuation

- **End punctuation (. ? !)** Leave no space before the end punctuation. Leave one space before the next sentence.

    . . . next year. After the term of . . .

- **Periods after abbreviations (.)** Leave no space before the period and one space after. When a sentence ends with an abbreviation, use only one period to indicate both the abbreviation and the period that ends the sentence.

    Dr. Smith was noted for . . .             . . . at 8 A.M. The next day . . .

- **Commas, semicolons, colons (, ; :)** Leave no space before the mark and one space after.

    happy, healthy child          John, a musician; Josh, a doctor; and . . .

- **Apostrophes (')** Leave no space within a word. At the end of a word, leave no space before the apostrophe, with one space after.

    don't                    boy's hat                    boxes' lids

- **Quotation marks (" " ' ')** Leave no space between the quotation marks and what they enclose, no space between double and single quotation marks, and one space afterward in the middle of a sentence.

    "No way" was his favorite expression.

    " 'Battle Hymn of the Republic' should be the last song on the program," she explained.

- **Hyphen (-)** Leave no space before or after. If the hyphen shows the connection of two prefixes to one root word, put one space after the first hyphen.

    a six-page report               the pre- and post-test scores

- **Dash (- - —)** In a typewritten paper, type two hyphens, with no space before or after. For handwritten papers, write a longer line than the hyphen, leaving no space before or after. For papers written on a computer, there may be a dash mark to use.

  Not one of us--Tobias, Matthew, or Nick--thought it mattered.
  Not one of us—Tobias, Matthew, or Nick—thought it mattered.

- **Slash (/)** Leave no space before or after except for marking lines of poetry, when one space is left before and after.

  and/or
  He read his favorite two lines from the poem, "slipping, sliding on his tongue / the sound of music in his soul."

- **Brackets, parentheses [ ] ( )** Leave no space before or after the material being enclosed.

  "When [the fund-raising group] presented its report (not previously published), the press covered the event."

- **Ellipsis (. . .)** Leave one space before each period, one space between, and one space after. If you are using four dots to indicate that you are omitting one or more sentences, treat the first dot like a period, with no space after the last word, and then space evenly.

  No one . . . noticed the error.
  Every worker signed the contract. . . . No one opposed the new guidelines for health care.

- **Underlining (<u>abcdef</u>) or italics (*abcdef*)** When using a typewriter or writing by hand, you can use underlining with or without breaks between words, but be consistent once you choose to use or not use breaks. If your computer has italic type, ask your instructor whether italics or underlining is preferred.

  <u>Wind in the Willows</u>          <u>Wind</u> <u>in</u> <u>the</u> <u>Willows</u>
  *<u>Wind in the Willows</u>*          *Wind in the Willows*

# B5 Document Design

The visual appeal of your pages is important because readers react to what they see as well as to what they read. When you see an overcrowded page with too little white space and long, unbroken sections of text, you are likely to react negatively. You are also missing helpful visual cues that sort out sections of the paper. To add visual appeal to your pages, especially with memos, reports, and résumés, consider the following guidelines:

- **Use white space to open up the page visually.** White space, well used, invites the reader into the page and offers some relief from the

heaviness of blocks of text. White space also helps to indicate sections or segments of the text.
- **Use lists whenever possible.** Instead of writing long paragraphs with many items, consider listing key points with bullets or dashes. This strategy also helps add white space to the page.

> The major parts of a proposal are the following:
>
> - Problem statement
> - Proposed project and  purpose
> - Plan
> - Evaluation

- **Use headings and subheadings to indicate sections.** For longer essays and reports, use words and phrases to announce new topics or segments of a topic (see B2).
- **Use visuals such as tables and charts.** Visuals convey information easily and succinctly. Tables present information in columns and rows and can include numbers or words. Figures, including pie charts, graphs, and drawings, are useful for indicating relationships. If you include a visual, refer to it in your text before it appears, and explain the main point it conveys.

# C Résumés (rés)

An effective résumé focuses on the particular organization to which you are applying. Choose the details that relate your particular skills and achievements to the specific job for which you are applying. If you intend to apply for several different jobs, you will need to revise your résumé so that it is tailored for each job.

## C1 Sections of the Résumé

Listed here are the major sections of a résumé. You can use any of these headings or make up new sections more appropriate for your special abilities.

### (a) Name

Generally, you should use your full name rather than initials or a nickname.

## (b) Address

Include both your college and permanent addresses if they are different so that your prospective employer can contact you at either place. Include phone numbers and the dates that you will be at both addresses.

### MARK DANIEL KANE

**COLLEGE ADDRESS**
421 Cary Quadrangle
West Lafayette, IN 47906
(317) 555-0224
(Until May 15, 1997)

**PERMANENT ADDRESS**
1523 Elmwood Drive
Nobleton, IN 46623
(317) 200-8749
(After May 15, 1997)

## (c) Career Objective

Relate this section directly to the job you want, and make sure to tie in the skills you have acquired from previous work experience, your education, and outside activities. Include the job title you seek and the type of work or skills you want to use, and in your résumé, include proof that you have those skills. Write a concise phrase or clause, not a full sentence.

A summer internship with a construction company that requires skills in field engineering, cost controlling, planning, scheduling, and estimating.

A systems analyst position, stressing technical, communication, and supervisory skills.

## (d) Education

This is a major section for most students. Include the following:

- Name of college(s) attended.
- Degree(s) and graduation dates(s) (month and year).
- Major, minor, or specialization.
- Grade-point average (optional). (Include your own GPA first, then a slash mark, and then the highest possible GPA at the school.) Or you can include your GPA in your major, then a slash mark, and then your overall GPA, as follows:
  GPA (major): 3.8/4.0

Put these in the order of whichever aspect you want to emphasize, the degree or the college.

Purdue University
Bachelor of Science, May 1999
Major: Electrical Engineering; GPA: 3.7/4.0

(or)

Bachelor of Science in Electrical Engineering, May 1999, Purdue University
GPA : 3.7/4.0

You may want to list some upper-level courses you've taken that are particularly significant to the job you are applying for, or courses that are different from those everyone in your major must take. Use a more specific heading, if possible, such as "Public Relations Courses" rather than "Significant Courses."

Under the heading "Special Projects," you can highlight unique features of your education that will help you to stand out from other job applicants. Describe special projects you've completed, reports you've written, or conferences you've attended, and briefly give the most important details.

### (e) Work Experience

This section can be arranged in several ways. Before deciding how to present this information, list the following items:

- Job titles, places worked, locations, and dates. Include part-time, temporary, and volunteer work as well as cooperative programs and internships.
- Duties you performed and skills you acquired, using action verbs.

You can organize this information as a functional, skills, chronological, or imaginative résumé. See C2 on résumé styles.

Research Analyst
Kellogg Co.; Montack, Michigan; Summer 1995
— Supervised 9 assistants gathering information on cows' eating habits
— Researched most recent information on cows' nutritional needs
— Analyzed data to determine how to reduce number of feeding hours while maintaining nutritional quality

If the company you worked for is particularly impressive, you may want to begin with the company's name to highlight it.

### (f) Skills

Not all résumés include a skills section, but this is a useful way to emphasize the skills you have acquired from various jobs or activities. To prepare this section, list the following for yourself:

- Jobs, club activities, projects, special offices or responsibilities.
- Skills you have developed from these experiences. For example, as president of a club you had to lead meetings, delegate responsibilities, coordinate activities, etc.

Group the skills under three to five skills categories that relate to the job you are seeking, as described in your goal statement, and use those categories as your skills headings.

Management
- Led a committee to prepare and institute new election procedures for Student Union Board.
- Evaluated employees' work progress for monthly reports.

Communication
- Wrote weekly advertisements for student government entertainment activities.
- Represented sorority in negotiations with university administrators.
- Spoke to potential funding groups for student-organized charity events.

Programming
- Analyzed and designed a program to record and average student grades for a faculty member.
- Designed a program to record and update items of sorority's $90,000 annual budget.

---

**HINT:** To make your skills section effective and to help the prospective employer see you as an active worker, use action verbs such as the following:

**Action Verbs**

| | | |
|---|---|---|
| act | generate | persuade |
| adapt | get | plan |
| administer | govern | prepare |
| advise | guide | present |
| analyze | handle | process |
| assess | head | produce |
| build | hire | program |
| calculate | implement | promote |
| catalog | improve | provide |
| compile | increase | raise |
| complete | initiate | recommend |
| conduct | install | recruit |
| coordinate | integrate | reorganize |
| create | maintain | represent |
| decide | manage | revise |
| define | market | schedule |
| demonstrate | modify | select |
| design | monitor | sell |
| develop | motivate | send |
| direct | negotiate | speak |
| distribute | obtain | supervise |
| edit | operate | survey |
| establish | order | train |
| evaluate | organize | transmit |
| examine | oversee | update |
| forecast | perform | write |

### (g) College Activities

This section demonstrates your leadership and involvement and can include college activities, honors, and official positions or responsibilities you have had. You may need to explain in a phrase or two what various organizations are because prospective employers will probably not be familiar with the fact that the Tomahawk Club is an honorary service organization on your campus or that Alpha Gamma Alpha is a first-year honors council at your school.

### (h) References

You can include three or four references on your résumé, but many people prefer to be selective about who gets a copy of their list. If you also wish to be selective, include the following statement on your résumé:

References available upon request.

List the names of your references on a separate sheet of paper that matches your résumé, and include their addresses, and phone numbers. Add a sentence or two to explain your connection with that person. You can then mail the list later if the potential employer asks for it.

# C2 Résumé Styles

Depending upon what information you want to highlight, you can choose from several different résumé styles: functional, skills, and chronological. Examples of these résumé styles are included here.

### (a) Functional Résumé

This style categorizes each job by function (for example, program designer, case worker, field consultant) with the most significant function listed first. Describe each function by detailing responsibilities held, actions taken, and results achieved. Subordinate employers' names and dates. This approach is useful if you have impressive job titles and duties to feature.

### (b) Skills Résumé

This style emphasizes skills and abilities gained through jobs, experiences, and school activities, and allows you to relate them to the job you want. Arrange the skills from the most relevant to the least. If appropriate, include the name and location of companies and dates of employment. This approach is particularly appropriate when the skills you've acquired are more impressive than the jobs you've had or when you want to highlight a significant skill acquired from different experiences and jobs.

## (c) Chronological Résumé

This style, which highlights your current job and employer's name, was once the standard approach, but it has been replaced in many fields. However, some conservative employers may still prefer it. It is also appropriate if you want to emphasize your current job as the most important, if your work experience is closely related to the job you are seeking, or if you are older and have extensive work experience to offer. When you are stressing extensive work experience as your strongest qualification, place "Work Experience" section before the "Education" section. You may prefer to include only your most recent jobs or those that best relate to the job you seek.

For this approach, begin each entry with the employer's name and your dates of employment. Then include a brief description of your job, including titles and responsibilities. Arrange this list chronologically, beginning with your most recent job.

---

**HINT: Résumé Checklist**

- **Organization** Put the most important sections of your résumé first. For example, is your work experience more important than your education? Are your college activities more important than your past jobs?
- **Visual appeal** Use white space and lists to make your résumé visually appealing, easy to read, and uncluttered. Highlight your headings with different kinds of type, underlining, boldface, capital letters, and indenting to show your organizing ability. But don't add clutter by using too many different fonts or types of headings.
- **Parallel headings** Be sure that your headings are all parallel.
- **Length** Many companies prefer one-page résumés, but this may vary according to your field and career objective.
- **Uniqueness** Your goal is not to make your résumé like all the others in the pile; instead, highlight your unique capabilities.

---

**HINT:** One place to look for a job is the Internet. Listed here are two of the many sites on the World Wide Web that post job openings.

- **Career Network: http://www.sgx.com/cw/**
  This site is a searchable database for jobs in areas such as finance, information technologies, marketing, and sales.
- **Online Career Center: http://www.occ.com**
  This is a large career center and employment data bank that can be searched by industry, city, state, and keyword. A résumé database can be searched by recruiters.

**LESLIE JAMES EDELON**

**CURRENT ADDRESS**
(until June 1, 1997)
230 Grant Street
West Grandville, KS 67608
(214) 743-9881

**PERMANENT ADDRESS**
(after June 1, 1997)
Route 2, Box 30-A
Rinard, KS 62339
(214) 681-0099

**CAREER OBJECTIVE**
An entry-level position in installment loans working toward a career as a farm loan officer

**EDUCATION**
**North Kansas State College, Bachelor of Science in Agriculture Finance, May 1997**
GPA: 4.02/5.00
**Areas of Study**
<u>Finance/Management</u>: Agriculture Finance, Financial Accounting, Financial Management, Farm Management, Farm Organization

<u>Sales/Marketing</u>: Marketing Management, Agri-Sales and Marketing, Grain Marketing, Managerial Accounting, Quantitative Techniques

**EXPERIENCE**
**Bookkeeper, Farmers & Merchants State Bank;** Summer 1996
- Answered customer inquiries and complaints
- Balanced customer checkbooks
- Verified $3,000-$5,000 currency daily

**Assistant Manager, Family Farm;** 1993-present
- Contributed management input
- Assisted in financial planning
- Operated heavy equipment

**Special Sales Chairman, State College Tractor Pull Foundation;**
August 1993
- Coordinated National College Tractor Pullers Association souvenir sales
- Sold advertising space on tickets

**ACTIVITIES**
Tractor Pull Foundation
Agriculture Economics Club
Alpha Zeta Professional Fraternity
Ceres Honorary Fraternity

**REFERENCES** Available on request

**Example of a functional résumé**

**ALETHA WATMAN**

**UNTIL** May 15, 1997
210 Waldron Drive
University City, LA  71213

**AFTER** May 15, 1997
12955 Bleekman Street
Pontosa, OK  75337

**PROFESSIONAL OBJECTIVE**
A career in personnel management that would involve coordinating, communicating, and training

**EDUCATION**
Carlman College: expected graduation, May 1997
Bachelor of Arts degree in Organization Psychology
Minor: General Management

GPA (6.0 scale): Major and Minor 5.9; Overall 5.6

Major-Related Courses:
Personnel Management, Interviewing, Labor Relations, Industrial Psychology, Organizational Communications, Persuasion, Public Relations, Psychological Testing, Business Writing, Marketing

**SKILLS**
**Coordinating**
- Planned and organized campaign for homecoming queen candidate
- Supervised dining room preparation at the Sheraton Plaza

**Communicating**
- Underwent 150 hours of training to learn peer counseling techniques
- Developed and delivered a seminar on peer counseling for the American Personal Guidance Convention, Washington, D.C., 1995
- Handled customer complaints

**Training**
- Supervised peer counseling program in college dormitory
- Instructed other employees in proper food and beverage service

**WORK EXPERIENCE** (paid for 100% of college expenses)
Waitress, Carlman Memorial Union; Fall 1994 to present
Salesperson, University Book Store, Carlman College; Fall 1993, Spring 1994, Spring 1995
Waitress, Sheraton Plaza, University City, Louisiana; Summer 1993

**ACTIVITIES AND HONORS**
Peer Counselor (Student Dormitory)
Campaign Manager for Homecoming Queen Candidate
Member of Psi Chi (Psychology Honor Society)
Dean's List (8 semesters)

**REFERENCES**
Available upon request

**Example of a skills résumé**

### NOAH ALLAN MARMOR

6545 Country Inn Lane
Fort Worth, TX   30101
phone: (314) 991-2387
fax: (314) 991-2380
e-mail: marmor@emet.com

## PROFESSIONAL OBJECTIVE
An engineering career in aircraft structural analysis or structural dynamics

## EDUCATION
**Milman Polytechnic Institute;** Oshkego, New York
**Bachelor of Science in Aeronautical Engineering,** December 1995
> Structures and Materials Major, Dynamics and Control Minor

**Significant Courses**
Advanced Matrix Methods, Mechanics of Composite Materials, Elasticity in Aerospace Engineering, Flight Mechanics, Aircraft Design I and II, Jet Propulsion Power Plants

**Special Projects**
- Proposed and performed wind tunnel test of composite laminates to study aeroelastic divergence
- Worked on a team designing a supersonic fighter aircraft with short takeoff and landing capabilities
- Learned to use a computer program to analyze aeroelastic stability of a wing

## WORK EXPERIENCE
**Bell Helicopter Textron,** Fort Worth, Texas: September 1995 to present
- Use flight dynamics simulation computer programs such as DNAW06 and C81
- Evaluate rotors and rotor-fuselage combinations

**Prisler and Associates,** Dallas, Texas: December 1994 to September 1995
- Draft rotor parts for research and flight test programs

**Hughes Aircraft,** Los Angeles, California (Engineering Co-op): January 1993 to July 1993
- Tested composite specimens to verify materials specifications
- Fabricated composite structures for research programs

## ACTIVITIES
Hillel Foundation Coordinator
Alpha Omicron (Engineering Honorary Society)
AIPAC Public Relations Chairman

**REFERENCES** Available on request

**Example of a chronological résumé**

**JILLIAN CHAPLER**
125 East Maynard Place
Gary, IN 46801
phone and fax: (312) 555-1818

**CAREER OBJECTIVE**
A career in the sales, marketing, or public relations department of a large and growing hotel chain

**WORK EXPERIENCE**
**Howard Johnson's O'Hare International** (Chicago): Sales
| | |
|---|---|
| Sales Manager | June 1991-present |
| Sales Representative | March 1988-January 1991 |
| Trade Shows Organizer | June 1987-February 1988 |

**Howard Johnson's** (Kokomo, IN): Management
| | |
|---|---|
| Management Office Staff | October 1980-April 1985 |
| Employee Training Supervisor | May 1979-September 1980 |

**Nippersink Manor Resort** (O'Dare Lake, MI): Management
| | |
|---|---|
| Scheduling Supervisor | May 1977-May 1979 |
| Promotional Staff | January 1974-May 1977 |
| Accounting Department | October 1973-December 1973 |

**Lakeview Manor** (Benton City, MI): Public Relations
| | |
|---|---|
| Public Relations Assistant | June 1972-October 1973 |

**EDUCATION**
**Northern Indiana State University** (Kendleberg, IN): Master of Arts in Restaurant and Hotel Management Major, 1985-1987

**Linton Community College** (Linton, IN): Liberal Arts Major, 1968-1972

**Degrees:** Bachelor of Science in Restaurant and Hotel Management, NISU, 1972
Associate of Arts and Sciences, L.C.C., 1970

**AFFILIATIONS**
American Management Association
American Society of Hotel Managers
National Hotel Association

**ACTIVITIES, AWARDS, INTERESTS**
Chairman of Awards: Outstanding Service Awards (Howard Johnson's)
Macintosh Users Club (Chicago)
President, Kokomo Chapter of National Hotel Association

**REFERENCES**
Available upon request

**Example of a chronological résumé that emphasizes extensive work experience rather than the education section**

# GLOSSARY OF USAGE

This list includes words and phrases you may be uncertain about when writing. If you have questions about words not included here, try the index to this book to see whether the word is discussed elsewhere. You can also check a recently published dictionary. (The dictionary used here as a source of information is the *Oxford American Dictionary*, Oxford University Press, 1980.)

**A, An:** Use *a* before words that begin with a consonant (for example, *a* cat, *a* house) and before words beginning with a vowel that sounds like a consonant (for example, *a* one-way street, *a* union). Use *an* before words that begin with a vowel (for example, *an* egg, *an* ice cube) and before words with a silent *h* (for example, *an* hour). See 19b.

**Accept, Except:** *Accept*, a verb, means "to agree to," "to believe," or "to receive."

> The detective **accepted** his account of the event and did not hold him as a suspect in the case.

*Except*, a verb, means "to exclude" or "to leave out," and *except*, a preposition, means "leaving out."

> Because he did not know any of the answers, he was **excepted** from the list of contestants and asked to leave.
> **Except** for brussels sprouts, which I hate, I eat most vegetables.

**Advice, Advise:** *Advice* is a noun, and *advise* is a verb.

> She always offers too much **advice**.
> Would you **advise** me about choosing the right course?

**Affect, Effect:** Most frequently, *affect*, which means "to influence," is used as a verb, and *effect*, which means "a result," is used as a noun.

> The weather **affects** my ability to study.
> What **effect** does too much coffee have on your concentration?

343

However, *effect,* meaning "to cause" or "to bring about," is also used as a verb.

> The new traffic enforcement laws **effected** a change in people's driving habits.

Common phrases with *effect* include the following:

> in effect        to that effect

**Ain't:** This is a nonstandard way of saying *am not, is not, has not, have not,* etc.

**All ready, Already:** *All ready* means "prepared"; *already* means "before" or "by this time."

> The courses for the meal are **all ready** to be served.
> When I got home, she was **already** there.

**All Right, Alright:** *All right* is two words, not one. *Alright* is an incorrect form.

**All Together, Altogether:** *All together* means "in a group," and *altogether* means "entirely," "totally."

> We were **all together** again after having separate vacations.
> He was not **altogether** happy about the outcome of the test.

**Alot, A Lot:** *Alot* is an incorrect form of *a lot.*

**a.m., p.m.** (or A.M., P.M.): Use these with numbers, not as substitutes for the words *morning* or *evening.*

> ❖ We meet every ~~a.m.~~ *morning at 9 A.M.* for an exercise class.

**Among, Between:** Use *among* when referring to three or more things and *between* when referring to two things.

> The decision was discussed **among** all the members of the committee.
> I had to decide **between** the chocolate mousse pie and the almond ice cream.

**Amount, Number:** Use *amount* for things or ideas that are general or abstract and cannot be counted. For example, furniture is a general term and cannot be counted. That is, we cannot say "one furniture" or "two furnitures." Use *number* for things that can be counted, as, for example, four chairs or three tables.

> He had a huge **amount** of work to finish before the deadline.
> There were a **number** of people who saw the accident.

**An:** See the entry for *a, an.*

**And:** While some people discourage the use of *and* as the first word in a sentence, it is an acceptable word with which to begin a sentence.

**And Etc.:** Adding *and* is redundant because *et* means "and" in Latin. See the entry for *etc.*

**Anybody, Any Body:** See the entry for *anyone, any one.*

**Anyone, Any One:** *Anyone* means "any person at all." *Any one* refers to a specific person or thing in a group. There are similar distinctions for other words ending in *-body* and *-one* (for example, *everybody, every body; anybody, any body;* and *someone, some one*).

> The teacher asked if **anyone** knew the answer.
> **Any one** of those children could have taken the ball.

**Anyways, Anywheres:** These are nonstandard forms for *anyway* and *anywhere.*

**As, As If, As Though, Like:** Use *as* in a comparison (not *like*) when there is an equality intended or when the meaning is "in the function of."

> Celia acted **as** (not *like*) the leader when the group was getting organized.   [Celia = leader]

Use *as if* or *as though* for the subjunctive.

> He spent his money **as if** [or **as though**] he were rich.

Use *like* in a comparison (not *as*) when the meaning is "in the manner of" or "to the same degree as."

> The boy swam **like** a fish.

Don't use *like* as the opening word in a clause in formal writing:

> **Informal: Like** I thought, he was unable to predict the weather.
> **Formal: As** I thought, he was unable to predict the weather.

**Assure, Ensure, Insure:** *Assure* means "to declare" or "to promise," *ensure* means "to make safe or certain," and *insure* means "to protect with a contract of insurance."

> I **assure** you that I am trying to find your lost package.
> Some people claim that eating properly **ensures** good health.
> This insurance policy also **insures** my car against theft.

**Awful, Awfully:** *Awful* is an adjective meaning "inspiring awe" or "extremely unpleasant."

> He was involved in an **awful** accident.

*Awfully* is an adverb used in informal writing to mean "very." It should be avoided in formal writing.

**Informal:** The dog was **awfully** dirty.

**Awhile, A While:** *Awhile* is an adverb meaning "a short time" and modifies a verb:

He talked **awhile** and then left.

*A while* is an article with the noun *while* and means "a period of time:"

I'll be there in **a while**.

**Bad, Badly:** *Bad* is an adjective and is used after linking verbs. *Badly* is an adverb.

The wheat crop looked **bad** [not *badly*] because of lack of rain.
There was a **bad** flood last summer.
The building was **badly** constructed and unable to withstand the strong winds.

**Beside, Besides:** *Beside* is a preposition meaning "at the side of," "compared with," or "having nothing to do with." *Besides* is a preposition meaning "in addition to" or "other than." *Besides* as an adverb means "also" or "moreover." Don't confuse *beside* with *besides*.

That is **beside** the point.
**Besides** the radio, they had no other means of contact with the outside world.
**Besides**, I enjoyed the concert.

**Between, Among:** See the entry for *among, between.*
**Breath, Breathe:** *Breath* is a noun, and *breathe* is a verb.

She held her **breath** when she dived into the water.
Learn to **breathe** deeply when you swim.

**But:** While some people discourage the use of *but* as the first word in a sentence, it is an acceptable word with which to begin a sentence.
**Can, May:** *Can* is a verb that expresses ability, knowledge, or capacity:

He **can** play both the violin and the cello.

*May* is a verb that expresses possibility or permission. Careful writers avoid using *can* to mean permission:

**May** (not *can*) I sit here?

**Can't Hardly:** This is incorrect because it is a double negative.

❖ She ~~can't~~ *can* hardly hear normal voice levels.

**Choose, Chose:** *Choose* is the present tense of the verb, and *chose* is the past tense:

Jennie always **chooses** strawberry ice cream.
Yesterday, she even **chose** strawberry-flavored popcorn.

**Cloth, Clothe:** *Cloth* is a noun, and *clothe* is a verb.

Here is some **cloth** for a new scarf.
His paycheck helps to feed and **clothe** many people in his family.

**Compared To, Compared With:** Use *compared to* when showing that two things are alike. Use *compared with* when showing similarities and differences.

The speaker **compared** the economy **to** a roller coaster because both have sudden ups and downs.
The detective **compared** the fingerprints **with** other sets from a previous crime.

**Could Of:** This is incorrect. Instead use *could have.*

**Data:** This is the plural form of *datum.* In informal usage, *data* is used as a singular noun, with a singular verb. However, since dictionaries do not accept this, use *data* as a plural form for academic writing.

**Informal:** The **data** is inconclusive.
**Formal:** The **data** are inconclusive.

**Different From, Different Than:** *Different from* is always correct, but some writers use *different than* if there is a clause following this phrase.

This program is **different from** the others.
That is a **different** result **than** they predicted.

**Done:** The past tense forms of the verb *do* are *did* and *done. Did* is the simple form that needs no additional verb as a helper. *Done* is the past form that requires the helper *have.* Some writers make the mistake of interchanging *did* and *done.*

❖ They ~~done~~ *did* it again. (or) They ₍*have*₎ done it again.

**Effect, Affect:** See the entry for *affect, effect.*
**Ensure:** See the entry for *assure, ensure, insure.*
**Etc.:** This is an abbreviation of the Latin *et cetera,* meaning "and the rest." Because it should be used sparingly if at all in formal academic writing, substitute other phrases such as *and so forth* or *and so on.*
**Everybody, Every Body:** See the entry for *anyone, any one.*
**Everyone, Every One:** See the entry for *anyone, any one.*
**Except, Accept:** See the entry for *accept, except.*
**Farther, Further:** While some writers use these words interchangeably, dictionary definitions differentiate them. *Farther* is used when actual distance is involved, and *further* is used to mean "to a greater extent," "more."

The house is **farther** from the road than I realized.
That was **furthest** from my thoughts at the time.

**Fewer, Less:** *Fewer* is used for things that can be counted (*fewer* trees, *fewer* people). *Less* is used for ideas; abstractions; things that are thought of collectively, not separately (*less* trouble, *less* furniture); and things that are measured by amount, not number (*less* milk, *less* fuel).

**Fun:** This noun is used informally as an adjective.

**Informal:** They had a **fun** time.

**Goes, Says:** *Goes* is a nonstandard form of *says*.

❖ Whenever I give him a book to read, he ~~goes,~~ *says* "What's it about?"

**Gone, Went:** Past tense forms of the verb *go*. *Went* is the simple form that needs no additional verb as a helper. *Gone* is the past form that requires the helper *have*. Some writers make the mistake of interchanging *went* and *gone*.

❖ They already ~~gone~~ away. *went (or) They had gone away before I woke up.*

**Good, Well:** *Good* is an adjective and therefore describes only nouns. *Well* is an adverb and therefore describes adjectives, other adverbs, and verbs. The word *well* is used as an adjective only in the sense of "in good health."

❖ The stereo works ~~good~~. *well*     I feel ~~good~~. *well*     She is a good driver.

**Got, Have:** *Got* is the past tense of *get* and should not be used in place of *have*. Similarly, *got to* should not be used as a substitute for *must*. *Have got to* is an informal substitute for *must*.

❖ Do you ~~got~~ any pennies for the meter? *have*     I ~~got to~~ go now. *must*

**Informal:** You have **got to** see that movie.

**Great:** This adjective is overworked in its formal meaning of "very enjoyable," "good," or "wonderful" and should be reserved for its more exact meanings, such as "of remarkable ability," "intense," "high degree of," and so on.

**Informal:** That was a **great** movie.
**More Exact Uses of *Great*:** The vaccine was a **great** discovery.
The map went into **great** detail.

**Have, Got:** See the entry for *got, have.*
**Have, Of:** *Have,* not *of,* should follow verbs such as *could, might, must,* and *should.*

❖ They should ~~of~~ *have* called by now.

**Hisself:** This is a nonstandard substitute for *himself.*
**Hopefully:** This adverb means "in a hopeful way." Many people consider the meaning "it is to be hoped" as unacceptable.

> **Acceptable:** He listened **hopefully** for the knock at the door.
> **Often Considered Unacceptable: Hopefully,** it will not rain tonight.

**I:** While some people discourage the use of *I* in formal essays, it is acceptable. If you wish to eliminate the use of *I,* see 16d on passive verbs.
**Imply, Infer:** Some writers use these interchangeably, but careful writers maintain the distinction between the two words. *Imply* means "to suggest without stating directly," "to hint." *Infer* means "to reach an opinion from facts or reasoning."

> The tone of her voice **implied** that he was stupid.
> The anthropologist **inferred** that this was a burial site for prehistoric people.

**Insure:** See the entry for *assure, ensure, insure.*
**Irregardless:** This is an incorrect form of the word *regardless.*
**Is When, Is Why, Is Where, Is Because:** These are incorrect forms for definitions. See Chapter 11 on faulty predication.

> **Faulty Predication:** Nervousness is when my palms sweat.
> **Revised:** When I am nervous, my palms sweat.
>
> (or)
>
> Nervousness is a state of being very uneasy or agitated.

**Its, It's:** *Its* is a personal pronoun in the possessive case. *It's* is a contraction for *it is.*

> The kitten licked **its** paw.
> **It's** a good time for a vacation.

**Kind, Sort:** These two forms are singular and should be used with *this* or *that.* Use *kinds* or *sorts* with *these* or *those.*

> This **kind** of cloud often indicates that there will be heavy rain.
> These **sorts** of plants are regarded as weeds.

**Lay, Lie:** *Lay* is a verb that needs an object and should not be used in place of *lie,* a verb that takes no direct object.

❖ He should *lie* ~~lay~~ down and rest awhile.

❖ You can *lay* ~~lie~~ that package on the front table.

**Leave, Let:** *Leave* means "to go away," and *let* means "to permit." It is incorrect to use *leave* when you mean *let*:

❖ *Let* ~~Leave~~ me get that for you.

**Less, Fewer:** See the entry for *fewer, less*.
**Let, Leave:** See the entry for *leave, let*.
**Like, As:** See the entry for *as, as if, as though, like*.
**Like For:** The phrase "I'd like for you to do that" is incorrect. Omit *for*.
**May, Can:** See the entry for *can, may*.
**Most:** It is incorrect to use *most* as a substitute for *almost*.
**Nowheres:** This is an incorrect form of *nowhere*.
**Number, Amount:** See the entry for *amount, number*.
**Of, Have:** See the entry for *have, of*.
**Off Of:** It is incorrect to write *off of* for *off* in a phrase such as *off the table*.
**O.K., Ok, Okay:** These can be used informally but should not be used in formal or academic writing.
**Reason . . . Because:** This is redundant. Instead of *because*, use *that*:

❖ The reason she dropped the course is *that* ~~because~~ she couldn't keep up with the homework.

> **Less Wordy Revision:** She dropped the course **because** she couldn't keep up with the homework.

**Reason Why:** Using *why* is redundant. Drop the word *why*.

❖ The reason ~~why~~ I called is to remind you of your promise.

**Saw, Seen:** Past tense forms of the verb *see*. *Saw* is the simple form that needs no additional verb as a helper. *Seen* is the past form that requires the helper *have*. Some writers make the mistake of interchanging *saw* and *seen*.

❖ They *saw* ~~seen~~ it happen.    (or)    They ∧ *have* seen it happen.

**Set, Sit:** *Set* means "to place" and is followed by a direct object. *Sit* means "to be seated." It is incorrect to substitute *set* for *sit*.

❖ Come in and *sit* ~~set~~ down.

*Set*
❖ ~~Sit~~ the flowers on the table.

**Should of:** This is incorrect. Instead use *should have.*
**Sit, Set:** See the entry for *set, sit.*
**Somebody, Some Body:** See the entry for *anyone, any one.*
**Someone, Some One:** See the entry for *anyone, any one.*
**Sort, Kind:** See the entry for *kind, sort.*
**Such:** This is an overworked word when used in place of *very* or *extremely.*
**Sure:** The use of *sure* as an adverb is informal. Careful writers use *surely* instead.

> **Informal:** I **sure** hope you can join us.
> **Revised:** I **surely** hope you can join us.

**Than, Then:** *Than* is a conjunction introducing the second element in comparison. *Then* is an adverb that means "at that time," "next," "after that," "also," or "in that case."

> She is taller **than** I am.
> He picked up the ticket and **then** left the house.

**That There, This Here, These Here, Those There:** These are incorrect forms for *that, this, these, those.*
**That, Which:** Use *that* for essential clauses and *which* for nonessential clauses. Some writers, however, also use *which* for essential clauses. (See 18b and Chapter 24.)
**Their, There, They're:** *Their* is a possessive pronoun; *there* means "in," "at," or "to that place"; and *they're* is a contraction for "they are."

> **Their** house has been sold.
> **There** is the parking lot.
> **They're** both good swimmers.

**Theirself, Theirselves, Themself:** These are all incorrect forms for *themselves.*
**Them:** It is incorrect to use *them* in place of either the pronoun *these* or *those.*

*those*
❖ Look at ~~them~~ apples.

**Then, Than:** See the entry for *than, then.*
**Thusly:** This is an incorrect substitute for *thus.*
**To, Too, Two:** *To* is a preposition; *too* is an adverb meaning "very" or "also;" and *two* is a number.

> He brought his bass guitar **to** the party.
> He brought his drums **too.**
> He had **two** music stands.

**Toward, Towards:** Both are accepted forms with the same meaning, but *toward* is preferred.

**Use to:** This is incorrect for the modal meaning *formerly*. Instead, use *used to*.

**Want for:** Omit the incorrect *for* in phrases such as "I want for you to come here."

**Well, Good:** See the entry for *good, well*.

**Went, Gone:** See the entry for *gone, went*.

**Where:** It is incorrect to use *where* to mean *when* or *that*.

❖ The Fourth of July is a holiday ~~where~~ *when* the town council shoots off fireworks.

❖ I see ~~where~~ *that* there is now a ban on shooting panthers.

**Where . . . at:** This is a redundant form. Omit the *at*.

❖ This is where the picnic is ~~at~~.

**Which, That:** See the entry for *that, which*.

**While, Awhile:** See the entry for *awhile, a while*.

**Who, Whom:** Use *who* for the subject case; use *whom* for the object case.

He is the person **who** signs that form.
He is the person **whom** I asked for help.

**Who's, Whose:** *Who's* is a contraction for *who is*; *whose* is a possessive pronoun.

**Who's** included on that list?
**Whose** wristwatch is this?

**Your, You're:** *Your* is a possessive pronoun; *you're* is a contraction for *you are*.

**Your** hands are cold.
**You're** a great success.

# GLOSSARY OF GRAMMATICAL TERMS

**Absolutes:** Words or phrases that modify whole sentences rather than parts of sentences or individual words. An absolute phrase, which consists of a noun and participle, can be placed anywhere in the sentence but needs to be set off from the sentence by commas.

> **The snow having finally stopped,** the football game began.
> *(absolute phrase)*

**Abstract Nouns:** Nouns that refer to ideas, qualities, generalized concepts, and conditions and that do not have plural forms. (See 41f.)

> happiness, pride, furniture, trouble, sincerity

**Active Voice:** See **voice.**

**Adjectives:** Words that modify nouns and pronouns. (See Chapter 19.) Descriptive adjectives (*red, clean, beautiful, offensive,* for example) have three forms:

> **Positive:** red, clean, beautiful, offensive
> **Comparative** (for comparing two things): redder, cleaner, more beautiful, less offensive
> **Superlative** (for comparing more than two things): reddest, cleanest, most beautiful, least offensive

**Adjective Clauses:** See **dependent clauses.**

**Adverbs:** Modify verbs, verb forms, adjectives, and other adverbs. (See Chapter 19.) Descriptive adverbs (for example, *fast, graceful, awkward*) have three forms:

> **Positive:** fast, graceful, awkward
> **Comparative** (for comparing two things): faster, more graceful, less awkward
> **Superlative** (for comparing more than two things): fastest, most graceful, least awkward

**Adverb Clauses:** See **dependent clauses.**

**Agreement:** The use of the corresponding form for related words in order to have them agree in number, person, or gender. (See Chapter 6, 10a, and 18b.)

> **John runs.**    [Both subject and verb are singular.]
>
> It is necessary to flush the **pipes** regularly so that **they** don't freeze.
>
> [Both subjects, *it* and *they*, are in third person; *they* agrees in number with the antecedent, *pipes*.]

**Antecedents:** Words or groups of words to which pronouns refer.

> When the **bell** was rung, **it** sounded very loudly.
>
> [*Bell* is the antecedent of *it*.]

**Antonyms:** Words with opposite meanings.

| *Word* | *Antonym* |
| --- | --- |
| hot | cold |
| fast | slow |
| noisy | quiet |

**Appositives:** Nonessential phrases and clauses that follow nouns and identify or explain them. (See Chapter 24.)

> My uncle, **who lives in Wyoming,** is taking wind surfing lessons in Florida.
>                       *(appositive)*

**Articles:** See **noun determiners.**

**Auxiliary Verbs:** Verbs used with main verbs in verb phrases.

> **should be** going        **has** taken
> *(auxiliary verb)*    *(auxiliary verb)*

**Cardinal Numbers:** See **noun determiners.**

**Case:** The form or position of a noun or pronoun that shows its use or relationship to other words in a sentence. The three cases in English are (1) *subject* (or *subjective* or *nominative*), (2) *object* (or *objective*), and (3) *possessive* (or *genitive*). (See 18a.)

**Clauses:** Groups of related words that contain both subjects and predicates and that function either as sentences or as parts of sentences. Clauses are either *independent* (or *main*) or *dependent* (or *subordinate*). (See Chapter 23.)

**Clichés:** Overused or tired expressions that no longer effectively communicate. (See 40b.)

**Collective Nouns:** Nouns that refer to groups of people or things, such as a *committee, team,* or *jury.* When the group includes a number of members acting as a unit and is the subject of the sentence, the verb is also singular. (See 6g and 17a.)

The **jury** has made a decision.

**Colloquialisms:** Words or phrases used in casual conversation and writing. (See 41b.)

**Comma Splices:** Punctuation errors in which two or more independent clauses in compound sentences are separated only by commas and no coordinating conjunctions. (See Chapter 5.)

❖ Jesse said he could not help, ∧ that was typical of his responses to requests.

*, but (or) ;*

**Common Nouns:** Nouns that refer to general rather than specific categories of people, places, and things and are not capitalized. (See 17a.)

basket    person    history    tractor

**Comparative:** The form of adjectives and adverbs used when two things are being compared. (See 19c.)

higher    more intelligent    less friendly

**Complement:** When linking verbs link subjects to adjectives or nouns, the adjectives or nouns are complements.

Phyllis was **tired.**        She became a **musician.**
  *(complement)*                  *(complement)*

**Complex Sentences:** Sentences with at least one independent clause and at least one dependent clause arranged in any order. (See 25b.)

**Compound Nouns:** Nouns such as *swimming pool, dropout, roommate,* and *stepmother,* in which more than one word is needed.

**Compound Sentences:** Sentences with two or more independent clauses and no dependent clauses. (See 25b.)

**Compound-Complex Sentences:** Sentences with at least two independent clauses and at least one dependent clause arranged in any order. (See 25b.)

**Concrete Nouns:** Words that refer to people and things that can be perceived by the senses. (See 41f.)

**Conjunctions:** Words that connect other words, phrases, and clauses in sentences. Coordinating conjunctions connect independent clauses; subordinating conjunctions connect dependent or subordinating clauses with independent or main clauses.

**Coordinating Conjunctions:** and, but, for, or, nor, so, yet
**Some Subordinating Conjunctions:** after, although, because, if, since, until, while

**Conjunctive Adverbs:** Words that begin or join independent clauses. (See 23a.)

consequently    however    therefore    thus    moreover

**Connotation:** The attitudes and emotional overtones beyond the direct definition of a word. (See 41g.)

The words *plump* and *fat* both mean fleshy, but *plump* has a more positive connotation than *fat*.

**Consistency:** Maintaining the same voice with pronouns, the same tense with verbs, and the same tone, voice, or mode of discourse. (See Chapter 10.)

**Coordinating Conjunctions:** See **conjunctions.**

**Coordination:** Of equal importance. Two independent clauses in the same sentence are coordinate because they have equal importance and the same emphasis. (See 12a and 23a.)

**Correlative Conjunctions:** Words that work in pairs and give emphasis.

both . . . and    neither . . . nor    either . . . or    not . . . but also

**Count Nouns:** Nouns that name things that can be counted because they can be divided into separate and distinct units. (See Chapter 50.)

**Dangling Modifiers:** Phrases or clauses in which the doer of the action is not clearly indicated. (See 8a.)

*Tim thought*
❖  Missing an opportunity to study, ∧ the exam seemed especially difficult.

**Declarative Mood:** See **mood.**

**Demonstrative Pronouns:** Pronouns that refer to things. (See **noun determiners** and 17b.)

this    that    these    those

**Denotation:** The explicit dictionary definition of a word. (See 41g.)

**Dependent Clauses (Subordinate Clauses):** Clauses that cannot stand alone as complete sentences. (See 23b.) There are two kinds of dependent clauses: adverb clauses and adjective clauses.

**Adverb clauses** begin with subordinating conjunctions such as *after, if, because, while, when,* and so on.
**Adjective clauses** tell more about nouns or pronouns in sentences and begin with words such as *who, which, that, whose, whom.*

**Determiner:** See **noun determiner.**
**Diagrams:** See **sentence diagrams.**
**Direct Discourse:** See **mode of discourse.**

**Direct and Indirect Quotations:** Direct quotations are the exact words said by someone or the exact words in print that are being copied. Indirect quotations are not the exact words but the rephrasing or summarizing of someone else's words. (See 30a.)

**Direct Objects:** Nouns or pronouns that follow a transitive verb and complete the meaning or receive the action of the verb. The direct object answers the question *what?* or *whom?*

**Ellipsis:** A series of three dots to indicate that words or parts of sentences are being omitted from material being quoted (See 33e.)

**Essential and Nonessential Clauses and Phrases:** *Essential* (also called *restrictive*) clauses and phrases appear after nouns and are necessary or essential to complete the meaning of the sentence. *Nonessential* (also called *nonrestrictive*) clauses and phrases appear after nouns and add extra information, but that information can be removed from the sentence without altering the meaning. (See Chapter 24.)

Apples **that are green** are not sweet.
> *(essential clause)*

Golden Delicious apples, **which are yellow,** are sweet.
> *(nonessential clause)*

**Excessive Coordination:** Occurs when too many equal clauses are strung together with coordinators into one sentence. (See 12a.)

**Excessive Subordination:** Occurs when too many subordinate clauses are strung together in a complex sentence. (See 12b.)

**Faulty Coordination:** Occurs when two clauses that either are unequal in importance or that have little or no connection to each other are combined in one sentence and written as independent clauses. (See 12a.)

**Faulty Parallelism:** See **nonparallel structure.**

**Faulty Predication:** Occurs when a predicate does not appropriately fit the subject. This happens most often after forms of the *to be* verb. (See Chapter 11.)

❖ ~~The reason he~~ *He* was late ~~was~~ because he had to study.

**Fragments:** Groups of words punctuated as sentences that either do not have both a subject and a complete verb or are dependent clauses. (See Chapter 7.)

❖ Whenever we wanted to pick fresh fruit while we were staying on my grandmother's farm ∧ *we would head for the apple orchard with buckets.* .

**Fused Sentences:** Punctuation errors (also called *run-ons*) in which there is no punctuation between independent clauses in the sentence. (See 5b.)

❖ Jennifer never learned how to ask politely ; she just took what she wanted.

**General Words:** Words that refer to whole categories or large classes of items. (See 41e.) See also **specific words.**

**Gerunds:** Verbal forms ending in *-ing* that function as nouns. (See **phrases, verbals,** and 16b.)

Arnon enjoys **cooking. Jogging** is another of his favorite pastimes.
*(gerund) (gerund)*

**Helping Verbs:** See **auxiliary verbs.**

**Homonyms:** Words that sound alike but are spelled differently and have different meanings. (See 38e.)

hear/here      passed/past      buy/by

**Idioms:** Expressions meaning something beyond the simple definition or literal translation into another language. For example, idioms such as "short and sweet" or "wearing his heart on his sleeve" are expressions in English that cannot be translated literally into another language. (See Chapter 53.)

**Imperative Mood:** See **mood.**

**Indefinite Pronouns:** Pronouns that make indefinite reference to nouns. (See 17b(5) and 18b(5).)

anyone      everyone      nobody      something

**Independent Clauses:** Clauses that can stand alone as complete sentences because they do not depend on other clauses to complete their meanings. (See 23a.)

**Indicative Mood:** See **mood.**

**Indirect Discourse:** See **mode of discourse.**

**Indirect Objects:** Words that follow transitive verbs and come before direct objects. They indicate the one to whom or for whom something is given, said, or done and answer the questions *to what?* or *to whom?* Indirect objects can always be replaced by a prepositional phrase beginning with *to* or *for.* (See 18a(2).)

Alice gave **me** some money.
*(indirect object)*

Alice gave some money **to me.**

**Infinitives:** Phrases made up of the present form of the verb preceded by *to.* Infinitives can have subjects, objects, complements, or modifiers. (See **phrases** and 16b.)

Everyone wanted **to swim** in the new pool.
*(infinitive)*

**Intensifiers:** Modifying words used for emphasis.

She **most certainly** did fix that car!

**Interjections:** Words used as exclamations.

**Oh,** I don't think I want to know about that.

**Interrogative Pronouns:** Pronouns used in questions. (See 17b.)

who    whose    whom    which    that

**Irregular Verbs:** Verbs in which the past tense forms and/or the past participles are not formed by adding *-ed* or *-d.* (See 16c(4).)

do, did, done    begin, began, begun

**Jargon:** Words and phrases that are either the specialized language of various fields or, in a negative sense, unnecessarily technical or inflated terms. (See 41d.)

**Intransitive Verbs:** See **verbs.**

**Linking Verbs:** Verbs linking the subject to the subject complement. The most common linking verbs are *appear, seem, become, feel, look, taste, sound,* and *be.*

I **feel** sleepy.    He **became** the president.
*(linking verb)*    *(linking verb)*

**Misplaced Modifiers:** Modifiers not placed next to or close to the word(s) being modified. (See 8b.)

                    *on television*
❖ We saw an advertisement ∧ for an excellent new stereo system with dual headphones ~~on television~~.

**Modal Verbs:** Helping verbs such as *shall, should, will, would, can, could, may, might, must, ought to,* and *used to* that express an attitude such as interest, possibility, or obligation. (See 16f and 47a.)

**Mode of Discourse:** Direct discourse repeats the exact words that someone says, and indirect discourse reports the words but changes some of the words. (See 10e.)

Everett said, **"I want to become a physicist."**
                    *(direct discourse)*

Everett said **that he wants to become a physicist.**
                    *(indirect discourse)*

**Modifiers:** Words or groups of words that describe or limit other words, phrases, and clauses. The most common modifiers are adjectives and adverbs. (See Chapter 19.)

**Mood:** Verbs indicate whether a sentence expresses a fact (the declarative or indicative mood), expresses some doubt or something contrary to fact or states a recommendation (the subjunctive mood), or issues a command (the imperative mood). (See 16e.)

**Noncount Nouns:** Nouns that name things that cannot be counted because they are abstractions or things that cannot be cut into parts. (See Chapter 50.)

**Nonessential Clauses and Phrases:** See **essential and nonessential clauses and phrases.**

**Nonparallel Structure:** Lack of parallelism that occurs when like items are not in the same grammatical form. (See 9b.)

**Nonrestrictive Clauses and Phrases:** See **essential and nonessential clauses and phrases.**

**Nouns:** Words that name people, places, things, and ideas and have plural or possessive endings. Nouns function as *subjects, direct objects, predicate nominatives, objects of prepositions,* and *indirect objects.* (See 17a.)

**Noun Clauses:** Subordinate clauses used as nouns.

> **What I see here** is adequate.
>  *(noun clause)*

**Noun Determiners:** Words that signal that a noun is about to follow. They stand next to their nouns or can be separated by adjectives. Some noun determiners can also function as nouns. There are five types of noun determiners:

1. Articles (see 51c): *the* (definite) *a,an* (indefinite)
2. Demonstratives: *this, that, these, those*
3. Possessives: *my, our, your, his, her, its, their*
4. Cardinal numbers: *one, two, three,* and so on
5. Miscellaneous: *all, another, each, every, much,* and others

**Noun Phrases:** See **phrases.**

**Number:** The quantity expressed by a noun or pronoun, either singular (one) or plural (more than one).

**Object Case of Pronouns:** The case needed when the pronoun is the direct or indirect object of the verb or the object of a preposition. (See 18a.)

| *Singular* | *Plural* |
|---|---|
| First person: *me* | First person: *us* |
| Second person: *you* | Second person: *you* |
| Third person: *him, her, it* | Third person: *them* |

**Objects:** See **direct objects** and **object complements.**

**Object Complements:** The adjectives in predicates modifying the object of the verb (not the subject).

The enlargement makes the picture **clear.**

*(object complement)*

**Object of the Preposition:** Noun or pronoun following the preposition. The preposition, its object, and any modifiers make up the *prepositional phrase.* (See 18a.)

For **Daniel**

*(object of the preposition* for*)*

She knocked twice **on the big wooden door.**

*(prepositional phrase)*

**Parallel Construction:** When two or more items are listed or compared, they must be in the same grammatical form as equal elements. When items are not in the same grammatical form, they lack parallel structure (this error is often called *faulty parallelism*). (See Chapter 9.)

She was sure that **being an apprentice in a photographer's studio** would be more useful than **being a student in photography classes.**

[The phrases in bold type are parallel because they have the same grammatical form.]

**Paraphrase:** Restatement of information from a source, using your own words. (See 44c.)

**Parenthetical Elements:** Nonessential words, phrases, and clauses set off by commas, dashes, or parentheses.

**Participles:** Verb forms that may be part of the complete verb or function as adjectives or adverbs. The present participle ends in *-ing,* and the past participle usually ends in *-ed, -d, -n* or *-t.* (See **phrases** and 16a.)

**Present participles:** *running, sleeping, digging*

She is running for mayor in this campaign.

**Past participles:** *walked, deleted, chosen*

The elected candidate will take office in January.

**Parts of Speech:** The eight classes into which words are grouped according to their function, place, meaning, and use in a sentence: *nouns, pronouns, verbs, adjectives, adverbs, prepositions, conjunctions,* and *interjections.*

**Passive Voice:** See **voice.**

**Past Participle:** See **participles.**

**Perfect Progressive Tense:** See **verb tenses.**

**Perfect Tenses:** See **verb tenses.**

**Person:** There are three "persons" in English. (See 18a.)

**First person:** the person(s) speaking (*I* or *we*)
**Second person:** the person(s) spoken to (*you*)
**Third person:** the person(s) spoken about (*he, she, it, they, anyone,* etc.)

**Personal Pronouns:** Refer to people or things. (See 18a.)

|  | **Subject** | **Object** | **Possessive** |
|---|---|---|---|
| **Singular**<br>First person<br>Second person<br>Third person | I<br>you<br>he, she, it | me<br>you<br>him, her, it | my, mine<br>your, yours<br>his, her, hers, its |
| **Plural**<br>First person<br>Second person<br>Third person | we<br>you<br>they | us<br>you<br>them | our, ours<br>your, yours<br>their, theirs |

**Phrasal Verbs:** Verbs that have two or three words following the verb that help to indicate the meaning. (See 47b.)

**Phrases:** Groups of related words without subjects and predicates. (See Chapter 22.)

Verb phrases function as verbs.

> She **has been eating** too much sugar.
> *(verb phrase)*

Noun phrases function as nouns.

> A **major winter storm**  hit **the eastern coast of Maine.**
> *(noun phrase)*                    *(noun phrase)*

Prepositional phrases usually function as modifiers.

> That book **of hers** is overdue at the library.
> *(prepositional phrase)*

Participial phrases, gerund phrases, infinitive phrases, appositive phrases, and absolute phrases function as adjectives, adverbs, or nouns.

> **Participial Phrase:** I saw people **staring at my peculiar-looking haircut.**
> **Gerund Phrase: Making copies of videotapes** can be illegal.
> **Infinitive Phrase:** He likes **to give expensive presents.**
> **Appostive Phrase:** You ought to see Dr. Elman, **a dermatologist.**
> **Absolute Phrase: The test done,** he sighed with relief.

**Plagiarism:** Action that results when writers fail to document a source so that the words and ideas of someone else are presented as the writer's own work. (See 44e.)

**Possessive Pronouns:** See **personal pronouns, noun determiners,** and 18a.

**Predicate Adjectives:** See **subject complement.**

**Predicate Nominatives:** See **subject complement.**
**Predicate:** Words or groups of words that express action or state of being in a sentence and consist of one or more verbs, plus any complements or modifiers.
**Prefixes:** Word parts added to the beginning of words. (See 38c(3).)

| *Prefix* | *Word* |
|---|---|
| bio- (life) | biography |
| mis- (wrong, bad) | misspell |

**Prepositions:** Link and relate their objects (usually nouns or pronouns) to some other word or words in a sentence. Prepositions usually precede their objects but may follow the objects and appear at the end of the sentence. (See Chapters 20 and 52.)

The waiter gave the check **to my date** by mistake.
*(prepositional phrase)*

I wonder **what** she is asking **for.**
*(object of the      (preposition)*
*preposition)*

**Prepositional Phrases:** See **phrases.**
**Progressive Tenses:** See **verb tenses.**
**Pronouns:** Words that substitute for nouns. (See 17b.) Pronouns should refer to previously stated nouns, called antecedents.

When **Josh** came in, **he** brought some firewood.
*(antecedent)   (pronoun)*

Forms of pronouns: personal, demonstrative, relative, interrogative, indefinite, possessive, reflexive, and reciprocal.
**Pronoun Case:** Refers to the form of the pronoun that is needed in a sentence. See **subject, direct objects, indirect objects,** and **case,** and 18a.
**Pronoun Reference:** The relationship between the pronoun and the noun (antecedent) for which it is substituting. (See 18b.)
**Proper Nouns:** Refer to specific people, places, and things. Proper nouns are always capitalized. (See Chapter 34.)

Copenhagen    Honda    House of Representatives    Spanish

**Quotation:** The record of the exact words of a written or spoken source, set off by quotation marks. (See 44d.)
**Reciprocal Pronouns:** Pronouns that refer back to individual parts of plural terms. (See 17b(8).)
**Reflexive Pronouns:** Pronouns that show someone or something in the sentence is acting for itself or on itself. Because a reflexive pronoun must refer to a word in a sentence, it is not the subject or direct object. If used to show emphasis, reflexive pronouns are called *intensive pronouns.* (See 17b.)

| *Singular* | *Plural* |
|---|---|
| First person: *myself* | First person: *ourselves* |
| Second person: *yourself* | Second person: *yourselves* |
| Third person: *himself, herself, itself* | Third person: *themselves* |

She returned the book **herself** rather than giving it to her roommate to
*(reflexive pronoun)*
bring back.

**Relative Pronouns:** Pronouns that show the relationship of a dependent clause to a noun in the sentence. Relative pronouns substitute for nouns already mentioned in sentences and introduce adjective or noun clauses. (See 17b.)

**Relative pronouns:** *that, which, who, whom, whose*

This was the movie **that** won the Academy Award.

**Restrictive Clauses and Phrases:** See **essential and nonessential clauses and phrases.**

**Run-on Sentences:** See **fused sentences** and 5b.

**Sentences:** Groups of words that have at least one independent clause (a complete unit of thought with a subject and predicate). (See Chapter 25.) Sentences can be classified by their structure as *simple, compound, complex,* and *compound-complex.*

**Simple:** One independent clause
**Compound:** Two or more independent clauses
**Complex:** One or more independent clauses and one or more dependent clauses
**Compound-complex:** Two or more independent clauses and one or more dependent clauses

Sentences can also be classified by their function as *declarative, interrogative, imperative,* and *exclamatory.*

**Declarative:** Makes a statement.
**Interrogative:** Asks a question.
**Imperative:** Issues a command.
**Exclamatory:** Makes an exclamation.

**Sentence Diagrams:** A method of showing relationships within a sentence.

Marnie's cousin, who has no taste in food, ordered a hamburger with cole-slaw at the Chinese restaurant.

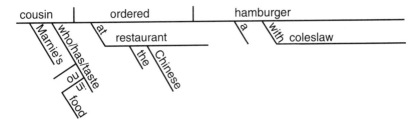

**Sentence Fragment:** See **fragments.**
**Simple Sentence:** See **sentences** and 25b.
**Simple Tenses:** See **verb tenses.**
**Slang:** Terms that are either invented or are given new definitions in order to be novel or unconventional. They are generally considered to be inappropriate in formal writing. (See 41b.)
**Specific Words:** Words that identify items in a group. (See 41e.) See also **general words.**
**Split Infinitives:** Phrases in which modifiers are inserted between *to* and the verb. Some people object to split infinitives, but others consider them grammatically acceptable.

to quickly turn     to easily reach     to forcefully enter

**Standard English:** Generally accepted language that conforms to established rules of grammar, sentence structure, punctuation, and spelling. (See 41a.)
**Subject:** The word or words in a sentence that act or are acted upon by the verb or are linked by the verb to another word or words in the sentence. The *simple subject* includes only the noun or other main word or words, and the *complete subject* includes all the modifiers with the subject. (See Chapter 21.)

**Harvey** objected to his roommate's alarm going off at 9 A.M.

[*Harvey* is the subject.]

**Every single one of the people in the room** heard her giggle.

[The simple subject is *one*; the complete subject is the whole phrase.]

**Subject Complement:** The noun or adjective in the predicate (*predicate noun* or *adjective*) that refers to the same entity as the subject in sentences with linking verbs, such as *is/are, feel, look, smell, sound, taste,* and *seem.*

She feels **happy.**        He is a **pharmacist.**
    *(subject complement*        *(subject complement)*

**Subject Case of Pronouns:** See **personal pronouns** and 18a.

**Subject-Verb Agreement:** Agreement in number and person between subjects and verb endings in sentences. (See Chapter 6.)

**Subjunctive Mood:** See **mood.**

**Subordinating Conjunctions:** Words such as *although, if, until,* and *when,* which join two clauses and subordinate one to the other.

> She is late. She overslept.
> She is late **because** she overslept.

**Subordination:** The act of placing one clause in a subordinate or dependent relationship to another in a sentence because it is less important and is dependent for its meaning on the other clause. (See 12b.)

**Suffix:** Word part added to the end of a word. (See 38c(3).)

| *Suffix* | *Word* |
|----------|--------|
| -ful | careful |
| -less | nameless |

**Summary:** Brief restatement of the main idea in a source, using your own words. (See 44b.)

**Superlative Forms of Adjectives and Adverbs:** See **adjectives** and **adverbs** and 18c.

**Synonyms:** Words with similar meanings.

| *Word* | *Synonym* |
|--------|-----------|
| damp | moist |
| pretty | attractive |

**Tense:** See **verb tense.**

**Tone:** The attitude or level of formality reflected in the word choices of a piece of writing. (See 10c and 41c.)

**Transitions:** Words in sentences that show relationships between sentences and paragraphs. (See Chapter 14.)

**Transitive Verbs:** See **verbs.**

**Two-Word Verbs:** See **phrasal verbs.**

**Verbals:** Words that are derived from verbs but do not act as verbs in sentences. Three types of verbals are *infinitives, participles,* and *gerunds.* (See 16b.)

**Infinitives:** *to* + verb

to wind    to say

**Participles:** Words used as modifiers or with helping verbs. The present participle ends in *-ing,* and many past participles end in *-ed.*

The dog is **panting.**      He bought only **used** clothing.
        *(present participle)*                    *(past participle)*

**Gerunds:** present participles used as nouns.

**Smiling** was not a natural act for her.
*(gerund)*

**Verbs:** Words or groups of words (verb phrases) in predicates that express action, show a state of being, or act as a link between the subject and the rest of the predicate. Verbs change form to show time (tense), mood, and voice and are classified as *transitive, intransitive,* and *linking verbs.* (See Chapter 16.)

- Transitive verbs require objects to complete the predicate.

    He **cut** the cardboard **box** with his knife.
    *(transitive verb)*      *(object)*

- Intransitive verbs do not require objects.

    My ancient cat often **lies** on the porch.
                *(intransitive verb)*

- Linking verbs link the subject to the following noun or adjective.

    The trees **are** bare.
        *(linking verb)*

**Verb Conjugations:** The forms of verbs in various tenses. (See 16c.)

*Regular:*
*Present*

**Simple present:**

| | |
|---|---|
| I walk | we walk |
| you walk | you walk |
| he, she, it walks | they walk |

**Present progressive:**

| | |
|---|---|
| I am walking | we are walking |
| you are walking | you are walking |
| he, she, it is walking | they are walking |

**Present perfect:**

| | |
|---|---|
| I have walked | we have walked |
| you have walked | you have walked |
| he, she, it has walked | they have walked |

**Present perfect progressive:**

| | |
|---|---|
| I have been walking | we have been walking |
| you have been walking | you have been walking |
| he, she, it has been walking | they have been walking |

## *Past*

### Simple past:

| | |
|---|---|
| I walked | we walked |
| you walked | you walked |
| he, she, it walked | they walked |

### Past progressive:

| | |
|---|---|
| I was walking | we were walking |
| you were walking | you were walking |
| he, she, it was walking | they were walking |

### Past perfect:

| | |
|---|---|
| I had walked | we had walked |
| you had walked | you had walked |
| he, she, it had walked | they had walked |

### Past perfect progressive:

| | |
|---|---|
| I had been walking | we had been walking |
| you had been walking | you had been walking |
| he, she, it had been walking | they had been walking |

## *Future*

### Simple future:

| | |
|---|---|
| I will walk | we will walk |
| you will walk | you will walk |
| he, she, it will walk | they will walk |

### Future progressive:

| | |
|---|---|
| I will be walking | we will be walking |
| you will be walking | you will be walking |
| he, she, it will be walking | they will be walking |

### Future perfect:

| | |
|---|---|
| I will have walked | we will have walked |
| you will have walked | you will have walked |
| he, she, it will have walked | they will have walked |

### Future perfect progressive:

| | |
|---|---|
| I will have been walking | we will have been walking |
| you will have been walking | you will have been walking |
| he, she, it will have been walking | they will have been walking |

*Irregular:*
## *Present*
### Simple present:

| | |
|---|---|
| I go | we go |
| you go | you go |
| he, she, it goes | they go |

### Present progressive:

| | |
|---|---|
| I am going | we are going |
| you are going | you are going |
| he, she, it is going | they are going |

### Present perfect:

| | |
|---|---|
| I have gone | we have gone |
| you have gone | you have gone |
| he, she, it has gone | they have gone |

### Present perfect progressive:

| | |
|---|---|
| I have been going | we have been going |
| you have been going | you have been going |
| he, she, it has been going | they have been going |

## *Past*
### Simple past:

| | |
|---|---|
| I went | we went |
| you went | you went |
| he, she, it went | they went |

### Past progressive:

| | |
|---|---|
| I was going | we were going |
| you were going | you were going |
| he, she, it was going | they were going |

### Past perfect:

| | |
|---|---|
| I had gone | we had gone |
| you had gone | you had gone |
| he, she, it had gone | they had gone |

### Past perfect progressive:

| | |
|---|---|
| I had been going | we had been going |
| you had been going | you had been going |
| he, she, it had been going | they had been going |

## *Future*

### Simple:

| | |
|---|---|
| I will go | we will go |
| you will go | you will go |
| he, she, it will go | they will go |

### Future progressive:

| | |
|---|---|
| I will be going | we will be going |
| you will be going | you will be going |
| he, she, it will be going | they will be going |

### Future perfect:

| | |
|---|---|
| I will have gone | we will have gone |
| you will have gone | you will have gone |
| he, she, it will have gone | they will have gone |

### Future perfect progressive:

| | |
|---|---|
| I will have been going | we will have been going |
| you will have been going | you will have been going |
| he, she, it will have been going | they will have been going |

**Verb Phrases:** See **verbs.**

**Verb Tenses:** The times indicated by the verb forms in the past, present, or future. (For the verb forms, see **verb conjugations** and 16c.)

## *Present*

**Simple present:** Describes actions or situations that exist now and are habitually or generally true.

I **walk** to class every afternoon.

**Present progressive:** Indicates activity in progress, something not finished, or something continuing.

He **is studying** Swedish.

**Present perfect:** Describes single or repeated actions that began in the past and lead up to and include the present.

She **has lived** in Alaska for two years.

**Present perfect progressive:** Indicates action that began in the past, continues to the present, and may continue into the future.

They **have been building** that parking garage for six months.

### Past

**Simple past:** Describes completed actions or conditions in the past.

> They **ate** breakfast in the cafeteria.

**Past progressive:** Indicates that past action that took place over a period of time.

> He **was swimming** when the storm began.

**Past perfect:** Indicates that an action or event was completed before another event in the past.

> No one **had heard** about the crisis when the newscast began.

**Past perfect progressive:** Indicates an ongoing condition in the past that has ended.

> I **had been planning** my trip to Mexico when I heard about the earthquake.

### Future

**Simple future:** Indicates actions or events in the future.

> The store **will open** at 9 A.M.

**Future progressive:** Indicates future action that will continue for some time.

> I **will be working** on that project next week.

**Future perfect:** Indicates action that will be completed by or before a specified time in the future.

> Next summer, they **will have been** here for twenty years.

**Future perfect progressive:** Indicates ongoing actions or conditions until a specific time in the future.

> By tomorrow, I **will have been waiting** for the delivery for one month.

**Voice:** Verbs are either in the *active* or *passive* voice. In the active voice, the subject performs the action of the verb. In the passive, the subject receives the action. (See 10d and 16d.)

> The dog **bit** the boy.    The boy **was bitten** by the dog.
> *(active verb)*             *(passive verb)*

# ANSWER KEY FOR EXERCISES

# PART TWO

## Exercise 5.1

(1) Cocoa beans have been grown in the Americas for several thousand years. (2) They were considered a treasure and were cultivated by the Aztecs for centuries before the Spanish discovered them in Mexico. (3) Cocoa reached Europe even before coffee or tea, and its use gradually spread from Spain and Portugal to Italy and France and north to England. (4) In 1753 the botanist Linnaeus gave the cocoa plant its scientific name, *Theobroma cacao,* the food of the gods. (5) The tree is cacao, the bean is cocoa, and the food is chocolate, but it bears no relation to coca, the source of cocaine. (6) Most cacao is grown within ten degrees of the equator. (7) In the late nineteenth century the Portuguese took the plant to some islands off Africa, and it soon became an established crop in the Gold Coast, Cameroon, and Nigeria, where the temperature and humidity are ideal for it.

## Exercise 5.2

*Some possible answers are as follows:*

1. There are many varieties of chocolate, but all varieties come from the same bean.
2. All varieties are the product of fermentation, and once fermented, beans must be dried before being packed for shipping.
3. Chocolate pods cannot be gathered when they are underripe or overripe, so they are usually harvested very carefully by hand.
4. Dutch chocolate has the cocoa butter pressed out and alkali added, and Swiss chocolate has milk added.
5. Chocolate is loved by millions of people all over the world, yet some people are allergic to chocolate.

## Exercise 6.1

1. is
2. do not
3. seem
4. become
5. attempts
6. are
7. study
8. conclude
9. are
10. insist
11. aren't
12. sets

## Exercise 7.1

A.  **1.** C     **5.** C     B.  **1.** C
     **2.** C     **6.** F      **2.** C
     **3.** F     **7.** C      **3.** F
     **4.** C     **8.** F      **4.** C
                                        **5.** F

## Exercise 8.1

According to some anthropologists, the fastball may be millions of years older than the beginning of baseball. <u>To prove this point</u>, prehistoric toolmaking sites, such as Olduvai Gorge in Tanzania, are offered as evidence. These sites are littered with smooth, roundish stones not suitable for flaking into tools. Suspecting that the stones might have been used as weapons, anthropologists have speculated that these stones were thrown at enemies and animals being hunted. <u>Searching for other evidence</u>, historical accounts of primitive peoples have been combed for stories of rock throwing. Here early adventurers are described as being caught by rocks thrown hard and fast. <u>Used in combat</u>, museums have collections of these "handstones." So stone throwing may have been a major form of defense and a tool for hunting. <u>Being an impulse that still has to be curbed</u>, parents still find themselves teaching their children not to throw stones.

## Exercise 8.3

(1) The man who was carrying the sack of groceries <u>with an umbrella</u> walked carefully to his car. (2) He <u>only</u> bought a small amount of food for his lunch because he was going to leave town that afternoon. (3) He whistled to his huge black dog <u>opening the car door</u> and set the groceries in the trunk. (4) The dog jumped into the trunk <u>happily</u> with the groceries.

## Exercise 9.1

One of the great American cars was the J-series Duesenberg. The cars were created by Fred and August Duesenberg, two brothers from Iowa <u>who began by making bicycles</u> and <u>who then gained fame by building racing cars</u>. Determined to build an American car that would earn respect for <u>its excellent quality</u> and <u>its high performance</u>, the Duesenbergs completed the first Model J in 1928. The car was an awesome machine described as having <u>a 265-horsepower engine</u> and <u>a top speed of 120 mph</u>. Special features of the car were its <u>four-wheel hydraulic brakes</u> and <u>extensive quantities of lightweight aluminum castings</u>. The masterpiece was the Duesenberg SJ, reputed <u>to have a 320-horsepower engine</u> and <u>to accelerate from zero to 100 mph in 17 seconds</u>.

## Exercise 10.1

Many people think that recycling material is a recent trend.

However, during World War II more than 43 percent of America's

newsprint was recycled, and the average person saved bacon grease and
*he (or she)*
other meat fat, which <u>they</u> returned to local collection centers. What
*a person did was*                                              *grease*
<u>you would do is</u> to pour leftover fat and other <u>greasy gunk</u> from frying

pans and pots into tin cans. Today, despite the fact that many trendy
*involved in*
people are <u>into</u> recycling, only about 10 percent of America's waste is
*people*
actually recycled. The problem is not to get <u>us</u> to save bottles and cans
*Manufacturers have*
but to convince industry to use recycled materials. <u>There is a concern</u>
*expressed concern*
<u>expressed by manufacturers</u> that they would be using materials of un-
*would*                                                        *manufacturers*
even quality and <u>will</u> face undependable delivery. If <u>the manufacturer</u>
*(this phrase can be omitted)*
would wake up <u>and smell the coffee</u>, they would see the advantages for
*the bigger profits they could make.*
the country and <u>bigger profits could be made by them</u>.

## Exercise 11.1

1. One way to relax is to grab a bowl of popcorn, put your feet up, and watch football on television for two hours.
2. Computer science is a field of study in which you learn how to program computers.
3. One of the most common ways to improve your math is to hire a tutor.
4. The next agenda item we want to look at is the question of finding out the cost of purchasing decorations.
5. His job consisted mainly of handling repetitious assembly line tasks.

## Exercise 12.1

*Some possibilities for rewriting this paragraph:*

Although most people think of pigs as providers of ham, bacon, and pork chops, they also think of pigs as dirty, smelly, lazy, stupid, mean, and stubborn. Because there's more to pigs than this bad press they've had, we should stop and reevaluate what we think of pigs. (2) President Harry Truman once said that no man should be allowed to be president who does not understand hogs. This lack of understanding indicates inadequate appreciation for a useful farm animal. (3) Some people are discovering that pigs make excellent pets. (4) In fact, because pigs have been favorite characters in children's fiction, many people fondly remember Porky Pig and Miss Piggy, the Muppet creation, as well as the heroic pig named Wilbur in E. B. White's *Charlotte's Web*. (5) Clubs for those who keep pigs as pets are now not just on farms, although pigs have long been favorite pets of farm children, who are likely to be fond of animals. (6) People with pigs as pets report that their pigs are curious, friendly little animals that are quite clean despite the "dirty as a pig" saying. However, pigs, which are not very athletic, also have a sweet tooth. (7) Pigs can be interesting pets and useful farm animals to raise.

## Exercise 12.2

*One possible paragraph is given here:*

Although plastic used to be considered a cheap, shoddy material, it is taking the place of traditional materials. In addition to cars made of plastic, there are also boats, airplanes, cameras, fishing rods, watches, suitcases, toothpaste tubes, and plates made of plastic. Plastic, which has replaced the glass in eyeglasses, the wood in tennis rackets, and cotton and wool in our clothing, seems new but has been with us for a long time. For example, amber is a natural form of plastic. Celluloid, which is a nearly natural plastic, was developed in 1868 as a substitute for ivory in billiard balls. However, celluloid proved to be too flammable. Now, because new types of plastic have mushroomed, the use of plastics has steadily increased. By the mid-1970s, in fact, plastic had become the nation's most widely used material.

## Exercise 13.1

1. 13a; 13b
2. 13e; 13f
3. 13d; 13e; 13f
4. 13b; 13c
5. 13a
6. 13b; 13e; 13f
7. 13e; 13f

## Exercise 13.2

*One suggested revision is as follows:*

(1) Until a few years ago Americans knew little about Australia beyond boomerangs and koala bears. (2) However, Australian movies such as *My Brilliant Career* and *Mad Max* have changed all that. (3) In addition, Paul Hogan, the Australian entertainer, has appeared on American TV commercials, reminding us that we lost the America's

Cup to the Australians. (4) Now, tourists from America are pouring into Australia, and most tourist agencies are offering package tours "down under." (5) Tourists are obviously happy to have discovered this new continent for sightseeing. (6 and 7) Sights to dazzle Americans are the Great Barrier Reef, which is a 1,250-mile reef teeming with tropical fish; the outback, a vast collection of deserts and bush country where the aborigines live; and lovely cities such as Sydney and Melbourne.

## Exercise 14.1

International airports may soon have a high-tech machine that is really an unusually reliable nose. <u>This</u> sophisticated <u>machine</u> sniffs for
*(3)*                                *(1)*
drugs and will provide a more accurate means of trapping narcotics smugglers than has been possible so far. <u>The walk-through narcotics vapor detector</u> pulls in air samples from a passenger's clothes as <u>he or she</u>
*(2)*
*(3)*
passes through. Several feet past the first sampling, the <u>passenger</u> is
*(1)*
again sampled by having <u>air</u> blown across <u>his or her</u> body. <u>Then</u>, <u>these</u>
*(1)*                        *(3)*            *(4)*    *(3)*
vapor <u>samples</u> are funneled into a device called a thermionic sensor. <u>If</u>
*(1)*                                                                *(4)*
the <u>sensor</u> sets off an alarm, the <u>passenger</u> is searched. <u>However</u>, it is not
*(1)*                            *(1)*                        *(4)*
always certain that <u>drugs</u> will be found because there can be an occa-
*(1)*
sional false alarm. <u>But</u> officials hope that the <u>electronic nose</u> will strike
*(4)*                                        *(2)*
fear in the hearts of would-be smugglers. <u>If so</u>, <u>this</u> <u>high-tech nose</u> will
*(4)*  *(3)*        *(2)*
act as a deterrent as well as a detector.

## Exercise 14.2

*One suggested version of paragraph 4 is as follows:*

Caring for houseplants requires some basic knowledge about plants. For example, the plant should be watered and its leaves should be cleaned. Moreover, since spring and summer bring a special time of growth, the plant can be fertilized then. In addition, the plant can be repotted, but the diameter of the new pot should be only two inches larger than the pot the plant is presently in. Some plants can be put outside in summer; however, some plants cannot. In sum, if you are familiar with basic requirements for houseplants, you will have healthy plants.

## Exercise 15.1

Paragraph 2 uses the following strategies to achieve sentence variety:
Sentence 1 combines the first three sentences of paragraph 1 (the second sentence has been turned into a *that* clause).
Sentence 2 combines sentences 4 and 5 of paragraph 1, adding the information from sentence 5 after the noun *chamber* in sentence 4.
Sentence 3 combines sentences 6 and 7 of paragraph 1, moving the adjective after the verb *is* in sentence 6 to the front of the new sentence so that it describes the subject. The predicates of sentences 6 and 7 can be joined because they have the same subject.
Sentence 4 is the result of changing sentence 8 of paragraph 1 into a dependent clause and joining it to sentence 9 of paragraph 1.
Sentence 5 is the result of combining sentences 10 and 11 of paragraph 1 into one longer sentence.

*One suggested version of paragraph 4 is as follows:*

While scientists neglect whistling, amateurs and hobbyists do not. There are whistling contests all over the United States, where accomplished whistlers whistle classical music, opera, jazz, Broadway show tunes, polkas, and even rock and roll. People whistle very differently. Some people pucker their lips while others use their throat, hands, or fingers to produce whistling sounds that resemble the flute. There are several advantages to whistling: it is a happy sound, whistlers never lose their instrument, their instrument doesn't need to be cleaned or repaired, it costs nothing, and it is easily transported. Because whistling is hard to explain, it is something you pick up either at a young age or not at all.

## PART THREE

## Exercise 16.1

(1) For a long time psychologists have wondered what memories are and where they are stored in the human brain. (2) Because it is the basis of human intellect, memory has been studied intensely. (3) According to one psychologist, memory is an umbrella term for a whole range of processes that occur in our brains. (4) In particular, psychologists have identified two types of memory. (5) One type is called declarative memory, and it includes memories of facts such as names,

places, dates, and even baseball scores. (6) It is (called) declarative because we use it (to declare) things. (7) For example, a person can declare that his or her favorite food is fried bean sprouts. (8) The other type is (called) procedural memory. (9) It is the type of memory (acquired) by repetitive practice or (conditioning,) and it includes skills such as (riding) a bike or (typing.) (10) We need both types of memory in our daily (living) because we need facts and use a variety of skills.

## Exercise 16.2

(1) To learn more about memory, a psychologist studied visual memory by watching monkeys. (2) To do this, he used a game that required the monkey to pick up a block in order to find the food in a pail underneath. (3) After a brief delay the monkey again saw the old block on top of a pail and also saw a new block with a pail underneath it. (4) The new block now covered a pail with bananas in it. (5) The monkey quickly learned each time to pick up the new block in order to find food. (6) This demonstrated that the monkey remembered what the old block looked like and also what distinguished the new block. (7) The psychologist concluded that visual memory was at work.

## Exercise 16.3

1. learn
2. begin
3. are
4. become
5. has studied
6. may represent
7. took
8. hopped
9. was going
10. concludes
11. sees
12. would not see
13. would conclude
14. failed

## Exercise 16.4

Last year, one of the most popular new attractions in Japanese recreation parks was a maze for people to walk through. For some people this could be twenty minutes of pleasant exercise, but others took an hour or two because they ran in circles. Admission cost about three dollars a person, an amount that made mazes cheaper than movies. Mazes also lasted longer than roller coaster rides. One Japanese businessman, first dragged there by his wife, said that he enjoyed it because it kept him so busy that he forgot all his other worries. Some people liked to amble in a leisurely way through the maze and let time pass, but most maze players tried to get out in the shortest time possible. At the entrance, a machine gave people a ticket stamped with the time they entered. Some people <u>quit</u> in the middle and <u>headed</u> for an emergency exit or <u>asked</u> a guard for help. But most <u>rose</u> to the challenge and <u>kept</u> going until they <u>emerged</u> at the other end, hoping to claim a prize.

## Exercise 16.5

1. is spent (passive)
2. may offer (active, subjunctive)
3. was marketed (passive); is being advertised (passive)
4. buy (active, command); could be (active, subjunctive); may reverse (active, subjunctive)

## Exercise 16.6

Retinoic acid <u>is</u> a promising new drug that <u>is being prescribed</u> by doc-
    *(active)*                                      *(passive)*
tors as a wrinkle cream. A company that <u>owns</u> it <u>calls</u> it a wonder drug.
                                         *(active)*   *(active)*
Although the Food and Drug Administration (FDA) <u>approved</u> it in
                                                       *(active)*
1971 as an acne cream, some users over thirty-five <u>told</u> doctors that it
                                                         *(active)*
<u>produced</u> side effects such as smoother, younger-looking skin. These
*(active)*
people <u>reported</u> that their skin <u>had</u> fewer wrinkles, but other users <u>said</u>
       *(active)*                  *(active)*                              *(active)*
the drug <u>irritated</u> their skin. Because the FDA <u>did</u> not <u>evaluate</u> the drug
         *(active)*                                *(active)*   *(active)*
as a wrinkle fighter, companies <u>are</u> now <u>testing</u> it for its ability to make
                                *(active)*   *(active)*
skin look younger. Since doctors <u>can determine</u> the appropriate use of
                                   *(active)*
the drug, they <u>can</u> prescribe it for its side effects and <u>recommend</u> it for
                *(active)*                                    *(active)*
uses not yet approved by the FDA.

## Exercise 17.1

It is a sad fact of life that what some people call the "everyday cour-
tesie<u>s</u> of life" are disappearing faster than finger bowl<u>s</u> and engineers⊙
slide rulers. People in movie theater<u>s</u> carry on loud conversation<u>s</u>, older
people on buse<u>s</u> rarely have anyone get up and offer them a seat, and
few shopper<u>s</u> bother to offer thank<u>s</u> to a helpful salesperson. Some people say that courteous way<u>s</u> seem to have lingered longer in small towns
than in big citie<u>s</u> and that some region<u>s</u>—notably the South—cling
more than other<u>s</u> to some remaining sign<u>s</u> of polite behavior. But more

often we hear complaints that courtesy is declining, dying, or dead. Says one New York executive: "There's no such thing as umbrella courtesy. Everybody ⊙s umbrella is aimed at my eye level." And a store owner in another city says that short-tempered waiters in restaurants and impatient salesclerks in stores make her feel as if she's bothering them by asking for service. Common courtesy may be a thing of the past.

## Exercise 17.2

Among the people who are most aware of the current lack of everyday politeness are airline flight attendants and newspaper advice columnists. Says one flight attendant: "Courtesy is almost zero. People think you're supposed to carry all their bags on and off the flight, even when you have dozens of other passengers to attend to." One syndicated advice columnist notes that courtesy is so rare these days that when someone is kind, helpful, or generous, it is an event worth writing about to an advice columnist. Some teachers blame television's poor example, especially the many rude detectives who shove people around, bang down all those doors, and yell in people's faces. Too many of our current movie heroes are not particularly gallant, thoughtful, or polite. As a psychologist recently noted, it is hard to explain to children what good manners are when they don't see such behavior on their television or movie screens.

## Exercise 17.3

Foreign tourists who travel in the United States often notice that Americans are not as polite as persons from other countries. Tourists from Europe, who are used to more formal manners, are particularly offended by Americans who immediately call tourists by their first names. Impoliteness in the United States extends even to objects. An English businessperson noted that in America public signs issue commands: "No Smoking" or "Do Not Enter." In England such signs would be less commanding: "No Smoking Please" or "Please Do Not Enter." Americans can also be rude without meaning to be. As a Japanese visitor noticed, the nurse who led him into the doctor's office said, "Come in here." In Japan, the visitor noted, nurses would say, "Please follow me." Foreign tourists, unfortunately, have a variety of such stories to take back to their countries.

## Exercise 18.1

Have you ever wondered how people in the entertainment industry

*I*

choose what you and me will see on television, read in books, and

hear on tapes and CDs? Some producers and publishers say that the executives in their companies and *they* ~~them~~ rely on instinct and an ability to forecast trends in taste. But we consumers cannot be relied on to be consistent from one month to the next. So, market researchers constantly keep seeking our opinions. For example, they ask *us* ~~we~~ moviegoers to preview movies and to fill out questionnaires. Reactions from *us* ~~we~~ and our friends are then studied closely. Sometimes, the market researchers merely forecast from previous experience what you and *I* ~~me~~ are likely to prefer. Still, some movies fail for reasons that the market researchers cannot understand. When that happens, *whom* ~~who~~ does the movie studio blame? The producer will say that the director and *he* *she* ~~him~~ or ~~her~~ did all they could but that the leading actor failed to attract *we* an audience. Sometimes, though, ~~us~~ movie goers simply get tired of some types of movies and want more variety.

## Exercise 18.3

**1.** X        **2.** C        **3.** X        **4.** X        **5.** C

## Exercise 18.4

Rising insurance premiums are taking their toll on the rock and
*these premiums are*
roll concert business, and ~~it is~~ likely to get higher before conditions improve. People who have been buying tickets for the last ten years are an-
*their tickets*
gry at paying five or six dollars more for ~~his or her ticket~~. But insurance companies say that instances of violence and injury at rock concerts and
*these higher insurance premiums*
the rising number of people who file claims are causing ~~it~~. Property damage has created an additional problem and has caused the number

of claims to increase tenfold over the last ten years. Each claim may be

for a large sum of money, and <u>it</u> is usually awarded by juries sympathetic
*the sum*

to damage caused by rock concert audiences. The situation has gotten

so bad recently that some concerts have been canceled when <u>they</u> could
*concert organizers*

not get insurance, and in one case, a particular act was cut from the

show because <u>they were</u> considered dangerous. <u>This</u> may cause the
*it was*        *These insurance problems*

number of rock concerts to decrease in the future.

## Exercise 19.1

We all know that when football players are very tired, their <u>con-</u>
<u>cerned</u> coaches call them back to the sidelines and give them pure oxy-
gen to breathe. But new evidence indicates that these <u>exhausted</u> players could just as well be saving their breath. It seems clear that 100
percent oxygen doesn't particularly help athletes. In a controlled test
some athletes breathed in very <u>rapidly</u> either normal air or pure oxygen. When tested as to how <u>quickly</u> the subjects revived, there was no
difference. Both groups said they felt <u>well</u> within about three minutes.
One of the players who breathed plain air even commented on the fact
that he felt <u>so well that he was ready to play again</u>. The biggest surprise
of all was that none of the players being tested could even tell whether
they had breathed <u>really</u> pure oxygen or just normal air.

## Exercise 19.3

| | | |
|---|---|---|
| **1.** a | **5.** a | **9.** an |
| **2.** an | **6.** an | **10.** a |
| **3.** a | **7.** a | **11.** an |
| **4.** an | **8.** an | |

## Exercise 19.5

(1) A new sport, already popular in Canada and sweeping across
the United States, is indoor box lacrosse. (2) It is faster, <u>more furious</u>,
and often a more brutal version of the field game of lacrosse. (3) Box
lacrosse is indeed an exciting game, as it is <u>speedier</u> and <u>rougher</u>
than ice hockey but requires the kind of teamwork needed in basketball. (4) Scores for box lacrosse are <u>higher</u> than those for field
lacrosse because the indoor game has a <u>smaller</u> playing area with
<u>more</u> opportunities for scoring. (5) The team in box lacrosse is also

<u>smaller</u> than that in field lacrosse; there are only six people on a side in the indoor game and ten people on conventional field lacrosse teams. (6) In addition, box lacrosse is played on artificial turf in ice-hockey rinks, and the sticks are <u>shorter</u> and <u>thinner</u> than conventional field lacrosse sticks. (7) Almost anything goes in this rough-and-tumble indoor sport.

## Exercise 20.1

The mail carrier knew she should <u>have</u> stayed away from the dog barking on the porch, but it was her first day on a new job. She was concerned <u>about</u> delivering all the mail she had in her bag and hoped she would not have to report any problems. Her co-workers had warned her <u>about</u> the animals along her route, especially that dog <u>on</u> Mayfield Street. <u>Among</u> all the problems she seemed to be having, she did not want to let her co-workers know that she was afraid <u>of</u> animals. But when she tried to put the mail <u>in</u> the mailbox, the dog jumped up and grabbed all of it in his mouth. No one had told her the dog was trained to collect the mail and bring it inside the house.

## Exercise 21.1

(1) <u>Humans</u> are unique in preferring to use the right hand. (2) Among other animals, each <u>individual</u> favors one hand or another, but in every species other than humans, the <u>split</u> between the right and the left hand is even. (3) Only <u>humans</u> seem to favor the right hand. (4) Even in studies of prehistoric people, <u>anthropologists</u> have found this preference. (5) For example, in ancient drawings over five thousand years old, most <u>people</u> are shown using their right hands. (6) This <u>evidence</u> suggests that <u>handedness</u> is not a matter of cultural pressures but perhaps of some genetic difference. (7) However, since <u>left-handedness</u> seems to run in families, <u>it</u> is not clear how hand <u>preference</u> is passed from one generation to the next.

## Exercise 21.2

(1) Almost every week of the year, <u>drunken teenagers</u> cause highway accidents that could have been avoided. (2) These <u>drivers</u> usually say that they thought they were in control, but the <u>cars</u> they drive still get away from them and cause damage. (3) Worst of all, <u>innocent people in other cars</u> are the real victims of these accidents because they are just as likely to get hurt. (4) Maybe <u>legislators</u> are right when they say that <u>teenagers</u> should not have driver's licenses. (5) There is <u>a lot</u> of wisdom in that statement.

## Exercise 22.1

(1) <u>Finding a place for our garbage</u> is a problem as old as human be-
*(1)*
ings. (2) On the Pacific coast there are <u>large, round shell mounds</u> where
*(5)*
for centuries Indians <u>had been discarding</u> the bones and clamshells
*(3)*
that constituted their garbage. (3) When people gathered together <u>in</u>
*(4)*
<u>cities</u>, they hauled their waste to the outskirts of town or dumped it <u>into</u>
*(4)*
<u>nearby rivers</u>. (4) In the United States the first municipal refuse system
was instituted in Philadelphia, <u>a well-organized city</u>. (5) Here slaves
*(6)*
were forced to <u>wade into the Delaware River</u> and toss bales of trash into
*(4)*
the current. (6) Eventually <u>this dumping into rivers</u> was outlawed, and
*(1)*
people looked for new solutions to the garbage problem. (7) Municipal
dump sites, <u>unused plots of land far away from houses</u>, were <u>a frequent</u>
*(2)*                                                    *(5)*
<u>answer</u>. (8) But the number of landfill sites <u>is decreasing</u> as many dumps
*(3)*
are closed because of health hazards or because of cost. (9) America, <u>a</u>
<u>land of throwaway containers and fancy packaging</u>, clearly faces a garbage
*(2)*
problem, <u>a problem without any obvious answers</u>.
*(6)*

## Exercise 22.2

1. Verb phrase
2. Phrase that is the subject of the sentence
3. Phrase that comes after a linking verb and completes the subject
4. Phrase that tells more about the subject
5. Verb phrase
6. Phrase that gives added information about the verb
7. Phrase that gives added information about another element in the sentence

## Exercise 23.1

(1) For years strange noises, <u>which would start in June and last until</u>
*(clause)*
<u>September</u>, filled the air around the waters of Richardson Bay, <u>an inlet</u>
<u>of water near Sausalito, California</u>. (2) The noise was heard in the
*(phrase)*
houseboats, <u>especially those with fiberglass hulls</u>, moored along the
*(phrase)*
southwestern shore of the bay. (3) <u>The noise was usually described as a</u>
*(clause)*
<u>deep hum like an electric foghorn or an airplane motor</u>. (4) The noise,
<u>which would start in late evening</u>, would stop by morning, <u>ruining</u>
*(clause)*
<u>people's sleep</u>. (5) <u>During the summer of 1984</u> <u>the hum was unusually</u>
*(phrase)*         *(phrase)*              *(clause)*
<u>loud and stirred investigations</u>. (6) Originally, suspicion centered on a
nearby sewage plant, <u>which was suspected of dumping sewage at night</u>
*(clause)*
<u>when no one would notice</u>. (7) Some others thought there were <u>secret</u>
*(clause)*
<u>Navy experiments going on</u>. (8) An acoustical engineer, <u>studying the</u>
*(phrase)*
<u>mystery sound for months</u>, kept thinking he would find the answer, <u>but</u>
*(phrase)*
<u>he didn't</u>. (9) Finally, a marine ecologist identified the source of the
*(clause)*
hum as the sound of the plainfin midshipman, <u>a fish also known as the</u>
*(phrase)*
<u>singing toad</u>. (10) <u>The male's singing</u> was the sound everyone heard, he
*(phrase)*
said, <u>though some people still suspect the sewage plant</u>.
*(clause)*

## Exercise 23.2

**1.** 3      **2.** 2      **3.** 2      **4.** 1      **5.** 2      **6.** 2

## Exercise 23.3

(1) The tiny lichen is an amazing plant. (2) It can survive in an incredibly difficult environment <u>because it can do things no other plant</u>
*(adverb clause)*

can do. (3) The lichen, <u>which can anchor itself on a bare rock by etch-</u>
*(adjective clause)*
<u>ing the rock's surface with powerful acids</u>, grows into the pits that it
burns out. (4) <u>Because lichens grow in cold climates above the tree line,</u>
*(adverb clause)*
they are frozen or covered by snow most of the year. (5) Unlike the cactus in the desert, the lichen has no way of retaining moisture. (6) Because of this, the sun dries lichens into waterless crusts during the day.
(7) <u>When there is a drought</u>, lichens may dry out completely for several
*(adverb clause)*
months. (8) Even under ideal conditions their total daily growing period may last only for an hour or two <u>while they are still wet with morn-</u>
*(adverb clause)*
<u>ing dew</u>. (9) The lichen, <u>which may take twenty-five years to grow to a</u>
*(adjective clause)*
<u>diameter of one inch</u>, can live for several thousand years. (10) These
amazing plants are able to live in all sorts of difficult places, but not
in cities <u>because the pollution may kill them</u>.
*(adverb clause)*

## Exercise 23.5

(2) <u>Within a decade, more than one-third of all homes in the United
States had VCRs</u> because people have found them such a convenient
source of entertainment. (3) When people want to go out in the
evening, <u>they can record their favorite programs and watch them at a
different time</u>. (4) <u>In addition, families can produce video histories of
weddings, anniversaries, and bar mitzvahs, or they can watch sporting
events and see replays whenever they want</u>. (5) <u>The price of a VCR</u>,
which fell about 80 percent in the first decade, <u>is another factor in making this new electronic gadget so popular</u>, and <u>videotapes can be rented
everywhere, from service stations and supermarkets to public libraries</u>.
(6) Because it is reasonably cheap, convenient, and a good source of entertainment, <u>the VCR will continue to be a visible part of the American
scene</u>.

## Exercise 23.6

**2.** 2    **3.** 1    **4.** 4    **5.** 3    **6.** 3    **7.** 1

## Exercise 24.1

(1) Art fraud, <u>a widespread problem</u>, is probably as old as art itself.
(N)

(2) Fourteenth-century Italian stonecarvers <u>who wanted to deceive their</u>
<u>buyers</u> copied Greek and Roman statues and then purposely chipped
(E)
their works so they could peddle them as antiquities. (3) Today forgers,
<u>who have become specialists in different kinds of fraud</u>, produce piles
(N)
of moderately priced prints, paintings, statues, and pottery. (4) The
people <u>whom they defraud</u> are usually beginning or less knowledgeable
(E)
collectors. (5) These people, <u>who usually can afford to spend only a few</u>
<u>thousand dollars at most for a work of art</u>, have not developed a skilled
(N)
eye for detecting fraud.

## Exercise 25.1

| | | | | |
|---|---|---|---|---|
| 1. CX | 3. CP | 5. CP-CX | 7. CX | 9. CX |
| 2. CX | 4. I | 6. S | 8. CP | 10. S |

## PART FOUR

## Exercise 26.1

An inventor working on a "flying car" says that traveling several hundred miles by commercial airplane is a fairly inefficient way to get around. First you have to drive through traffic to the airport, and then you have to park your car somewhere in order to board a plane. You fly to another crowded airport outside a city, but then you have to take another automobile to your final destination in town. A more practical solution would be a personal commuter flying vehicle. The inventor, working in a company supported by several government agencies, has developed a vertical takeoff and landing vehicle that has the potential to allow everyone to take to the air. The vehicle can take off and land vertically, and it travels five times faster than an automobile. The most recently developed model looks more like a car than a plane; however, it operates more like a cross between a plane and a helicopter. Above 125 mph in flight, it flies like a conventional plane, and below 125 mph, it maneuvers like a helicopter. It has a number of safety features, such as six engines; therefore, it can recover if it loses an engine while hovering close to the ground.

## Exercise 26.3

(1) A recent study showed that small cars are tailgated more than big ones. (2) Moreover, the drivers of subcompact and compact cars also do more tailgating themselves. (3) In the study, traffic flow at five different locations was observed, and various driving conditions were included, such as two-lane state roads, four-lane divided highways, and so on. (4) In all, more than 100,000 vehicles were videotaped. (5) Although subcompact and compact cars accounted for only 38 percent of the vehicles on the tape, their drivers were tailgating in 48 percent of the incidents observed. (6) In addition to having done all this tailgating, these drivers were the victims of tailgating 47 percent of the time. (7) Midsize cars made up 31 percent of the cars on the tapes but accounted for only 20 percent of the tailgaters and 24 percent of the drivers being tailgated. (8) Having considered various reasons for this difference, the researchers suggest that drivers of other cars may avoid getting close to midsize cars because of the cars' contours. (9) Because midsize cars have more curves in their sloping backs and trunks, people may have more trouble seeing around them.

## Exercise 26.4

| | | |
|---|---|---|
| **1.** C | **3.** B | **5.** C |
| **2.** B | **4.** B | **6.** A |

## Exercise 26.5

The use of technical advisers for TV programs is not new. For medical, legal, and police dramas <u>that attempt to be realistic,</u> producers
(E)
have long called on experts to check the scripts. These experts, <u>who</u>
<u>read the scripts before production,</u> make sure <u>that TV surgeons, lawyers</u>
(N)                                              (E)
<u>and police officers use the right terminology and follow standard</u>
<u>procedures.</u> Now network shows are also calling on social scientists as consultants to add realism in sitcoms and to help networks conform to criteria <u>that are required by (FCC) standards.</u> The FCC, <u>a federal</u>
(E)                                                        (N)

regulatory agency, says <u>that TV shows with a potential audience of child-</u>
(E)
<u>ren even if they are not aired until after the early evening family viewing</u>
(N)
<u>time,</u> must offer some content with educational value. But<u>, of course,</u> TV
(N)
still wants to entertain, and sometimes there is some conflict with the

writers. On the whole<u>, though,</u>television scriptwriters have come to rec-
(N)
ognize and value advice from social scientists and psychologists, <u>partic-</u>
(N)
<u>ularly on important topics such as how children react to divorce, how</u>

<u>parents might handle children's drug abuse, or how families deal with</u>

<u>emotional crises.</u>

## Exercise 26.7

Imagine not being able to recognize the face of your sister, your boss, or your best friend from high school. Imagine looking into a mirror, seeing a face, and realizing that the face you see is totally unfamiliar. Though this may sound impossible, a small number of people do suffer from a neurological condition that leaves them unable to recognize familiar faces. The condition is called prosopagnosia and results from brain damage caused by infection or stroke. Many people with this problem who have been studied have normal vision, reading ability, and language skills. They know that a face is a face, they can name its parts, and they can distinguish differences between faces. But only through other clues—hearing a familiar voice, remembering a specific feature like a mustache, hearing a name, or recalling a particular identifying mark such as an unusual scar—can the people who were studied call up memories of people they should know. Researchers studying this phenomenon have found evidence suggesting that the step leading to conscious recognition of the face by the brain is somehow being blocked.

## Exercise 26.9

New computer technology has revolutionized the work of secretaries. Previously, dictaphones, electric typewriters, and copy machines made the office an easier⊙more efficient place to work, but secretaries say that e-mail is the breakthrough that has changed the modern⊙large office. Years ago, when a secretary had to mail an inter-office memo, it would be a very tedious job. Printing, collating, addressing, and stuffing envelopes with copies of the memo was a big ⊙ time-consuming job. Now, with e-mail, a secretary can distinguish a memo with a simple ⊙ quick computer command. But e-mail has some disadvantages too. Some secretaries say that they used to be the center of all important⊙inside information because all memos and correspondence passed through them. Now, bosses can send their own messages, and secretaries can be left out of the loop with important matters. Moreover, a secretary's personal ⊙ private messages can mistakenly get sent to the whole company.

## Exercise 26.11

The United States Government Printing Office has a catalog of thousands of popular books that it prints. If you'd like a copy of this catalog, write to the Superintendent of Documents, United States Government Printing Office, Washington, DC 20402. There are books on agriculture, business and industry, careers, computers, diet and nutrition, health, history, hobbies, space exploration, and other topics. To pay for the books, you can send a check or money order, but more than 30,000 customers every year set up deposit accounts with an initial deposit of at least fifty dollars. Future purchases can then be charged against this account. There are also Government Printing Office bookstores all around the country where you can browse before buying. They do not stock all 16,000 titles in their inventory, but they do carry the more popular ones. For example, if you live in Birmingham, you can find the Government Printing Office bookstore in Roebuck Shopping City, 9220-B Parkway East, Birmingham, AL 35206. There are other bookstores in Cleveland, Ohio, and Jacksonville, Florida.

## Exercise 26.13

Have you ever thought about where all those oranges in your orange juice come from? You'd probably say that they come from Florida, wouldn't you? Some oranges may, but the world's largest producer of orange juice is now Brazil. Says one of Florida's biggest orange growers, "We're going to regain the market sooner than those rookie Brazilians think." Florida growers predict that overplanting and plunging prices have set the stage for a damaging glut in Brazil, not in Florida. "We have never had excess juice," claims a major Brazilian grower, "and I don't think we ever will." Know-how from American juice companies, along with subsidies from the Brazilian government, is helping Brazilian growers stay on top of the market. Brazilian growers are confident, knowing that Florida is more prone to drought and hard freezes. So it looks as if our orange juice will remain partly Brazilian for the foreseeable future.

## Exercise 26.15

Although the dangers of alcohol are well known, and have been
                                                    *(X)*
widely publicized, there may be another danger that we haven't yet realized. Several controlled studies of drunken animals have indicated to
researchers, that in an accident there is more swelling and hemorrhag-
          *(X)*
ing in the spinal cord, and in the brain, if alcohol is present in the body.
        *(X)*                    *(X)*
To find out if this is true in humans, researchers studied the data on
more than one million drivers in automobile crashes. One thing already known is, that drunks are more likely to be driving fast, and to
          *(X)*                                          *(X)*
have seat belts unfastened. Of course, their coordination is also poorer
than that of sober people, so drunks are more likely to get into serious
accidents. To compensate for this, researchers grouped accidents according to type, speed, and degree of vehicle deformation, and found
                                                    *(X)*
that alcohol still appears to make people more vulnerable to injury. The
conclusion of the study was, that the higher the level of alcohol in the
                          *(X)*
person's body, the greater the chance of being injured or killed. In
minor crashes, drunk drivers were more than four times as likely to be
killed as sober ones. In average crashes, drunk drivers were more than
three times as likely to be killed, and in the worst ones, drunks were almost twice as likely to die. Overall, drunks were more than twice as likely
to die in an accident, because of the alcohol they drank.
                          *(X)*

## Exercise 27.1

Although teachers commonly use tests to grade their students' learning, taking a test can also help students learn. People's memories seem

to be more accurate after reading some material and taking a test than after merely reading the material with no testing. In fact, studies have shown that students who take several tests learn even more than those who take only one test after reading material. Although everyone's ability to memorize material generally depends on how well the material was studied, scientists' research does indicate that test taking aids memory. The type of test is also important because multiple-choice exams help us to put facts together better while fill-in-the-blank questions promote recall of specific facts. These questions' ability to test different types of learning suggests that teachers ought to include different types of tests throughout the semester.

## Exercise 27.3

Magazine racks used to be for magazines, but that was before mail-order catalogs began invading the market. In 1985, when some catalogs began taking paid ads for such products as liquor and cologne, the line between magazines and catalogs began to blur. In some cases it's hard to distinguish the difference. And customers have good reasons to prefer buying catalogs when there's the advantage of having discount coupons tucked in. The catalogs that began appearing on magazine racks in '85 sold for $1 to $3 apiece, but customers would get a $5 discount on their first order. National distributors now estimate that more than five thousand stores and newsstands stock catalogs for such well-known companies as The Sharper Image and Bloomingdale's. Waldenbooks was among the first to display these catalogs on its magazine racks. It's big business now, and magazines have a tough rival to beat.

## Exercise 27.5

In the late 1970's the M.B.A. became one of the most desirable degrees awarded by American universities. In large part this was due to the high salaries offered to new graduates. Students graduating with B.A.'s or B.S.'s in most fields could expect starting salaries thousands of dollars below the pay of new M.B.A.'s, especially those graduating at the top of the class from the more prestigious universities. It was a case of having those hard-earned A's translate into better salaries. When huge numbers of M.B.A.'s began flooding the market in the mid-1980's, the value of the degree declined somewhat.

## Exercise 27.7

Erica Johns, a recent contestant on one of the game shows, was embarrassed to see herself in the reruns. There she was on the screen, yelling out the answer and claiming the big prize was hers, even when someone else sounded the buzzer before she did. "It's difficult," she said, "not to act foolish when so much money is involved." But she did win some dance lessons and a cute puppy with its own diamond-studded leash. Still, she wished she had pushed the buzzer and answered the question worth $2000.

## Exercise 28.1

Even before children begin school, many parents think they should take part in their children's education and help the children to develop mentally. Such parents usually consider reading to young toddlers important; moreover, they help the children memorize facts such as the days of the week and the numbers from one to ten. Now it is becoming clear that parents can begin helping when the children are babies. One particular type of parent communication, encouraging the baby to pay attention to new things, seems especially promising in helping babies' brains develop; for example, handing the baby a toy encourages the baby to notice something new. Some studies seem to indicate that this kind of activity helped children score higher on intelligence tests several years later. Parents interested in helping their babies' brain development have been encouraged by this study to point to new things in the baby's environment as part of their communication with their babies; thus, their children's education can begin in the crib.

## Exercise 28.3

In the not-too-distant future, when airline passengers board their flights, they will be able to enjoy a number of new conveniences; such as *(X)* choosing their snacks and drinks from on-board vending machines; selecting movies, TV programs, or video games from screens mounted on the seat in front of them; and making hotel and car-rental reservations from an on-board computer. Such features are what aircraft designers envision within the next five years for passenger jets. Their plans, though, may not be realized until much further in the future; if ever. But the ideas *(X)* reflect the airline industry's hopes. If fare wars stop and ticket prices stabilize, passengers may begin choosing different airlines on the basis of comfort, not cost; if that happens, airlines will have to be ready with new and better in-flight features. A Boeing Company executive says

that "cabin environment will be a major factor;" that is, designers must
*(X)*

make the cabin so attractive that it will offset lower fares on other air-

lines. The problem, however, is added weight caused by some of the
*(no punct.)*

suggested features; such as; computers, video screens, and more elaborate
*(X)*        *(X)*

kitchens. Added weight will mean that the plane consumes more fuel; thus
*(X)*

driving up the price of the ticket. Still, some carriers, determined to find

answers, are studying ways to use the new services to generate income;
*(X)*

particularly in the area of commercial-supported or pay-as-you-use video

entertainment.

## Exercise 29.1

When the Apollo astronauts brought back bags of moon rocks, it was

expected that the rocks would provide some answers to a perennial

question; the origin of the moon. Instead, the Apollo's moon rocks
*(X)*

suggested a number of new theories. One that is gaining more supporters
*(no punct)*

is called: the giant impact theory. Alan Smith, a lunar scientist, offers an
*(X)*

explanation of the giant impact theory: "Recently acquired evidence

suggests that the moon was born of a monstrous collision between a

primordial, just-formed Earth and a protoplanet the size of Mars." This

evidence comes from modeling such a collision on powerful super-

computers. The theory proposes the following sequence of events: (1)

as Earth was forming, it was struck a glancing blow by a projectile the size

of Mars; (2) a jet of vapor then spurted out, moving so fast that some of it escaped from Earth and the rest condensed into pebble-sized rock fragments; and (3) gravitational attraction fused this cloud of pebbles into the moon. There are several reasons that make some scientists favor this theory, for example, it dovetails with what is known about the moon's *(X)* chemistry, and it explains why the moon's average composition resembles Earth's. Another lunar scientist says, "We may be close to tracking down the real answer."

## Exercise 30.1

Remember Silverton wine coolers? Silverton, like hundreds of other products that appeared in the same year, was pulled from the shelf after it failed to gain a market. "Silverton didn't seem to have any connotation as a cooler," explains G. F. Strousel, the company's vice-president in charge of sales. Every year new products appear briefly on the shelf and disappear, and established products that no longer have customer appeal are canceled *(X)*                    *(X)* as well. Either way, experts say, the signs that point to failure are the same. *(X)*          *(X)*          *(X)*                                        *(X)* Companies looking to cut their losses pay attention to such signs. In a recent newspaper article titled "Over 75% of Business Ideas Are Flops," T. M. Weir, a professor of marketing, explains that products that don't grow but maintain their percentage of the market are known as "cash cows," and those that are declining in growth and in market share are called "dipping dogs." Says Weir, "Marketers plot the growth and decline of products, especially of the dipping dogs, very closely." According to several sources at a New York research firm that studies new product development,

the final decision to stop making a product is a financial one. When the red
*(X)*                                                          *(X)*            *(X)*
ink flows, the product is pulled.
*(X)*

## Exercise 31.1

For health-conscious people who cringe at the thought of using a toothpaste with preservatives and dyes, there are now alternative toothpastes made entirely from plants. One brand of these new, all-natural toothpastes advertises that its paste includes twenty-nine different herbs, root and flower extracts, and seaweed. Some of these toothpastes have a
*(X)*
pleasant taste and appearance, but the owner of a San Francisco health-food store decided not to carry one brand because it is a reddish-brown paste. "When squeezed from a tube, it resembles a fat earthworm," she explained. She prefers a brand made of propolis, the sticky stuff bees use to line their hives, and myrrh. Another brand, a black paste made of charred eggplant powder, clay, and seaweed, is favored by the hard-core macro-biotic crowd. This interest in natural toothpastes may be cyclical, explains the director of an oral health institute. He recalls a gray-striped, mint-flavored paste from the Philippines that sought to capitalize on a spurt of interest several years ago. It was a big seller for a few months and
*(X)*
then disappeared.

## Exercise 32.1

Several years ago the nation's print and broadcast media joined with advertising agencies to launch a massive media campaign against drugs.

Some, like ABC-TV, announced that they would donate prime time **TV**
                                                              *(X)(X)*
spots, but CBS Inc., while agreeing to cooperate, announced its intention

to continue to commit funds for campaigns for other public issues such as

AIDS prevention. James R. Daly, a spokesman for the antidrug cam-

paign, said, "We were glad to see other companies joining in to help the

campaign." For example, the Kodak Co. donated the film needed for TV
     *(X)*
spots, and in Washington, D.C., a group of concerned parents volunteered

to do additional fund raising. In the first two years of this media cam-

paign, more than $500 million was raised. Says Dr. Harrison Rublin, a

leading spokesperson for one of the fund-raising groups, "One effective

thirty-second ad aired at 8 P.M. is ten times more effective than a hun-

dred brochures on the subject."
                          *(X)*

## Exercise 32.3

Oxford University has a chancellor, but members of the Oxford faculty

wonder whether anyone in the general public knows who the chancellor

is. As the principal of one of the colleges said, "Does anyone care?" The
*(X)*                                                              *(X)*
post of chancellor at Oxford is mostly ceremonial, carrying very few re-

sponsibilities. One previous chancellor, Lord Curzon, did try to get

involved with running the university but was soon discouraged from

such unseemly action. When Prime Minister Harold Macmillan was

installed as chancellor, he delivered a speech in Latin saying that he

was quite clear on the point that it was not one of his duties to run
                                                              *(X)*

the university. He underscored his recognition of the heavy duties of his new job by wearing his cap backward throughout the whole proceedings. Many old Oxonians fear that they'll never see his lackadaisical like again. Is there anyone who can be trusted to keep a campaign promise when he or she says, "If elected, I won't stir things up"?
_(X)_

## Exercise 32.5

At the end of winter, when gardeners are depressed from the long months indoors, plant catalogs start flooding the mail. With their large type the catalogs blare out their news to hungry gardeners. "Amazing!"
_(X)_
"Fantastic!" "Incredible!" The covers always belong to some enormous
_(X)_     _(X)_
new strain of tomatoes. "Bigger than Beefsteaks!" or "Too Big to Fit on This
_(X)_
Page!" they yell. Even the blueberries are monsters. "Blueberries as big
_(X)_
as quarters!" the catalogs promise. All you do, according to these enticing catalogs, is "Plant 'em and stand back!" On a gloomy February after-
_(X)_
noon, many would-be gardeners are probably ready to believe that this year they too can have "Asparagus thicker than a person's thumb!"
_(X)_

## Exercise 33.1

Businesspeople, laborers, children, private clubs, and senior citizens—these are some of the groups who sponsor floats in the New Orleans Mardi Gras parade. Every year more than fifty different parading organizations trundle their floats through the streets. All kinds of difficulties have to be anticipated—including rain, tipsy float riders who will fall off, and mechanical failures in the tractor engines pulling the floats—and have to be overcome. Rain can slow the parade—but not stop it. Too much money, time, and dedication go into parade preparation to let anything prevent it—or so the parade organizers say.

## Exercise 33.6

The last two lines of Archibald MacLeish's poem "Ars Poetica" (written in 1924) are often quoted as his theory of poetry. "A poem should not mean / But be," he wrote. In his notebooks, he expanded on this statement: "The purpose of the expression of emotion in a poem is not to recreate the poet's emotion in someone else". . . . The poem itself is a finality, an end, a creation." G. T. Hardison, in his analysis of MacLeish's theory of poetry ("The Non-Meaning of Poetry," *Modern Poetics* 27 [1981]: 45), explains that "when MacLeish says the poem 'is a finality, an ending [sic],' he means that a good poem is self-sufficient; it is, it does not mean something else. One might as well ask the meaning of a friend or brother."

## PART FIVE

## Exercise 34.1

1. Every spring when the Madison Avenue advertisers compete for Clio Awards for the best commercials, my cousin Bert makes bets on who will win.
2. At the Dallas-Fort Worth International Airport, the Pan Am plane landed with a cargo of Dutch cigars and African diamonds.
3. When Marta signed up for an advanced course in psychology, she was already familiar with Freudian psychology and various twentieth-century views on dream interpretation.
4. Shanta Prabil, a Washington, D.C., physician, has recently completed his study of the effects of asthma as his contribution to a task force convened by the National Institutes of Health.
5. When Aleen drove south from Minnesota to Tennessee, she wondered whether "every restaurant, including McDonald's, would serve grits."

## Exercise 35.1

Some forms of illegal fishing are hard to define. For example, "noodling," the practice of catching fish by snagging them in the gills or flesh, is illegal in most places in the <u>United States</u>. However, in a recent case, a man who had caught two fish, weighing <u>twenty-five</u> and <u>thirty-one pounds,</u> in a Texas lake argued that he wasn't noodling when he dived under water with a fishing pole <u>and</u> a very short line. This was not noodling, he claimed, because he poked his rod <u>and</u> baited hook into catfish nets instead of dragging his lines through the water to snag fish the way noodlers do. The local game warden charged the angler with noodling, a misdemeanor that carries a fine of up to $250. Residents of the area, near Cloud Creek Lake, <u>Texas,</u> agreed that he was fishing illegally. But, after much debate, the man won his claim that although his unusual method was very close to noodling, he was innocent.

## Exercise 37.1

Because of her interest in the influence of the media on people's attitudes, Sarah chose as the topic for her research project the media's image of the Japanese during the last ten years. For source material Sarah began by reading newsmagazines such as <u>Time</u> and <u>Newsweek</u>, but she found them less likely to portray attitudes than features in magazines such as <u>People</u> and <u>Fortune</u>, which have articles on sushi bars, Japanese electronics, and karate. The index to the <u>New York Times</u> also led her to articles such as "The Japanese Influence on American Business" and "Japanese Technology in America." Sarah also read reviews of old television programs, including the short-lived series <u>Ohara</u>, which featured a Japanese-American detective, and old movies, such as <u>The Karate Kid</u>. Sarah rapidly found herself buried under mounds of notes and decided to limit her topic to one of the media, though she couldn't decide which one.

## Exercise 38.1

Turkish people <u>don't</u> think of St. Nicholas as having reindeer or <u>elves</u>, living at <u>the</u> North Pole, or climbing down chimneys with gifts on <u>Christmas</u> Eve. <u>Except</u> for a twist of history, Santa Claus might well speak Turkish, ride a camel, dress for a <u>warmer</u> climate, bring gifts of oranges and tomatoes, and appear on December 5 instead of Christmas Eve. According to the story of the Turkish church about his <u>background</u>, Nicholas was the <u>first</u> bishop of Myra, on the coast <u>of</u> Turkey. Turkish scholars say he was known far and wide for his <u>piety</u> and charity. He was killed around A.D. 245, and after his martyrdom, on December 6, <u>tales</u> of his good deeds lived on. His <u>fame</u> was so great that in the eleventh <u>century</u>, when the Italian branch of the Catholic church began a drive to bring to Italy the remains of the most famous saints, <u>thieves</u> stole most of Nicholas's bones from the church tomb in Turkey and took them to a town in <u>southern</u> Italy. Nicholas was abbreviated to Claus, and St. Nick became Santa. Since there are no <u>documents</u> or records of the original Nicholas of Myra, some <u>scholars</u> doubt his <u>existence.</u> But others are convinced there really was a St. Nicholas, even if he didn't have reindeer or live at <u>the</u> North Pole.

## Exercise 38.2

1. eight
2. received
3. niece
4. thief
5. conceited
6. chief
7. piece
8. freight, neighbors
9. neither
10. believe
11. ceiling
12. weigh
13. receipt
14. field
15. counterfeit

## Exercise 38.3

Last week Michael <u>planned</u> to have his bicycle repaired, though he admitted that he was <u>hoping</u> he had stopped the leak in the front tire with a patch. Even though he <u>concealed</u> the patch with some heavy tape, he found that he had to keep <u>taping</u> the patch back on the tire. Yesterday, when Michael looked at the bicycle on the way to his first class, he could see that the front tire had become flatter than it should be because it was <u>losing</u> air. With no time to spare, he <u>jogged</u> off to class, resolved that he would take the bicycle to a shop that afternoon.

## Exercise 38.5

1. rising, guiding, coming
2. likely, surely, truly
3. careful, useful, stressful
4. continuous, courageous, nervous
5. desirable, noticeable, knowledgeable

## Exercise 38.6

1. trays
2. apologies
3. allied
4. steadying
5. accompanying
6. studying
7. merciful
8. funnier
9. monkeys
10. burial
11. likelier
12. stories
13. loneliness
14. varied
15. ninetieth
16. studious
17. prettiness
18. employer

## Exercise 38.7

1, 3, 4, 8, 11, 12, 13

## Exercise 38.8

1. affects
2. too
3. quiet
4. any one
5. envelope
6. everyday
7. advice
8. any way
9. than
10. by
11. it's
12. stationary
13. all together
14. may be
15. passed
16. assistance
17. all right
18. fourth
19. cite
20. their

## PART SIX

## Exercise 39.1

*One possible revision is as follows:*

In the curricula of most business schools, the study of failure has not yet become an accepted subject. Yet average business <u>students</u> need to know what <u>they</u> should do when a business strategy fails and how <u>they</u> can learn from <u>their</u> mistakes. Even the <u>chairperson</u> of one Fortune 500 company says that the average <u>business executive</u> can learn more from ~~his~~ $_\wedge$ mistakes than from $_\wedge$ ~~his~~ successes. Yet the concept of studying failure has been slow in catching on. However, a few business schools and even engineering management majors at one university in California now confront the question of how anyone can recover from <u>his or her</u> mistakes. Student papers analyze how a typical failed entrepreneur might have better managed <u>his or her</u> problems. Sometimes, perceptive <u>students</u> can even relate the lessons to <u>their</u> own behavior. One of the typical problems that is studied is that of escalating commitment, the tendency of a manager to throw more and more $_\wedge$ ~~of his~~ financial resources and <u>personnel</u> into a project that is failing. Another is the tendency of a hapless executive not to see that <u>an</u> idea is a bomb. For this reason, computers are being enlisted to help <u>executives</u>—and <u>their</u> superiors—make decisions about whether <u>to</u> bail out or stay in. The study of failure clearly promises to breed success, at least for future <u>business executives</u> now enrolled in business schools.

## Exercise 40.1

*One possible revision is as follows:*

   Researchers note a growing concern among psychologists that as more working parents entrust infants to day care centers, some of these babies may face psychological harm. The research findings focus on children younger than eighteen months of age left in day care centers more than twenty hours a week. For children at that formative age, say the researchers, day care seems to increase the feeling of insecurity. One of the foremost researchers in this field says he isn't sure how the increase in insecurity happens, but he guesses that the stress a child undergoes each day as a result of the separation from the parent can be a contributing factor. Studies of infants in day care for long periods each week have shown that more of these infants exhibit anxiousness and hyperactivity. These findings challenge the older view that day care does not harm a young child.

## Exercise 40.3

When learning good study habits, some students are <u>sharp as a tack</u>. They know how to make study sessions <u>short and sweet</u> by concentrating on only the most important material. <u>First and foremost</u>, they look at chapter headings and subheadings <u>to get a fix on</u> what the main ideas are. <u>Getting down to business</u> means <u>getting in there</u> and <u>seeing the big picture</u>. Once that is <u>crystal clear</u>, they review arguments or add details. <u>Slowly but surely</u> they go through the material, asking themselves questions that <u>get down to the nitty-gritty</u>. <u>Climbing the ladder of success</u> in college means <u>putting your nose to the grindstone</u> and working hard.

## Exercise 40.4

*One possible revision is as follows:*

When learning good study habits, some students are very knowledgeable. They know how to make study sessions concise by concentrating only on the most important material. First, they look at chapter headings and subheadings to get a clear idea of what the main ideas are. They get to work by looking for the major ideas. Once that is clear, they review arguments or add details. They methodically go through the material asking themselves questions that focus on basic points. Being successful in college means expending effort and working hard.

## Exercise 41.3

*One possible revision is as follows:*

To eliminate sexual harassment in the workplace, companies should <u>construct</u> clearly defined guidelines that help <u>employees</u> <u>recognize</u> actions to avoid. Merely telling people not to engage in sexual harassment <u>does not adequately</u> illustrate <u>specific acts employees should avoid</u>. Therefore, to sensitize their personnel, some companies hold seminars in which employees who have complaints act out unpleasant or demeaning <u>actions</u> directed at them by their <u>supervisors</u> or fellow workers. Seeing such actions portrayed often helps the offender recognize how insulting some act was, even if the offending person <u>did not intend any disrespect</u>. Discussions that <u>follow</u> also help people realize how their actions affect those they work with, and further definitions or memos often <u>are not</u> needed.

## Exercise 41.4

*Possible revisions:*

**1.** Revised to a more formal tone:

An appropriate measure would be to exert pressure on automobile manufacturers and force them to increase the fuel efficiency of the current models, which consume excessive amounts of gasoline.

**2.** Revised to a more formal tone:

However, a more rapid method of reducing fuel consumption would be to increase taxation on gasoline.

**3.** Revised to a less formal tone:

People interested in protecting the environment are also asking for tighter limits on smokestacks pouring out sulfur dioxide, a major cause of acid rain.

**4.** Revised to a more formal tone:

However, states currently producing high-sulfur coal are expressing concern about the resulting damage to their economies.

## Exercise 41.5

*Some possible answers are as follows:*

| General | Specific | More Specific |
|---------|----------|---------------|
| **1.** music | song | *Star-Spangled Banner* |
| **2.** book | novel | *David Copperfield* |
| **3.** animal | cat | Siamese kitten |
| **4.** clothes | pants | white linen shorts |
| **5.** field of study | economics | agricultural economics |
| **6.** machine | saw | chain saw |
| **7.** car | sports car | Honda CRX |
| **8.** food | bread | dark rye bread |
| **9.** place of business | grocery store | fruit and vegetable market |
| **10.** athlete | football player | linebacker |

## Exercise 41.7

*Possible answers are as follows:*

| Most Positive | Neutral | Most Negative |
|---------------|---------|---------------|
| **1.** puppy | canine | mutt |
| **2.** law-enforcement officer | police officer | cop |
| **3.** economical | inexpensive | cheap |
| **4.** ornate | embellished | garish |

| | | |
|---|---|---|
| **5.** replica | copy | counterfeit |
| **6.** scholar | intellectual | egghead |
| **7.** uncompromising | determined | stubborn |
| **8.** apprehensive | scared | paranoid |
| **9.** explanation | reason | excuse |
| **10.** chatty | talkative | gabby |

## PART SEVEN

## Exercise 44.2

*One possible revision is as follows:*

Another important concern in city planning is to formulate propos-als to eliminate or reduce problems caused by automobiles. As Marcia D. Lowe notes, "Cities with streets designed for cars instead of people are increasingly unlivable" (56), for cars cause congestion, pollution, and noise. Providing more public transportation can reduce these problems, but it is not likely that city dwellers will give up owning cars. Therefore, solutions are needed for parking, which already uses up as much as 20 to 30 percent of the space available in downtown areas (Lipperman 99), and for rush hour traffic, which now extends to more than twelve hours in Seoul and to fourteen hours in Rio de Janeiro (Lowe 57). Pollution, another urban problem caused partly by cars, needs to be controlled. As Irwin Lipperman points out, automobile emissions cause lung disorders and aggravate bronchial problems (108). In addition, noise from auto-mobiles must be curbed. Noise has already become a health problem in cities such as Cairo, where noise levels are already ten times the accept-able standard for human health (Lowe 57).

## PART EIGHT

## Exhercise 47.1

*visit*
(1) When people from other countries <u>will visit</u> the United States, they

find a bewildering variety of words that can be used for the same thing.

*ask*
(2) In some parts of the United States, a salesperson will <u>asked</u> the cus-

*wants*
tomer if she <u>would want</u> the item in a "sack." (3) In other places, the sales-

*want*
person might ask, "Did you <u>wanted</u> this in a 'bag'?" (4) It is hard for

tourists who don't understand to <u>bring up it</u> *bring it up* when they don't know if

there is a difference. (5) Or a tourist may ask, "<u>May</u> I take this metro to *"Can*

First Avenue?" in a city where the underground train is called the sub-

way. (6) If I <u>was</u> one of those tourists, I <u>could</u> always keep a dictionary in *were* *would*

my pocket to use when the situation <u>calls it for</u>. *calls for it.*


## Exercise 47.2

**1.** to encourage
**2.** talk
**3.** will learn
**4.** asking
**5.** to talk;
**6.** to respond (or) responding; both are correct
**7.** to have (or) having; both are correct
**8.** must be


## Exercise 49.1

(1) When students <u>are</u> looking for part-time work, one difficulty is that they want the job to be after class hours. (2) Another difficulty for students is that <u>they</u> want the job to be near their school so that <u>they</u> don't have far to travel. (3) But that means <u>there</u> are many students who want to work at the same time and in the same area of ~~a~~ town. (4) The competition for the jobs that exist ~~it~~ causes too many students to be unable to find work. (5) Some counselors ~~they~~ tell their students to try looking for jobs that have flexible hours or for work that ~~it~~ can be done at home. (6) <u>It</u> is also worth trying to look farther away from the campus.


## Exercise 50.1

**1.** Americans
**2.** coffee
**3.** restaurants
**4.** stores
**5.** coffees
**6.** flavors
**7.** dozens
**8.** ice cream
**9.** milk
**10.** cream
**11.** problems
**12.** information
**13.** Advertising
**14.** drinkers


## Exercise 51.1

**1.** six famous old sports stars
**2.** her favorite old Hispanic song
**3.** a new German steel knife
**4.** a strange small square box
**5.** nine large yellow balls

## Exercise 51.2

One of the most interesting physicists of this century was Richard Feynman. He wrote a best-selling book about his own life, but he became even more famous on television as the man who was a member of the team that investigated after an accident happened to Challenger, the space shuttle that crashed in 1986. People watched on television as he demonstrated that a faulty part in the space shuttle probably caused the accident. Feynman's greatest achievement in science was the theory of quantum electrodynamics, which described the behavior of subatomic particles, atoms, light, electricity, and magnetism. The field of computer science also owes much to the work of Feynman. Many scientists consider Feynman to be one of the geniuses of the twentieth century.

## Exercise 52.1

(1) Table tennis used to be a minor pastime *at* [*in*] America, but a little [*few*] years ago it began to develop into an important sport. (2) Newcomers to the United States from countries such as Nigeria, Korea, and China, where table tennis is a major sport, have helped the United States become a respectable contender *at* [*in*] world competition. (3) Much [*Many*] new residents who are very good *in* [*at*] this sport have brought their skills to this country. (4) Now there are specialized table tennis parlors where players play *in* [*on*] tables with special hard surfaces. (5) Players no longer use some [*any*] sandpaper paddles. (6) Instead, much [*many*] paddles are made of carbon fiber and have special coatings *in* [*on*] the hitting surface. (7) At [*In*] the past, America was often *on* [*in*] last place in international competitions. (8) But now, with many strong players, often born *at* [*in*] China, the United States is beginning to win.

# Using Compare and Correct and Question and Correct

When you know the terms you want to look up, you can use the table of contents or the index to this book. But when you do not know the term, there are two ways you can find the section you need.

## 1. Compare and Correct

On the following pages you will find examples of problems or errors that may be like those you want to correct. When you recognize a sentence with a problem similar to one in your sentence, you will be referred to the chapter in this book that will help you make the needed revision. The examples are grouped in sets as follows:

- About sentences
- About punctuation
- About mechanics and spelling
- About problems with words
- About ESL concerns

## 2. Question and Correct

Inside the back cover of the book is a series of questions writers often ask. When you read a question similar to the one you have in mind, you'll find a reference to the book chapter that will give you the answer. Though the topic headings will help you locate your question, there is also an alphabetized list of Key Topics on the foldout back cover to speed your search. The questions are grouped in sets as follows:

- About writing papers
- About sentences
- About punctuation
- About mechanics and spelling
- About style and word choices
- About research and documentation
- About paper format (document design)

# COMPARE AND CORRECT

| **Examples of Sentence Problems** | **Problem and Corresponding Chapter Number** |
|---|---|
| 1. We decided to shift to a zone defense, this gave us better coverage on Maravich.<br>**Revised:** We decided to shift to a zone defense, *and* this gave us better coverage on Maravich. | 1. Comma Splice. See **5a.** |
| 2. Senator Levadi led the fight against salary hikes in Congress he hoped in that way to attract public favor.<br>**Revised:** Senator Levadi led the fight against salary hikes in Congress; he hoped in that way to attract public favor. | 2. Fused or run-on sentence. See **5b.** |
| 3. Usually Tim *ride* his bike to class.<br>**Revised:** Usually Tim *rides* his bike to class. | 3. Incorrect subject-verb agreement. See **6a.** |
| 4. Either the book or the magazines *is* a good source of information on that topic.<br>**Revised:** Either the book or the magazines *are* a good source of information on that topic. | 4. Incorrect subject-verb agreement. See **6d.** |
| 5. One hundred miles *are* a long distance between gas stations.<br>**Revised:** One hundred miles *is* a long distance between gas stations. | 5. Incorrect subject-verb agreement. See **6d.** |

6. *Living Legends sound* like a collection of sport stories.
   **Revised:** *Living Legends sounds* like a collection of sports stories.

6. Incorrect subject-verb agreement. See **6i.**

7. There *is* so many problems with the television set that I'll return it to the store.
   **Revised:** There *are* so many problems with the television set that I'll return it to the store.

7. Incorrect subject-verb agreement. See **6k.**

8. She is one of those teachers who *give* you in-class quizzes every day.
   **Revised:** She is one of those teachers who *gives* you in-class quizzes every day.

8. Incorrect subject-verb agreement. See **6l.**

9. Owning a pet has many advantages. *Such as learning to care for an animal and learning responsibility.*
   **Revised:** Owning a pet has many advantages, *such as learning to care for an animal and learning responsibility.*

9. Sentence fragment. See Chapter **7.**

10. *Being in Chem. 114, it was* useful to have a calculator at all times.
    **Revised:** *Being in Chem. 114, I found it* useful to have a calculator at all times.

10. Dangling modifier. See **8a.**

11. The weather reporter announced that a tornado had been sighted *on the evening news.*
    **Revised:** The weather reporter announced *on the evening news* that a tornado had been sighted.

11. Misplaced modifier. See **8b.**

12. In the training camp our mornings started with 6 A.M. *wake-up calls and eating breakfast at 8 A.M.*
    **Revised:** In the training camp our mornings started with 6 A.M. *wake-up calls and breakfasts at 8 A.M.*

12. Faulty parallelism. See **9b.**

13. The best way to spend *one's* free time is to work on an activity *you* haven't done for a long time.

13. Shift in person. See **10a.**

**Revised:** The best way to spend *your* free time is to work on an activity *you* haven't done for a long time.

14. The hardest part for beginning skiers is keeping *their* skis pointed straight forward. To succeed *you* have to concentrate on the skis.
**Revised:** The hardest part for beginning skiers is keeping *their* skis pointed straight forward. To succeed *they* have to concentrate on the skis.

14. Shift in person. See **10a**.

15. Suddenly, as we *were driving* along, smoke or steam *starts* coming out from under our hood.
**Revised:** Suddenly, as we *were driving* along, smoke or steam *started* coming out from under our hood.

15. Shift in verb tense. See **10b**.

16. We *were riding* along, enjoying the scenery and not thinking about how long it had been since we stopped for gas. Suddenly, the motor *dies*.
**Revised:** We *were riding* along, enjoying the scenery and not thinking about how long it had been since we stopped for gas. Suddenly, the motor *died*.

16. Shift in verb tense. See **10b**.

17. It was desirable for all the candidates to have fluent speaking abilities, good social skills, and a *with-it* appearance.
**Revised:** It was desirable for all the candidates to have fluent speaking abilities, good social skills, and *fashionably current clothing*.

17. Shift in tone. See **10c**.

18. The boy had to stay home and do his homework, but *this was not wanted by him*.
**Revised:** The boy had to stay home and do his homework, *but he did not want to do this*.

18. Shift in voice. See **10d**.

19. The secretary said *that her boss was busy* and *could you* wait in the reception area.

19. Shift in discourse. See **10e**.

**Revised:** The secretary said *that her boss was busy* and *that they could* wait in the reception area.

20. Loneliness *is when* you have no real friend to turn to.
    **Revised:** Loneliness *is a condition in which you find you have* no real friend to turn to.

20. Faulty predication. See Chapter **11**.

21. He drank too much on the job, *and* he was fired.
    **Revised:** *Because* he drank too much on the job, he was fired.

21. Inappropriate coordination. See **12a**.

22. The crowd objected to the referee's decision, *and* they began yelling insults, *so* the referee blew her whistle to call for quiet, *but* people didn't stop their hooting and stomping.
    **Revised:** *When* the crowd objected to the referee's decision, they began yelling insults. *As a result,* the referee blew her whistle to call for quiet. *But* people didn't stop their hooting and stomping.

22. Excessive coordination. See **12a**.

23. *When* I finally decided to major in public relations and advertising, it was a difficult decision.
    **Revised:** I finally decided to major in public relations and advertising, *which* was a difficult decision.

23. Inappropriate subordination. See **12b**.

24. *The future is bright for* the high school vocational agriculture student *who* has training in microcomputers *because* computers are necessary on the modern farm, *which* requires planning and record keeping.
    **Revised:** The high school vocational agriculture student *who* has training in microcomputers has a bright future. Computers are necessary on the modern farm *because* farming requires planning and record keeping.

24. Excessive subordination. See **12b**.

**25.** Instead of *a motorcycle helmet,* which I would have preferred, *a dictionary* was what my aunt chose for my *graduation present.*
**Revised:** For my *graduation present,* my aunt chose a *dictionary,* though I would have preferred a *motorcycle helmet.*

**25.** Sentence moves from unknown to known material. See **13a.**

**26.** Automobile commercials that *do not* compare their brand to another one tend *not* to create as much audience interest.
**Revised:** Automobile commercials that compare their brand to another one tend to create more audience interest.

**26.** Negative language. See **13b.**

**27.** She *couldn't hardly* refuse the gift.
**Revised:** She *could hardly* refuse the gift.

**27.** Double negative. See **13c.**

**28.** *Selection* of the candidates was the next item on the committee's agenda.
**Revised:** The next item on the committee's agenda was *selecting* the candidates.

**28.** Uses a noun instead of a verb. See **13d.**

**29.** *It* was the wish of my parents that I would go to college.
**Revised:** *My parents* wished that I would go to college.

**29.** Sentence subject is not the intended subject. See Chapter **13.**

**30.** A *mistake was made* in my sandwich order *by the waiter.*
**Revised:** The *waiter made a mistake* in my sandwich order.

**30.** Uses passive instead of active. See Chapter **13.**

**31.** The tension in the arena was obvious. The crowd was not cheering noisily or tossing popcorn boxes around. We knew that without Terry our team wouldn't be able to win and go on to the semifinals. We tried to psych ourselves up anyway.

**31.** Needs transitions. See Chapter **14.**

**Revised:** The tension in the arena was obvious. *For example,* the crowd was not cheering noisily or tossing popcorn boxes around. We knew that without Terry our team wouldn't be able to win and go on to the semi-finals. *But* we tried to psych ourselves up anyway.

32. The homecoming queen waved enthusiastically to the crowd. She was teary-eyed but happy. She kept smiling at the TV camera as she rode by. It was easy to see how happy she was.
    **Revised:** *Teary-eyed but happy,* the homecoming queen waved enthusiastically to the crowd. *As she rode by,* she kept smiling at the TV camera. It was easy to see how happy she was.

    32. Monotonous sentence rhythm. See Chapter **15**.

33. He has *broke* his bike light and *need* a new one.
    **Revised:** He has *broken* his bike light and *needs* a new one.

    33. Incorrect verb form and ending. See **16c.**

34. Mr. Villus is one of those people who *is* never on time.
    **Revised:** Mr. Villus is one of those people who *are* never on time.

    34. Incorrect subject-verb agreement. See **6k.**

35. The library has a dozen *computer* and some *printer* for students to use.
    **Revised:** The library has a dozen *computers* and some *printers* for students to use.

    35. Incorrect use of plurals. See Chapter **17**.

36. The committee had to make a choice between *him and I.*
    **Revised:** The committee had to make a choice between *him and me.*

    36. Incorrect pronoun case. See **18a.**

37. In Hollywood, *they* think that movie-goers are too conservative to appreciate really interesting background music.

    37. Vague pronoun reference. See **18b.**

**Revised:** In Hollywood, *composers who write music for movies* think that moviegoers are too conservative to appreciate really interesting background music.

38. Whenever the class does experiments with the lab assistants' measuring devices, *they* end up leaving *their* equipment all over the lab tables.
    **Revised:** Whenever the class does experiments with the lab assistants' measuring devices, *the students* end up leaving *the lab assistants'* equipment all over the lab tables.

    38. Unclear pronoun reference. See **18b.**

39. He learned how to play the bass guitar *real* well.
    **Revised:** He learned how to play the bass guitar *very* well.

    39. Incorrect use of adjective. See **19a.**

40. It will take *a* hour to finish this project.
    **Revised:** It will take *an* hour to finish this project.

    40. Incorrect use of article. See **19b.**

41. Taking the main street through town is *more quicker* than the bypass road.
    **Revised:** Taking the main street through town is *quicker* than *taking* the bypass road.

    41. Incorrect comparison. See **19c.**

42. She was bored *on* the subject of safe driving.
    **Revised:** She was bored *with* the subject of safe driving.

    42 Incorrect preposition. See Chapter **20.**

## Examples of Punctuation Problems

**Problem and Corresponding Chapter Number**

43. Kari studied the catalog of summer courses and she decided she should sign up for an introduction to anthropology.
    **Revised:** Kari studied the catalog of summer courses ⊙ and she decided she should sign up for an introduction to anthropology.

    43. Comma needed in compound sentence. See **26a.**

**44.** When the sun had set the owls started to hoot.
**Revised:** When the sun had set ⊙ the owls started to hoot.

**44.** Comma needed after introductory clause. See **26b.**

**45.** Laura who is my cousin's daughter is coming for a visit.
**Revised:** Laura ⊙ who is my cousin's daughter ⊙ is coming for a visit.

**45.** Comma needed to set off nonessential clause. See **26c.**

**46.** Jerrys old VW is faster than my car but not hers'.
**Revised:** Jerry⊙s old VW is faster than my car but not hers.

**46.** No apostrophe with the possessive pronoun. See **27a.**

**47.** The jury announced it⊙s decision.
**Revised:** The jury announced its decision.

**47.** Apostrophe incorrectly used with possessive pronoun *its*. See **27b.**

**48.** Wade showed up on time for the meeting ⊙ however, it was the wrong day.
**Revised:** Wade showed up on time for the meeting ⊙ however, it was the wrong day.

**48.** Semicolon needed between independent clauses. See **28a.**

**49.** He preferred health foods, such as ⊙ whole wheat bread, organically grown vegetables, and caffeine-free drinks.
**Revised:** He preferred health foods ⊙ such as whole wheat bread, organically grown vegetables, and caffeine-free drinks.

**49.** Unnecessary colon. See **29f.**

**50.** Was Karl the one who said, "I'll bring the beer⊙"
**Revised:** Was Karl the one who said, "I'll bring the beer"⊙

**50.** Incorrect use of question mark with quotation. See **32b.**

**51.** The 6 P.M. news announced that ⊙ the White House said it would not confirm the truth of this story. ⊙
**Revised:** The 6 P.M. news announced that the White House said it would not confirm the truth of this story.

**51.** Incorrect use of quotation marks with a quotation. See **30a.**

**52.** "I would like to learn more about how tornadoes form," I said. "Here's a useful book," responded the librarian.
**Revised:**
　"I would like to learn more about how tornadoes form," I said.
　"Here's a useful book," responded the librarian.

**52.** Incorrect presentation of dialogue. See **30a**.

**53.** He always writes cheers at the bottom of his e-mail notes.
**Revised:** He always writes "cheers" at the bottom of his e-mail notes.

**53.** Quotation marks needed. See **30c**.

**54.** She was a well known medieval historian. She was not, however, as well-known as her husband, a musician.
**Revised:** She was a well-known medieval historian. She was not, however, as well known as her husband, a musician.

**54.** Incorrect hyphenation of two-word units. See **31c**.

**55.** They were hardly ever a-part after they met.
**Revised:** They were hardly ever apart after they met.

**55.** Incorrect word division at the end of a line. See **31a**.

**56.** The puppy returned with some black and white shreds in its mouth—my morning newspaper. I gulped—again.
**Revised:** The puppy returned with some black and white shreds in its mouth—my morning newspaper. I gulped, again.

**56.** Overuse of dashes. **See 33a**.

## Examples of Problems with Mechanics and Spelling

**Problem and Corresponding Chapter Number**

**57.** I took two *Economics* courses this semester and one *History* course.
**Revised:** I took two *economics* courses this semester and one *history* course.

**57.** Incorrect capitalization. See Chapter **34**.

**58.** 43 more names were added to the list.
**Revised:** Forty-three more names were added to the list.

**58.** Incorrect use of numbers. See Chapter **36**.

**59.** One of his favorite old movies, ☺Casablanca,☺ was on the late show last night.
**Revised:** One of his favorite old movies, *Casablanca,* was on the late show last night.

**59.** Needs italics. See **37a**.

**60.** When winter comes, I always enjoy *planing* a trip to warm beaches, even if don't always go.
**Revised:** When winter comes, I always enjoy *planning* a trip to warm beaches, even if *I* don't always go.

**60.** Needs proofreading. See **38a**.

**61.** She *recieved* a B.A. in the *feild* of art history.
**Revised:** She *received* a B.A. in the *field* of art history.

**61.** Spelling error (*ie/ei*). See **38c**.

**62.** She *discribed* the hill she would climb *tommorow.*
**Revised:** She *described* the hill she would climb *tomorrow.*

**62.** Incorrect prefixes. See **38c**.

**63.** Echo Bay is a *desireable* place to go *picnicing.*
**Revised:** Echo Bay is a *desirable* place to go *picnicking.*

**63.** Incorrect suffixes. See **38c**.

**64.** Of all the various electronic *mediums,* broadcasting via *radioes* is the most popular.
**Revised:** Of all the various electronic *media,* broadcasting via *radios* is the most popular.

**64.** Spelling error (plurals). See **38d**.

**65.** *There* train *past* through *to* quickly to see much of the town *accept* the station.
**Revised:** *Their* train *passed* through *too* quickly to see much of the town *except* the station.

**65.** Incorrect sound-alike words. See **38e**.

| **Examples of Problems with Words** | **Problem and Corresponding Chapter Number** |
|---|---|
| **66.** In the last ten years, the *mailman has* had an increased work load because of the tide of bulk mail *he* must deliver. **Revised:** In the last ten years, *mail carriers have* had an increased work load because of the tide of bulk mail *they* must deliver. | **66.** Sexist language. See **39b.** |
| **67.** At 8 A.M. *in the morning* I *first* began to feel ill. **Revised:** At 8 A.M. I began to feel ill. | **67.** Unnecessary words. See **40a.** |
| **68.** Tina is usually a *quick study* and can master new skills with *lightning speed,* but the computer programming course was *over her head.* **Revised:** Tina is usually a *quick learner* who masters new skills *in jet-speed time.* But the computer programming course, she *groped helplessly,* unable to cope with the material that was too advanced for her. | **68.** Clichés. See **40b.** |
| **69.** The legal system is intended to protect the average *guy's* rights. **Revised:** The legal system is intended to protect the average *person's* rights. | **69.** Mixture of formal and informal language. See **41c.** |

| **Examples of ESL Concerns** | **Problem and Corresponding Chapter Number** |
|---|---|
| **70.** I have *starting* my homework. **Revised:** I have *started* my homework. | **70.** Verb forms with helping verbs. See **44a.** |
| **71.** If Mr. Patel had more time, he *may* join us. **Revised:** If Mr. Patel had more time, he *would* join us. | **71.** Verbs with conditionals. See **44a.** |

**72.** He *cut up it.*
**Revised:** He *cut it up.*

**72.** Phrasal verbs. See **44b.**

**73.** Miranda appreciates *to join* the group.
**Revised:** Miranda appreciates *joining* the group.

**73.** Verbs with *-ing* and *to* + verb. See **44c.**

**74.** Mussah going to visit his cousin lives in Denver.
**Revised:** Mussah *is* going to visit his cousin *who* lives in Denver.

**74.** Omitted words. See Chapter **45.**

**75.** The book she was reading *it* was very helpful.
**Revised:** The book she was reading was very helpful.

**75.** Repeated words. See Chapter **46.**

**76.** Sumanas was not used to the *weathers* in Minnesota.
**Revised:** Sumanas was not used to the *weather* in Minnesota.

**76.** Count and non-count nouns. See Chapter **47.**

**77.** His favorite snack is a *red big* apple.
**Revised:** His favorite snack is a *big red* apple.

**77.** Adjective order. See Chapter **48.**

**78.** Whenever Mr. Tran sees book on geography, he wants to buy it.
**Revised:** Whenever Mr. Tran sees *a* book on geography, he wants to buy it.

**78.** Articles (*a/an/the*). See **48c.**

**79.** He had *much* problems with his computer.
**Revised:** He had *many* problems with his computer.

**79.** Incorrect choice of *much/many.* See **48d.**

**80.** The meeting will be *at* Monday.
**Revised:** The meeting will be *on* Monday.

**80.** Incorrect preposition. See Chapter **49.**

# INDEX

| Symbol | Error Explanation | Chapter |
|--------|-------------------|---------|
| ab | abbreviation | 35 |
| ad | adjective/adverb | 19 |
| agr | agreement | 6 |
| awk | awkward construction | |
| ca | case | 18 |
| cap | capitalization | 34 |
| comp | computers and writing | 4 |
| coord | coordination | 12a |
| cs | comma splice | 5a |
| dm | dangling modifier | 8a |
| emph | needs emphasis | |
| frag | sentence fragment | 7 |
| fs | fused sentence | 5b |
| hyph | hyphenation | 31 |
| ital | italics/underlining | 37 |
| lc | use lowercase | 34 |
| mm | misplaced modifier | 8b |
| num | number use | 36 |
| ¶ | new paragraph | 3 |
| // | parallelism | 9 |
| para | paragraphs | 3 |
| pl | plural needed | 17a |
| pred | predication | 11 |
| p | punctuation | 26–33 |
| purp | purpose and audience | 1 |
| . | period | 32a |
| ? | question mark | 32b |
| ! | exclamation point | 32c |
| , | comma | 26 |
| ; | semicolon | 28 |
| : | colon | 29 |
| ' | apostrophe | 27 |
| " " | quotation marks | 30 |
| — | dash | 33a |
| ( ) | parentheses | 33c |
| [ ] | brackets | 33d |
| . . . | ellipses | 33e |
| / | slash | 33b |
| ref | reference | 18b |
| shft | shift | 10 |
| sp | spelling | 38 |
| subord | subordination | 12b |
| sxt | sexist language | 39 |
| t | tense | 16c |
| trans | transition needed | 14 |
| v | verb | 16 |
| var | variety needed | 15 |
| w | wordy | 40 |
| wc | word choice | 41 |
| w pr | writing process | 2 |
| ww | wrong word | 41 |
| x | obvious error | |
| ∧ | insert | |
| ∿ | transpose | |
| ℒ | delete | |